BREADWINNERS AND CITIZENS

BREADWINNERS AND CITIZENS

Gender in the Making of

the French Social Model

LAURA LEVINE FRADER

DUKE UNIVERSITY PRESS

Durham and London

2008

© 2008 DUKE UNIVERSITY PRESS

All rights reserved. Printed in the United

States of America on acid-free paper ∞

Designed by Amy Ruth Buchanan

Typeset in Minion by Keystone Typesetting, Inc.

Library of Congress Cataloging-in-Publication Data

appear on the last printed page of this book.

CONTENTS

ACKNOWLEDGMENTS

Over the years this book has been in preparation, I have accumulated a large debt of gratitude to many friends and colleagues who have provided encouragement, assistance, conversation, and critique along the way. I have been especially fortunate to benefit from the generosity of librarians and archivists in Paris, who made the task of research a pleasure. At the Bibliothèque du Musée Social in Paris, Collette Chambelland and Françoise Blum generously shared their knowledge of aspects of my topic, as well as their own work, and graciously accommodated yet another request for yet another dusty volume. Brigitte Lanay, archivist at the Archives de la Ville de Paris, provided invaluable assistance directing me to relevant materials in the archives' branch at Villemoisson-sur-Orge. Others at the Archives nationales and the Biblibiothèque nationale in Paris likewise provided essential research assistance as did the staff at the Bibliothèque Marguerite Durand, a treasure trove of material on women's and gender history. The staffs of the Confédération générale du travail (CGT) archives in Montreuil tirelessly lugged boxes of materials for me up from storage, as did those of the Archives départmentales du Nord in Lille, and the librarians at the library of the Musée de la Poste in Paris. Françoise Cribier, director of the project "Jeune provinciaux d'hier, vieux parisiens d'aujourd'hui," at the Laboratoire d'Analyse statistique et méthodologique appliqué à la sociologie (LASMAS), turned me loose in her office at the Institut de Recherches sur la Société contemporaine (IRESCO), where I was able to use her collection of interviews for the project, and generously provided me with a massive volume of data analysis.

In addition to librarians and archivists, over the years, the Center for European Studies at Harvard, where much of this book was written, provided me with as stimulating an intellectual environment as one could hope for. My thanks go to Abby Collins and Patricia Craig, associate directors, as well as to directors Stanley Hoffmann, Charles Maier, Peter Hall, George Ross, and David Blackbourn. In Paris, I benefited from the support of Pascal Perrineau, director of the Centre de la Vie Politique française (CEVIPOF), where I wrote very early drafts of a couple of chapters, as well as that of his staff. Seminars and discussions with colleagues at both of these research institutes have shaped my thinking about politics and society sometimes in unexpected ways. At the Ecole des hautes études en sciences sociales (EHESS) on the Boulevard Raspail, I benefited from many conversations with both faculty and students in the Centre de Recherches historiques in the course of the seminars I gave during my month as a Visiting Professor in 1997. Other colleagues provided much needed responses to my work in the Centre national de recherche scientifique (CNRS) seminars "Etat et Rapports sociaux de sexe" at Paris VII, "Genre et Rapports sociaux" and "Précarisation sociale, travail, et santé" (conjointly with the Institut national de la Santé et de la recherche medical) at the Institut de Recherches sur la Société contemporaine (IRESCO).

I have especially benefited from lively discussions with my French, American, Canadian, and British colleagues and friends: Nancy Green, Jane Jenson, George Ross, Eleni Varikas, Michelle Perrot, Michele Riot-Sarcey, Herrick Chapman, Helen Chenut, Laura Downs, Antoinette Burton, Michele Zancarini, Jacqueline Heinen, Danièle Kergoat, Helena Hirata, Eléonore Lépinard, Sonya O. Rose, Eileen Boris, Mary Lewis, Judith Surkis, Béatrice Appay, Anne Thébaud-Mony, and Sîan Reynolds. Claire Duchen, a fast friend and colleague, regrettably died too soon to see this book in its final form. In Paris, Isabelle Martelly and Jeffrey and Ulla Kaplow gave freely of their much-appreciated hospitality and great friendship.

The German Marshall Fund of the United States provided generous research support in 1995 (Grant #A-0222), and Northeastern University granted leaves in 1994, 1995 and 2002–2003 that made it possible to conduct the research for the project. I thank Oxford University Press for permission to reproduce in chapter 5 portions of my article "Social Citizens without Citizenship," *Social Politics* 3 (Summer/Fall, 1996): 111–35; and the International Institute of Social History for permission to reproduce portions of my article "From Muscles to Nerves: Gender, 'Race,' and the Body at Work in France, 1919–1939," *International Review of Social History* 44 (supplement, 1999): 123–47. Research assistants Nuala McGeogh, Susan McCain, and Nora Weberova provided invaluable help at an early stage of the project.

Through the latter stages of this book no one gave me more support and intellectual companionship than Jim Cronin, first as a friend and then as my husband. He read and commented on more drafts than either of us cares to contemplate. It is to him that I dedicate this book with love and gratitude for his patience and wisdom.

GENDER IN THE MAKING OF

THE FRENCH SOCIAL MODEL

During the lively campaign surrounding the French vote on the European constitution in May 2005, much of the discussion centered on whether or not a vote "oui" or "non" would protect the "French social model" from the advance of unbridled Anglo-Saxon liberalism.[1] Indeed, at the same time as the European Union has sought to extend broad social protections to its member states, the viability of that model was thrown into question not only during the campaign over the constitution but also in October and November 2005 when French youths rioted in working-class towns around Paris and in other major cities. The debate about the "social model" and its ability to survive in an era of intense global competition and persistent social exclusion is one of the central questions that vexes the separate states and publics of Europe, as well as the European Union itself. Characterized by a broad array of social policies, particularly state-generated welfare provisions, family policies, employment protections, labor agreements, and pensions designed to alleviate the effects of economic fluctuations and social changes on families and individuals, that model has been based on notions of social solidarity and rights that include the state's obligation to provide for the welfare of its citizens—what came to be known as "social citizenship" in the language of the British sociologist T. H. Marshall.[2]

The historical process by which social groups realized full citizenship in Marshall's construct is by now reasonably well known.[3] A first stage involved the acquisition of civil rights such as the rights to work and make contracts, the right to bodily integrity, and the rights to freedom of speech and religion. In the second stage, states extended political rights to male citizens, primarily through the granting of suffrage. But because the extension of civil and political rights failed to eliminate major gaps in economic and social status, twentieth-century states recognized the need to take responsibility for reducing social inequality by providing certain minimum standards of life for all, including "the organization and financing of care for the old, the sick, children, and the disabled."[4] In this way, states took account of "social citizenship," Marshall's third stage in the acquisition of rights. In France, the process of establishing this new relationship between the state and society by granting social rights did not conform precisely to the historical stages of Marshall's model. The French state began to implement the social rights of citizenship piecemeal beginning in the late nineteenth century and continuing into the twentieth century through complex interactions between the state, employers, and organized labor, long before all French citizens achieved political rights, or even civil rights.[5] "Social citizenship" in France—the notion that the state had the obligation to ensure all citizens under the French Republic the fundamental right to food, shelter, and care—notably preceded the granting of full political rights to women in 1944. The scope of social rights expanded considerably in the decades following World War II, but although France had one of the most extensive programs of social protections on the European continent by the late twentieth century, the French model of social citizenship persistently incorporated significant gender inequality.

This book offers a new interpretation of the construction of the family and welfare components of the social model in France on the basis of struggles to define the roles of breadwinners and especially the position of women in economic and social life in the two decades following World War I. Several assumptions guide this study. First, although French welfare policies began in the nineteenth century incorporating republican solidarists' ideas about the state's responsibility for its citizens, the foundations of the late-twentieth-century model emerged more fully in the 1920s and 1930s, particularly in the domain of policies concerning the family and reproduction.[6] The broad process of postwar reconstruction during the 1920s, in which France rebuilt its labor force and modernized its economy, recovered from the destruction of war, and deployed new forms of labor management, generated important practices and policies that came to underscore the social model. These practices and policies were further elaborated when the Depression of the 1930s provoked new social choices over work and support for the unemployed. Second, although many historians and sociologists who have studied the history of the French welfare state have highlighted the state's and employers' roles in framing social policy, a closer investigation suggests that new ways of thinking about work and about the relationship between work, the family, and rights helped to create the foundations of that model in the years between the world wars.[7] These relationships were of fundamental importance in France, where many of the social rights of the French welfare state that were developed in the 1920s and 1930s were linked to employment.

The third assumption that guides this study is that questions of gender as well as race and ethnicity proved central to the creation of post–World War I society. The massive mobilization of the First World War had thrown women as well as men into new situations at work and in society. Whether the end of the war would mean the further transformation of social roles and divisions of labor or the reassertion of prewar gender norms and the establishment of new patterns of inequality would be central to the social politics of the next two decades. Both in terms of French economic and social life and in cultural terms, the postwar period saw serious debates about gender roles. Tremendous mortality during the war contributed to France's ongoing demographic crisis, provoking fresh anxieties about the problem of low fertility from across the political spectrum, and led to measures designed to encourage population growth. Government and popular concerns about France's demographic deficit implicated women directly in the effort to boost French population, and these concerns, already in evidence before and during World War I, emerged after the war with renewed vigor in popular novels, debates within the ranks of organized labor, and in employers' practices at the same time as it colored the policy discourses of political representatives and government officials.[8] Additionally, France experienced unprecedented immigration from its colonies in North Africa and Southeast Asia, as well as from Eastern and Southern Europe through the 1920s and 1930s. The presence of large numbers of colonial and foreign workers on French soil contributed to discussions of population renewal as well as the process of economic reconstruction and led to the extension of citizenship rights to certain groups of foreign workers during the 1920s. This book revisits how these critical issues together contributed to constructing the meanings of citizenship and essential features of social policy between the world wars. It is not a book about the welfare state as such; rather, it examines the political and social practices that underpinned the French model of state-society relations.

Over the past twenty-five years, numerous scholars have examined the relationship between gender, work, social policy, and citizenship in various combinations. Although for some time historians assumed that French social policy was less developed than that of other countries, it is clear that before World War I, France had passed a variety of major social provisions that included labor laws regulating child and women's labor, maternity leaves for working women, and social insurance, among other provisions.[9] These initiatives expanded in the period following World War I through legislation fixing new criminal penalties for the practice of abortion and for distributing birth control or information about contraception, through state incentives to bear children, the enhancement of maternity leaves, expansion of family allowances, a broad package of social insurance legislation passed in 1930, and the state's extension of family allowances to all working people two years later.

Scholars who examined the construction of the French welfare state in the twentieth century have pointed to the pronatalist objectives that lay at the heart of both private employer initiatives and state policies and have shown how employers advanced their economic interests while simultaneously promoting the reproduction of the labor force through family allowances.[10] Susan Pedersen's important work on Britain and France, for example, examined how employer strategies were crucial to the emergence of the welfare state in France. The family allowance system that was so central to French social provision began with employers' initiatives designed to promote the reproduction of their labor force, while simultaneously keeping wages low, linking family allowances to childbearing and regularity of employment. The practice of granting allowances spread from Catholic textile entrepreneurs to employers all over France until the state finally assumed control of the system in 1932.[11] Pedersen argued that in contrast to Britain, where a male breadwinner norm influenced the shape of welfare policies, the French developed a "parental welfare state" designed to redistribute benefits from those who were childless to those who had families and simultaneously recognized women's rights as wage earners. The French system was based on a relatively weak male breadwinner norm that supported women's high rates of employment with maternity leaves, family allowances, direct payment of allowances to mothers that implicitly recognized their status as workers, and ultimately a range of child-care options (after 1945). In this respect Pedersen's interpretation followed that of feminist scholars who compared other European welfare regimes and their effects on women, although she argued that gender relations were not at the heart of French and British policies but rather concerns about children and "assimilating children to other 'risks' to be shared."[12]

Other research has focused on the relationship between the gender division of labor and the development of industrial welfare in the private sector. In her work on employer strategies in British and French metalworking, Laura L. Downs discussed how metalworking entrepreneurs in the Paris region refined the gender division of labor during and after World War I and hired factory superintendents to supervise women in newly rationalized small metalworking factories to promote the health and hygiene of their female charges.[13] Thus, at the same time as they rationalized metalworking, breaking down the labor process and "deskilling" formerly skilled jobs in order to hire women, employers extended their rationalization initiatives to the private sphere and the regulation of reproduction and maternity. Downs argued that employer-based industrial welfare in this single industry fit with the pronatalist objectives of French employers and the state in the decades following the war, by attempting to reconcile women's labor force participation with pregnancy and motherhood. These policies and practices initiated by both employers and the state underscored the extent to which, in postwar France, public and private domains intersected, particularly as the state and employers made the private domains of maternity and the family more open to public scrutiny than ever before, and as public agents of the state intruded on and regulated the private sphere of the family.

If initiatives that permitted women to reconcile childbearing and motherhood with work made the French welfare state seem friendly to women, feminist scholars have also pointed to its failure to achieve gender equality.[14] In the nineteenth century, for example, protective labor legislation pointed to the incompatibility of women's work and maternity.[15] Treating women as a special category of worker, it undermined women's ability to claim equal treatment with men in terms of wages or access to certain kinds of jobs. At the beginning of the twenty-first century, French women overall still earned 24 percent less than men; women in administrative posts—*cadres*—earned 33 percent less than their male counterparts. Women also experienced higher unemployment rates and the percentage of women employed in part-time work was almost six times as high as that of men. Although in March 2000 the French National Assembly adopted a law designed to reinforce 1983 legislation condemning gender discrimination at work, most agree that it has not been adequately enforced.[16] In other domains as well, the "social state" had ambiguous gender effects. Women in France have held formal political rights only since 1944 and have remained vastly underrepresented in democratic legislative bodies as well as in labor organizations.[17] Until 1975, when birth control was legalized in France, they lacked the civil right to bodily integrity inherent in reproductive rights. Recently feminist analysts have examined the relationship between social citizenship, work, and care and have critiqued the failure of welfare states to address gender-specific forms of care and care work, even or perhaps especially in France, where maternalist arguments played such a large role in the formulation of family policies.[18]

Alongside their social rights and their late accession to political and civil rights in the late twentieth century, women in France have lacked full *economic* citizenship. The concept of economic citizenship, understood as the right to work at the occupation of one's choice and as the right to economic independence, was not part of T. H. Marshall's original formulation of rights; as the American historian Alice Kessler-Harris has noted, Marshall included these rights within the package of basic civil rights. Yet, "subsuming economic rights in the civil arena obscures their interactive influence on political and social citizenship."[19] As Kessler-Harris writes, although "democratic citizenship was closely tied to earning . . . the right to work constituted a rather precarious guarantee even for skilled free white men and none at all for women of any race."[20] In France, women's lack of economic citizenship had important consequences for how the French social model was elaborated over time. Indeed, the question of economic citizenship, who the state and employers consider a legitimate breadwinner, who works, when, and where are of profound importance to questions of inequality and hence of need, risk, and dependency that social models across Europe have sought to address. The fact that social protections in France have historically been tied to employment is reason enough to examine afresh how the cultural practices of gender difference in work shaped the expansion of social rights and political and social citizenship in the twentieth century.

This book reassesses the allegedly weak or moderate French male breadwinner norm and argues that amid intense debates about the relationship between gender, family, and work, the process of reconstruction in France following World War I refined gender divisions and gave fresh support to the male breadwinner ideal.[21] In this respect it departs from much recent comparative work on social policy that has claimed that French women's historically relatively high labor force participation, the high percentage of dual wage-earner families, and practices such as direct welfare payments to mothers have signaled the relative absence or weakness of the male breadwinner norm. Although French women's strong statistical presence in the labor force has been a persistent feature of French life, that perspective masks the strong historical ambivalence surrounding women's work and the persistent efforts to contest and contain women's rights as wage earners that began in the nineteenth century and continued during World War I (in spite of or perhaps because of women's employment in "nontraditional" defense work) and into the interwar years. Indeed, looking at the period 1914–19, debates about the female body at work, the consequences of women's wartime industrial work on reproduction, and policies designed to facilitate motherhood all demonstrated that far from liberating French women, the war reinforced prewar gender norms. The employment of women in jobs previously gendered male during World War I disrupted earlier gender divisions of labor, but only temporarily. As the historians Laura Downs, Susan Grayzel, and Mathilde Dubesset, Françoise Thébaud, and Catherine Vincent have shown, far from eradicating gender difference, the employment of women in nontraditional jobs in the defense industries produced new and resilient gender divisions of labor and inequalities.[22] To be sure, war provoked major cultural challenges to gender roles and relations, but it is not clear that these cultural challenges, as important as they were, positively influenced the lives of the vast majority of French women or that the war constituted as much of a watershed for women as some historians have claimed.[23] The male breadwinner ideal in France, moreover, was not only promoted by political conservatives; it received support from across the political spectrum. State officials, employers, and organized labor in the 1920s and 1930s incorporated strong ambivalence about women's status as breadwinners and helped to sustain patterns of gender inequality that became inscribed in French social life.

This study makes three claims. First, it asserts that the meanings attached to masculinity and paternity alongside those attached to femininity and maternity profoundly shaped postwar reconstruction, efforts to redefine citizenship in the 1920s and 1930s, and policies that addressed France's demographic deficit and the family.[24] In this regard, culture and the cultural practices of gender assumed as much importance as the statistical distribution of men and women in the labor force. This point is crucial for understanding how work influenced the French social model, for the relationship between work and gender helped determine who had the right to rights. Criticism of and skepticism about women's right to work on the basis of their role in social reproduction, their status under the law, and their ability to master skills and achieve professional competence—all symptomatic of the denial of full economic rights to women—arguably undermined their status as wage earners and had enormous repercussions for gender inequality beyond the labor force. Notions of rights and political participation—the very idea of political citizenship itself—emerged from social and cultural understandings about masculine and feminine roles in private and public realms. Women's relative lack of power in formal politics and the privileging of male political and civil citizenship resulted from the ways in which politics and the capacities of citizens were defined.[25] Policymakers' efforts to enhance paternal power both inside and outside the family shaped perceptions of the new social rights that emerged after World War I and recast citizenship claims. The cultural practices of gender, sometimes alongside ethnicity and race, influenced policies that addressed the family and employment, such as tax incentives for prolific fathers, family allowances, and unemployment benefits during the Depression.

World War I left a legacy of destruction marked not only by dramatic damage of the industrial and agricultural infrastructure but also by real and symbolic devastation of the body of the nation. The human and physical evidence of war was everywhere to be seen: men on crutches, men with missing limbs, the arm of an empty jacket tucked neatly into a pocket; the *mutilé de guerre* constituted a constant, public reminder of the hecatomb during the interwar years. But women, for the most part, survived without extensive physical damage, despite the dangers of the munitions factories and exposure to combat of men and women who faced German bombs that fell on French soil. The contrasts between the bodies of men who returned from the war maimed or shell-shocked and women who remained healthy and whole couldn't have been more dramatic. The war exposed the fragility of the hegemonic meanings of masculinity and femininity in ways that continued to have an impact on French society throughout the following two decades. In this context, ideas about manhood and the importance of paternity proved critical to reestablishing men's position in a reconstituted postwar society and to thinking about the intersections of citizenship and work. But in the postwar period, the meanings of gender were not always stable, especially when applied to foreign and colonial bodies.

Second, the French labor force had been bled dry by the war, forcing employers to call upon unprecedented immigration. The war had indeed exposed the racial and ethnic tensions that accompanied encounters between women workers and colonial workers of color and fears of sexual mixing.[26] Following the war, alongside the relative stability of its gender composition, the labor force became increasingly foreign and unskilled.[27] Although much scholarship on gender in post–World War I France has left aside race and ethnicity or has focused on the history of immigration while excluding its gender dimensions, this book argues that the changing ethnic and racial contours of the labor force in postwar France alongside women's strong labor force participation between the wars shaped the social and political dimensions of citizenship.[28] If the white male worker erroneously came to represent the universal worker in the nineteenth century, this model of the paradigmatic worker proved even less appropriate in the 1920s and 1930s.

Finally, in a major addition to the existing literature, this book asserts that Depression-era policies incorporated assumptions about gender and nationality that contributed to the inequalities embedded in the social model. The Depression put to an end the period of spectacular economic growth that characterized the French economy of the 1920s (a rate of 9 percent for French industrial growth between 1921 and 1929). France during the 1920s had witnessed substantial shifts in economic structure and productive apparatus, represented by the fact that by the end of that decade, the majority of wage earners worked in enterprises employing over 100 workers (in 1906, 60 percent of wage earners worked in shops of fewer than 100 employees).[29] Alongside older, less dynamic industries like textile, garment, and leather production, the aggressive food, automobile, and metalworking industries deployed extensive mechanization and rationalization to modernize and expand. In the Paris suburbs, for example, the locus of small metalworking and manufacturing since the end of the nineteenth century, huge automobile factories blossomed. Renault, Citroën, and Berliet employed several thousand workers at the end of the war but employed around 30,000 by the end of the 1930s. These massive factories included large numbers of women and immigrants alongside French male workers. The growth of the state sector caused the number of public service workers to increase by 50 percent during the 1920s, reflecting the tremendous expansion of postal and telephone services, primary schools, and state bureaucracy, all of which employed large numbers of women.[30] Indeed, the state played a larger economic role than ever by providing credits for the reconstruction of industrial infrastructure, facilitating the employment of contract immigrant labor, providing public housing, and spurring the development of the aviation industry among others. Yet the economic development and prosperity of the 1920s that protected France from the immediate effects of the worldwide Depression of the 1930s did not immunize France against serious economic downturn or its differential effects on women, men, and foreign workers. Policies that attempted to deal with these effects incorporated social inequalities that subsequently influenced the gendered forms of French social citizenship.

During the comparatively brief twenty-year period between the world wars, the combined processes of economic modernization, expansion, and contraction rendered the nature and meanings of work in France increasingly complex. In examining these developments, this book draws on a rich history of women and work. Scholarship on France between the world wars has examined the expansion and diversification of women's work throughout the economy in metalworking, automobile production, garment manufacture, and in the new industries that were linked to the economic growth of the interwar period—consumer goods, pharmaceutical manufacture, and food processing—as well as the expanding service sector in teaching and in the postal and telephone services.[31] Research has also chronicled women's exclusion from jobs on the basis of gender, has pointed to the obstacles they faced within organized labor, and has examined women's professional trajectories and occupational mobility in the 1920s and 1930s.[32] Finally, still in its infancy, historical work on women during the Depression of the 1930s has shown how women experienced the economic crisis differently from men, focusing on the structural position of women in the economy and on the attendant complexities of measuring women's unemployment. Variations between industrial sectors, as well as geographically and between firms influenced women's experience of the Depression.[33]

These developments occurred within a context of profound political volatility as French governments lurched back and forth between conservative and progressive political formations.[34] The Bloc national government of immediate postwar period (1919–24) brought together a heterogeneous collection of war veterans, conservative Catholics, radicals, and a handful of center-leaning socialists who struggled between the competing drives of embracing modernity and returning to a mythic prewar stability. Although legislation in 1919 established the eight-hour day, the government also proved ready to crush massive strikes in 1919 and 1920, gave the offensive to employers to embark on reconstruction on their own terms, and took the first steps toward the promulgation of conservative family and social policies. The alternation between the reactionary politics of the Bloc national (1919–24) and the progressive Radical-Socialist Cartel des gauches (1924–26) is but one example of shifts in the political terrain that would characterize the entire period up to World War II.

The efforts of the more left-leaning Radical-Socialist Cartel to pursue a social agenda of extending rights to workers and enforcing labor laws constituted a brief interlude in a period of troubled Radical governments that rose and fell with alarming rapidity. A 1924 law authorized the unionization of public sector workers and the government threw its weight behind application of the eight-hour day. The Cartel not only arbitrated a major strike of Breton cannery workers; it even provided financial assistance to strikers' families. In 1925, it expanded the maternity leave benefits for working women inaugurated by the 1913 Strauss law.[35] These efforts demonstrated the state's willingness to support social rights. Under the leadership of Raymond Poincaré, the subsequent Union nationale government stabilized (in 1926) and subsequently devalued (1928) the franc, placing it at one fifth of its previous value. These measures temporarily ended financial instability but included new taxes (on beverages, automobiles, and income, among other things) and severe belt-tightening in the growing public sector, much to the distress of French workers. Just before the government passed major social insurance legislation in 1928 (further developed in the 1930 social insurance law), conservatives swept back into power where they remained to oversee the Depression, with the exception of the period from 1932 to 1934 and the Popular Front.[36] The most important experience of state regulation in the period, the Popular Front, provided real and lasting gains to workers over a brief two-year period, establishing compulsory arbitration of labor disputes, paid vacations for all French workers, and new collective contracts between workers and employers, as well as nationalizing banks, among other measures. Yet in spite of the Popular Front government's real and durable measures of social solidarity, gender inequality proved tenacious and even left-leaning governments failed to integrate women fully into all the rights of political, social, or economic citizenship.

The following chapters examine how the state, employers, and organized labor contributed to the mixed record that underpinned the French social model, by focusing on the relationship between work, citizenship, and rights. Chapter 1 explores how postwar reconstruction simultaneously addressed France's demographic deficit, massive labor shortage, and the redeployment of labor. In the politically conservative climate of the 1920s, reconstituting the national body—not only to rebuild the labor force and increase population but also to rebuild the nation in symbolic terms—loomed large on the agenda of government officials and social observers. At the war's end, visions of women's return to home and family predictably accompanied employers' and state planners' efforts both to promote population growth and to engineer men's reinsertion into the labor market. These groups supported men's authority in the family and promoted policies that attempted to expand fathers' rights through tax breaks for married men with children and proposals for a family vote, while simultaneously punishing unmarried men with a tax on bachelors. At the same time, immigration of one million, largely male, colonial workers and foreign nationals to France between 1919 and 1924 made ethnicity and nationality part of the social landscape in which discussions of national regeneration and economic recovery occurred.[37] Some social observers argued that French women's labor force participation could counteract the influence of foreigners. Others saw foreign workers as a substitute for women who could otherwise devote themselves to bearing and rearing the nation's children. These debates shaped the family-centered social policies of the 1920s.

Having outlined how government officials and social observers defined the contours of postwar reconstruction, chapters 2 and 3 turn to how employers contributed to the foundations of the twentieth-century social model by reinforcing gender divisions and promoting the position of male breadwinners. In the postwar years when "science" promised "modernity," a more efficient workplace, and greater productivity, employers used rationalization and industrial physiology to raise productivity and in the process refine gender and/or ethnic divisions of labor. Chapter 2 expands on previous historical research, using archived factory superintendents' reports and studies of scientific management to show how employers implemented new management techniques more broadly across the economy than historians have previously recognized. The small metalworking industries upon which Laura Downs's excellent study focused demonstrate how rationalization and the creation of more refined gender divisions proceeded in one industry. Yet similar techniques of gender-based rationalization in varying degrees permeated dozens of other industries in which women worked, such as automobile manufacturing, textiles, and the food industries. Training and apprenticeship programs revealed employers' assumptions about the gender and race of breadwinners in efforts to reconstitute a skilled industrial labor force and create a new "citizen-worker."

Chapter 3 examines the contribution of industrial physiology (ergonomics) to refining racial or ethnic and gender divisions of labor. Although existing scholarship on the science of work and fatigue has focused on male European industrial workers, this chapter shows that physiologists made use of gender difference and overlapping racial categories in analyzing workers' responses to fatigue. As a form of rationalization, industrial physiology offered a new way of thinking about the deployment of immigrant and colonial workers as well as French workers. Scientists promoted gender and racial divisions in the interest of increasing workers' efficiency, while claiming to address the "human factor" that scientific management had ostensibly ignored. Their research influenced employment practices, creating a new category of "foreign worker" alongside the "woman worker," further complicating an already complex and stratified division of labor within both industry and the growing service sector. The refinement of the gender division of labor that resulted from the deployment of rationalization and industrial physiology did not translate directly into support for male breadwinners. Women's employment itself constituted recognition of women's right *to* work, but it did not constitute recognition of women's rights *as* workers. The effects of more highly refined gender divisions that systematically relegated women to less remunerative, unskilled jobs in industry or the service sector did have an impact on women's ability to support their families. Employers' use of aptitude testing and vocational guidance, both by-products of the science of work, contributed to defining the gender of breadwinners and reinforcing social inequalities.

Chapter 4 discusses how organized labor simultaneously supported women's right to work, contested the "scientific organization of labor," and defended the male breadwinner. Analysis of the labor press, labor congresses, and the writings of contemporary social observers shows how anxieties about the family, immigration, and gender roles emerged in organized labor's reactions to rationalization. Some male workers targeted shift work as destructive of family life; others feared displacement by women and foreigners; and women and men across the economy protested against the overwork that resulted from rationalization. At the same time, male labor leaders favored aspects of the emerging social model: the state's promotion of family and population growth and privileging of fathers' rights in families. The chapter shows how workers' responses to scientific management and their discussions of family, population, and the meaning of a living wage were directed at sustaining the privileged position of male breadwinners between the wars.

Chapter 5 shows how the state incorporated ideas about gender and family in expanding political and social rights during the later 1920s in two ways: first, by facilitating the naturalization of thousands of immigrants who entered the French labor market in the 1920s, thus broadening political citizenship, and second, by expanding social provisions for families that marked France as a leader in the formation of the modern European welfare state. This chapter shows how population and concerns about family and fertility eased the attainment of political citizenship rights for some men and the achievement of social rights for women. In contrast to the Marshallian model of citizenship, women in France achieved social rights before they attained full political rights. Economic citizenship remained elusive. Although the voices of working women, so critical to both reproduction and production, often were heard only indirectly in the formulation of social policies that were delivered "from the top down," working women claimed rights based on their status as both workers and mothers, linking the maternal body to the welfare of the nation. However, the logic of women's claims also threw into relief the frailty of the social model for women, as the Depression demonstrated.

Chapter 6 examines how, following on employers' and organized labor's support for male breadwinners, the French state's management of the Depression of the 1930s contributed to a gendered model of rights. Although historians still debate the exact dimensions and causes of the Depression in France, until recently this scholarship has tended to ignore its gender dimension.[38] This chapter shows how, in a manner consistent with postwar reconstruction policies and the extension of rights, in developing measures to deal with the Depression, employers, the state, and organized labor threw into question women's rights as wage earners and the rights of immigrant workers. Based on archival research and contemporary economic analyses, the chapter demonstrates that the Depression pushed to the foreground a major debate over who should be a family provider, with implications for the disbursement of unemployment benefits. Despite the fact that the Popular Front government of Leon Blum made important gestures in the direction of gender equity, overall the state reinforced rather than diminished gender inequalities with regard to employment during the Depression. Thus, the social policies of the 1930s built on those of the 1920s to create a distinctly French package of social rights with mixed consequences for women.

The conclusion reviews the significance of these historical developments for the later development of the French social model and explores some of the ramifications of inequalities in work for employment-based social policies. It suggests that the patterns of more refined gender and ethnic divisions at work and decisions about who counted as a breadwinner and a citizen that emerged in the 1920s and 1930s undermined the French social model's broader goals of solidarity in the post–World War II welfare state as seen particularly in the gendering of care work.

CHAPTER ONE

RECONSTRUCTION AND REGENERATION

AFTER WORLD WAR I

Massive mortality, destruction of industrial infrastructure in the north, and widespread food shortages constituted only a few of the challenges France faced in the aftermath of World War I. In contrast to Britain, where a discourse of "a return to normalcy" defined the project of post–World War I recovery, France embarked on a much broader and more deliberate process of national reconstruction and regeneration that encompassed efforts to stimulate population growth, rebuild economic infrastructures, contain social unrest, and reconstitute the labor force in the wake of massive wartime losses. Over 16 percent of French enlisted men had died—the highest casualty rate of any of the European combatants with the exception of Germany and Russia.[1]

Demobilization and reconstruction involved the Herculean task of rebuilding industrial infrastructure and redeploying the wartime labor force in the midst of a dramatic labor shortage. It also implied the regeneration of the social body in real and symbolic terms in a country whose birthrate was the lowest in Western Europe (18.1 per thousand in 1914; 12.6 in 1919). The loss of some one and a half million lives and the injury or maiming of another one and a half million also profoundly marked efforts to reestablish social stability, the family, and men's and women's places both in the home and in civil society. By 1919, labor shortage and widespread industrial unrest accompanied men's reinsertion into the labor market and corresponding visions of women's return to home and family. Massive immigration brought over one million foreign workers into France between 1919 and 1924, their numbers nearly tripling by 1931, challenging the contours of French "identity."[2] This chapter examines how employers, workers, and the state dealt with these competing challenges in the process of reconstituting French society after the war. It looks specifically at the reaffirmation of gender difference through social policies and the debates they elicited. Tension between the desire to reinforce the position of male breadwinners and fathers on the one hand and the need for women's labor in key sectors on the other hand constituted an important legacy of the war. Anxieties about gender that ultimately underscored France's social model were played out at the intersecting sites of culture, the family, and work.

The paradigm of a gendered reserve army of labor has influenced much thinking about the effects of wars on periods of postwar reconstruction: women would take on "male jobs" during wartime and withdraw from the labor force following wars as men returned to their former positions. Yet this model does not capture the nuances of French recovery following World War I. The war arguably disrupted gender divisions at work and shattered the fragile boundaries between public and private realms. It also destabilized prewar assumptions about gender and power as women expanded their arenas of expertise and authority in men's absence. Some 500,000 women contributed to the war effort as armaments workers, machining metal on laths and loading shell; by sewing military uniforms; by volunteering in hospitals and canteens; and by driving Red Cross ambulances in the field, counting for fully 46 percent of the labor force in 1918 (from 38.2 percent in 1911).[3] But the apparent suppression of gender difference during the war proved to be partial and superficial. As Laura Downs has shown, gender difference remained central to the wartime organization of labor. Employers mobilized what they defined as women's gender-specific skills to rationalize wartime defense production and create unskilled "women's work" in the defense industries.[4] During the war, as women left behind domesticity and "feminine" occupations, debate raged over the effects of munitions work on women's childbearing capacities and employers and government officials scrutinized their morality as they worked alongside colonial workers.[5] Although government officials and social observers marveled at their abilities and applauded women's labor as essential, they never viewed it as "normal." This would become strikingly apparent at the end of the war. As wartime industries shut down at the end of 1918 and women shifted out of armaments production, despite a drop in women's labor force participation, their presence in paid employment remained strong (see table 1, page 47).

At the war's end, conservatives and liberals alike participated in reestablishing gender boundaries as many came to see the reconstitution of masculinity and femininity as central to the task of national reconstruction.[6] Postwar literary representations of women embodied a devastating critique of the shift in women's employment, reproductive choices, and fashion.[7] Concerns about gender relations saturated writing about soldiers' return from the front as novelists and essayists depicted efforts to reconstitute male authority and power in domestic life. At the end of the war, soldiers described their anxieties about coming home, their fears of a sea change in conjugal relations, and humiliation at their loss of authority as breadwinners. The novelist Gaston Rageot described how some men, returning from the front felt compelled to relieve and care for their wives, whereas "others felt a confused humiliation because they were no longer the breadwinners. All were persuaded that they would never find their wives exactly as they had left them: some would be lost and the best would have become authoritarian and imperious, playing at being the boss."[8] As one soldier wrote, "Coming home victorious . . . will it be fair to return to a deserted hearth where our authority, so hard-won, will no longer be recognized? . . . Pushed out of his age-old role as protector at the moment when he has just qualified once more for the title, will [the returning soldier] have to put up with sharing civil and political struggles with women?"[9] Although the novelist and country doctor Ernest Perochon praised women as the guardians of hearth and home in his 1924 postwar romantic evocation of peasant life, *Les gardiennes,* he too mourned the loss of male control: "The virile fist was gone and the capricious beings upon whom it ultimately weighed now sought to emancipate themselves."[10]

Whereas some criticized women's independence and control in men's absence, other writers targeted women's alleged sexual promiscuity and charged that women had been "living it up" at home while men perished at the front.[11] Louis Barthas, a corporal in the 81st infantry, illustrated this view of women as egotistical pleasure seekers as he bitterly observed that Parisian women, "with their *décolleté* dresses and short skirts, bare arms and shoulders seemed [only] to care about looking attractive" while the Big Berthas rained bombs on France and soldiers fell right and left.[12] Indeed, the contrast between women's comparative safety on the home front and the horrors of the real front produced no end of war and postwar bitterness and resentment, culminating in the cultural critique of the independent woman of the 1920s that has been described so vividly by Mary-Louise Roberts.[13]

Descriptions of gender anxiety constituted a revealing dimension of the cultural challenges of postwar reconstruction. While femininity has been subject to much historical analysis, less historical work has analyzed the reassertion of masculinity to reestablish that "virile fist."[14] Yet the war not only provoked a critique of the independent woman; it also raised concerns about men's resumption of their dominant position in a new postwar order. This chapter argues that postwar attempts to reestablish *both* hegemonic ideals of femininity and motherhood alongside masculine authority and fatherhood underscored the social and economic reconstruction of the postwar years. Yet policymakers and social observers who sought to reaffirm gender divisions did not simply reproduce prewar gender ideals and cultural practices but established them on new foundations in response to the demands of particular postwar dilemmas and conjunctures. France's demographic deficit proved to be especially salient to reconstruction and led to innumerable debates about and initiatives designed to regenerate the national body—initiatives that proved fundamental to casting the origins of the French social model.

Regenerating the National Body

Historians have long noted how states have used the politics of sexuality and reproductive policy in furthering national and nationalist aims.[15] The project of healing the French nation after World War I was no different. In a political environment dominated by the conservative Bloc national government, doctors, social observers, and the state officials mobilized around demographic recovery. Pronatalist agitation predated World War I and France's historically low birthrate preoccupied social observers in the last decades of the nineteenth century.[16] Following France's defeat in the Franco-Prussian War, in the context of intense anti-German sentiment, numerous works appeared on the subject, raising the specter of national degeneration. Émile Zola denounced France's chronic low population growth, and particularly infanticide, in his 1899 novel *La fécondité*. Social critics targeted high infant mortality, usually framed as a class issue and linked to attacks on women's work outside the home, as the source of prewar demographic stagnation and France's loss of international prestige.[17] As in 1870, the invasion of northern departments in late 1914 and the rapid French defeat during World War I immediately turned attention to the problem of low French fertility as responsible for the weakness of the French army. Doctors simultaneously debated the compatibility of women's defense work with maternal health.[18] Following the war, an explosion of proposals and policies designed to promote population growth and regenerate the national body resurfaced.[19] Public discussions, debates, and policies in this domain deployed and in turn constituted notions of masculinity and fatherhood alongside femininity and motherhood. The deeply troubling wartime atrocities, particularly the rape of French women by German soldiers, and the fate of the children who resulted from these rapes, played a brief, but telling role in these debates.[20]

Atrocities perpetrated by enemy soldiers on French women in the first three months of the war and the production of "children of the barbarians" constituted one of several forms of violent intrusion of foreigners upon the national body.[21] The maternal bodies of raped women became a symbolic battlefield. The little that scholars have written on the subject has focused on women's victimization and the debate over whether women who had been raped by German soldiers and became pregnant should be permitted to abort, or on the representation of rape as a violation of the (female) nation and the French race.[22] Although feminists, deputies, and doctors supported allowing victims of rape to abort, proposals that the laws penalizing abortion be relaxed for French women in the occupied departments who had been raped never saw the light of day. Rather, the government ordered public assistance hospitals to admit raped and pregnant women free of charge and pledged to pay the expenses of home deliveries by a midwife. French maternity stood at the center of this debate, and from the perspective of doctors and others opposed to abortion, bearing these children gave mothers an opportunity to perform a kind of national service by raising them as French citizens. French mothers' milk could make them French.[23] At the same time, as Ruth Harris and Stéphane Audoin-Rouzeau have pointed out, rape not only constituted the humiliation of French women; it constituted an assault on the masculinity and honor of French men, powerless to defend their homes and families.[24] Documentary sources as well as visual and literary representations of rape portrayed German men as a "race" of aggressive barbarians embodying masculine force and violence. They also depicted French men as helpless victims of French moral frailty and decadence as well as of the rape of their wives and daughters.[25]

The pregnancies that resulted from these rapes raised further questions about the power of French fatherhood and motherhood in wartime and the eugenics dimension of these debates showed how concerns about biological regeneration in France intersected with concerns about racial purity and national stability.[26] Indeed, in 1915, a French labor activist writing under the name of Jehan Rictus racialized the German rapist in the pages of *La Bataille syndicaliste*: the "German race" is "an inferior and unworldly race. Whatever they do they will remain gorillas, orang-outangs. . . . The child of the German can only become . . . a brute and a criminal degenerate."[27] Both of these issues appeared in discussions of telegony or "physiological impregnation," the theory that once impregnated with German sperm, a woman's body was altered forever; "once violated, French women might also pass on Teutonic heredity to subsequent children conceived with French husbands."[28] Indeed some of the most eminent physicians were convinced that "the propagation of [the French] race is menaced . . . for . . . the [result of] rape and pregnancy . . . [is] a fetus that bears, in large part, the traits of the male progenitor."[29] Embedded within concerns about telegony and threats to "racial" purity were fears about French men's ability to transmit their traits to offspring and hence concerns about masculine sexual and reproductive potency. As Harris has written, the effort to repopulate France can also be construed as "[men's] means of re-appropriating French women, the French family, and French national territory."[30] Arguably, concern about rape and the fate of the potential offspring of these unions was most intense during the early stages of the war, as German troops swept over the north of France. But historical evidence suggests that the threat to masculine identity produced by German soldiers' rapes of French women and the debate over whether women could bear children who would carry the genetic imprint of the father also endured as part of the war's cultural legacy.[31] Ultimately, the larger issue of replacing France's enormous losses overshadowed the memory of German atrocities.

The French state emerged from the war with unprecedented authority in both the public and private spheres, and the dilemmas of postwar recovery rendered the private sphere more public and more subject to state scrutiny than ever before. As historians have shown, concerns about promoting the family and recovering French population proved critical in shaping France's nascent welfare state from the end of the war through the 1930s and beyond. A combination of public and private initiatives created the foundations of the social model. After a brief recovery in 1920 (to 20.4 live births per thousand from 12.6 in 1919), French fertility dropped steadily through the 1920s and 1930s, reaching a low of 14.6 live births per thousand in 1939.[32] Demographic recovery stood high on the agenda of the men who entered the new postwar center-right Bloc national government, many of whom had ties to the Alliance nationale pour l'accroissement de la population française (National Alliance for French Population Growth), or the French Eugenics Society, both founded before the war. At the end of the war (1919) the government created the Conseil supérieur de la natalité (High Council on Fertility), designed to oversee population policy, and promoted the activities of the Institut d'études démographiques, (National Demographic Institute) to study and document the problems and progress of French fertility. In 1920 the government created the first health ministry, the Ministère de l'Hygiène, de l'Assistance, et de la Prévoyance sociale (Ministry of Hygiene, Assistance and Social Planning), headed by socialist deputy from the Orne and member of the Alliance nationale, Jean-Louis Breton. Other natalists such as Adolphe Landry, André Honnorat, and August Issac took up ministerial posts: Landry as Minister of the Navy, Honnorat as Minister of Public Works, and Issac as Minister of Commerce.[33] Historians have argued that maternity and motherhood became more central than ever to the constitution of postwar femininity. Doctors' and reformers' concerns about the effects of women's work during the war had their logical outcome in postwar policies that attempted to regulate women's sexuality and effectively placed upon them the burden of national regeneration.[34] The 1920 law on birth control and abortion fixed new criminal penalties for practicing or distributing information about abortion or contraception. By making it easier for judges to rule against the purveyors of information or devices, or to punish practitioners, the law effectively closed off the possibility of legal family limitation for millions of French men and women until 1975. Accompanying this coercive measure were the well-publicized arrests of prominent birth control advocates. The firing, arrest, and imprisonment of a schoolteacher, Henriette Alquier, in 1927 for publishing an article in favor of birth control (she was later acquitted) and the imprisonment of Jeanne and Eugène Humbert of the Ligue malthusienne for advocating birth control exemplified the repressive dimension of postwar sexual politics.

Most measures addressed women specifically and provided positive encouragement to childbearing and motherhood. Under the leadership of Adolphe Pinard, obstetrician and a vice president of the French Eugenics Society, the government created the Ecole de puericulture (Infant Care School) and by 1923 all French schoolgirls were required to take a course in infant care.[35] In 1928, after years of debate, Raymond Poincaré's Union nationale government pushed through a progressive social insurance law that also expanded the 1913 Strauss Law on obligatory maternity leaves for working women to provide them with twelve weeks of paid leave, government-sponsored delivery and postnatal care, and a monthly nursing allowance.[36] Meanwhile, the growth and development of French medicine and public health in the 1920s and 1930s led to new standards of hospital-based care for pregnant women and their newborn children.[37] Symbolic rewards for mothers also encouraged and celebrated prolific maternity, such as the Medal of the French Family, established in 1920 by the postwar Center-Right coalition government of Alexandre Millerand, which rewarded mothers of large families with bronze, silver, and gold medals according to the number of children, honoring them for their patriotism and national service.[38] Subsequently, the Union nationale government established Mother's Day as an annual celebration in 1926; pronatalist groups held parades in 1933 and 1938; and in 1938 the government unveiled a Monument to the French Mother on the Boulevard Kellerman in Paris.[39]

Parallel interventions of Catholic familialists, pronatalists, and feminists promoted maternity and women's domestic vocation. As Karen Offen and Anne Cova have shown, Catholic and non-Catholic defenses of maternity dated at least since the Franco-Prussian War, when nationalist reactions to the French defeat raised the specter of French "racial decline" and made mothers the defenders of the race.[40] Before the war, social reformers who looked askance at women's public wage labor encouraged working women to return to home and family duties. After World War I, these arguments intensified in the context of pronatalist hysteria. As they stepped up the campaign to raise the French birthrate, Catholic familialists likewise promoted maternity as women's "natural" duty and also as vital to reconstituting the national body. The Catholic Union féminine civique et sociale (UFCS; Feminine Civic and Social Union), founded in 1925 by Andrée Butillard and boasting more than 10,000 members, was an especially vocal promoter of this view.[41] Butillard and others like Eve Baudouin not only argued for women's withdrawal from wage work and their return to the home but in the 1930s led an aggressive campaign for an unwaged mother's allowance that would provide state support to married women who stayed at home in order to care for their infant children.[42]

Although the French feminists Cécile Brunschvicg, Marguerite Witt-Schlumberger, and other "maternal feminists" argued that women would be better mothers if they had the full complement of civil and political rights, unlike the UFCS, they never argued that women's work was incompatible with motherhood or unnatural.[43] At the end of the war, Madeleine Vernet founded a monthly revue, La Mère éducatrice, which glorified maternity and simultaneously promoted feminist pacifism.[44] Brunschvicg argued that mothers had a crucial role to play in remaking French society after the war by fighting against infant mortality. A series of articles in the feminist newspaper La Française praised the activities of "des mères viriles" (literally, virile mothers), working mothers who had kept the country going during the war.[45] The term illustrated how women's assumption of male duties and occupations in wartime had led to a new form of republican motherhood based on aggressive and restorative maternity. Feminist maternalists also argued for the importance of state supports for motherhood, picking up on prewar and wartime demands for protection for pregnant and nursing mothers, and demanded measures that would permit the reconciliation of work and motherhood.[46]

Alongside policies that rewarded maternity and women's movements that promoted motherhood, others, such as Paulette Bernège, sought to revalorize domesticity and elevate homemaking to professional status in the 1920s.[47] Whereas pronatalist groups saw the return of working women to home and motherhood as an end in itself, Bernège, inspired by American promoter of home economics and household science, Christine Fredericks, argued that by rationalizing the household and providing home economics training, women could become more effective mothers and homemakers and gain social influence.[48] Her application of scientific management techniques involved performing time-measurement studies of cooking and cleaning, arguably a major departure from the domesticity of the prewar years. Her efforts were paralleled by the annual Salon des Arts ménagers that opened in 1923 with a dazzling array of cooking ranges, washing machines, and refrigerators, promising modernization and convenience to homemakers and designed to seduce women to adopt new domestic technology.[49] In the same year Bernège created the Institut d'organisation ménagère; a few years later she formed the Ligue de l'organisation ménagère and had founded a journal, *Mon chez moi*, devoted to providing information on the organization of kitchens and laundry rooms, housing, and keeping its readers informed of parallel developments in the United States and elsewhere in Europe.[50] By 1930 she had acquired enough support to open an Ecole de haut enseignement ménager in Paris.

While Bernège campaigned for the rationalization of the household, social Catholic agrarian activists appealed to rural women to become the "gracious missionaries of the return to the land" and lead the battle against social decadence, individualism, and rural population decline.[51] Although this movement began prior to the war, numerous manuals of rural domestic economy appeared after the war, some of them reissued editions of earlier publications, praising women's rural domesticity, lauding the virtues of dairying, poultry raising, vegetable and flower gardening, and filled with mouthwatering recipes for jams, conserves, and stews.[52] Although in other contexts social Catholics deplored women's industrial labor (while simultaneously organizing them in Catholic trade unions), they praised women's labor in the countryside: competent wives could keep men and families home on the farm. From 1919 on they multiplied their efforts to mobilize rural women, combining religious retreats with courses in home economics, housekeeping, cooking, accounting, horticulture, and animal husbandry.[53] Along with right-wing agrarians they spearheaded the founding of agricultural home economics schools and circulating home economics training programs, initiatives that the French government later supported.[54] More than merely educating women in the skills of dairying or cheese making, agricultural home economics educators now attempted to professionalize home economics to make it more attractive to women by dispensing certificates and diplomas. Fully aware that the farm woman's long, sixteen-hour days alienated even those most enamored of rural life, the Countess Keranflech-Kernezne, a major figure in the rural home economics movement and head of the women's section of the Société des agriculteurs de France, applied a Taylorist model, encouraging her audiences to undertake their own time-management studies to rationalize farm labor in order "to make the farm woman a specialized, qualified professional."[55] The efforts of Bernège and other right-wing agrarians to rationalize the household and professionalize the housewife responded to multiple postwar social and economic objectives. They could reeducate the independent woman by creating an alternative feminine career, halt demographic decline, and potentially stimulate the growth of a burgeoning consumer economy.

Alongside measures that specifically addressed women, other social policies were more gender-neutral. Before the war, legislation in 1913 provided for aid to needy large families, the beginning of a much more far-reaching set of state supports for families with at least three children regardless of financial situation, in order to encourage young couples to have children. Although its application was cut short by the war, other legislation passed in 1918 and 1921 established the first birth bonuses. Birth-conscious Catholic textile entrepreneurs in the Nord and the department of the Vosges as well as the Michelin rubber company offered family wage bonuses to their male and female workers and the first birth bonuses financed by the départments appeared in 1920. Eventually the state provided an impressive array of financial incentives: state-sponsored family allowances went into effect in 1923 to aid poor families with more than three children—a policy that was expanded and finally generalized to all by legislation in 1932 that established state authority over privately administered allowances.[56] In the postwar years, in addition to the Medal of the French Family, no fewer less than six prizes existed to honor and financially assist large families and support French

Christian families: the Bernard Prize; Barnoud Prize; a special prize created by Auguste Issac, pronatalist businessman who became Minister of Commerce in 1919; the Prix Lamy; and two prizes established by the Cognacq-Jay family.[57] By this time, a panoply of private associations existed to promote population growth and lobby government officials. These included the Alliance nationale pour l'accroissement de la population française (National Alliance for French Population Growth), later known in the 1930s as the Alliance nationale contre la dépopulation (National Alliance Against Depopulation), the conservative Ligue des droits de la famille (Family Rights' League), local Associations des familles nombreuses (Associations of Large Families), the Fédération nationale des familles nombreuses (National Federation of Large Families), and a Groupe parlementaire de la famille et de la natalité (Parliamentary Group on Family and Fertility) which included 220 deputies by 1932.[58] These groups also sponsored pronatalist policies that addressed fathers and contributed to the revalorization of procreative masculinity in civil society and the family in ways that overlapped with concerns about French racial purity.

Masculinity and the Population Question

Leaders of pronatalist groups Jacques Bertillon, Fernand Boverat, August Issac, Charles Richet, and Adolphe Pinard naturally supported postwar measures that punished childlessness. They also privileged prolific fathers and promoted fatherhood with progressive inducements to patriotism by drawing comparisons between men's duty to perform military service and their duty to produce children. Their interventions participated in shaping ideas about gender, and especially generative manhood, in the interwar period; they also promoted a particular racial logic in the work of reversing postwar demographic decline.

From the late nineteenth century, many writers and social observers had tied their notions of respectable French masculinity to men's roles as fathers. In 1897, Jacques Bertillon, chief demographer at the Bureau du travail statistique de Paris (Paris Statistics Bureau) and one of the founders of the Alliance nationale pour l'accroissement de la population française, had targeted men as responsible for France's low birthrate. For Bertillon the duty of men to procreate was every bit as important as their duty to defend their country. But he believed that the legal requirement of partible inheritance and high inheritance taxes kept fathers from having more than one or two children, in order to maintain family wealth intact.[59] Bertillon argued for reducing inheritance taxes for large families and argued that men with more than three children be exempt from taxes entirely.[60] Although pronatalist legislators never actually went this far, Bertillon's proposals and subsequent measures showed how gender influenced initiatives to place a greater tax burden on those who failed to perform their reproductive duty. Following this logic of redistribution, the June 25, 1920, income tax law established a 25 percent surtax on the incomes of single men and women and a 10 percent surtax on the incomes of childless couples who had been married for two years, thereby reallocating the burden of taxation.[61] Historians have understandably emphasized how legislators promoted women's economic dependence in the debates over the status of single women as taxpayers. Admitting that single women should pay the surtax posed the problem of implicitly acknowledging women's right to work (still a matter of debate in the postwar years), but unmarried women were only relieved from the obligation to pay the surtax in 1937.[62] On the other side of the ledger, easing the financial burden on those who replenished France, the income tax law of 1930 significantly increased deductions for dependents and reduced inheritance taxes for families counting four or more children.[63]

Natalist legislators invoked the virtues of procreative manhood in attempting to reconcile the need to generate new sources of revenue through revised taxation with the financial burdens of large families. In the debate over the 1920 income tax law, M. de Tinguy de Pouët, deputy and mayor of a small town in the conservative Vendée department, supporter of the surtax, and member of his local "groupe des familles nombreuses," spoke in the Chamber of Deputies in favor of a 2,000-franc deduction after the third child as a reward for procreative fathers, "to render to France what is owed to her. . . . fathers, in giving her children, have fulfilled their sacred duty; . . . in furnishing the nation with future citizens and taxpayers, they have acquitted a sacred debt."[64] It was only reasonable, legislators argued, that childless men and bachelors pay more, since they had fewer mouths to feed and because they paid lower indirect taxes (they presumably consumed less). In the words of Tinguy de Pouët, the surtax constituted a measure of "fiscal justice," designed "to surcharge more or less egoistic taxpayers" and equalize the burden of aggregate taxation.[65] But the surtax on bachelors and the implicit encouragement to men to marry and multiply constituted only one of multiple postwar legal initiatives designed to regenerate the postwar family and reinstate gender norms.

In enacting other legislation, like the law establishing a family allowance for families with at least three children debated in 1921 (and enacted in 1923), members of Parliament likewise criticized childless bachelors who lived sumptuous, pleasure-filled lives, whereas "the father of eight children has to feed ten mouths with the same amount of money the bachelor uses for himself, alone."[66] The bill established a national system of allowances designed to modify earlier legislation applicable only to poor families by creating uniform standards, thus removing the requirement that poor fathers establish need by going before their municipal councils. Deputy Joseph Delachanel's presentation of the bill prepared by the Commission de l'assistance et de la prévoyance (Assistance and Planning Commission) showed how the masculine honor of family men was at stake: "is it not humiliating to oblige fathers to seek help like beggars (*Très bien! Très bien!*), by submitting to the assessment of the municipal council which will then determine whether the family is poor enough to receive assistance?"[67] But the social obligation of procreative fatherhood explicit in the bill included a particular distributive logic. "Solely from the point of view of patriotic duty," Delachanel argued, "parents should have a minimum of three children. After the fourth, they really begin to serve and fortify the country. At this point, the cost of raising children should fall upon bachelors and fathers with fewer than three children, who have not completely fulfilled their social obligation."[68] These deputies promoted a new notion of respectable manliness solidly tied to the fulfillment of a moral duty in the family. Although some objected that the proposal to place the cost of support on those men who had not been sufficiently procreative would involve a heavy financial burden, the idea that the state had an obligation to support procreative virility in a period of demographic deficit prevailed.

Questions of men's authority in the family also emerged in the debate over which family member should receive the allowance. The Commission's proposal called for distributing the allowance to the mother, on the grounds that "it's the mother who takes care of the household, buys the clothes and food that the child needs. It is she who carries the responsibility of the large family; it is her virtue that makes her accept the weight of multiple pregnancies. It is only just that the nation pay homage to her."[69] Although the idea that mothers could be recipients of the allowance rested on the belief that this provision would enable mothers to carry out their domestic obligations, it also provoked a huge stir in the Chamber and constituted another battleground on which different notions of gender were elaborated and reproduced. Speaking to abundant applause, the Health Minister, Leredu, argued against giving the allowance to the mother because this would constitute a major blow to the very core of the family and paternal authority. "The family is not simply the mother; the normal family is both the father and the mother. Moreover, the Civil Code, in marriage law, has spelled out perfectly clearly the respective rights and duties of spouses. At the head of the family is the father: let him occupy his natural place."[70] August Issac, head of the Conseil supérieur de la natalité and one of the leaders of the Association nationale des familles nombreuses, echoed Leredu, arguing, "We must put respect for the family, the authority of its head at the forefront of this law and not simply sympathy for the mother burdened with children. The family must have respect and the family, until further notice, is represented by a head, who is the father."[71] Deputy Louis Duval-Arnould, later vice-president of the Conseil supérieur de la natalité, concurred that "it would be inadmissible that the law deprive the father of his rights as family head, rights that have been consecrated by every French tradition, as well as by the Civil Code."[72] This issue, object of one of several key debates over the bill, was finally resolved ten days later when the Commission agreed to pay the 350-franc allowance to the father as family head, unless a widow headed the family.[73] Finally, an additional amendment proposed by the natalist activist and deputy Abbé Jules Lemire incorporated into the bill the nationalist and class dimensions of natalism by specifying that only French families would be eligible to receive the allowance. Lemire simultaneously condemned working women as the real culprits in the French fertility crisis and made a counterproposal for an unwaged mother's allowance to encourage French mothers to stay at home. "Every working mother of French nationality [toute mère de nationalité française et de profession ouvrière] will receive from the State an annual allowance of 360 francs per child under 16 on the condition that she no longer leaves her home to work outside of the family."[74] In a long speech justifying the unwaged mother's allowance, Lemire praised the Flemish slogan "kind, keuken, kirk," as he extolled the virtues of homemade soup as the key to keeping French husbands close to home.[75] Too many working-class husbands fled to the café in order to wash down their indigestible, cold meals with a shot of alcohol ("un coup de piston d'alcool"), he argued. "Consider the man who goes to the cabaret because he's not enticed to stay at home by well-prepared food; this is a man who has not been caught by the mouth [pris par la bouche] like all men are, sooner or later (laughter and applause)." But a woman who was "a real guardian of the hearth, a queen, a governess, a housewife, who carried her children in her arms close to her heart," knows how to keep her husband out of the café.[76] Paying mothers an allowance to stay at home, Lemire believed, would help keep men committed to supporting the family. Lemire's counterproposal failed (although the unwaged mother's allowance was later incorporated into the French Family Code of 1938), but the message about the mutually reinforcing attributes of gender was clear: good housewives would make good family men.

Other measures, such as the advantages accorded to fathers in military service, worked in similar fashion to reinstate the power and authority of fathers heading *familles nombreuses,* large families with more than three children. The Ligues des familles nombreuses had made reduction of military service for the sons of large families part of their platforms, just as, before the war, the Alliance nationale pour l'accroissement de la population française had argued that the *impôt de sang* (the blood tax, that is, military service) be treated as the equivalent of the *impôt sur le revenu* (income tax). During the war, fathers of three children or more were the last to be mobilized and fathers of six children or more were permitted to return home. After the war lively debates occurred in the legislature over the military service of such fertile fathers and their sons. The law of April 1, 1923, reduced the military service for the oldest son in a family of at least five children to a year (with the next younger sons eligible to benefit from this disposition of the oldest had not already done so). It also relieved fathers of large families from military service (a father of eight children, for example, was discharged of all military obligations from the age of thirty-five).[77] Subsequent legislation in 1928 permitted soldier / fathers to be assigned to the garrisons closest to their homes and allowed families to receive an allowance for each son who was mobilized.[78] In much the same vein, the progressive Loucher housing law of 1928 that provided for the construction of new low-income housing gave fathers of at least three children land outright rather than requiring that they pay for the land on which the housing was built (*dispensation de l'apport du terrain*) and provided a substantial allowance for each child.[79] Finally, in 1936, while France continued to suffer the effects of the Depression, the Ministry of War granted the Alliance nationale contre la dépopulation the right to take its pronatalist appeals to military barracks. Natalists could now lecture a captive audience of young soldiers on the virtues of marriage and childbearing, inform them of family policies, and show films made by the Alliance describing the joys of family life.[80] Thus the state acknowledged its duty to promote the family and in some contexts privileged fatherhood and service to family as a form of male patriotism and duty to the state, alongside military service. These measures underscored state support for male breadwinners and ultimately became embedded in French social policy.

It is only fair to note that in spite of how pronatalists' incitements to reproduce dominated discussions of national regeneration, this was not the only discourse on sexuality in the 1920s and 1930s. At the same time that legislators debated policies, and in addition to initiatives that promoted maternity, a Catholic pronatalist literature on paternity also addressed the qualitative aspects of fatherhood and men's moral responsibilities in procreation.[81] Moreover, as Martine Sevegrand has shown, Catholic writers on marriage did not insist on fecundity as an absolute duty for couples; fecundity was rather the logical consequence of fulfilling one's "conjugal duty." The Catholic exaltation of chastity meant that husbands and wives could renounce their right to the body of their spouse and abstain from sex altogether. But middle-class Catholic men and women struggled with sexual desire in the face of Catholic doctrine, and undoubtedly others did as well. At the same time that the Church sought to channel desire toward reproduction, the project of reconstituting the national body was complicated by postwar demographic shifts.[82]

Immigration and Population

For many pronatalists unprecedented immigration of foreign (largely male) workers to France in the 1920s also meant tremendous changes in the composition of the social body and raised concerns about the purity of the French "race." The 1920s witnessed the unprecedented immigration of North Africans, Africans, Indo-Chinese, and Europeans from every corner of the continent. Racial and ethnic difference that occupied a relatively small place in French society prior to the war now proved more difficult to ignore, especially given widespread concerns about population decline. Race and nationality thus became part of the discursive landscape within which discussions of social regeneration occurred. The French eugenics movement, already active in the nineteenth century, emerged from the war with new vitality. In the 1920s for instance, it undertook a parliamentary campaign for a premarital examination, with Adolphe Pinard's 1926 proposal specifying that any French male citizen wishing to marry or to remarry would be obliged to undergo a medical examination to demonstrate that he carried no contagious diseases, on the assumption that men, not women, were the active partners in the reproductive act. Although the French parliament seriously debated Pinard's proposal, it did not become law until the Vichy government adopted it in 1942.[83] But it signaled a larger concern about the composition of French population that surfaced in the 1920s not only in the French Eugenics Society but also in the National Alliance for French Population Growth, linked to the intersecting "problems" of immigration, gender, and class.

Contemporaries' concerns about ethnic and racial mixing focused not only on working-class immigrants from French African and North African colonies and Asians, as yet relatively small in number, but also on the much larger numbers of "white immigrants," working-class Poles, Italians, Belgians, and Spanish.[84] Immigration in the service of national economic reconstruction could potentially disrupt the project of national repopulation unless it was carefully controlled and immigrants were carefully selected not only for their ability to work but also for their ability to increase the French population. For the Alliance immigration was not altogether bad as long as the government practiced a principle of selection: undesirables—those too old to reproduce, or groups that eugenicists and pronatalists believed could not easily be assimilated—had to be eliminated and admission of "desirables" had to be encouraged in order to promote population growth. Drawing the color line, in 1923, Fernand Boverat, prominent member of the Alliance and later its general secretary, argued for careful selection of "acceptable" workers, those from Spain, Italy, Czechoslovakia, Poland, and Romania—considered "white." Greeks, Levantines, and Kabyles, on the other hand, constituted "second order immigrants," and men of color were to be avoided at all costs "lest we experience the racial conflicts that have exploded in the United States with such disastrous consequences."[85] In his 1928 work on France and foreigners, Charles Lambert, deputy from the Vosges, former High Commissioner for Immigration and Naturalization, and an author of the 1927 Naturalization Law, similarly argued for selection in the "renovation of the French race." He advised the selection of "good stock," the Spanish, Italians, and Belgians as well as Slavs and Nordic peoples, Czechs, Poles, Russians, Swedes, the Dutch, and the Swiss, "prolific and strong," who would mix well with the French. On the other hand, Africans and Asians, "races which cannot melt [into the French race]," should be avoided. Apart from already formed large families, Lambert especially favored young immigrant men who could marry and father children.[86] In 1931, as France began to feel the effects of the Depression and debates over immigrant workers intensified, Boverat argued that foreign bachelors or childless married men above the age of forty could be turned back at the border; it was unlikely that they would contribute to increasing French population. Young family men, on the other hand, would most likely set roots into French soil and produce descendents who could become French, as would those groups who had the "natural potential to procreate," especially Spanish, Italians, and Poles, "white foreigners." Family life civilized young men and assured that they would contribute to repopulating France.[87] In the eyes of ardent pronatalists, immigrant male bodies, if appropriately selected, could contribute to the regeneration of the French social body.

Dozens of writers supported these ideas. Members of the French Eugenics Society promoted selective admission of immigrant workers, distinguishing desirables from undesirables and warning against admitting too many Africans and Asians. The vice-president of the Society, Eugène Apert, promoted such views, as did Georges Papillaut, vice-president of the Société d'anthropologie, who argued, "The productive white races can be considered capable of furnishing to France good elements of immigration."[88] But not all agreed on which groups of foreigners would make desirable immigrants. Doctors meeting at the annual congress of the Society for Public Medicine in 1926 heard a paper by a delegate of the Ministry of Interior and a departmental health inspector that raised the specter of immigration leading to the "decline of the white race." The authors quoted the French racist eugenicist Georges Vacher de Lapouge: "The first waves of Orientals and Slavs that are breaking on France presage the invading flood which threatens to submerge that which is left of our civilization and the health of our race."[89] Such strident defenses of the French "race" were arguably tied to the class dimensions of immigration and probably could not easily be dissociated from it, but they also appealed to anxieties about population decline and about the "dangers" of foreign intrusion.

Dr. René Martial, a prominent public health physician and authority on immigration was only one of numerous writers on immigration and population decline in the 1920s and 1930s who likewise raised the specter of Asians and Africans overrunning French borders and who supported selective immigration.[90] But his views on immigrant labor, developed in over twenty-two books and articles published between 1924 and 1942, helped to shape the discursive climate in which discussions of reconstituting the national body took place. While siding with Boverat and the Alliance on the merits of selective immigration, Martial's views of selective breeding situated him close to a small group of eugenics advocates. Noting that all peoples emerged from some form of racial mixing historically, Martial proposed "interracial grafting," involving assimilating immigrants into French society and selecting those who would best graft to French stock and contribute to strengthening the French race.[91] Basing his theory on biological and horticultural models of grafting, and making no secret of his racist and anti-Semitic views, Martial argued that he had found a scientific way to select potential racial grafts, drawing on the relatively new biochemical indices that eugenics practitioners had developed to classify blood types. He rejected Asians and Africans out of hand as unassimilable. Holding up the Jews as examples of a "race" whose mixing with other races produced negative results, Martial argued, "Jews could be much more easily assimilated to French society intellectually, politically, and economically, than physically." Because of the predominantly male character of immigrant labor, Martial's examples presumed a union between a male foreigner and a French woman. Some advocates of interethnic marriages believed that a French woman could civilize or Gallicize a foreign spouse, much as after the war, some believed that mother's milk could Gallicize the child of a French woman raped by a German soldier. In Martial's view, however, French women did not have the force of conversion when it came to Jews.[92] A marriage between a Jew and a French woman, he argued, often "produces degenerate offspring in whom Jewish characteristics and intellect dominate." Similarly, in "métissage [mixing] between [French] and Negroes or yellow-raced people, the products are often very inferior."[93] Martial's proposals thus illustrated that the reconstitution of the national body involved a racial dimension alongside appeals to French men to procreate and the revalorization of maternity. Racial selection would permit the French to draw on immigrants to replenish French population. Although not all agreed about using selective breeding toward that end, most concurred that rewarding reproductive men with enhanced social benefits was justified.

Rethinking Citizenship

The same groups that argued for the revalorization of virile French manhood in the postwar years and developed taxation and other policies to reward men's reproductive prowess also proposed redefining the parameters of citizenship in the service of reconstituting the national body. The campaign for the family vote, a major challenge to the republican notion of citizenship and individual rights, came in the context of a revival of suffrage agitation in the immediate postwar years, as French feminists sought to capitalize on the international wave of postwar women's suffrage law. Throughout Europe (including Britain), in Russia, in Sweden, and in the United States women won the right to vote as the result of long political struggles and because the victory of democracy over monarchies demanded it. By 1920, twenty-four countries had granted women suffrage. Although the Chamber of Deputies voted in favor of full suffrage for women in May 1919 (by a 77 percent majority), not until November 1922 did the proposition come up for debate in the Senate. Thus began a protracted period of alternation between positive and negative votes in each house that lasted until World War II. Not surprisingly, in the pronatalist climate of the 1920s, right-wing and Catholic legislators revived proposals for the family vote that had been unsuccessfully presented before the war. Although historians have emphasized the arguments made by feminists linking maternity to women's suffrage, arguments for family suffrage turned on privileging male citizenship on the grounds of men's status as prolific fathers.[94] Some proponents acknowledged women's right to vote alongside the father's right to extra votes for each minor child; others, mindful of women's independence during the war, somewhat predictably accused women of egoism and selfishness and argued for extra votes for the father as an alternative to women's suffrage. Others rejected proposals for women's suffrage out of hand.[95] But in spite of differences on other issues, all sought to amend the concept of the abstract male individual as the rights bearer within the regime of republican citizenship by claiming that a man's position in the family conferred additional rights. The deputy abbé Jules Lemire, a major proponent of family suffrage in the Chamber, argued for giving married men one more vote than bachelors, as well as an additional vote if the father was the head of a large family. In words that echoed those of Rousseau almost two centuries earlier, he declared, "Woman is made for the family and the child. She governs the home. That has been her mission since the world began."[96] Although natalist groups such as the Alliance nationale pour l'accroissement de la population française and familialist social Catholics constituted the main forces behind the family vote, the notion enjoyed support across party lines (with the exception of socialists and communists). Prime Minister Poincaré briefly supported the idea, as did the presidents of the French Chambers of Commerce.[97] In 1921 the Chamber of Deputies' Universal Suffrage Commission unanimously adopted the proposition: "Each family head will possess, in addition to his own vote, as many votes as he has living minor legitimate or recognized children in his care."[98] Family vote proposals sought to replace the individual right of citizenship with a collective right, exercised by the father.[99] However, this reward to procreative male household heads arguably broadened the notion of male citizenship to include fertility—not as a defining feature of citizenship but as a condition of the exercise of citizenship. The father's status as household head, his authority under the Civil Code, his responsibility for minor children, and his position as defender of his children's civil rights all gave him the right to exercise suffrage in the name of the family.[100] Fatherhood conferred a guarantee of morality and indicated a degree of experience, wisdom, prudence, and probity lacking in childless men.[101] Virile manhood, not previously included as an argument for male suffrage, now appeared as the counterpart to motherhood and as a justification for men's exercise of political power through the family.[102]

Although the family vote movement temporarily fizzled out when Poincaré ended the 1923 parliamentary session before discussion of a final bill could take place, the campaign revived the following year and spilled beyond parliamentary debates well into the 1930s. In his preface to André Toulemon's *Le suffrage familial ou le suffrage intégral,* Georges Pernot, president of the Fédération nationale des associations des familles nombreuses de France, criticized the absence of a role for the family in French political life under a system in which only the individual could be a voter.[103] Bachelors and fathers of small families, he argued, more numerous than fathers of large families, carried more political weight even though they provided fewer producers and defenders of the nation. Toulemon agreed with this picture of injustice. A majority of nonreproductive bachelors destroyed the rights of families and children "who represent the race and the future of the country."[104] But Toulemon went further than most family vote advocates: he believed it would not only preserve the authority of men in families but help French men to maintain authority over immigrant men who threatened France with racial degeneration. Against this picture of national decline, Toulemon held up two positive examples of successful family voting. In Tunisia, from 1922 the Resident General of France established the practice of voting for the French Section of the Tunisian General Council whereby the head of a family having at least four minor children would receive a supplemental vote. The same practice was incorporated into the election of the governmental council of Morocco.[105] This effort to ensure French racial domination in the protectorates, he implied, could work just as well in the metropole and would restore paternal authority in the family as well. But this was not to be. Despite the fact that six different bills appeared on the floor of the Chamber, the movement stalled during the Popular Front as conservative proponents lost momentum and succumbed to their own divisions. The parliamentary campaign, however, like other attempts to reward women's and men's efforts to regenerate the national body, constituted another site at which contemporaries forged ideas about gender privilege and attempted to put them into practice. These conservative gender and racial discourses framed the demobilization and likewise influenced the reconstitution of labor in postwar France.

Reconstituting Labor

Although French men's access to the postwar labor market was never questioned, the position of women workers proved to be more complex: ideas about family, femininity, and masculinity had mixed effects on industrial demobilization and the reconstitution of the French labor force. The end of the war forced hundreds of thousands of women out of work; by 1919, almost 500,000 women working in armaments production were encouraged to leave. At the gunpowder works at Puteaux, outside Paris, three quarters of the women workers left with severance pay, although 2,000 stayed on in the chemical manufacture division. At the military factories at Vincennes, 2,000 out of 2,500 women left, and at Citroën's Javel plant, of the 11,700 workers (half men and half women), only 3,300 men remained by February 1919.[106] Although many women were rehired in the fall of 1919, they were given jobs in unskilled work at much reduced wages.

During the war, male labor leaders and activists had expressed deep reservations about and outright opposition to women's work and voiced anxieties about women's "invasion" of "male jobs."[107] As Jean-Louis Robert has argued, during the war, within the main labor confederation, the Confédération générale du travail, CGT (General Confederation of Labor), men's critique of women's work largely reflected their anxieties over their ability to maintain authority in the household. The war arguably contributed to efforts to reassert working-class masculine identities, underscoring the persistence of ideas about the gender of jobs. For some, women's wartime activities constituted an invasion of male space and a menace to male virility.[108] During the war, metalworkers expressed their anxiety about how wartime employment of women disrupted the gender order of the workplace in the pages of the Metalworkers' Federation newspaper, *L'Union des métaux.* One wrote, "Disorder reigns when these . . . little hands load missiles onto factory trucks. . . . Exploitation . . . is inevitably worsened by employing our own native [women] workers, [and leads to] the masculinization of women. . . ."[109] Another complained about women's loss of femininity, "We think it much better for little fairy's hands to dust or fashion a hat than to turn out the same piece of metal on a machine day after day, to perfume themselves with coconut grease or to be covered with globs of oil." The complaint that women had "usurped men's work" underscored how ideas about the gender of jobs persisted during the war in a highly masculine profession.[110] The executive committee of the Metalworkers' Federation reasserted the primacy of women's domestic, procreative role in September 1917. "The systematic introduction of women into [metalworking] workshops is absolutely opposed to the existence of the home and family . . . the increasingly generalized absorption of women into all forms of industry totally contradicts the demand to procreate."[111] Working-class men anticipated the concerns of postwar legislators, denouncing women's work as a threat to the survival of families and of the "race."[112]

Ambivalence about the desirability of unionizing women, long a theme in the history of French labor, also surfaced. Even though some men supported the principle of "equal pay for equal work" during the war to prevent employers from undercutting men's wages, others feared that unruly women, with their "sensitive, nervous character," would get out of hand and "escape our control."[113] The language in which they expressed their opposition was filled with images of defensive masculinity that portrayed the unions as arenas of military combat and struggle between men, in which women had no place. As one argued, "The union is a fighting organization and what good is a voluntary combatant if he doesn't know what he is fighting for . . . ?" Another insisted that in order to organize women, "you'd have to virilize their brains!"[114] Men also questioned the durability of women's labor activism. Following strikes of garment workers and metalworkers in May–June 1917, the executive commission of the Metalworkers' Federation took a stand against women's work in the metals industries on the grounds that after the strikes women left the unions.[115] But French unions had a bad record of unionizing women before the war (women made up just under 10 percent of union members in 1914) and in contrast to their British counterparts were too weak to make deals with employers to protect male jobs after the war.

After the war, automobile workers, food workers, railway men, laborers, office and chemical workers confronting reinsertion into the labor force continued vigorously to defend an ideal of "separate spheres," where women took responsibility for the family and men worked outside the home. In April 1919, male workers at Citroën discussed striking for higher wages for skilled men and for firing women whom Citroën planned to hire to work on lathes. They argued that "women never worked in metallurgy before the war and if Citroën continues to employ them, it is only in order to drive down men's wages."[116] Renaudel, head of the Syndicat des employés de la région parisienne (Paris Region Clerk's Union), argued for the family wage in July 1919. "A man must be paid enough to cover his family's needs so that his wife can stop all work in order to devote herself to her social role as wife and mother."[117] And a tract issued by the Syndicat général des industries chimiques (General Union of Chemical Industries) in early 1920 proclaimed, "In a properly ordered society . . . the woman, man's companion, is made first of all to have children, to keep them clean, to tidy the house, to educate her little ones, and to make her companion's life as happy as possible so that he will forget that he is a victim of monstrous exploitation. For us, this is her real social role."[118] But their defense of the male breadwinner did not tell the whole story.

Demobilization in the immediate postwar years produced a general debate over the "problem" of women discharged from munitions and military uniform factories. Despite some male metalworkers' vigorous defense of the workplace and unions as male terrain, the problem of transition following the end of the war did not produce a knee-jerk reaction against women workers from all quarters. Employers and government officials wanted to lay off women quickly with severance pay so that they could reclassify them at lower skill levels and at lower wages. They believed that these steps would keep women from competing with men and help restore gender divisions in the postwar workplace.[119] Some foresaw rehiring women at "women's jobs" and concurred that postwar labor reorganization demanded the reconciliation of work and motherhood.[120] Those who raised the specter of female unemployment defended women's right to work at the same time as they defended traditional gender divisions of labor based on women's and men's perceived natural inclinations and gender privilege. Writing in January 1919, Leon Abensour, for example, supported women's right to work and at the same time argued for the redistribution of women and gender-segmented labor markets. Professional training and technical courses should be used to place women in "appropriate feminine jobs," especially in the garment and fashion industries, bookbinding, silver and gold plating, ceramic and toy manufacture, decorative arts, and jewelry.[121] Albert Thomas, the former Minister of Armaments, argued that employers needed time to reclassify women workers. In St. Etienne and Lyon, for example, where women were moving out of metalworking into the ribbon-making and silk industries, employers couldn't hire women until they rehired some three hundred men as mechanics and adjusters to restart those industries.[122] Interestingly, Thomas also argued against part-time work for women—a solution to the "problem" of women's work favored by some—on the grounds that, although it would allow them to reconcile work and motherhood more easily, it would lead to lowering wages and deadly competition between the sexes. His program for the postwar reorganization of labor incorporated a utopian vision of recovery in which the workday would be reduced to seven and even six hours for both sexes, employers would provide day care centers and nursing rooms, and ultimately, "vast worker estates, with comfortable and affordable apartments, collective daycare and meals [would] free women workers from domestic tasks."[123]

The auto manufacturer André Citroën came closest to fulfilling Thomas's vision of the reconciliation of work and motherhood by providing nursing rooms, day care centers, and medical facilities for workers in his factories. Full of optimism for the future, Citroën claimed that although some women would undoubtedly choose to leave work, some 70 percent of his female labor force would remain employed. The explosion of a consumer economy, he thought, would provide jobs for them in the production of automobiles, small trucks, bicycles, sewing machines, agricultural machinery and spare parts, which men produced before the war and which women could now manufacture, thanks to rationalization and the simplification of tasks.[124] Pierre Juquelier, doctor in chief of nursery schools in the department of the Seine, mindful of his colleagues' objections to women's wartime armaments work, also argued for the reconciliation of women's labor force participation with pronatalist goals. Following the thinking of Thomas, Juquelier put the onus on employers to take account of women's "special needs" for shorter hours and make provisions to enable them to reconcile work and mother-hood. He also argued that given the tremendous male mortality during the war, the state and employers had to provide for single women unable to marry and forced to support themselves.[125] Finally, Jacques Valdour, a con-servative journalist who wrote of his own work experiences, pointed to the complexity of gender dynamics in postwar factories, openly suggesting how men's anxieties about preserving a monopoly on certain kinds of work shaped their views of women workers. Although some men verbally ha-rassed women on the job and complained that they didn't belong in the factory "when there's so little work to go around," men and women also worked side by side on lathes and treated each other to drinks after work. Women sang bawdy songs and mercilessly teased the men, hazing them with antics like sewing the sleeves of their jackets together.[126] Moreover, in the period of demobilization, within the labor movement clear signs emerged that some labor leaders and rank and file workers previously hostile to women in the labor force were now more willing to defend women's right to work as long as it did not threaten men's dominance of skilled labor or tasks defined as male.

Organized Labor, Immigrant Workers, and Women

Léon Jouhaux, general secretary of the CGT, addressing the problem of wom-en's postwar labor force participation, argued that employers had a respon-sibility to redeploy women; the eight-hour day could provide a partial solution to potential unemployment.[127] Even in a trade previously openly hostile to admitting women, the printing industry, labor leaders debated the problem of women's postwar work in new terms. At the 1919 congress of the Fédération française des travailleurs du livre (French Federation of Printing Workers), Auguste Keufer, secretary general of the Printers' Federation, who prior to the war aggressively opposed women's presence in the trade, defended women's work in printing. Keufer pointed to the shortage of male labor (the Federation had lost over 1,600 male workers in the war) and to the plight of single women and widows without support who were obliged to provide for their families and injured husbands or fathers. Praising women's labor activism during the war, he presented a resolution proposing the admission of women into the printing trade as long as their numbers were proportionate to men's in different branches of the trade, and as long as the Federation insisted on the principle of equal pay for equal work. Following a long debate with interventions from labor leaders all over France supporting women's right to work, the resolution passed by 120 votes to 34.[128] By 1927, the communist-dominated Fédération unitaire des ouvriers et ouvrières sur métaux (United Metalworker's Federation) dropped its opposition to women metalworkers and shifted its rhetoric to grouping all workers in the struggle against capital. A resolution passed at the 1927 national congress asserted that the Federation would henceforth cease to demand eliminating women from factories as a solution to the problems of wage competition and unemployment.[129]

A similar shift in rank and file workers' view of women's status as workers also appeared in workers' demands for severance pay at demobilization. In November 1918 the government promised to award all workers—about half of the 80,000 employed in the department of the Seine were women—who left the munitions industries by December 5 with a month's salary in severance pay that was to be no less that 180 francs per month and no more than 250 francs. In addition, newly discharged workers became eligible for 140 francs per month government unemployment compensation.[130] By January 1919, at public meetings of up to 6,000 unemployed workers, some composed entirely of women, workers protested employers' failure to accord severance pay and to demand higher unemployment compensation. Organized by the CGT as part of a unionization initiative, the meetings of the unemployed echoed with men's defense of women's demands. At a meeting of over 1,000 unemployed women on January 3, 1919 for example, male labor leaders Maxime Loze (Chemical Workers' Union), Maurice Millerat (Garment Workers' Union), Fournier (Metalworkers' Federation), and others promoted women's claims and urged them to use the unions to struggle for higher unemployment compensation.[131] A week later at a meeting of 2,000 men and women at the Paris Bourse du Travail, workers heard speeches in favor of increasing the unemployment allowance by Mme. Geoffroy, secretary of the Military Garment Workers' Union, and by Hélène Brion, socialist feminist and peace activist. Robert Lefèvre, president of the Union des Syndicats de la Seine, the department of the Seine labor organization, Millerat, (Garment Workers' Federation), and Alfred Leclerc (Railway Car and Aviation Workers) all supported women's claims. The resolution adopted at the meeting demanded the immediate payment of a demobilization allowance (severance pay) of 250 francs to both men and women plus a minimum unemployment allowance of 3 francs a day and an allowance of 1 franc 50 for each child, and the immediate provision of work that would permit men and women "to live from their work and not on charity."[132] At a meeting of 6,000 demobilized women and men on January 25, Joseph Couergou of the Metalworkers' Federation, influential in eventually obtaining severance pay for women of the war industries of the Paris region, encouraged women to keep up the fight once they received unemployment compensation, and a few days later, *La Bataille* (formerly *La Bataille syndicaliste*), the CGT weekly, reported that the "Mécaniciens de la Seine" passed a resolution expressing their indignation that neither women nor men had been given adequate severance pay.[133] By the end of February, the government acted to extend unemployment benefits, originally intended to last until the first of March, to the end of March and agreed to reimburse employers up to 100 francs for every 200 francs of severance pay.[134] Arguably linked to their postwar organizing drive, labor leaders' support for women's demands departed from other workingmen's defense of the family wage ideal and work as a male duty.

A similar tension between recognition of women as independent workers and their right to severance pay on the one hand, and older ideas about women's dependence on a male breadwinner on the other hand, appeared among government officials such as members of departmental general councils and prefects and employers who regulated postwar labor demobilization and redeployment. The distinction they made between severance pay and unemployment allowances illustrated how this tension entered the calculus of postwar reconstruction. Whereas employers gave severance pay directly to all workers, the government paid the unemployment allowance "to the head of household (*chef de la famille*). If his companion (female) is also unemployed, she will receive one franc [per day] for herself personally." Children under sixteen had a right to the same amount.[135] Thus, although the government recognized the right of the individual worker to compensation at demobilization, it effectively ignored the independent wage-earner status of the unemployed female worker living in a household and assumed her dependence on a male breadwinner. As long as she was a member of a family, she had no right to receive the full allowance. In this way, the government privileged the male breadwinner over the individual female wageearner. In a similar vein, government officials and employers meeting at a conference on departmental placement offices and unemployment in early February 1919 made it clear that male workers would be given priority in job placement, even though placement offices also had to take into account the "special situation" of certain categories of labor: women, the war-wounded, and those exempt from military service because of physical infirmities (*réformés*).[136] Including women in the category of those who were "damaged" and therefore not fully competent to work demonstrated how gender meanings operated in classifying and marginalizing some workers and in establishing the parameters of government support. A government committee on redeployment recommended that demobilized men in the highest ranks of the military (*les vieilles classes*) would also be given priority in placement. Each father would be treated as a soldier of the highest rank and would automatically get two years of job seniority per child. Fatherhood thus could be defined as a form of national service and rewarded with work, essential to maintaining the ideal of a male breadwinner.[137] At the same time employers and department administrators raised concerns about the place of foreign workers alongside women in the context of the postwar labor shortage and the project of national economic reconstruction.

Male Immigrant Labor and the Problem of Women's Work

As scholars have shown, having relied on some 440,000 immigrant workers during the war, French employers began planning for immigration to serve postwar labor needs and immediately after the war formed a private organization to manage immigration with the cooperation of the state, the Société générale d'immigration.[138] At the end of the war, a permanent "Conférence sur la main d'oeuvre étrangère" served as the governmental instrument for negotiating labor contracts with foreign countries and directing immigrant labor to specific occupations. Although immigrants counted for 2.8 percent of the population in 1911, by 1921 they made up 4 percent, and 6.6 percent by 1931, when they constituted 12 percent of the labor force. Over two thirds of immigrants were workers.[139] Although women made up 39 percent of total immigrants, they counted for less than a fifth (19.2 percent) of immigrants in the labor force, and according to an estimate from the 1931 census there were 2.03 foreign men for every foreign woman.[140] About 28 percent of immigrant women worked as domestic servants, but even more worked in fishing, agriculture, and industry and immigrant women were especially prominent in the textile and garment industries.[141] Initially, large numbers of Italian and Polish men were directed to mining and construction jobs, but by 1931 almost half of all immigrant workers worked in industry; 14 percent worked in commerce and transport; and 2.6 percent held professional occupations.[142] The presence of foreign workers on French soil complicated but also potentially facilitated the reconstruction of the national body. Pronatalists' concerns about maintaining the "purity" of the French race by selecting immigrants according to their racially or ethnically specific ability to assimilate arguably conflicted both with industrialists' interests in labor recruitment and their desire to avoid labor conflicts on the grounds of competition between French and foreign workers. French workers had already reacted against the threat of immigrant labor before the war, sometimes violently; riots had broken out between French and foreign workers before, during, and just after the war.[143] In 1918, as the war wound down, Dr. Edouard Toulouse, specialist on the physiology of work, praised the potential of eugenics to make France "a nation of élites, a people of leaders, foremen, and creators; . . . unskilled work should be left to our colonial subjects until the day when machines replace men almost everywhere."[144]

At the same time, the prospect of immigrant labor recruitment had implications for the gender composition of the labor force. Writing on the postwar problem of men's reinsertion into the labor force in *Les Métiers blessés,* Pierre Hamp, for example, spoke against employers' recruitment of single immigrant men, especially blacks and Chinese. "This practice," he wrote, "will lead to social difficulties if Africans and 'Asiatics' are hired in order to dampen [*mater*] the spirit of the French worker" and if "the just price of labor is cast aside by the preference for servile men." If immigrants were necessary, he argued, entire families should be brought over, lodged, and allowed to put their roots into French soil. But overall, it would be better to hire women: "It is up to us to choose: Chinese men or French women."[145] Likewise, Pierre Juquelier, in supporting women's right to work and arguing for reconciling work and maternity, believed that the presence of women in the labor force might stem a rising tide of male immigrants. "Must French industry limit its production for lack of a labor force, or should it put itself at the mercy of foreign elements too dense to melt into the native population?

It would be reduced to one or the other of these options if women, who were capable of becoming mothers were also kept out of factories, and it would be in either case dangerous for the future of the country."[146] Women could preserve French racial singularity by remaining in the labor force if employers allowed women to combine motherhood with wage labor.

Finally, after the war social observers and workers also voiced concern about competition from immigrant workers in the transitional period of job scarcity that mirrored pronatalists' fears of foreign contamination of French population. Writing in *La France libre,* the socialist Eugène Morel proposed limiting immigration of foreign and colonial workers in order to mitigate the effects of rising unemployment among women discharged from the war industries, implying that immigrants and women would compete for the same unskilled low-paying jobs.[147] Indeed, concerns about how immigrant workers might or might not compete with French workers, female and male, intensified in the early 1920s—concerns that occasionally resulted in xenophobic reactions. Jacques Valdour implied that Arab workers were potential thieves when he described locking up his belongings because those who didn't do so saw things disappear. In speaking about the labor hierarchy at work ("electricians think they are above everyone else") he averred that "everyone distrusts the Arabs," who complained endlessly and were only concerned about money.[148] Valdour's view was probably shared by many of his contemporaries, but did not reflect the official position of organized labor.

It is probably true, as Gary Cross has argued, that the problems plaguing the labor movement—a disastrous general strike in May 1920 and the subsequent departure of the majority communist-dominated Confédération générale du travail unitaire (CGTU; United General Confederation of Labor) from the CGT in 1921—left little room for debates about foreign labor.[149] But from 1922 on, activists and leaders in both confederations began to address the position of immigrants with some regularity. Both established commissions to oversee the organization of foreign workers in the mid-1920s. In the immediate postwar years, the CGT leadership accepted the inevitability of immigrant labor recruitment provided that it did not threaten French workers.[150] The Confederation argued for organizing immigrant workers and defending their rights; it demanded that foreign workers work at the same wages and under the same conditions as French male workers and that employers cease to hire foreign workers as strikebreakers.[151] The position of the Communist confederation did not differ substantially; it viewed immigrant labor as a problem of international labor solidarity, arguing for "equal pay for equal work." Although the CGTU leadership argued against xenophobia, local labor leaders relayed the fears of rank and file workers in thoroughly male trades such as heavy metallurgy and lumber who saw immigrants working for lower wages in order to get jobs, and called for regulation as well as organization. On balance, the CGTU responded to local concerns about job and wage competition with ever more concerted efforts to organize foreign male workers. It created ethnic sections in the major unions, interunion committees, and departmental unions (such as the Union des Syndicats de la Seine) and trade federations and published tracts in foreign languages. It also created the position of Secretary of Foreign Labor and an Office of Foreign Labor within the Confederation.[152] Most of these efforts had little effect, but on balance the labor movement kept anti-immigrant sentiment under wraps even if hostility to foreigners occasionally escaped unions' control.

Efforts to organize foreign labor had mixed results—legal reprisals threatened foreign workers who openly joined unions or participated in labor activities. At the same time, organized labor more aggressively attempted to mobilize women. Both confederations established commissions to oversee the organization of women, the CGTU in 1923 and the CGT in 1929 (although from the early 1920s, Jeanne Chevenard served as women's propaganda delegate for the CGT). The Union des Syndicats de la Seine, which eventually came under the umbrella of the CGTU, established a Women's Commission in 1922 charged with gathering information on women's labor with a view to organizing women more effectively.[153] The CGTU followed the directives of the Profintern (the Red International of Trade Unions) to defend women workers and bring them into the "army of social revolution." It addressed its appeals to both women and men, established women's columns in the labor press, and created women's committees at the regional and local levels. As one delegate to a CGTU National Congress pointed out, when organizers tried to recruit workers at the factory gates, it was not enough to issue directives "that women workers will not understand"; they had to speak their language.[154] L'Humanité, the Communist Party paper, published a "Tribune féminine," and the CGTU established a newspaper devoted entirely to women, L'Ouvrière. On balance women workers gave voice to their demands and concerns within the framework of the women's commissions much more frequently than immigrant men, who feared arrest or repatriation for union activities.

In the immediate postwar years, working women developed their own utopian vision of the modern twentieth-century household, demonstrating how their subjective identities as workers differed from the domestic modernity promoted by Pauline Bernège. They supported not a rationalized household but an egalitarian one, in which women would no longer be educated to be "men's slaves," where men would treat women as equals, and where all members of the family would share household tasks.[155] They vigorously defended women's right to work. As Germaine Goujon, a textile worker from the Basse-Seine, proclaimed, "How is it that [men] cannot understand that women will stay in industry? The fact that [women] have been called into production demands that they defend their lives and the lives of their children just as men do."[156] They demanded that the state recognize motherhood as a social function, with social policies that would permit them to combine work and childcare.[157] Interestingly, in the context of rampant inflation and the flurry of organizing that followed the end of the war, the CGT appealed to working women who were also mothers and housewives to join unions, "the only real protector[s] of their feminine rights and freedoms."[158] But this utopian vision of the household did not become the dominant influence on what later would be called the French social model. In the postwar debates on immigration and gender it became clear that both the government and employers were more willing to shift the nationality of the French labor force than they were to shift its gender distribution. In the end foreign male workers probably did not compete with French women for jobs. Because of the ways that gender divisions in the labor force became more refined in the postwar years, women and immigrant men remained separate categories of labor with their own terrains of employment.[159]

Women in the Labor Force

Although some historians have pointed to World War I as the beginning of a decline in French women's labor force participation, this is scarcely surprising given the problems of postwar industrial conversion. Women's aggregate labor force participation, 38.2 in 1911, declined from an estimated 46 percent in 1919 to 42.3 percent in 1921 to 37.2 percent in 1926 (see table 1). Some of that decline reflected the withdrawal of women from agricultural work (some 1,300,000 women between 1921 and 1931). Yet what is striking is that in spite of intense debate about women's work, the rights of male breadwinners, and fathers, neither pronatalist hysteria nor the male breadwinner ideal prevailed as constraints on women's actual economic activity, although they probably influenced women's *distribution* within the labor force. Between 1926 and

Table 1. Employed women as a percentage of all persons employed, France, 1911–36

Employment sector	1911	1918	1921	1926	1931	1936
			YEAR			
Agriculture	38.0	—	44.2	41.7	41.8	40.8
Industry and transport	34.8	[40.0]	31.3	27.8	26.9	26.1
Trade	40.6	[55.0]	43.5	40.0	42.5	42.0
Services	27.5	—	37.0	36.4	38.3	39.3
Domestic	83.0	—	87.0	86.0	86.0	87.0
All sectors	38.2	[46.2]	42.3	37.2	37.3	37.1

Source: République française, Statistique générale de France. *Résultats statistiques des recensements* (Paris: Imprimerie nationale, 1911, 1921, 1926, 1931, 1936). Estimates are bracketed. Table adapted from Robert, "Women and Work in France During the War," 262.

1936 women's labor force participation remained relatively stable, between 37.2 and 37.1.[160] When women's nonagricultural labor force participation is examined, it also looks surprisingly stable for the period between 1921 and 1931 (increasing from 4,600,000 in 1921 to 4,700,000 in 1931), even if this increase did not match men's growing numbers in the nonagricultural labor force (from 8,530,000 in 1921 to 9,201,000 in 1931).[161] Moreover, as Sylvie Zerner has shown, if building and public works are excluded, the proportion of women in manufacturing industries (*industries de transformation*) increased slightly between 1921 and 1931 from 25.04 percent to 25.53 percent.[162] Meanwhile, women's employment, viewed by age, remained surprisingly stable. Although the employment of women between fourteen and twenty-four years of age declined between 1921 and 1931 by 70,000 as more women remained in school, and although women over fifty-five left work in public service jobs, banking, and transportation, where they benefited from good retirement benefits, the number of women in the labor force between twenty-five and fifty-five years of age remained constant at 3.6 million.

Even more interesting are the shifting distributions of women between different economic sectors. Throughout the interwar years, for example, the proportion of women in "ordinary" metalworking in the Paris region, a center of light metal production, increased from 14 percent in 1921 to nearly

Table 2. Women as a percentage of economically active population by selected branches

	YEAR			
Industry	1921	1926	1931	1936
Manufacturing				
Food	29.6	28.7	31.8	29.8
Textiles	61.3	58.5	60.1	56.8
Chemical	18.6	20.5	22.5	23.3
Small metals	9.1	10.0	10.4	10.1
Government service	24.3	25.5	26.9	27.2
Commerce	45.1	41.2	42.6	41.6

Source: Deldyke, Gelders, and Limbor, *La Population active et sa structure*, 172–73.

20 percent in 1931.[163] Although women's presence in garment industries declined by 230,000 between 1921 and 1931 with the development of mass production techniques, women remained strongly represented in textiles (60 percent of all textile workers in 1931). They also became prominent in the food industries (just under a third of all workers in 1931) and in the chemical industry, where they represented over a fifth of all workers in 1931 (see table 2).[164]

New production processes, the electrification of factories, and modernization of equipment in the 1920s reduced the requirement of physical force and facilitated their industrial employment. The numbers of women working as "employees," in banking, secretarial and clerical jobs, and small commerce, although they declined by 139,000 between 1921 and 1926, had increased by 243,000 by 1931; women constituted the vast majority of telephone operators. Indeed, women's increasing share of jobs in government services (from 24.3 percent in 1921 to 27.2 percent in 1936) was suggestive of the trend away from industrial jobs.[165] Women's shifting employment patterns reflected the gendering of jobs that accompanied industrial restructuring in the 1920s, economic instability, and the Depression of the 1930s, topics that I examine in the following chapters.[166] Indeed, it was the movement between sectors of the labor market and the relative stability of women's labor force participation that marked the years between the two world wars. At the war's end, demobilization did not drive women from the labor force but rather provoked a redistribution of men and women.

Dramatic events such as wars almost inevitably lead to attempts to reestablish "things as they were." But wartime mortality, demographic decline, the demands of industrial restructuring, and redeployment of labor in a shifting political context made return to a mythical prewar age impossible, even as the postwar period saw strong elements of continuity. Efforts to reassert the boundaries of gender immediately after World War I on the part of social observers, policymakers, and the state had complex results. Ideas about gender difference played an important role in the state's negotiation of postwar reconstruction but on new terms. Under conservative governments, family and male authority constituted the object of deliberate policy initiatives far more than before the war. Reproductive policies that proclaimed women's dependence in families simultaneously reinforced men's power and authority and attempted to confer citizenship rights. These initiatives profoundly marked the character of state-society relations and the resulting vision of the French welfare state. Chapter 2 examines in more detail why, although male breadwinner ideology did not decisively shape the *composition* of the French labor force, ideas about masculinity and femininity profoundly influenced the *distribution* of men and women and women in work, as planners and employers attempted to deal with the shortage of workers in the wake of war.

CHAPTER TWO

GENDER DIVISION, THE FAMILY, AND

THE CITIZEN-WORKER

Describing her first day on the job making batteries at Thomson-Houston, a Parisian metalworking factory, Eugénie Rey wrote, in June 1921,

> . . . for hours, days, months, and years, each worker repeated the same gesture and the same work. [With] repetition, the fingers developed remarkable agility and output was extraordinary. But what monotony in work and how could all these human beings put up with the uniformity of their existence? [My] task . . . was simple: wrap in heavy muslin (*tarlatan*) the tablets for flashlight batteries which were about four centimeters high and fifteen millimeters in diameter. . . . A woman on my right made around 1,500 a day and many girls from sixteen to eighteen years succeeded in making their 2,000. They were paid 68 centimes per hundred and when they made more than 1,200, they got a 10 centime bonus for the first hundred, 20 centimes for the second hundred, 30 centimes for the third, and so on. . . . All the women were seated on stools; only pregnant women had the right to a chair. It was horribly tiring to sit without support for my back for four hours and a half in the morning and three hours and a half in the afternoon.[1]

Rey's description of repetitive and monotonous piecework at one of the major electrical equipment companies of the Paris region demonstrated that whether wrapping and boxing chocolates, polishing shoes, cutting metal on a press, supervising bobbin winding for a self-acting loom, or working as a telephone operator, women's modern industrial work obeyed not only the rhythm of the clock, but also that of the stopwatch and the assembly line as never before. Indeed, in spite of contemporary ambivalence about the gender composition of the labor force, new forms of deskilling work combined with postwar labor shortages and prewar gender divisions facilitated women's relatively strong labor force participation throughout the French economy after World War I and into the 1920s. Political and cultural assertions of masculinity and femininity in the aftermath of the war continued to influence profoundly the kinds of work that men and women performed, the conditions of recruitment, and training. In the process of rationalizing production, employers redefined skill demands and created new forms of unskilled labor in both industry and the service sector. The accentuation of gender and racial divisions of labor between the world wars constituted one reason why French male workers generally dropped their opposition to women's labor force participation in the 1920s and tolerated foreign workers, in spite of occasional protests about competition from both. At the same time, the male breadwinner ideal, weak in its influence on women's *presence* in the labor force, continued to have salience as ideology and exerted powerful influence on the social meanings of work and the value of men's and women's work. These contradictory forces eventually underscored the social policies of the 1920s and 1930s that later came to be incorporated into the French social model.

In the period between the wars, two sets of alternately competing and complementary initiatives created new divisions in the workplace and confirmed the validity of older divisions on the basis of gender: technical training and rationalization on the one hand, and industrial physiology and vocational guidance on the other. Historically, these techniques for increasing productivity developed together in the process of applying modern science to the assessment of the skills and aptitudes necessary for certain kinds of jobs, and employers drew upon them in varying degrees while attempting to maximize efficiency. Science, in the years following World War I, held the promise of "modernity," a powerful if multivalent term that included many things such as increased industrial production, consumption, reduced fatigue for the worker, and a better, prosperous life for all.[2]

This chapter examines how technical training and rationalization refined the gender division of labor and shaped concepts of the wage in postwar industrial work in the process of creating a new citizen-worker. It argues that the refinement of gender divisions of skill, the product of both employer initiatives and organized labor's efforts to reduce competition from women and foreign workers, facilitated the employment of both sets of workers while simultaneously perpetuating gender-based inequality. Chapter 3 considers how industrial psychology and vocational guidance participated in creating the new worker of the 1920s in public service sector work, where the state and bureaucratic rationality governed the organization of postwar work and wages. The separation of these different rationalizing processes for the purpose of analysis, however, is not meant to imply that they were entirely discrete management alternatives in the twentieth-century workplace. French employers adopted elements of technical training, Taylorism, Fordism, industrial physiology, and vocational guidance in overlapping and piecemeal fashion to increase productivity and create a modern twentieth-century labor force of citizen-workers.

Reinstating the Gender Division of Labor

Feminist scholarship on labor history of the late 1970s and 1980s examined the importance of the gender division of labor and occupational segregation, debated their historical origins, and theorized their reproduction over time. Whereas some scholars emphasized the primacy of male dominance in the family ("patriarchy") as accounting for gender inequalities in the division of labor, others argued for the primacy of capitalist relations of production in the emergence of gender segregation at work. Still others treated capitalism and gender as two intersecting and mutually reinforcing systems, following the important work of Heidi Hartmann.[3] These debates and studies attested to the complexity of forms of occupational segregation. All called attention to the importance of gender difference in capitalist economic development and influenced much historical work on women and men in the economy. Building on this work, feminist historians, economists, and sociologists also examined how "skill" was constituted historically and in gender-specific ways. Anne Phillips and Barbara Taylor, for example, drew upon Hartmann's critique of the gender-blindness of Marxist explanations for economic inequality and the gender division of labor. They argued that what constituted skill was not "objective economic fact" but rather "an ideological category imposed on certain types of work by virtue of the sex and power of the workers who perform it." As they wrote, "[T]he classification of women's jobs as unskilled and men's jobs as skilled or semiskilled frequently bears little relation to the exact amount of training or ability required for them. Skill definitions are saturated with sexual bias. The work of women is often deemed inferior simply because it is women who do it. Women workers carry into the workplace their status as subordinate individuals, and this status comes to define the value of the work they do."[4] The social constructedness of skill applied not only to women but also to certain kinds of men, for example, African men or Asian men in the Western European economy. Moreover, as Phillips and Taylor pointed out, new technologies alone were not responsible for changes in the organization of work and the gender differentiation of skill; these changes were also the product of tension and struggles between employers and workers and between men and women workers. Men's claims to monopolize skilled labor and to control access to jobs and opportunities accompanied their attempt to preserve dominance in the household.

Charles Tilly's theorization of "durable inequality" added to these models. Tilly attempted to map some of the common patterns in the gender typing of skills and their consequences for wage differences, arguing that the explanation for lasting inequalities rests not on individuals but on "organized social relations."[5] Tilly maintained that gender divisions do not by themselves explain inequality. "Durable inequality among categories [such as male/female, black/white, citizen/foreigner] arises because people who control access to value-producing resources solve pressing organizational problems by means of categorical distinctions."[6] In this model three factors are at play: "first, employers install categorical boundaries between jobs requiring more or less occupation-specific training time, offer lower pay on the lesser training side of the boundaries, and channel women into those jobs whether or not they could actually perform the jobs that require more training; second . . . gender sorting begins before or during the acquisition of occupation-specific training; and third . . . both of these mechanisms are in operation . . ."[7] Moreover, the inequality in rewards results from the operation of these mechanisms "throughout the job allocation process," not just at the point of hiring or determination of pay.[8] Here we are interested particularly in how ideas about sexual difference entered into the training and employment of different categories of workers.

Empirical studies have illustrated how these mechanisms have operated historically with respect to gender. The historian Sonya O. Rose, for example, has shown how in nineteenth-century Britain the gender typing of skill occurred as a historical process, particularly in the transition from home-based to factory-based production. In the English hosiery industry, men, threatened with loss of control over jobs as work moved from households to factories, challenged women's ability to run certain machines and pressured employers to exclude women, claiming that only men had the skill sufficient to run those machines. Employers went along with their demands in order to avoid labor conflict and benefited from hiring lower-paid women for less skilled machine jobs.[9] Rose demonstrated how gender ideology shaped the distinctions between "men's work" and "women's work" at a crucial moment in the transition to factory production. Employers supported workingmen's "opportunity hoarding," invoking existing ideas about gender difference to create new distinctions between jobs and ultimately substantial differences in skill and wages.[10] Laura Downs likewise examined the historical contingency of skill definitions in munitions and metalworking, showing how in Britain and France employers created unskilled jobs from formerly skilled jobs in order to employ women in defense work during World War I. Downs showed how employers used preexisting assumptions about gender difference to create a new classification of workers and new categorical boundaries between jobs through the simultaneous deskilling and feminization of labor—classifications and categories that persisted through the 1920s and created new forms of inequality.[11]

Closer study of gender and work in twentieth-century France reveals how perceptions of sexual difference influenced the practices of employers and state actors and shaped male workers' claims in reinforcing divisions of labor in areas beyond metalworking in a period of labor scarcity and recovery. Gender as well as racial or ethnic difference played a fundamental role in economic restructuring. As this chapter argues, the constitution of new gender divisions in large part accounts for the relatively strong labor force participation of French women and the fact that a male breadwinner model did not actually deter women from entering the labor force—even though the ideal of a male family wage continued to have discursive salience.

The employment of women during the war, at first resisted by employers, disrupted and disturbed traditional notions of gender abilities but did not displace ideas about gender difference on the job, as Laura Downs has shown for the wartime metalworking industries. Indeed, wartime labor inspectors' astonishment at women's capacities, even at "heavy work requiring muscular force to which one hesitated to assign them," and at women's higher quality output and "more regular productivity than that of men," showed how officials' assumptions about sexual difference shaped their expectations about job performance.[12] Inspectors' repeated comparisons of women with men and their attention to the physical consequences of women's work showed how they assumed gender difference as a given. Thus they praised women's ability to perform well at "exceptional work . . . including professional jobs demanding a high level of skill, such as fitting, running steam engines, welding, linotype composition, attaching threads in cotton spinning, series machining, accessory forge work, brick manufacture, dying [in textiles], laboratory work, and occasionally surveillance."[13] In textiles, they marveled

at how women replaced men running looms formerly considered too difficult for them to operate in Limoges, Toulouse, and Lyon, and in numerous
stocking-knitting factories women were even initiated on the Cotton Patent
looms, a machine that only men were allowed to run prior to the war.[14] Yet
even where women excelled at skilled work, employers and labor inspectors
saw it as exceptional and temporary. What is significant is not merely *that*
gender divisions were reconstituted after the war, since they never really
disappeared, but *how* they were redeployed and refined in the "modern"
economy of the 1920s. The experience of the war spoke eloquently to the fact
that the meanings of skill often had more to do with the gender of the worker
than with the actual demands of jobs. Employers and government officials
assumed men's right to "ownership" of certain jobs and women's "ownership" of other jobs as employers met their needs for workers.[15]

During World War I not only did perceptions of gender difference never
completely disappear; indeed, in key sectors such as the defense industries, as
Downs has shown, the gendering of jobs accelerated as employers hired
unskilled women with no previous training or expertise in metalworking
and armaments production. Rationalization in metalworking and the key
defense industries permitted employers to create new categories of skilled
and unskilled jobs and modify some tasks requiring exceptional physical
strength by adapting machines or by using moving belts and carts.[16] Revealing the malleability of perceptions of what constituted "skill," employers
created new unskilled jobs designed specifically for women and thereby
contributed to "manufacture inequality" in the labor force.[17] Although apprenticeships and training existed for male workers in the metalworking
industries, employers refused to establish training programs for women;
most employers were reluctant to train women for jobs at the war's end and
expected women to learn on the job.[18] Since "skill often is [a cultural and]
ideological category imposed on certain forms of labor by virtue of the
gender and power of those who perform it," changing the demography of the
labor force during the war did not fundamentally change perceptions of the
kinds of work that men and women could perform.[19] Employers effectively
established a ceiling on the skill levels that women could attain and the lack
of training proved to be part of the construction of a separate, low-paid
category of labor.

Similar processes in the 1920s and 1930s refined gender divisions in other
areas of the industrial economy and also in newly rationalized service work.
In fact, one of the conditions of women's relatively stable labor force par-

ticipation in the interwar period was the invention of new job categories that were defined as feminine. Technical training and rationalization constituted two solutions to employers' need to recruit skilled workers and get unskilled workers to work at optimum efficiency. Several sets of initiatives illustrate how dominant ideas about gender characteristics shaped changes in training and employment. Refining the gender division of labor so as to keep unskilled women and immigrant men in the labor force seemed an alternative to a male breadwinner model in the 1920s. But basing structural divisions on cultural perceptions of sexual difference in arenas as diverse as textiles and service sector work helped to perpetuate tremendous gender inequalities.

Creating the Citizen-Worker

The need to provide workers with technical training had occupied labor leaders and reformers for much of the nineteenth century, particularly as the practice of apprenticeship declined over the course of the century. Employers and middle-class reformers argued that well-trained and well-educated workers could be weaned from the violence and contestation of organized labor. Moreover, some believed that technical training could not only improve skills but make workers into good citizens.[20] However, neither training nor citizenship was open to everyone. The majority of initiatives addressed boys and young men and the view of technical training as an asset to citizenship clearly referred only to men. Municipalities and employers established training programs that incorporated their ideas of appropriate work for women. At the end of the nineteenth century, for example, the city of Paris opened six schools to teach "women's skills" like sewing, embroidery, dressmaking, working with feathers, artificial flower making, and painting porcelain.[21] Women's employment throughout the economy combined with their lack of training and their status as unskilled, underpaid workers allowed employers to hire them as strikebreakers, as they did during strikes of male printing workers in Paris in 1909. But employers' perceptions of gender difference did not always lead them to behave rationally in training and assigning jobs, as the work of the industrial physiologist Jean-Marie Lahy demonstrated. Lahy was scandalized by men's and women's unequal apprenticeships, where young men were apprenticed for three years at a wage proportional to their progress, while women underwent a much shorter, unpaid apprenticeship.[22] Lahy found in his experiments on the output of male and female linotypists that women's productivity almost uniformly exceeded men's. His observations also proved emblematic of how gender difference in training and apprenticeship marked the postwar deployment of labor.

Despite the employment of women on "men's work" during World War I, labor leaders never completely abandoned their gender-differentiated view of technical training. They proposed an extra year of school for boys at ages 13 and 14 as a form of pre-apprenticeship, adding technical training to manual instruction, "since it is at this point that they are ready to embrace a profession and become a worker committed to progress."[23] For labor leaders in the CGT, the technical training of young boys also had a moral component that recalled the rules of medieval and early modern guilds, where professional training included socialization into the fellowship of male workers and produced a form of male bonding.[24] During World War I, labor leaders demanded that young male apprentices be kept away from "all temptations to drink and [their instructors] had to use proper language [*un langage correct*; that is, no profanity]." For women, it was incumbent upon employers to determine the categories of work of which they were capable "in relation to their physical strength and physiological constitution. Like the war wounded they should enjoy certain privileges and avoid work that is too extenuating, like night work. Their wages must never compete with men's and measures of morality and health must be of the utmost importance."[25] Again, the comparison of women with a group with a limited capacity for work—the war wounded—demonstrated how organized labor viewed women as imperfect workers. These perceptions of gender difference carried over into specific trades such as printing. After the war, the leadership of the Fédération française des travailleurs du livre (French Federation of Printers) agreed to admit women to the printing trades at all levels. Yet some male rank and file members proposed limiting extensive training on the linotype machine to men, thus demarcating male skill and the gender of the machine in a way that would effectively exclude women and preserve the division of labor.[26] For some contemporary observers, however, women's work constituted a defense against the presence of foreign workers in the French labor force.

In writing about the dilemma of demobilization and France's postwar labor shortage, Léon Abensour maintained that French women and immigrant men constituted two alternative and interchangeable labor pools and argued that women must remain in the labor force so that "the country doesn't give a preponderant place to the efforts of foreigners in its industrial renaissance."[27] The war had shown that women could undertake the most difficult tasks. However, he believed that employers should not expect them to work at either metallurgy, which required great muscular force, or in chemical manufacture, "which can kill the germ of life." Decorative arts, luxury trades, fashion, bookbinding (which involved sewing), and jewelry manufacture constituted appropriate employments, where "women can find the qualities that are truly those of the French woman: good taste, ingenuity, and the inventive spirit."[28] If by some accident they did work in the metal industries, women could polish, burnish, and solder, but chiseling should be confined to men. In textiles, women could work as supervisors, but a weaver, who created cloth from an artist's drawing via the correct disposition of threads on the loom, had to be a man. For Abensour, technical training and mandatory courses for all workers from fourteen to eighteen years of age was the key to maintaining the gender division of labor. But postwar plans for retraining and reviving apprenticeship were also based on the central place accorded to the male citizen-worker in postwar French society.

The July 1919 Astier Law on apprenticeship attempted to respond to the paucity of skilled workers (the so-called apprenticeship crisis) in postwar France. The law encouraged local chambers of commerce to create free technical training courses to youths of both sexes under eighteen with government support and urged employers to provide formal training to their workers as well.[29] Deputy Placide Astier, whose bill had been passed in the Senate just before the war, spelled out his utopian vision of an army of workers that would permit France to assume leadership among the industrial nations of the world. Astier noted that although mechanization had led to enormous deskilling in some areas, new machines and production techniques had also created a need for a new corps of skilled workers capable of building, maintaining, repairing, and adjusting machines. Moreover, the luxury trades, electrical construction and building industries, and countless others still demanded a skilled labor force imbued with the specialized knowledge that came with apprenticeship or systematic training.[30] Astier believed that training not only produced good workers but encouraged the development of citizenship and civic responsibility. Good professional training would produce social peace.

> . . . we have often criticized workers for their impulsive movements, their infuriating docility in the face of appeals to violence, without asking if society has sufficiently put them on guard against their own inclinations. When the State has taken responsibility for their technical education, developing in them simultaneously the man and the citizen, an entirely

new mentality will substitute itself for the old one. The worker will obey less his nerves than his judgement. Popular agitators and sycophants will play less of a role in his decisions than his well considered interests and in this way he will truly become the artisan of his own destiny.[31]

Astier envisioned three levels of training, employing the metaphor of military hierarchy. "Advanced technical training would train the top officers, engineers, chemists, physicists, bankers, exporters, and large employers. Secondary training would develop the lower ranks of officers, such as supervisors, small employers, artisans, businessmen and salesmen: the essential intermediaries between the employers and workers or the clientele, who would ensure harmony between production and consumption and between capital and labor. Basic training would educate the mass of 'soldiers:' workers of every profession, all kinds of employees, whose naturally intelligent activity could, served by the appropriate knowledge, give marvelous results and also receive better pay."[32] It was to the latter group that Astier addressed his legislative proposal: professional courses that would allow all youths the training necessary to meet the demands of modern industrial production and enable France to successfully confront international economic competition.

Alongside Astier's conviction that job training could produce a class of responsible male citizen-workers, beliefs about women's and men's specific characteristics and roles fundamentally shaped training opportunities in the postwar period under the terms of the Astier Law. As one observer remarked, implying the age-old gender difference between "nature" and "culture,"

> Men are usually employed at more difficult work than women and they need a certain scientific culture. On the contrary the young woman is normally called upon to form a household and in devoting herself to her home will sooner or later leave industrial work. . . . Wouldn't it be better to emphasize general instruction [for her] which would include, apart from knowledge acquired in primary school, an entirely feminine and particularly useful science: household science?[33]

Beliefs such as this, however, far more than merely reflecting past practices, also helped to confirm the constitution of the female worker as a gendered subject for the future postwar world and as a subject who stood outside the model of the citizen-worker. By the early 1920s, some Catholic textile employers in the north of France established home economics courses for their young workers as an alternative to technical training. The Lepoutre Wool Spinning manufacture in Roubaix gave workers sewing courses so that they could sew their own wedding trousseaux; the Thiriez Spinners in Lille established its own home economics school in the factory, and the Agache factory had its own housekeeping school where each evening after work fifty young women came to learn sewing and cooking under the supervision of nuns.[34] Support for home economics training under the rubric of "apprenticeship" also came from the emerging social services professions that included women factory superintendents. Mlle. de Robien, general secretary of the Institut social familial ménager (Paris), speaking at the first Conférence internationale du Service social held in Paris in July 1928, promoted employers' sponsorship of home economics training for young working-class women.[35] Perhaps not surprisingly, the *Guide de l'apprenti* issued by the Société de protection des apprentis et des enfants employés dans les manufactures included home economics training for girls in its list of apprenticeship workshops and schools in Paris, along with sewing, embroidery, lacemaking, laundry and ironing, artificial flower and feather making, sales, and corset making. Alongside these initiatives, which complemented the family wage bonuses (*sursalaires familiales*) that Catholic textile manufacturers pioneered for workingmen and women with children, industrial municipalities also promoted such training.[36]

Gendered Forms of Training and Apprenticeship

State promotion of home economics under the rubric of technical training attempted to equate the crisis of "family apprenticeship" (in women's training in home economics) to the crisis of professional apprenticeship in the crafts and trades.[37] In the Paris region, towns such as Courbevoie, Epinay, Plessy-Robinson, Fresnes, Ivry, and Levallois-Perret, where industry existed side by side with small market gardening, established home economics training in schools for women alongside courses in rural housekeeping.[38] If at the same time the Ecole d'enseignement technique féminin (Women's Technical Training School, subsidized by the City of Paris and the Paris Chamber of Commerce) taught girls industrial drawing and tracing and trained them to be chemists, assistant chemists, and technical secretaries, this was the exception, rather than the rule.[39] In the city of Vienne, in the Isère, a textile firm established obligatory home economics courses in sewing, washing, and domestic economy for young women workers under the age of eighteen.[40] Local municipalities and employers thus contributed to the exclusion of women from skilled work already in place in many trades and reproduced the gendered social construction of competence.

Wartime labor needs had occasionally worked in women's favor to bring them into what employers defined as skilled work in some textile industries and allowed them to run machines that had previously been defined as "men's machines." Following the war, however, men reclaimed work on those machines and older gender divisions returned in force.[41] Helen Chenut's study of the hosiery industry in Troyes has shown that "by the 1920s, women workers spent three to six months acquiring the skills and speed necessary to earn their living at piecework. This relatively short training period implied lower skill content and contrasted noticeably with the longer training required for men's work." As Chenut suggests, with the exception of the fine needlework of women who identified flaws and mended knitted goods, increasing fragmentation of the labor process and mechanization meant that "women learned little more than specialized, mechanical high speed tasks, such as operating buttonholing and button sewing machines."[42] But it wasn't mechanization that made these tasks "unskilled"; rather, a combination of factors caused employers to define them as such, despite the fact that this work required strong concentration, accuracy, speed, and knowledge of the machines. These factors included some male workers' insistence on performing other varieties of higher-paid work requiring training or apprenticeship and the fact that employers believed that women could be hired at lower rates.

Other sectors of textile production illustrated further how gender shaped the historical process of skill differentiation. In the ribbon industry, for instance, rationalization separated pattern design (defined as highly skilled male labor) from execution of patterns by unskilled women on mechanical looms. In addition, men worked as mechanics and machine adjusters; women performed preparatory work, threading and bobbin winding for example, which employers defined as highly skilled. In one area, however, women did receive technical training—in the complex and delicate warping of looms for weaving fine ribbons (*ourdissage*) based on drawings that male designers had produced. The process involved aligning fine silk threads in preparation for warping the loom—something for which employers preferred to hire young women on the grounds of their manual dexterity.[43] In 1920, ribbon manufacturers in St. Etienne in south central France responded to a shortage of skilled workers capable of performing this work by setting up a technical training school (l'Ecole d'ourdissage), where each year about twenty young women learned this skilled trade in an apprenticeship that lasted from six months to a year.[44] This kind of apprenticeship was exceptional, but once women completed the training, manufacturers still paid them well below the rates of skilled male workers. Specialized warping was not at all like women's work on assembly lines in the metalworking and food industries. However, this example of a step in the historical evolution of gender-based skill differentiation shows that the same dynamics of gender and skill that were characteristic of the Paris region metalworking industries after the war also reached into other professional domains.[45] In textiles, the woman worker was defined primarily by her gender, no matter what level of skill her work demanded, unlike the male worker, whose wages and role in production were defined by the skill required by his work, as well as by gender. In silk weaving, even apprenticeship in a skill did not remove the indelible gender markers with which women were stamped. For even though women received training in skilled warp preparation, it was "natural" manual dexterity that made them good at it and the work remained undervalued.

Indeed, most initiatives that provided training for women did so in the context of bolstering gender divisions of skill in a variety of other jobs in the postwar period. In the Paris region at the same time that small-garment manufacturing declined during and after the war, haute couture, the high fashion industry, regained its earlier dynamism in the 1920s and a dozen or so new manufacturers rose to prominence alongside the prestigious, well-known houses of Chanel, Lanvin, Worth, Poiret, Doucet, Vionnet, and Drécoll. They specialized in coats and dresses, with diverse models ranging from expensive high fashion products to "ordinary," relatively inexpensive clothing.[46] In this growing trade, manufacturers sought to reestablish the position of French couture in the international market and responded to the lack of skilled seamstresses by reviving apprenticeship and professional training. Parisian schoolgirls were encouraged to take up sewing as a "naturally" feminine occupation in the manual training and home economics courses that existed throughout the Paris schools, bolstered by the emerging "science" of vocational guidance. After leaving school, they could enter an apprenticeship either in the workshop itself or in a separate apprenticeship workshop such as those operated by the manufacturers Jean Patou and Jeanne Lanvin, and in complementary technical training courses where they received training in design, cutting, sewing, and technology. For example, in 1931 the fashion manufacturer Pacquin took on eight thirteen-year-old girls as apprentices and Madeleine Vionnet took on twenty-three girls between the ages of thirteen and fifteen for periods from two to three years. All were the daughters of working-class men—a baker, a laborer, a mechanic, a cabinetmaker, and locksmith. These employers had an interest in training young women themselves to the specific standards of their fashion houses.[47] Mme.

G., for example, who came to Paris from Burgundy after the war, underwent a three-year apprenticeship in the highly stratified fashion industry in the 1920s. Large fashion houses had sometimes as many as twelve workshops—one that created the designs and then distributed them to the others where women sewed. She described the division of labor between men and women in making hats: men created the forms using special steam presses; women embroidered and decorated the hats.[48] Young women whose parents could afford to do so also sent them to professional training schools such as those run by the City of Paris.

Rising wages for seamstresses working in both the high fashion houses and those in the ordinary, ready-to-wear market that blossomed in the inflationary, consumer-conscious 1920s accompanied these initiatives. The wages of a "*première main*" (first-hand seamstress) in the Paris needle trades rose from 72 francs weekly in 1919 to 189.6 francs in 1928; those of a woman who prepared the cloth for sewing, a "*première apprêteuse*" in the high fashion industry (*mode*) who did not take her meals in the workshop, rose from 270 francs a month in 1919 to 749 francs a month in 1927.[49] These relatively high wages reflected market trends and skill. In contrast to the deskilling and task fragmentation (what the French call "specialization") that occurred in most trades in this period, the opposite occurred in the fashion industry. The adoption of the simple straight "chemise" dress meant that no longer did the seamstress specialize in making one piece of the dress (the bodice, skirt, or sleeves) as she had before the war; she now made the entire dress from start to finish. Thus she had to have a "knowledge of design, proportion, and the harmony of lines which was useless to the bodice-maker before the war; . . . more numerous models, with more frequent modifications means that habit cannot take the place of skill."[50] Similarly, the high fashion manufacturers of the popular 1920s "cloche" hats required that the size be perfect; the hat maker had to be capable of making an entire hat according to the precise specifications of a drawing or model, following exact measurements. To a "natural sense of good taste" she had to be able to bring dexterity, skill, and a perfect knowledge of execution.[51] But the high fashion industry was an exception amid the multiplicity of jobs at which women labored in the 1920s and 1930s. Although women were given the opportunity to learn skills and rise in the ranks, haute couture was a profession that had *already* been gendered female. Fashion houses' preference for women's allegedly "natural dexterity" excluded men from some sectors of the industry. Training programs in the high fashion houses thus reproduced the gender segregation of the labor market.

The mass-market ready-made garment industry presented an even more complex picture of gender and ethnic divisions. As Nancy Green has shown, the gender of skill in the ready-made industry overall was extremely unstable and sewing could be men's as well as women's work. Men cut and sewed fur coats and made suits in men's garment manufacture at least from the nineteenth century forward. In Paris, immigrant Russian and Eastern European Jewish men made up almost half of all male garment workers in the interwar years.[52] Work shifted constantly between immigrant men and French men or French and immigrant women although employers viewed the skill of immigrant men as "imported" rather than linked to "natural" physical attributes as in the case of women.[53] Moreover, even though women could learn sewing in home economics training programs established by municipal governments and employers and men and women could take courses in vocational training programs and high schools (*collèges d'enseignement technique*), much sewing "skill" in the ready-made clothing industry was not learned through a formal apprenticeship but on the job, "from older relatives and co-workers."[54] This did not prevent one factory inspector from remarking on the skill of the woman machine sewer in 1928,

> The ready-made clothing worker is now only rarely the mechanical worker or finisher who repeats indefinitely the same monotonous gesture and whose only skill consists in her ability to work fast. She is now called upon to exercise her intelligence, her good taste, her lively spirit, at the same time as her manual skill. To be a good worker, she has to know a thousand professional details; the styles are so numerous, so different, and follow one another so rapidly, that the same kind of work only rarely repeats itself.[55]

Even though in principle professional training might have enabled women to obtain skills in professions that previously offered them no training, in practice, the Astier Law and employer initiatives had a limited effect in this regard. In general, employers' views of what counted as "skill" meant that most believed that women didn't need special training for "what came naturally," with the result that women remained confined to the same gender-typed trades as before the war. Even if in the fur and leather industries women were now allowed to become cutters (a job reserved for men before the war and in some areas confined to men after the war), before 1929, no professional training courses were set up for women to complement their apprenticeship in the trade, reflecting the common perception that in this trade women occupied a secondary position alongside men.[56] Within a wide range of industries ranging from food processing to machining nuts and bolts, women learned on the job, with only minimal instructions.

Indeed, reports of women factory superintendents-in-training suggest that none of the women they saw in their factory internships received training for their jobs. Eugénie Rey described how she learned on the job to make batteries at Thomson-Houston after the team head (*chef d'équipe*) briefly showed her the work. The fact that she was seated next to a young woman with more seniority and experience in soldering enabled her to pick up the work by watching her neighbor.[57] Marthe Teyssot, employed as a factory superintendent-in-training at a small metalworking factory outside Paris, in 1920, received no training for her job, which consisted of producing the threads on bolts with the aid of a threading machine. She found that she had to expend more energy than was probably necessary to do the job and put out such muscular effort to work the machine that her whole body ached. Teyssot implied that had she been properly trained she would have been able to do the work more effectively without the physical discomfort.[58] Mademoiselle Renard likewise remarked on the lack of formal training during her internship in the weaving and warping departments of the Textilose rayon factory in Chambéry. She argued that it was necessary that the workers be given at least a minimum of training; doing so would lead to fewer errors and interest the women in their work.[59] But the relative paucity of training programs does not by itself explain women's relegation to unskilled work or the devaluation of the skilled work they did. Even when women received training, apprenticeship occurred in areas of the labor market that were already sex-segregated and was tied to prior assumptions about what kinds of work women could perform. Cultural discourses of gender predictably influenced employers' views of which workers could be effectively trained.

Numerous writers and industrialists illustrated the durability of views regarding the limits of women's expertise. Writing in 1926, a labor inspector, Marcel Frois, argued, "Women are not constituted to perform work where muscular force plays a large role; nor should they be assigned to jobs requiring a [prolonged] physical effort. On the other hand, they distinguish themselves by their courage, their capability at work that demands fine motor skills, and rapid and precise movements."[60] In June 1933, an unnamed industrialist spoke to the Union féminine civique et sociale and remarked on women's gender-specific aptitudes. Taking for granted the gender division of labor as so many of his contemporaries did, he noted that it was just a fact that women had always worked in the textile industry, where they were "in the domain of their special aptitudes."[61] Now, however, although the jobs for women had expanded, the idea that women possessed special capacities for certain kinds of delicate work persisted. This could also be seen in electrical construction for making the rotors for motors, in crystal manufacture, the manipulation of cigarettes, and sorting paper: " . . . women's work in sorting is more rapid and better than that of men; their dexterity, the precision of their movements make them more capable of handling small trucks. In assembly line work, women . . . produce more and better . . . [than men]."[62]

Such views were surprisingly persistent. In 1945, Charles Labriffe, a member of the textile industry's Committee on Professional Qualification, deplored the lack of professional training in the textile industry and proposed the expansion of apprenticeships: " . . . one must think of forming the future man, alongside the man, the worker, and alongside the worker, the textile worker."[63] Taking the example of weaving, Labriffe argued for a naturalized gender division of trades:

> In weaving we find capable women weavers in silk, both solid and Jacquard; in dress fabric and drapery . . . but there are few women weavers of furniture fabrics and rugs. This would raise questions about sex in apprenticeship if women's movements did not already display a natural specificity: the housewife, the woman at light work; the man at work requiring more effort, otherwise stated, a judicious distribution of effort in work. Whatever happens in the future, there is a fact that no one can change: there are professions that are better for some than for others and what is important is that everyone has their place.[64]

Thus, social characteristics and naturalized aptitudes dictated capacities for skilled labor. But if gender and lack of training restricted the range of jobs open to women, it was also true that neither gender nor technical training made skilled work available to all French men.

The growing number of men attending schools such as the Ecole nationale professionnelle (National Vocational School) and the Ecoles pratiques de commerce et d'industrie (Practical Commercial and Industrial School) constituted an elite whose technical training led them to become not skilled workers but engineers and managers. As Director of Technical Education E. Labbé pointed out in 1927, "thanks to [the professional training schools] each year several hundred intelligent, hard working young men, armed with solid scientific and technical knowledge, are ready to become good technicians and managers."[65] Julien Fontène, director of vocational guidance in the Services d'orientation professionnelle à la direction générale de l'enseignement technique (General Office of Technical Education) confirmed this view.

He believed that managers could be selected from the skilled workers in these programs to direct operations on the shop floor and increase productivity.[66] The Diderot School in Paris, for example, had been created as a model of technical training but by 1931 turned out young male managerial personnel rather than skilled workers. In spite of political leaders' and reformers' rhetoric about the need to form skilled workers, at best technical training produced "worker-technicians" rather than citizen-workers, thus adding a new level to the ongoing differentiation of male labor.[67]

Even the technical training courses set up by municipal governments failed to attract a significant number of young men. In order to get employers to accept the terms of the Astier Law, reformers and legislators agreed that the courses would be given after work, so that employers would not have to sacrifice productivity during the normal workday. But the young men who were supposed to attend the courses viewed them as a supplemental, unremunerated obligation, and the courses' theoretical emphasis often failed to connect with the realities of work on the shop floor. Moreover, most employers were reluctant to either invest in their own training programs or require that their workers attend municipal programs. Some believed that it was best to keep adolescents and women at the bottom of the skill ladder and use them for "specialized" (that is unskilled) work and never even considered training unskilled immigrants hired on fixed-term contracts.[68] By 1928, only 173 male workers in the factories of manufacturers belonging to the Groupement des industries métallurgiques (GIM), the association of large metal manufacturers, were enrolled in the courses given by the French mechanics,' boilermakers,' and foundry workers' union; this was an exceptionally low number given the thousands of workers employed in these industries.[69] And although the Paris city government opened pre-apprenticeship classes in woodworking and metalworking for boys aged twelve to fifteen (no parallel initiative existed for girls), trade schools enrolled 2,300 students in 1927 and only 2,700 ten years later.[70] The passage of the Apprenticeship Law of 1928 that envisioned a measure of state regulation of apprenticeship left many loopholes that employers seized upon to avoid training their workers. On balance, employers preferred to invest in training a small cadre of élite skilled French men and to rely on semiskilled and unskilled French and immigrant men and women as the "shock troops" of industrial development in the prosperous 1920s.

As Aimée Moutet has argued, automobile manufacturers, metallurgical firms, and employers in the naval construction and electrical construction industries that adopted methods of rationalization also developed the most extensive programs to train skilled male workers, whose professional expertise was linked to the needs of individual firms.[71] To meet the postwar need for skilled workers, the Citroën automobile manufacture established an apprenticeship program in 1920 to train workers' sons from the age of thirteen for the mass production of automobiles.[72] When this program proved insufficient to meet the demand for skilled automobile workers, Citroën set up workshop schools in 1927 at his Javel factory outside Paris where two groups of young men took a combination of theoretical and practical courses designed to produce three types of skilled worker. The first group consisted of young men recruited from those leaving primary school for a two-year course in the factory. The second, even more highly skilled, followed a one-year apprenticeship that reversed the Taylorist process of labor management and would enable the trainee to "escape the division of labor that separates design from [execution] . . . he incorporates rational organization in all of its details and is prepared to take his place in the organization with in-depth training."[73] At the third level were the "cadres supérieurs"—upper-level managers—recruited from higher educational training institutes like the Ecole nationale des arts et métiers (National School of Arts and Trades). In an effort to encourage the training of skilled workers and labor force stability, Citroën gave workers' sons scholarships to attend his workshop schools. In addition to the workshop schools at Javel, at his other factories Citroën established training programs in time-measurement, machine regulation, metal stamping, metal plating (tôlerie), and a program for training supervisors.[74] As Moutet argues, Citroën did the most to advance technical education by developing apprenticeship within the factory and a school open to students from upper-level primary schools. Maurice Lacoin, in charge of professional training at Citroën, believed that Citroën could "transform the factory atmosphere in the service of professionalism and social peace." The school was designed to create future regulators, demonstrators, and the skilled male workers who would undertake time-measurement, by training them in equipment, the running of new machines, and assembly. Thus Citroën attempted to create an élite of skilled workers who would direct the mass of unskilled workers and implement scientific management on the shop floor.[75] But these employers resisted training women or immigrant men, whom they preferred to hire for unskilled repetition work or the sort of dirty industrial jobs that French men were disinclined to do. Selective training helped to produce gender differentiation of skills and in turn reproduced cultural perceptions of sexual difference.[76] These goals were entirely consistent with the selective adoption of scientific management techniques in the 1920s and 1930s.

Rationalizing Work, Managing the Worker

In the postwar years, rationalization rather than technical training facilitated the entry of women as well as many unskilled men—especially immigrants—into industry, especially in metalworking and automobile production. In late-nineteenth and early-twentieth-century France, scientific management attracted the interest of large employers eager to render workers more productive and efficient.[77] Taylorism, imported into France shortly after Frederick Winslow Taylor's publication of *The Principles of Scientific Management* in 1898 and other works in the United States, focused on managers' capacity to organize work effectively and efficiently by measuring the motions of the body through time and regulating the body according to plan.[78] Shop foremen circulated on the factory floor with clipboard and stopwatch, timing workers' motions to document the efficiency of the working body with the goal of increasing productivity. Engineers attempted to reorganize the factory to cut down on time-wasting trips between one part of the factory and another or to make it possible for workers to reach tools more effectively. Taylor's model of scientific management was not simply about measuring the body's effective and efficient performance of tasks. It also involved a new model of managerial authority aimed at the reorganization of the entire labor process through a more refined and intensified division of labor in which the design and planning of production were clearly differentiated from the execution of work.[79] It could even be applied in the home. Henri le Chatelier, a major proponent of scientific management, believed that rationalization could as effectively be applied to women's domestic work in the kitchen by reducing recipes to simple formulas and by more precisely estimating cooking times—simple techniques that could be taught in housekeeping schools and home economics courses.[80] But many employers did not agree with le Chatelier's views of traditional gender roles. For those who sought to adopt some of the "principles of scientific management," women's labor was an asset to the rational workplace.

As historians have noted, gender difference and division played a fundamental role in technological modification and deskilling of the labor process, in the increasing use of piecework, and in new management techniques designed to integrate workers into manufacturing and stabilize the labor force.

Although rationalization was most visible in the large metalworking and automobile plants of the Paris region and elsewhere (at Peugeot in Montbeliard, for example), employers in food processing, textile production, and the state postal, telephone, and telegraph services (PTT) also adopted elements of scientific management hoping to increase efficiency and productivity. The Citroën automobile plants in the northwestern extremity of Paris in the 1920s stood as the most highly rationalized of the automobile factories in the Paris region, and while hardly typical, they illustrate processes that were repeated elsewhere. Citroën had been one of the largest arms manufacturers during the war and in wartime women made up almost 87 percent of the workforce at Citroën's Javel plant alone. Despite Citroën's optimism about the redeployment of women workers after the war, in the first wave of rehiring in 1919, women made up only 10 percent of his new recruits, reflecting gender divisions already in place. About a third of these women worked as semiskilled solderers or mechanics, having learned these trades during the war; 49 percent were unskilled laborers or assembly-line workers.[81] In the period of immediate postwar reconstruction, skilled French men, adjusters, turners, and sheet metal workers made up two-thirds of the workforce. Foreign workers counted for less than 4 percent and included no colonial workers; this would change later in the 1920s as the number of unskilled workers, including foreign men at Citroën, increased and the overall workforce multiplied by a factor of seven.[82]

Citroën attempted to create a finely tuned workforce in which the division of labor meant that each worker was responsible for a particular job. As Downs has shown in her study of small metals manufacture, categorizing workers based on refinements in the division of labor constituted a central element in the rationalization process and in turn had important implications for how employers determined workers' skill competencies and, ultimately, their wages. A 1919 list of professional categories at Citroën listed 186 different categories of unskilled and skilled workers.[83] In the early 1920s, in the mechanical casting department (*atelier de fonte mécanique*) seventy unskilled women and thirty unskilled men worked on simple machines, making nuts and bolts and parts for automobile gas filters (*noyautage*), producing 800 bolts an hour and 960 gas filter parts. On the other hand the highly skilled work of trimming was entirely male, and occupied 123 men at filing by hand, with pneumatic files or sand, working at huge rotating tables, in barrels, or closed cabins. Likewise, some 200 skilled men worked at sheet metal; no women were to be found in this area of work.[84] Eventually, the introduction of metal presses for the manufacture of chassis made the skill and knowledge of these male workers obsolete. In the mid-1920s, Citroën began to apply time-measurement techniques (*chronométrage*) to analyzing work, establishing time norms for manufacturing cars in order to increase individual workers' productivity and overall assembly-line production.

The introduction of assembly-line work in the manufacture of automobile seats illustrates the gender shifts that occurred in the process of transforming work once performed by skilled male workers. In 1926 Ernest Mattern's "methods" service at Citroën established uniform procedures for cutting the upholstery fabric in order to minimize waste and put the entire operation of making the seats on an assembly line. This step became possible once seat construction had been disassembled into its component parts.[85] Mattern standardized the production of seat armatures so that by moving along the line, machines could be deployed for bending and connecting the armature; machines cut the cloth, and workers assembled the cushions and fitted upholstery. Standardization enabled Mattern to replace two highly skilled male workers—one to assemble the seat frame, the other to assemble the cushions—by forty unskilled women, each of whom was responsible for a different task along the line.[86] This kind of transformation—which involved not merely the substitution of women for men but the creation of new unskilled forms of labor—helps to explain why, following the war, in the newly reconstructed industries of the Paris region, women's presence in metalworking reached 17.4 percent in 1931.[87] In similar fashion, refining the gender division of labor in the process of rationalizing the manufacture of clocks and gauges at the Jaegar Company involved replacing highly skilled male workers by unskilled women on assembly-line production. About 150 women worked on the line and a relatively small number of men were employed as team heads or as skilled clockmakers. As one factory superintendent in training noted, "The head of each workshop was an overseer who directed each team [of] . . . women linked by the assembly line. Thus in [my] workshop . . . a team included fourteen women . . . at each table. The pieces passed automatically down the length of the table, where each worker completed them. [The pieces] then traveled down to the next table and the next up to the testing table, where the correct operation of each device was tested."[88]

The unskilled assembly line worker, whether female or male, forced to repeat the same movement minute after minute, day after day, found this mindless assembly-line work exhausting. Simone Weil's well-known description of her experience in a metal factory in 1934 described the inexorable pace of repetitive piecework in terms even more disheartening than that of superintendent-in-training, Eugénie Rey.[89] Weil, a teacher and revolutionary syndicalist activist, took a job as an unskilled machine operator in order to experience for herself the life of a worker. Page after page of her factory journal documented the number of pieces she was able to turn out in a single workday, including the imperfect pieces that didn't count, and how much she was paid.

[Monday 17 December] Afternoon—[Work on the] press: pieces very difficult to place, [lost 56 centimes]. [Made] 600 from 2:30 to 5:15 p.m. with a half hour to readjust the machine which had gone out of adjustment because I had left a piece in the tool. Tired and disheartened. I feel like a free being for 24 hours (Sunday) and have had to readapt to a servile condition. Disgust because of the 56 centimes, causing [me] to become tense and exhaust myself with the certainty that I'll be yelled at for not working fast enough or for botched pieces . . . I feel like a slave.

Wednesday 19 [December] Work stopped from 7 to 11. From 11 to 5 [pm used the] heavy press to make rounds in a bronze bar with Robert (2 francs per hour, 2 francs 28 for a thousand rounds). Violent headache, finished the work almost continuously in tears . . . However no disasters; only 3 or 4 botched pieces. Insightful advice from the supply man: work the pedal only with your leg, not with the whole body; push the band [of metal] with one hand and hold it steady with the other instead of pulling and keeping it steady with the same hand. Work is related to athletic skill.[90]

Exhausting, physically taxing work like this caused industrial physiologists to charge that Taylorism had failed to account for the "human factor" in work.

Aimée Moutet has distinguished the different levels of unskilled work in automobile production and assembly work. She argues that not all women were to be found at the bottom of the labor hierarchy and that some women may have viewed machine work positively. Women specialized workers—*ouvrières spécialisées,* or o.s.—occupied an intermediary level between the skilled worker and the ordinary laborer (*manoeuvres ordinaires*). Foreign workers were almost never recruited for these jobs, except for jobs in foundries, for example, that French workers balked at.[91] The unskilled women who worked at assembly-line production and serial manufacture in automobile, electrical construction, and precision mechanics, she argues, were relatively well integrated into the factory, whereas the common laborer—especially the immigrant worker—was considered the "maid of all work."[92] It is not implausible, as Moutet has suggested, that even unskilled machine work gave women a certain independence and pride in the sense of mastery of the machine, something that may not always have been available to immigrant male workers. "If she lacked skill, [she nonetheless] possessed a special touch, acquired by habit, but also by her intelligence at work. Integrated into production, the woman machine worker wound up adhering to professional values and to the pride in a job well done."[93] It was even possible (although not especially common) for women to acquire skills and a certain amount of independence on the job in large factories. At the same time, "in the rotor workshop (*atelier de bobinage*) at Thomson . . . a year's apprenticeship was necessary to produce satisfactory work. But this knowledge was rarely recognized as a real skill."[94] This example illustrates the contingency of skill and of what employers recognized as "useful knowledge" on the job. Even if unskilled women occupied a position a notch above that of the unskilled male immigrant laborer, gender played an enormous role in whether or not employers defined work as skilled. And if women could and did rise in the ranks to become overseers, they did so only in workshops employing women exclusively.[95]

Gender segregation in the factory persisted and even became more rarified in the early-twentieth-century economy than it had been before World War I. By 1935 the "Métallurgie, Voiture, Aviation" section of the Office départemental de placement de la Seine (Seine Departmental Placement Office) listed women as the most numerous among those placed in the jobs designated as least skilled: as machine and lathe operators, as "specialized" (unskilled) workers, and as polishers and nickel platers. Although during World War I women had worked as skilled fitters (*ajusteurs*), none worked at this job in the highly masculine metalworking and aviation trades in 1936, nor did they appear among the ranks of skilled lock makers, boiler and pipe fitters, tin platers, forgers, or ironworkers.[96] Although some women machinists arguably took pride in their work, within the highly stratified automobile factory most unskilled workers, especially women, found themselves dependent upon male skilled workers, team leaders, and overseers for the adjusting and regulation of machines—a job over which men maintained a monopoly. In most factories, overseers also had the power to fire a worker for shoddy work (even if it was the fault of a poorly regulated machine) or insubordination.[97] The gender division of labor in the rationalized factory not only deprived women and some men of more prestigious skilled jobs; it also created new relations of dependency of unskilled women and men on skilled men.

Feminization was not only a *product* of rationalization but *facilitated* rationalization. The same assumptions about women's innate ability to perform monotonous, repetitive work that led employers to create new women's jobs designated as "unskilled" also allowed employers to speed up machines, following time-measurement studies in order to speed up production. In the food processing industry, one woman described how fast she had to work to keep up with the machine cutting sugar cubes in the Say sugar refinery in the 1930s: "The knife kept going without stopping for cutting the sugar into pieces. For the woman manipulating the bar of sugar to be cut (*la lingoteuse*) it was really hard because she had to fill the squares so that the arranger could put them into boxes. She filled six squares in two seconds!"[98]

In textile manufacture the high proportion of women already employed in unskilled work facilitated the piecemeal adoption of techniques of scientific management and refinement of the gender divisions of skill in the 1920s. Rationalization took the form of gender-specific task specialization. Since the end of the nineteenth century, nationally women had been a majority of textile workers and at the end of the war they counted for 62 percent of all textile workers; in 1926 and 1931, they constituted 59 percent. In the arrondissement of Lille, a major center of linen and cotton manufacture, postwar mechanization caused women's share of jobs in textiles to decline and then rise slowly from 49 percent in 1921 to 50 percent in 1926 and to 52 percent in 1936, shifts that reflected a more sophisticated gender division of labor.[99] During the war, unlike metalworking, textile work was neither massively rationalized nor deskilled. Indeed, many factories in the occupied zones shut down or cut back on their workforce. Women substituted for men on skilled men's jobs, working as "attachers" (*rattacheuses*), reaching inside the looms to piece together broken threads. They ran carding machines and the Cotton Patent machines that were previously considered skilled "men's machines."[100] Employers introduced technical modifications to speed up production and began the process of rationalization that continued through the interwar years. At the end of hostilities, new English machines—new two-meter wide looms—and automatic combing machines allowed for increased productivity and workers now supervised four instead of two looms.[101]

But wartime rationalization did not have the same effects in all industries. Unlike metalworking or automobile manufacture, in the textile industry new production processes and technologies did not allow women to remain in men's jobs in the 1920s and 1930s. Rather, the postwar and interwar years saw the restoration of skilled work to men that women had performed during the war.[102] In fact the industry became more divided between skilled and unskilled work. Certain areas like combing and dying functioned perfectly well with a staff of male managers and unskilled laborers, whereas spinning and weaving continued to require an experienced and skilled labor force.[103] In weaving alone, six different apprenticeships corresponded to the skills required for weaving different fabrics: solid fabric cotton and linen on *excentrique* looms with one shuttle; weaving of dress and drapery fabric on mechanical looms with several shuttles; weaving on automatic looms; Jacquard loom production for dress fabric, furniture textiles, and rugs; weaving of velvet; and carpets. Charles Labriffe, professor of industrial education and member of the Commission on Professional Qualification listed nineteen jobs in weaving, fourteen of which he designated as women's preparatory or finishing jobs. Four were jobs that either men or women could fill and five were specifically designated as men's jobs.[104] In this highly mechanized industry, as weaving and spinning modernized, employers hired skilled male adjusters and mechanics whose technical knowledge was necessary to running and maintaining more sophisticated machines.[105] But employers believed that women made especially good bobbin winders and that women's allegedly good eyesight enabled them to observe the bobbins especially carefully. They could work with two hands at once and repeat the same movement frequently. Their sense of responsibility and foresight meant that they would grease and maintain the machines well; they were orderly and would put away the finished bobbins neatly; their perseverance meant that they could be expected to learn gradually on the job. Dexterity and fine motor coordination would stand them in good stead.[106] Labriffe recommended that time and motion studies of bobbin winding, warping, weaving, and a host of other jobs could vastly improve the efficiency of textile production. He urged textile manufacturers to invest in such studies as well as in aptitude testing of workers with a view to training them in more efficient techniques. But in textiles, rationalization accentuated gender divisions already in place. In one Lille textile firm after World War II, the gender division of skill had changed little. Men made up 88 percent of the "*agents de maîtrise,*" highly skilled technical personnel, and 87 percent of skilled workers. Women counted for 66 percent of the "specialized"—unskilled—workers, men and women were distributed evenly among the lowly specialized laborers, and common laborers and women made up 90 percent of the secretarial staff (there was one man).[107]

Likewise, in the hosiery industry following the war, men reclaimed the prestigious and skilled work on Cotton Patent machines. Chenut points out how in nineteenth-century Troyes these machines became identified as "men's machines" largely because of the muscular strength needed to shift the heavy gears. Yet before World War I, the addition of an automatic gearshift removed the need for physical strength; "the operator became more of a machine minder and a supervisor of the knitting process."[108] Nonetheless, male workers continued to undergo substantial apprenticeship in running the machines and retained their status as skilled workers despite the fact that the physical and technical demands of the job shifted in the postwar years. Here, then, is another case in which the designation of "skill" was linked less to physical or mental labor requirements than to the gender of the worker and persisted despite the fact that the original requirements of "skill" no longer existed.

In virtually all areas of textile production, the gender division of labor varied according to the fabric. In linen weaving, for example, women performed most of the preparatory operations, whereas in jute weaving men beat and softened the heavy fibers by hand and processed raw cotton.[109] In wool textiles women supervised five to six combing machines at a time as the combed wool was wound onto large rollers. Although men were responsible for wool dyeing, women washed and combed after dyeing; women generally worked in spinning and twisting and in running the machines that put the thread onto bobbins.[110] Men, however, monopolized the work of warping the mechanical looms, which required "heavy manipulation." A division of labor also existed in wool weaving, which was entirely mechanized and demanded no particular strength. Women and men both ran looms that wove canvas, cottons, and drapery. Wide weaves or complicated patterns, such as those produced on the Jacquard looms, in carpet weaving, and upholstery, were men's work.[111] These distinctions, established in the nineteenth century in the transition to factory production, were replicated in the post–World War I years, even though the work no longer required significant muscular strength. The association of running large machines as "men's work" persisted, even if the principal tasks in weaving consisted of starting up the loom, surveillance, and tying up broken threads.[112] Here is a case, then, where discourses of gender difference took precedence over the rational deployment of labor on the basis of real abilities.

Finally, a refined gender division of labor had long existed in other sectors of textile production. Although some women in the silk ribbon manufacture around Lyon underwent an apprenticeship in order to become warpers in the early 1920s, employers maintained the distinction between design (male) and execution (unskilled female and male) that had existed since the nineteenth century, as Mathilde Dubesset and Michèle Zancarini-Fournel have noted. Jules Simon, in the course of his lengthy study of women silk workers, had expressed surprise to find no women among the designers in the Lyonnais ribbon industry in 1860. "One would have at first thought that the job of textile design was made expressly for women. It's nice, sedentary work, not very tiring, well paid, which to all appearances requires only good taste. And who know better than women how to choose a design or colors?" Simon himself provided the answer to this apparent paradox: women did indeed have "taste," but they could not *create*.[113] As Dubesset and Zancarini-Fournel point out, over half a century later, at the Ecole de Beaux Arts in St. Etienne, where designers trained for the industry, no women were to be found in the courses devoted to textile design and application. Although a course for women opened in 1919, no women were hired as designers for another twenty years.[114] As in other areas of the textile industry, employers reserved weaving exclusively for men. No women attended the weaving courses in the Ecole professionnelle; women, apart from the few warpers who were trained in the early 1920s, ran errands or worked as "folders," winding the finished ribbons on rectangular cards or on cylinders, ready for the market. At the same time, women often escaped rigid divisions by force of necessity. As much as male employers and workers defended the gender division of labor and men's prerogative over skill ("there are some things that are simply men's work"), women's ability to learn rapidly on the job meant that they could learn to repair and regulate their machines. As men began to leave the ribbon industry for other jobs in the late 1920s and early 1930s, women increasingly learned to replace broken machine parts or resolve mechanical problems, in stark contrast to employers' representations of their competence. But women had already internalized the norms that often attached skilled work to the gender of the worker rather than to the tasks performed, and described their work repairing and adjusting as *bricolage,* or fiddling, rather than as skilled labor as men would have done.[115] This example illustrates how powerfully masculine and feminine work identities shaped the perception of skill.

Finally, the case of telephone manufacture provides an additional illustration of how employers participated in reducing the skill designation of jobs in ways that corresponded not to the actual work performed but to the gender of the worker—a process that Downs noted for armaments manufacture during World War I. As Catherine Omnès points out, in 1926 the Groupement des industries métallurgiques, the principal organization of metalworking and metallurgical employers, reclassified all women's jobs in telephone manufacture that had previously been grouped as "ouvrières professionnelles" and grouped them with "manoeuvres spécialisées." As Omnès observes, this "declassification was the result of a more restrictive—but also more arbitrary—definition of the skilled worker, a definition that left little room for acquired experience. Henceforth, only someone who possessed a skill and whose apprenticeship was sanctioned by a certificate of expertise could be considered skilled. Absent an adequate system of training for girls, women had almost no opportunity to recover the status that their professional experience had formerly assured them."[116]

Following the labor inspector Marcel Frois, many employers believed that women's "innate dexterity"—their nimble fingers—and deftness, their fine motor skills, "nervous constitution," and good eyesight made them ideal for the manipulation of miniscule pieces, in the assembly of gauges, turning, and a myriad of other tasks throughout the economy. They could be rapid machine workers in food processing and good bobbin winders. Employers believed that "women's patient execution of rapid, detailed work sprang from some set of qualities intrinsic in women" rather than from deskilled, rationalized, and repetitive jobs for which they were hired.[117] These "qualities" and "innate abilities" kept them in the labor force but condemned them to unskilled work. If, on rare occasions they conferred "skill," women's professional competence was not recognized and remunerated as such since employers essentialized it as a product of "nature." Thus, women supervisors rarely benefited financially from supervisory work because they were only employed in gender-segregated workshops supervising women. Just like semiskilled women working in all women's workshops, they suffered from the general devaluation of women's work that contemporary sociologists have noted is a product of gender segregation and segmentation.[118] Organizing work along scientific principles also had implications for how sexual difference influenced wages and wage inequality.

Rationalizing the Wage

Ideas about family, masculinity, and femininity influence not only the kinds of work that men and women do but how work is valued. In interwar France, the same ideas about sexual difference that accompanied the rationalization of the labor process influenced thinking about the wage. In the 1920s and 1930s, wage policies, linked to gender-based labor stratification, incorporated assumptions about workers' relationship to the family as well as their relationship to the labor market. I have already suggested that training and "opportunity hoarding" were crucial in shaping gender divisions of labor.

Two additional practices proved crucial in evaluating work, productivity, and wages. First, in the productivist climate of postwar economic reconstruction, rationalizing employers aggressively applied old forms of payment like piece rates and used teamwork to get workers to produce at maximum capacity. Employers also increasingly used time-measurement studies (*chronométrage*) to determine what a worker was capable of producing in a given amount of time and set wages accordingly. Although employers had begun to use time measurement before the war in automobile manufacturing and encountered strong opposition from male workers, after the war the weakness and division of the labor movement made workers powerless to resist successfully this technique of increasing production. Because this system of payment took no account of mechanical breakdowns, unforeseen stoppages could cost a worker not minutes but hours. Simone Weil, working in electrical and mechanical construction in 1934–35, earned an hourly wage that corresponded to the price of the pieces of the particular order she was supposed to fill, determined by time-measurement studies. Part of her wage (the *taux d'affutage*) was based on her level of skill; the rest (the *boni*) was a function of her output. When her productivity was good, her wages rose; if she failed to fill the order, she lost part of her wage.[119] This form of payment —potentially highly unstable for the worker—affected both men and women, but employers' perceptions of gender difference in workers' capacities for sustained repetition work led them to apply these techniques especially aggressively to increase women's output. Moreover, because women received no formal training and had to wait for male adjusters to repair and restart a broken machine, they were more vulnerable to the vagaries of this form of payment. But this was only one of several payment systems that accompanied rationalization.

Employers at the Jaegar clock and gauge firm outside Paris paid male and female assembly line workers according to the Bedaux system, a form of wage management designed to increase the individual workers' productivity by paying them according to a formula based on output per minute.[120] Other employers preferred the Rowan system, which paid workers on the basis of a combined hourly wage and piece rate. Although these systems were used to pay both men and women, in the minds of employers, women fit perfectly within these logics of payment. Women, employers believed, could withstand the monotony of endless repetition work better than men and would produce as much as humanly possible within a given period of time in order to make a living wage.[121] Indeed, according to Marcel Frois, "Women are . . . economical and provident by nature and ever keen to earn more. A small increase in their wages is sufficient to get them to work above and beyond their capacity."[122] Employers' decisions to use certain forms of payment were thus designed to take advantage of preconceived notions of the relationship between gender and skill.

Unsurprisingly, pay scales reflected gender-based professional categories that were already divided and stratified according to gender, even for workers who were paid a weekly wage. At Citroën, the wage demands made by the metalworkers' Comité d'entente in 1919 listed both men and women laborers at the very bottom of the adult wage scale at 110 francs per week and specialized (unskilled) men and women at 132 francs per week. Only when men and women performed the same unskilled or semiskilled work did they earn the same wage: male and female welders would have earned 150 francs a week, while male electrical welders and female tin welders would earn 132 francs. But this apparent wage equity at Citröen did not reflect the experience of all categories. Male file trimmers earned 150 francs a week, whereas women earned 100 francs. No woman could earn more than 132 francs a week, 45 percent less than the most highly paid male nonprofessional modelers who would have earned 240 francs a week, and 87 percent less than the most highly paid male designers who would have earned 1,000 francs.[123] As Downs points out, employers exercised tremendous flexibility "by simply moving the line that divided men's work from women's work. Indeed, employers' insistence on the technical distinctions between male and female forms of skill dovetailed with the notion that women are, by definition cheap labor."[124] This flexibility enabled employers to sustain and benefit from gender-based wage inequality.

Textile employers, like automobile manufacturers, also employed piece rates and added the obligation of surveillance on multiple looms.[125] In addition, employers introduced a system of double rotating teams according to which two teams worked for six hours each on multiple looms that ran for twelve hours. As the textile industry entered a period of depression at the end of the 1920s, some employers used triple teams in order to keep looms running for eighteen hours at a stretch. Although rising wages in the 1920s allowed the wage gap between men and women to narrow from 75 to 84 percent, because of the rotating team system (combined with the effects of the Depression of the 1930s) women's wages fell by 10 to 30 percent between the wars. And workers bitterly resented the system for the way in which it disrupted family life. If more than one family member was employed, which was often the case, family members working on different teams barely saw one another during the week. Moreover, although employers of the Lille-

Roubaix-Tourcoing region proclaimed the principle of "equal pay for work of equal quality and quantity" where men and women performed the same work, a highly refined division of labor on the shop floor helped to maintain wage inequality.[126]

A second aspect of thinking about the wage and wage practices concerned the relationship between gender, family, and work—a relationship that had important consequences for both state and employer-initiated social policies. In addition to these new methods of calculating wages, in the 1920s wages became linked to the worker's status as a family member, not only to his or her individual productivity. This new way of thinking about wages occurred in the context of rampant inflation that caused prices of consumer goods to skyrocket between 230 and 300 percent from prewar levels, widespread concern about demographic crisis, and the reaffirmation of the importance of both motherhood and fatherhood in the postwar years. The notion that a worker was not merely an individual but a member of a family—increasingly prevalent in these years of demographic deficit—challenged the idea that all wage earners were independent, freely contracting individuals. The gender of the worker governed even those allowances that were added to the wage but were not part of the wage in the sense of constituting remuneration for actual work performed. Cost of living allowances, paid by French employers well into the 1920s to cope with inflation, sometimes incorporated an assumption that the deserving recipient was a male breadwinner. Male workers for the Société des transports en commun de la région parisienne (STCRP), for example, received a cost of living allowance at the rate of one franc per day for 365 days. Women however, received only a 50 centimes allowance based on the number of hours they actually worked for the company—a discrepancy that arguably reflected employers' assumption of a male breadwinner model.[127]

In addition to providing cost of living allowances, pronatalist and paternalist employers took major initiatives to meet the multiple objectives of stimulating the reproduction of the French labor force, containing wages, tying workers to the firm, and heading off labor conflict. Many employers— metalworking and textile firms were prominent examples—provided a family bonus (*sursalaire familiale*) to workers who had worked for one month in their factory on the basis of the number of children they had to support. Workers with two children could add as much as 25 percent to their wages; those with six children received double wages.[128] Unlike the working-class ideal of the family wage, based on the labor of the working man and on the obligation of "honest family heads" to provide for their dependents, the *sursalaire familiale* constituted a wage supplement, payable to both men and women.[129] It was based not on an individual worker's labor but on the number of dependents he or she had to support and therefore was not the same for all workers. It also contrasted sharply with organized labor's efforts in this period to establish unified wage scales over which they could exercise some control in bargaining with employers, and understandably often drew opposition from unions. The *sursalaire,* however, was only one of a series of allowances begun by pronatalist employers in the 1920s that included birth bonuses, available to workers employed by a firm for three months, and nursing bonuses, payable to nursing mothers employed by the firm or whose husbands were employed by the firm, and marriage bonuses, among others.[130] These initiatives were part of the more general system of regulating labor, promoting childbearing, and modulating employers' wage payments through the provision of social services and financial benefits that accompanied rationalization. But although they could be paid to either men or women, some employers clearly saw them as linked to the father's role in the family as breadwinner. Indeed, some metalworking employers conceptualized the wage not only as a reward for the individual worker's production but in relation to the father's social reproduction—that is, in relation to his needs as a family provider. Robert Pinot, for instance, reporting on the social provisions of metalworking firms in the early 1920s, summed it up this way:

> The idea of family allowances was born of the economic crisis that the war produced. Increases and fluctuations in the cost of living have made the position of fathers more difficult than ever. The inequality between the bachelor worker who has only himself to think of and the [father] who must provide for his wife and children has . . . awakened a vague feeling of injustice. . . . With increasing prices, especially food prices, the costs of raising a child have become heavier and heavier. In this respect, even wage increases can only provoke awareness of the injustice of the incomparable situations of father and bachelor. [Metalworking employers] have thus sought a formula better adapted to the necessities of this new situation and the idea of family allowances was born of this concern.[131]

Although family allowances did not formally constitute part of the wage and were at least partially inspired by employers' efforts to resist wage inflation, some employers chose to think of them as such. This constituted a significant departure from the prewar years when wages were tied to production, not to the family lives of individual workers. Now, a certain number of employers believed that the wage should take account not only of productivity on the job but of a worker's family situation. Both employers' and workers' views of allowances revealed how both groups saw work as tied to the masculine duty of the breadwinner. Thus, after the war, when Lyon metalworkers struck for higher wages, the organization of metallurgical employers argued that "the value of the minimum wage situated at the bottom of the scale should be designed to satisfy the minimum needs of the least educated and least productive bachelor. Minimum wages should be graduated in relation to professional capabilities and qualities . . . [and] an adjustment [should be added to them] taking account of the worker's family responsibilities . . ."[132] The belief that the wage should take into account employees' family needs also governed thinking about the wages of bachelors and single women who, some believed, could get by on very little. One observer, Pierre Paraf, commented that women living by themselves could make ends meet by virtue of domestic skills that enabled them to take care of their laundry, clothing, and other household details. Women, he wrote, could save money by making their own meals whereas men tended to eat out.[133] This view reproduced over a century of thinking that assumed that women's domestic activities had no wage value in and of themselves but constituted "labors of love" that could compensate for low wages. Convictions about women's alleged ingenuity in "making ends meet" constituted one of the beliefs that arguably shaped employers' views of women's wages historically and ultimately influenced French social policy. In practice, the marital and domestic situation of both men and women could influence how workers were paid, paradoxically separating the wage from individual labor and productivity and linking it to the family and domestic activity.

This way of thinking about wages was not new. During the war, Charles Piquenard and William Oualid redefined the wage with their concept of the *salaire vital* that took account of workers' "social needs." "Because workers had different needs, their remuneration varied even when they did identical work." Some employers initiated family allowances during the hostilities to provide precisely this form of selective compensation.[134] Following the war, the mining and metals industries employers' consortium, the Groupement des industries minières et métallurgiques (GIMM) followed this practice to hold down inflation. Pierre Richemond, head of the GIMM, delivered a speech to the GIMM general meeting in March 1923, where he advocated family allowances as a form of industrial wage policy. "Family allowances permit us to place our comparisons of prewar and postwar wages on a more just . . . foundation . . . on wages, no uniform changes: if certain individual cases are below average . . . then some adjustment can be made on an individual basis, but there can be no general increases."[135] However, these practices were hardly gender-neutral, and some employers incorporated assumptions about the gender of breadwinners.

Although Pedersen and others have been correct to point out that the *objective* of employer-administered family allowances was to stimulate births and the reproduction of the labor force while restraining wages, the *implementation* of policies was arguably gender-specific. Some employers specifically earmarked benefits as a form of unwaged mother's allowance. The Schneider metallurgical firm at Creusot was one of a small number of employers that "by means of a just and rational increase in wages made it possible for every worker or employee to be affluent enough to permit his wife to remain at home and raise her children herself."[136] Pierre Magnier de Maisonneuve suggested that because of the generous allowances provided by the joint family allowance fund (*caisses de compensation*) of the textile consortium of Lille-Roubaix-Tourcoing, an economical housewife could manage to make ends meet on her husband's wages, alone.[137] Other employers' applications of family allowances showed how they privileged the male breadwinner in issuing benefits. The public sector Paris Electrical Distribution Company (Compagnie parisienne de distribution d'électricité), for instance, had an extensive system of allowances that augmented the wage significantly, including a marriage bonus, birth bonus, nursing bonus, and generous family allowance. The nursing bonus amounted to a sizeable 5,400 francs for the first year of the infant's life and was paid directly to the mother, "so that the husband would not be able to keep it for the satisfaction of his own needs." But in order to receive it, the woman employee or wife of an employee had to promise not to work, even at home, while she was nursing. "The rest period was given to her for the sole purpose of taking care of her child."[138] Subsidies like this could constitute valuable and progressive complements to the wage for working-class families but they came with a set of social meanings about economic rights that contributed to shaping the gender inequalities of the labor market.

Other benefits distributed by employers reproduced different forms of labor force inequality. Because the labor market of the 1920s was so volatile, some employers instituted loyalty bonuses (*primes de fidelité*) in order to limit labor mobility and encourage workers to stay with firms. But such bonuses did not benefit everyone. Foreign workers in some enterprises not only found themselves disadvantaged by the absence of training programs, poor opportunities for advancement, and low wages; they were also excluded from the loyalty bonuses that French workers received. Thus, in the Dressoir shoe factory, the bonus that French workers received after ten years of service was not available to a French woman who had worked for ten years but who had married a Belgian.[139] Until the 1927 reform of the nationality code allowed French women to retain their nationality upon marriage to foreigners, women automatically adopted the nationality of their foreign husbands; thus this woman had effectively become a foreigner. Designed to encourage the formation of a stable labor force in a period of labor shortage, the loyalty bonus at Dressoir could amount to a substantial addition to salary—25 francs per trimester after ten years, 50 francs per trimester after 15 years, and 75 francs per trimester after 20 years. But since employers viewed foreign workers as an inherently unstable labor force and preferred to retain flexibility to hire and fire them, even those who remained loyal to the firm were not rewarded. Such practices contributed to maintaining foreigners as a separate and unequal category of labor.

Immigrant Workers and the Division of Labor

Racial or national difference influenced the social meanings of skill as much as gender. Like French women, male immigrants provided much of the unskilled labor that facilitated economic recovery in the 1920s and figured prominently in industrial rationalization. In some areas of industry immigrant men made up a greater proportion of the labor force than French women and worked at the same unskilled jobs that French women did. They also worked at jobs that employers believed were too dangerous or too dirty for French women or that French men refused to do. By 1931, almost 60 percent of immigrant workers worked in industry (as against one third of French workers), the majority (68 percent) as unskilled laborers.[140] The vast majority of these workers were men; immigrant women tended to be concentrated in textiles, garment production, and domestic services.[141] In the Paris region 35 percent of the immigrant workforce worked in metals manufacture, and Russian and Armenian men worked especially in automobiles.[142] According to one estimate, Russian men made up one third of the labor force at Renault in 1930.[143] In the textile industry of the Nord, Belgian and Polish men provided essential labor in mining; Belgian men and women and the wives and daughters of Polish mineworkers worked in the mills. In 1929, in order to take advantage of gender-differentiated patterns of employment and labor migration, employers of the textile consortium of the Lille-Roubaix-Tourcoing agglomeration organized special trains from the mining town of Lens to transport some 500 Polish women to work in the Lille mills. But Belgians constituted by far the largest number of textile immigrants. By

1930 some 40,000 Belgians, many of them day migrants, made up 40 percent of the textile workers in Lille-Roubaix-Tourcoing.[144] As one observer noted in the early 1930s, this was a "hardworking and hardy race that doesn't skimp on effort."[145] In Lille alone, Belgians counted for some 14 percent of the labor force in 1936 (with a roughly equal proportion of men and women), higher than the percentage of immigrants in the labor force nationally (12 percent) at roughly the same time.[146]

The French government also facilitated the employment of Belgians in the Nord crucial to postwar reconstruction by means of international agreements. In 1924 an accord with Belgium provided that workers of either nationality could work in the other country under the same conditions and at wages equal to those of indigenous workers. Immigrants benefited from workmen's compensation (*réparations des dommages résultants des accidents au travail*) and social insurance. The French accorded Belgians the same rights in purchasing property as French nationals, and Belgian workers could avail themselves of the same conciliation and arbitration during labor conflicts as French workers and in theory could benefit from unemployment benefits.[147] In July 1928 the government issued work permits to Belgian workers that required them to carry identity cards, issued after they presented a confirmation of their moral standing and a certificate from a French employer that had been signed by the French employment office (Bureau de Placement). This new requirement provided a means of accounting for the numbers of *frontaliers*—daily cross-border migrants—and to regulate entries on the basis of market needs.[148]

Regarded as "almost French" and the most able to assimilate of all foreigners working in France by contemporary observers of the racial dimensions of immigration such as René Martial, Belgian workers often melted seamlessly into the French population of the Nord, marrying French workers and settling in the textile cities where they found work. Unskilled for the most part, they labored at the same unskilled jobs as women and common French male laborers; as rationalization in the industry increased, immigrants found themselves supervising as many as eighteen or twenty-four looms at once.[149] Because they viewed Belgian workers as an expendable labor force (even though many put down roots in France's northern textile cities), employers refused to invest in technical training for immigrants. In the Nord, where employers kept looms running far into the night on rotating shifts, immigrant Belgian men worked the night shifts closed to French women by the 1892 law on night work.[150] The fact that immigrant men could be employed interchangeably at women's jobs was a measure of flexibility that enabled textile manufacturers to keep looms running on multiple shifts. French male workers, eager to preserve control over jobs, occasionally resisted this use of foreign labor. Although the organized labor movement's leadership papered over workers' hostility to immigrants and fear of competition, hostility often spilled out, as it did in Roubaix-Tourcoing during the recession of 1921, when French textile workers struck briefly to demand priority in hiring.[151]

Immigrant colonial workers—Algerians and sometimes Moroccans—in the food-processing industries of the Paris region similarly worked at unskilled jobs that employers didn't give to women, such as handling. In the Say and Lebaudy sugar refineries, they pushed heavy wagons filled with sugar and worked, naked to the waist because of the intense heat, in rotating teams on shifts that lasted as long as sixteen hours.[152] Immigrant labor also figured prominently in the automobile industry of the Paris suburbs, where companies in Boulogne, Issy-les-Moulineaux, Courbevoie, Asnières, and St.-Ouen employed from 6,000 to 8,000 foreign workers, notably North Africans and Africans, Russians, and Poles.[153] Citroën's expansion of its unskilled labor force in the 1920s drew in large numbers of foreign male workers. At its Clichy factory, for example, foreigners made up 39 percent of the work force in November 1928. The majority were unskilled North African men, Algerians, and Moroccans (25 percent). By January 1930, Citroën employed some 7,000 Kabyles; the company also employed Polish, Belgian, Portuguese, Spanish, Russian, and Italian men. Most (60 percent) worked at unskilled heavy work in the foundries and ironworks, in handling and loading, or at sandblasting metal in preparation for painting or enameling—all areas in which French workers avoided the heat, dirt, work accidents, burns, and respiratory infections.[154] As one Russian worker at Renault recounted,

> My work consisted of placing a single pin in a transmission gear and opening the sides [of the pin] with a pair of pliers. Voilà. That's it. Pin in the morning, pin in the afternoon, pin in the evening. I became the champion of the pin. I saw pins everywhere. Occasionally my eyes bothered me, my rhythm slowed, but the assembly line marched on without pity. The overseers yelled at me, fined me; after six months I couldn't handle it any longer; I gave up pins![155]

Although the majority of foreign workers were unskilled, in the automobile industry, European immigrants, considered closer to the French than colonial workers, performed skilled jobs. According to one estimate, 22 percent of Russian men working at Renault in 1926 were skilled, although by 1931 the progressive automation of the industry caused the percentage of skilled Russians to decline to 14 percent.[156] Some immigrant men—especially in the garment trades—were themselves employers; these workers constituted a distinct minority.[157]

Employers generally considered the majority of immigrant men, like women, to be expendable and paid them at the very bottom of the wage scale, unless international accords stipulated equal wages. As Stéphane Sirot notes, colonial North Africans at the Say sugar refinery in Paris earned between 12 and 14 francs per day in 1923, in contrast to the 30 francs average daily wage of French men. By 1929, in the same establishment, foreign workers' average wage was 162 francs 50 for a five-and-a-half day, fifty-three-hour week, (29.50 francs per day), whereas the French workers' average was 270 francs per week (50.80 francs per day).[158] Employers hired many on piece rates on the assumption that their desperation to earn a living wage would drive them to work faster. Ernest Mattern, the chief architect of rationalization at Citroën in the 1920s, described how he used piece rates with Arab workers. "[H]andling was paid by the piece according to a formula I developed . . . [the workers were] Arabs; the worst among them were eliminated by the best. It was remarkable to see how otherwise lazy Arabs raced at unloading the trucks."[159] Mattern's view of Arab workers' response to Taylorization was not dissimilar to Marcel Frois's observations about women's "inherent ability" to keep up with fast-paced repetition work in order to make a living wage. In this industry, however, in spite of postwar claims to the contrary, the work of most women and immigrant workers was not interchangeable.

Both immigrants and women found themselves at the lowest levels of the labor hierarchy, but the work that most immigrant men—especially colonial workers—performed in automobile manufacture, metallurgy, or food processing threw into relief the different levels of gender division of even unskilled labor. Gender difference prevailed at the lowest levels of work. No employer expected women to perform backbreaking foundry work in enormous heat or sandblast metals. The fact that immigrants would perform the dirty unskilled work that even the least-skilled French laborer refused to do allowed French male workers to remain masculine and French women workers to remain feminine. At the same time, it is not implausible that the presence of unskilled foreign labor at the lowest rungs of the labor ladder permitted French male workers to think of themselves as occupying the upper echelon of labor even if they were themselves unskilled. French citizenship and job status together constituted differentiating markers of status.

Citroën, counseling his future production team heads, advised them that "knowing how to command is all about psychology," but one had to give orders with an appropriate tone to French workers, "whose subtle and refined spirit doesn't want to be insulted by officiousness."[160] By specifically addressing his advice to the treatment of *French* workers, Citroën implied that immigrant workers lacked a "subtle and refined spirit" and could be treated differently. As the next chapter suggests, the questions that work scientists and social observers raised about the masculinity of immigrants reinforced the view that French workers were superior to foreigners. But not all foreign workers were the same.

Just as eugenics advocates believed in the differential capacities of foreigners to assimilate to French society, so too did observers differentiate between the capacities of foreign workers. The ambiguous status of French colonial workers in France, who lacked both nationality and citizenship and were subject to a special regulatory system, the *code de l'indigénat,* made them especially vulnerable to the whims of employers. The fact that colonial North African workers were given the worst jobs led some to believe that they were especially useful to the French economy and did not pose a threat to much more qualified French workers. Norbert Gomar, writing about Algerian migration to France between the world wars, argued that it was better that the French face competition from Kabyles rather than from "foreigners." The latter, he claimed, have professional capacities closer to those of the French, whereas Kabyles complement rather than compete with the French.[161]

> If it is true that their standard of living is low, their mediocre professional abilities prevent them from supplanting French labor. The latter increasingly specializes and becomes a high quality labor force, a sort of worker aristocracy, whereas inferior work is given to a level of less evolved worker and whom Kabyle workers typify exactly. [In addition] . . . in periods of unemployment, the Algerian *indigènes* are almost always the first to be laid off, it becomes clear that they do not compete with French workers at all and that they constitute a very useful element for the metropolitan labor force.

The members of the metalworking employers' organization, the Groupement des industries métallurgiques de la région parisienne, agreed. In responding to a government inquiry about the employment of foreign workers during the Depression, they claimed that although they tried to substitute French workers for immigrants, they had reached their limit because of the "repulsion of national labor for hard work." Moroccan workers, on the other hand, "have shown themselves to be particularly good at hard, unpleasant labor."[162] But the male colonial worker was quite possibly in a more delicate position than that of the European male immigrant, for he was already bound to the system of colonial domination that rendered him in every respect subject to the authority of the French state and French employers. He was not only a distinct category of labor; he was easily replaceable.[163]

Delegating to immigrant male workers the most undesirable unskilled labor that French common laborers refused to perform illustrates the influence of racial and national thinking, alongside gender, on attitudes toward and employer policies on immigrant labor. Ernest Mattern would undoubtedly have agreed with some contemporary employers that the output of North African men was inferior to that of French or other Europeans. Georges Mauco, for example, in his lengthy 1932 work on the place of immigrant workers in the French economy argued that North Africans were poorly prepared for the rapid, disciplined, sustained, and regular work of modern, rationalized industry due to "the physical weakness of certain Arab tribes, their poor nutrition resulting from excessive parsimony, the absence of all professional preparation, the utter lack of hygiene [and] climatic differences . . ."[164] Mauco tried to bolster his case for the inferiority of North African workers with data gathered in 1924 and in 1928–29 in 350 metalworking factories all over France, where employers and supervisors judged 60,000 immigrant workers as either "good," "mediocre," or "inadequate." Those with the highest scores were Belgians, Italians, Spanish, Poles, and Portuguese. North Africans had the lowest scores of any, and the Belgians' "good" score was almost four times the score of the North Africans. Mauco was not surprised to find a similar result in another study carried out by an anonymous "important automobile manufacturer" which employed 5,075 foreigners (30 percent) in a labor force of 17,000. In this study, a dozen division heads (*chefs de service*) were asked to rank the immigrant workers, with the highest score a 10. Whereas the Belgians scored 9, the North Africans came in at 2.9, the lowest score of the eleven nationalities ranked.[165] But this was far from the only problem with immigrant labor, according to Mauco. Immigrant laborers also lacked the discipline of French workers. Foreigners, argued Mauco, needed authority and guidance; left to their own devices they were completely at loose ends and much less productive than French workers. Slowness and passivity characterized virtually all foreigners, whether it was southern laziness (common to the Spanish, Portuguese, and North Africans), Nordic ponderousness (found among the Poles and Dutch), or a certain resignation to fate seen in Slavs and Arabs. According to Mauco, some metallurgical employers attempted to change these attitudes by training unskilled foreigners to work more efficiently. But this did not prevent the high turnover also characteristic of immigrants: " . . . the particularly dirty and thankless jobs that were only suitable for the least evolved foreigners led to high turnover, especially in mining."[166] But Mauco also believed that on the whole French employers had failed utterly to understand the psychology of the foreign worker—this was especially important in the highly rationalized large modern factory. At the same time, from the employers' perspective turnover and the flexible deployment of immigrants and women posed both advantages and disadvantages for production and stability. Strategies that addressed French women and to a lesser extent French men and foreign women demonstrated how employers tried to ensure discipline, efficiency, and loyalty to the firm, while simultaneously addressing the reproduction of the labor force. Employers' firm-based social policies constituted an important foundation stone of the French social model.

Flexibilization and Integration: Manufacturing Consent

In the 1920s it was not uncommon for unskilled women to move from job to job within the factory according to the business cycle and production demands of the firm. In this sense they served as a kind of "reserve army of labor," permitting employers tremendous flexibility, another factor that contributed to the persistence of gender division in the labor force. Indeed, in the settlement of a major strike in the northern textile city of Halluin in 1928, employers specified their right to move workers from job to job as conditions required.[167] The fact that women could be rotated from one unskilled job to another as needed was another reason, alongside employers' conviction that women lacked the ability to perform highly skilled work, that employers did not bother to train them for stable, skilled positions, and the boredom of monotonous unskilled work did not make women inclined to stay in one place very long. Thus in the Dressoir shoe manufacture, in the early 1920s, within the space of just a few months one young woman moved from the finishing workshop to scraping leather (*grattage*) to polishing.[168] Women's movement from factory to factory also accelerated in the period of prosperity and labor shortage of the 1920s, offering both women and manufacturers the same kind of flexibility. Mme D, a Parisian, began making gas masks at the age of thirteen during the war. When the war ended, she worked at a variety of jobs, doing housework, sewing, working in a pharmacy, and eventually in a pharmaceutical laboratory.[169]

According to Catherine Omnès's study of Parisian working women, turnover of the female working population accelerated alongside the increasing integration of women into the Parisian labor market (an increase of nearly 20 percent in the number of women working in the manufacturing industries of the Seine between 1921 and 1931).[170] Omnès's examination of mobility in a sample of over 600 women who worked in the Paris region between the two world wars shows that turnover increased from 54.9 percent of those hired in 1920 to 76.8 percent of those hired in 1930. At the Panhard automobile company, for example, turnover averaged 53.1 percent between 1919 and 1929 and rose to 72.7 percent in 1929 alone. Half of the women workers at Panhard lasted less than seven months in any single job.[171] Omnès argues that growing female turnover in the 1920s stemmed from the increasing rationalization of work following the stabilization of the franc (1926–28), along with the knowledge that in a period in which work was relatively plentiful they would have little trouble finding a new job.[172] Mlle V, a factory superintendent-in-training who worked as an intern at Panhard in 1928, reported that the majority of women who left the firm did so because of the "brutalizing repetition" of the assembly line.[173] Likewise, of the men and women who left Citroën in November 1928, 25 percent did so because they couldn't stand the discipline and the working conditions.[174] But although such labor mobility could be tolerable for workers in the booming labor market of the 1920s and was useful for employers' management of slowdowns and depressions, from management's perspective it could also interfere with the productivist norms of the postwar economy.

In the process of rationalizing work, employers deployed new management techniques designed to both regulate and stabilize the labor force. Through social benefits that firms first administered, employers anticipated the broad features of what later became the French welfare state. As the historian Sylvie Schweitzer has pointed out, "The new impulse given to social benefits (*des oeuvres sociaux*) corresponded . . . to integration, to the 'socialization' indispensable for this unskilled labor force that was the product of rationalization."[175] Employing women factory superintendents was one such strategy. First seen in the metalworking industries of the Paris region during World War I, women factory superintendents attempted to ensure that munitions work would not lead women workers to sacrifice maternity and family. As Laura Downs has shown, both during the war and after, middle-class women factory superintendents in metalworking attempted to reconcile wartime and postwar employment of women with what most agreed was women's "maternal vocation."[176] Reflecting a growing concern about public health and hygiene that intersected with French concerns about fertility and population, employers expected women factory superintendents and nurses to penetrate working-class homes with information on infant care while at the same time scrutinizing domestic hygiene. Inside the factory, dressed in their khaki uniforms, circulating on the shop floor or maintaining a presence in their offices, the factory superintendents oversaw maternal health and welfare and paid attention to the "special needs" of women workers. In the interwar years, they expanded their sphere of influence to include hiring and the promotion of home economics training. Although they were relatively few in relation to the size of French industry (85 women were placed in factories in 1923), their numbers doubled in five years (172 placements in 1928), and by 1935, 191 superintendents worked in factories and some in service-sector jobs.[177] These women embodied the new thinking about the links between work, family, and society that marked the interwar years.

As well as supervising women in the wartime defense industries, superintendents also worked in other areas of the industrial economy and in the growing service sector during the 1920s and 1930s. Outside of the automobile and small metalworking industries where they were most numerous (54 percent of those placed in industry in 1928 worked in metalworking), superintendents also worked textile factories, in electrical and mechanical construction factories, shoe manufacture, food processing, bookbinding, pharmaceutical products, and department stores, as well as in public and private administration (in hospitals, prefectures, and ministries). Their increasing presence in public and private administration (90 placements in 1928 as opposed to 79 in industrial factories) reflected the broadening definition of their social-service capacities.[178] In private administration, 18 percent of those placed in administrative jobs in 1928 worked in the *caisses de compensation,* the employer-administered funds for the distribution of family allowances.[179] In service-sector jobs as well as in textiles, electrical construction, and the food industries, they initiated social welfare programs just as broad as those developed by the superintendents in metalworking. Working to reconcile capital and labor, the superintendent stood as a living example of twentieth-century solidarism; her task was to bring workers under the beneficent wing of the employer with the dual aim of making the factory or the administrative service for which she worked a smoothly running machine.[180] Indeed, the administrative council of the Association des surintendantes included the feminist and founder of the Ecole des surintendantes Cécile Brunschvicq, Brunschvicq's husband Léon Brunschvicq, Max Lazard, Jules Siegfried, and Bertrand de Mun, all prominent members of the solidarist community. A textile industrialist from the Vienne revealed clearly the paternalist dimension of solidarism in an address to the Assocation in 1928. The superintendent's job was to "let the worker know just how much effort employers expended to assure regular (and not always profitable) work to the greatest number of workers. . . . And having brought one of your antagonists down from his ivory tower, and having brought him to regard his employer as a good master, you will hold in your women's hands the two hands of the worker and go to work in confidence . . ."[181]

This employer's vision of the superintendent's role also illustrated the idea that harmony between workers and employers was important not only for the smooth operation of the factory but for the health of the working-class family and fit squarely within the familialist, pronatalist national model of state-society relations that emerged after the war. "Never forget that the vital core of the social and national question is the Family. Everything resides in this [social] cell. It is thus towards it that all your efforts must be directed."[182]

In the Amieux food processing company, for example, where women processed preserves, chocolate, mustard, and fruits, the superintendent assisted in hiring and worked to promote infant protection, welfare, and mutual aid. She also developed and implemented leisure activities. All fit within the firm's desire to ensure harmonious relations between labor and capital and corresponded to employers' recognition that attention to the health and well-being of workers was the best route to social peace and a reliable labor force from whom employers could then, in good conscience, extract a maximum amount of labor. As Monsieur Amieux himself stated,

> The woman superintendent's role is to assist the personnel to overcome the difficulties they encountered in life outside of questions of work, properly speaking; to give them information in the event of sickness, marriage, birth and death; to give any advice that that will help them to avoid the problems that families often face; to supervise the application of rules for the maintenance of hygiene and well-being on the shop floor. Everyone should be able to speak in complete confidence to the superintendent, who will strive to be a guide and resource for all.[183]

As a welfare worker, the superintendent was to serve as a source of information, since "workers lack the leisure to study the multiplicity of laws that exists to regulate their relations with their employers [and] protect them from social risks . . ." Her role as a psychological confidant and, above all, as a moral force emerged repeatedly in the reports of superintendents-in-training and in employers' observations on their work.[184] But superintendents also had a role in employment and especially in mitigating high turnover.

At Amieux the factory superintendent played a role in maintaining employer flexibility in hiring in this highly seasonal industry, particularly in attempting to alleviate the effects of irregular employment, for "she can only be thinking about the best conditions of work in which to place the personnel." Amieux also expected his superintendent to take account of the family situation of the worker in hiring: "preference is given to mothers who want to leave the hearth for a short period in order to supplement the household's resources." She was also responsible for monitoring the relationships between work and health, for overseeing a dispensary where a doctor recommended shifting women from one job to another for health reasons.[185] As in metalworking, part of her job involved regulating workers' domestic lives. Home visits, to look in on a sick worker or after the birth of a child, facilitated regulation, for by visiting the working-class home she could take account of the condition of "housing, linens and toiletries [*articles d'hygiène*], and give advice" about each where appropriate. She provided future mothers with a "birth kit" composed of linens, toiletries, and medicine, and with a layette for their babies, all at the company's cost, and implemented the employer-based maternity leaves that complemented the state-sponsored maternity leaves from which French working women benefited. Women at Amieux or the wives of male workers received eight weeks of paid maternity leave, four weeks before and four weeks after the birth and in addition received birth and nursing bonuses from the company's welfare fund (*caisse de compensation*). Amieux believed that these measures would tie working-class families to the company and encourage mothers to prolong their absence from work following a birth, in the interest of the child. It was also clear that in this seasonal industry, prolonged rest after birth not only benefited the nursing mother and her child but allowed the employer more flexibility in managing labor. In addition to these initiatives, the superintendent supervised a daycare center for the children of personnel and leisure facilities for children and adults including a park, tennis courts, a library, billiard room, and movie theater. Finally, she oversaw the distribution of welfare and insurance benefits provided by the company—especially medical insurance, where members of mutual aid societies were reimbursed for three-quarters of their medical costs and all prescription drug costs.[186] These kinds of employment-based rights served as a powerful model for the future French welfare state.

The package of social services provided by Amieux was probably more extensive than those provided by most companies that hired women superintendents. Still, other large firms established leisure and sports facilities for their workers, medical services, housekeeping courses, cooperative grocery stores, butchers, bakeries, low-cost housing, theater and film programs, as well as retirement funds.[187] The automobile industry, the most highly rationalized of any by the mid-1920s, was a leader in this regard. Peugeot's superintendent at his Montbéliard factory supervised a sports center for women (where workers could participate in Swedish gymnastics or women's basketball) as well as a factory clinic (which maintained relations with the anti-tuberculosis and anti–venereal disease dispensary in Montbéliard) and a visiting nurse service that conducted home visits.[188] In Paris, Citroën's social services program included a summer camp for the children of his employees, opened in 1928, and from 1931 the company sponsored bicycling, football, rugby, basketball, and swimming clubs as well as an orchestra and musical society. If the effort to build employee loyalty while promoting workers' health and hygiene was unmistakable, these social services also served as vehicles of regulation. Citroen's private insurance fund made no secret of sending superintendents to workers' homes to verify that they really *were* in fact ill when they made such claims.[189]

Superintendents' activities in public administration were no different from their roles in industry, marked by the same confluence of regulation and consent. Mlle Javel, superintendent at the welfare fund of the Construction and Public Works Service of the department of the Seine, pointed this out in her report to the Association of Surintendantes in 1923. "The employer owes his workers something else besides a salary; it is his duty to pay attention to their moral and physical condition, and this entirely moral obligation which no wage can replace must take priority over [all other] considerations . . ."[190] Although Mlle Javel refered to herself as a worksite superintendent (*surintendante de chantier*), in fact her main activities concerned overseeing the distribution of nursing allowances for women and the child-health services of the Public Works and Construction Service. She conducted home visits to "gain the confidence and become the friend and counselor of mothers," and establishing trust with workers enabled her to operate as a vital gear in the mechanism of twentieth-century employer "maternalism." At the same time she played on her perceptions of class difference in ministering to her working-class inferiors.[191] Once inside the door of the working-class household, she asserted her class authority to give advice about health and hygiene to the future working-class mother "who knows nothing or almost nothing about care and precautions, who most of the time ignores everything about the help she can receive."[192] Once the child was born, she provided advice about childcare and encouraged the new mother to nurse her baby and take her child regularly to the doctor. In households with older children, the superintendent provided vocational guidance and advice about apprenticeship, affirming the links between family and company.

Although the majority of superintendents were attached to industries that employed large numbers of foreign workers, they paid almost no attention to immigrants. Their pronatalist vision did not include the broader notion of metropolitan population regeneration advanced by those who argued for the integration of some immigrants into French society. They did, however, carry their activities to French colonies, Algeria and Tunisia, where some of them became visiting nurses (*infirmières sociales*) and feminized the French civilizing mission. The French Colonial Exposition of 1931 had turned public attention to all the ambiguities of "la plus grande France" at the very moment that the superintendent began to expand the range of her social services to include what we would today call social work. Praising her activities in the colonies, Cécile Brunschvicq, vice-president of the Association des Surintendantes in 1931, noted, "In Algeria, [she] not only does a social service, but a French service, because social work is, so to speak, the only way to penetrate indigenous families [*des familles indigènes*], to lead them little by little to understand health and hygiene, and to appreciate the benefits of our civilization."[193] Brunschvicq pointed to the superintendent's potential attention to *enfants assistés*—illegitimate children of interracial marriages between European men and Arab women. These children were given over to "indigenous families who most often live in squalid districts and repulsive houses [*des quartiers infects et des maisons répugnantes*]. Just think of this backward civilization [*civilization à rebours*]) that allows young Europeans to be raised by the natives so that instead of becoming French, they become little Arabs." Here the activity of the superintendent became more that of a social worker who, along with feminist organizations, could address the issue of child marriage, where girls as young as ten were married off "against their will to Arabs old enough to be their grandfathers."[194] As Mlle. Fromentin, superintendent in Tunis, also recognized, drawing on the experience of factory superintendents' regulation of working-class domesticity in France, these social workers might overcome the cultural obstacles to penetrating the Muslim home. For if the Muslim home remained closed to French women, Muslim women increasingly frequented the French social worker's dispensary and sent their girls to the French home economics schools. This was "the surest road to the liberation of the Arab woman and the way to adapt these ignorant populations to our civilization."[195] Thus in the colonies a superintendent cum social worker could attempt to elicit the confidence of Arab women, much as she sought to counsel working-class women—and families—at home.

Back in the métropole, alongside their emphasis on the importance of motherhood and their attention to the care of future mothers, mothers, and children, superintendents participated in reproducing the gender division of labor. Mme Fromentin, who began her career at the Lorraine Dietrich metallurgical firm in Lunéville, stated in 1923 that once children had graduated from school at age thirteen, boys entered the factory as apprentices while girls learned "that science far too neglected today that our fathers appreciated the most in women: household science." The Lorraine Dietrich employers established their own home economics school (*école ménagère*) for girls, run by the superintendent; boys, on the other hand, took obligatory vocational training courses inside the factory for a five-year period, and at eighteen they became workers.[196] At Peugeot, following primary school the majority of school-age girls in the Peugeot housing developments attended a sewing and home economics school run by the superintendent.[197]

Finally, although their main purpose was unquestionably to protect women working in "unfeminine" occupations and to safeguard motherhood, superintendents also aspired to the moral and hygienic regulation of men as fathers and family heads, allegedly "rekindling in the hearts of men the family spirit that modern industry had killed."[198] This goal fit well with their other pronatalist and family-based activities and reinforced employers' view of men as family providers. Mademoiselle Javel included the male construction worker in her vision of the superintendent's role: "The construction workers who we need so badly deserve to be encouraged in their trade and supported in their family responsibilities."[199] At the AlsThom electrical construction factory in St. Ouen, a superintendent supervised men, making sure that they did not suffer from health problems that would interfere with their efficiency. Indeed, during the 1920s and 1930s, employers gave increasing attention to industrial hygiene and to preventing work accidents as a corollary of promoting productivity. At this factory, male apprentices were weighed and measured twice a year and examined by a local doctor. In the interests of preserving workers' health and effectiveness on the job, superintendents could remove a young man from apprenticeship if his health appeared to be compromised.[200] Finally, the director of the Decré department stores in Nantes, reporting to the Association des surintendentes in 1930, made it clear that in the selection of employees, his superintendent paid as much attention to hiring and training men as she did to hiring women for appropriate jobs in the store and consulted with both on matters of housing and social benefits. When a young girl confided her intention of marrying, the superintendent would try to meet the young man and find him stable work.[201] "The efforts of our *surintendante* will continue to be directed towards this goal: to make the [male] employee or worker a man who is satisfied with himself and is happy at home; as well as someone who loves his work."[202]

Overall, then, the factory superintendent became a linchpin of the rational organization of labor and the maintenance of its gender divisions to facilitate both labor flexibility and stabilization while simultaneously protecting women as mothers and men as fathers. In this sense her work blurred the boundaries between regulation and welfare. Arguably the visits to workers' homes when a worker was ill or after the birth of a child represented a form of regulation, as did the home economics courses that many employers expected superintendents to conduct.[203] The provision of maternity benefits such as birth and nursing bonuses, day care centers, medical services and clinics, sports facilities and movie theaters, and access to housing, unquestionably marked employers' efforts to elicit cooperation from workers otherwise brutalized by the system of rationalized labor. Thus, the superintendent participated in employers' strategy of manufacturing *consent* (in Gramsci's terms) by providing a range of social services unheard of in most contemporary workplaces and by extending regulation of the worker into the domestic sphere.[204]

French employers deployed apprenticeship, technical training, and scientific management to transform work and create a new citizen-worker adapted to the demands of economic recovery in the postwar years, while at the same time reproducing and refining gender divisions of labor. Divisions between French and foreign male workers and between French male workers also grew more acute. Skill continued to be as closely linked to the ascription of gender characteristics to workers as before and during World War I and gender ideals profoundly influenced perceptions of what constituted appropriate work for men and women. Employers' assignment of gender divisions, as arbitrary as they might seem, were neither arbitrary nor always entirely rational. Employers' economic calculus drew upon prevailing gender norms and simultaneously perpetuated and reinforced those norms. In these respects France did not differ appreciably from Britain and the United States or from other European countries where definitions of skill also remained highly contingent upon the gender of the worker.

The implementation of new techniques of rationalization and consent also drew on ideas about masculinity and femininity and about the gender of breadwinners in modernizing industry even if not all French employers adopted scientific management techniques as the route to productivity. Historians have argued that overall, with the exception of metalworking and automobile construction, until about 1926 French manufacturers attempted to restore profits more through exports than through major modifications of equipment and management of their labor force.[205] Entrepreneurs relied on the development of foreign and colonial markets, while they employed colonial workers in France more extensively than ever before in the production of the very industrial goods they would sell to the colonies and elsewhere. But the stabilization of the franc in 1926 and the slowing of exports inspired employers to see rationalization as the key to economic modernization. Many adopted elements of rationalization piecemeal, such as new methods of payment and bonuses and automation, without engaging in the extensive implementation of scientific management seen in the automobile industry or in food-processing plants.

The refinement of gender divisions of labor arguably created jobs for women in postwar France but simultaneously confined women to the lower rungs of the labor ladder. As employers attempted to modernize industry and increase production and efficiency, they also carried forth assumptions about the value of women's wage work as a supplemental contribution to the family alongside their maternal and domestic "vocation" and about the importance of the male breadwinner. These discourses translated into firm-based social policies designed to ensure a stable, compliant, and healthy labor force, protect maternity, and further women's roles in social reproduction. Provisions for worker's leisure, health care, cost of living allowances, and family wage bonuses directed at promoting fertility and, in some cases, to encouraging women to stay at home helped to constitute a new vision of the relationship between work and family and new set of employment-based rights. Some of these allowances paid to mothers who stayed at home to care for children also arguably functioned as a form of employment policy as employers sought greater flexibility.

As interest in industrial hygiene as the counterpart to efficient production grew, scientists and employers also paid attention to the problem of worker fatigue engendered by the new productivism and looked to other ways to increase worker efficiency. In addition to adopting scientific management, scientists and employers turned their attention to the body of the worker and new ways to select the best worker for the job. New modes of selection contributed to reinforcing the gender-differentiated labor force that underscored the French model of state-society relations later in the twentieth century.

CHAPTER THREE

MANAGING THE HUMAN FACTOR

The process of building a stable economic and social order in postwar France rested not only on new technologies of managing labor and engineering consent but on the promise of science as the agent of efficiency. Drawing on the work of eugenics experts and physiologists active prior to World War I, French engineers, doctors, scientists, and employers turned their attention to the working body and the problem of fatigue at work.[1] These new agents of reform argued that the industrial rationalization that produced exhausting repetitive work (described so effectively by Simone Weil in her factory journal of 1934–35) failed to take account of "the human factor."[2] Their focus on the body in the years around and after World War I took on new poignancy as disfigured and dismembered bodies returned from the battlefields, and one of the most prominent of this group of industrial physiologists, Jules Amar, developed prosthetic devices that would allow disabled men to return to the labor force.[3] Employers, seduced by the promise of "modernity" and the seemingly endless possibilities of science and mechanization to increase efficiency and productivity, were drawn to physiological research, as was a French state eager to modernize public services. Both mobilized industrial physiology to identify the allegedly "natural" qualities that made gendered and racialized workers suitable for certain kinds of jobs and excluded them from others.[4] Although historians have tended to treat the "science of work" as gender- and race-neutral, assumptions about the race and gender characteristics of workers ran throughout industrial physiology and its applications in the 1920s and 1930s, as French physiologists envisioned the potential uses of French women's and male colonial labor in the context of postwar immigration of Poles, Italians, Spanish, Africans, North Africans, and Eastern Europeans.[5] At the same time, scientists' efforts to ascertain the physical endurance of colonial male workers and French male and female workers relied on both the *durability* of gender with regard to white French workers and the *instability* of gender in assessing the abilities of workers of color.

This chapter discusses how gendered and differently raced and national immigrant working-class bodies became sites of postwar rationalization under the scrutiny of industrial physiologists.[6] Understanding gender, race, and class to be mutually constitutive rather than separate and parallel categories of difference, it further investigates how perceptions of racial and ethnic difference alongside gender helped to create new categories of workers and further divisions of labor.[7] These divisions ultimately shaped the thinking about the gender of breadwinners that underpinned the social model. The fluid meanings of "race" and the common uses of racial vocabulary in France between the wars arguably differed from the meanings of this term in other national contexts. This fluidity introduces another level of complexity into discussions of how race operated as a marker of difference. The French notion of race was strongly linked to membership in the national community —to Frenchness or non-Frenchness.[8] Although "race" had long been part of the French vocabulary, consciousness of racial difference emerged more publicly, at least from the seventeenth century, with the expansion of an overseas colonial empire. Indeed, it is likely, as Alice Conklin has pointed out, that in France the categories of whiteness and blackness and the boundaries between white and black became more refined in the 1920s and 1930s in the context of threats to the stability of the French colonial empire. Debates over the redefinition of French citizenship showed that "skin color increasingly became a decisive marker of Frenchness."[9] Efforts to distinguish between differently gendered, raced, and national workers reinforced differences in the labor market that ultimately influenced employment-based social policies and underscored the French model of welfare provision.

In spite of their claims to "science"—a term that still, in the early to mid-twentieth century, signified neutrality and objectivity—the social and medical investigators who practiced and promoted industrial physiology in the period from 1900 to 1939 hardly treated the body as a neutral biological entity. As Sandra Harding has observed, science itself is constituted by historical and cultural meanings and practices that are lodged in its very epistemological foundations. For centuries, science has been complicit in perpetuating racist and gendered as well as Eurocentric assumptions and beliefs.[10] As the object of physiologists' investigations into fatigue and endurance, the working body could never be separated from its gendered, racial, or cultural meanings, and those meanings permeated their investigations.[11] The task here is to look at how employers and the state deployed those meanings to select and hire workers. The French state also paid attention to the body at work in organizing public-sector service work, where ideas about gender and race characteristics influenced employment policy and contributed to maintaining gender and racial inequalities at work. This chapter first examines scientists' experiments and observations; it then looks at their applications in industrial and service-sector work; and finally it analyzes how vocational training attempted to render career selection for men and women scientific and rational while reproducing the cultural meanings of gender difference. These efforts contributed to the state's and employers' growing interest in promoting the rational selection of workers and to an interwar model of state-society relations that privileged male breadwinners.

Science, the Working Body, and War

At the same time that Frederick Winslow Taylor's methods of scientific management attracted interest from French industrialists and engineers, important critiques of Taylor's techniques emerged from a small but growing group of psychologists and physiologists who focused directly on the human body as the site of investigation and regulation. This was not an entirely new development historically; from the late eighteenth and early nineteenth centuries various forms of industrial discipline regulated workers to conform to the pace of the clock and the rhythm of machines.[12] But the particular focus on the body of the worker intensified at the end of the nineteenth century and in the years around World War I. Anson Rabinbach has shown how, in late-nineteenth-century France and Germany, thermodynamics became the model for new ways of thinking about work and about the body as a human motor. As Rabinbach has argued, "The science of labor was certainly not, like Taylorism, simply an ideology of management. . . . Rather, it represented a third stage in the political struggle over the working body . . . [and] over the intensity of labor power within a fixed duration of labor time and in the context of mechanization and factory organization. It was a struggle over energy and fatigue rather than time and money."[13]

In France, the physiologist Jean-Marie Lahy recognized the importance of the scientific organization of labor, especially given the loss of labor power due to wartime mortality and the employment of women in jobs formerly defined as "men's jobs."[14] However, Lahy argued that Taylor's focus on productivity led him to assimilate human beings to machines and ignore the "human factor," especially the problem of fatigue. For Lahy, whose socialist and later communist politics also informed his critique of Taylor, this amounted to another step in the exploitation of the worker. As for Taylor's idea about enhancing the division of labor and stimulating workers to work faster by means of piece rates, Lahy argued that Taylor underestimated the fact that some workers actually bring taste to their jobs and tools that are "practically fashioned for their bodies."[15] Lahy attempted to determine the fit between workers and their jobs by analyzing their psychophysiological signs of professional inclination—research that ultimately led to the development of professional aptitude testing. Additionally, Lahy believed that attention to endurance and fatigue would allow workers to reduce wasted motions, use their energy more effectively, and become more productive.[16] In their laboratory experiments on efficiency, fatigue, and endurance, conducted largely on French males, Lahy's fellow industrial physiologists Armand Imbert, Auguste Chauveau, and Jules Amar, head of the Laboratoire des recherches sur le travail musculaire professionnel (Research Laboratory on Professional Muscular Work) followed the earlier work of Etienne-Jules Marey and Charles Frémont and applied the principles of general mechanics to the human machine, measuring carbon dioxide–oxygen exchange and muscular effort and charting the body's motions in different occupations ranging from mechanics to public speaking.[17] Auguste Chauveau measured energy expenditure in lifting various weights and tracked caloric consumption; Armando Mosso developed the *ergographe* to refine the measurement of muscular fatigue.

Jules Amar's work on the "human motor," *Le moteur humain et les bases scientifiques du travail professionnel,* illustrated the application of the principles of physics to the study of the human body. Amar began with a 117-page section on the principles of general mechanics and then discussed the application of these principles to work in laboratory studies of energy expenditure. He investigated the caloric output and respiratory exchange of men pedaling a monocycle and the labor of men carrying a 45-kilogram weight during a seven- to eight-hour march.[18] Unlike Lahy, Amar saw his experiments as prolonging and extending Taylor's ideas, with the goal of applying physiological studies to the scientific organization of labor.[19] To this research on the body, the psychotechnicians Alfred Binet, Charles Henry, and Edouard Toulouse added the notion that because overwork and fatigue seemed inevitable in modern labor, industrial physiology could help industry effectively use its human capital by developing methods of selection. Although these scientists and their medical and psychologist allies constituted a minority in France, by the eve of World War I they had established a broad international network that included journals and conferences.

World War I arguably forced scientists' attention to the problem of working bodies. In the 1880s, when popular anti-German sentiment over the
French defeat in the Franco-Prussian War still had purchase, industrial physiologists examined soldiers' marching patterns and promoted gymnastics
training for French schoolboys in the interest of military preparedness.[20]
Scientists linked improving the health and stamina of the French male body
to national strength and proposed the rational application of physiology to
physical education and diet.[21] These ideas inspired Jean-Marie Lahy's subsequent studies of machine gunners' reaction times and fatigue in order to
understand the "cold-bloodedness" of soldiers—their ability to withstand
the psychological as well as the physical duress of war.[22] As historians have
shown, during World War I scientists collaborated with employers and the
state to reconcile the disturbing incongruity of women's work in jobs formerly gendered male with the strategic objective of stimulating war production in the defense industries.[23] Wartime industrial physiologists were divided, however, in their estimation of women's capabilities for work. Marcel
Frois, for example, investigated the impact of work on the female body in the
wartime defense industries for the French Ministry of Armaments and War
Manufactures and concluded that although women's bodies disqualified
them for work requiring muscular strength or sustained physical effort, their
allegedly great motor sensibility (*grande sensibilité motrice*) meant that industry could employ them effectively in jobs requiring rapid and precise
movements. Frois encouraged employers to modify machinery and production processes in order to hire them.[24] He also documented occupational
health and safety, including fatigue, mortality, exposure to toxic chemicals,
work-related accidents, housing, food, night work, working hours, wages,
and the professional aptitudes and production levels of women workers, as
well as the effects of rationalization in both private and state-administered
industries. In one experiment, measuring the energy expenditure, muscular
fatigue, and reaction times of a group of women during a normal workday,
he concluded that although the work required some 18,000 rapidly executed
movements, it did not require excessive effort; although the women were
tired, they usually recovered by the next day.[25] Frois's attention to the effects
of women's work on their childbearing capacities and maternity led him to
argue that although hygiene was important for all workers, it was even more
important for women factory workers, whose bodies, if they were not weaker
than men's, certainly required more care than men's.[26] But this did not
disqualify women from performing defense work.

Jules Amar, however, disagreed about the employability of women in "male" jobs. He reviewed differences in the cardiograms of French men and women responding to the sound of a two-kilogram weight falling. He found that the cardiograms showed strong changes in the women tested but negligible or no change in the men—the difference he attributed to women's allegedly greater sensation of fear and powerlessness and their greater emotional susceptibility.[27] Amar's conclusions blurred assumptions about the social meaning of gender difference and observed performance. In this respect they were strikingly similar to conclusions drawn by scientists using anthropometric data in the 1860s and 1870s who argued for women's inferiority to men on the grounds of measures of height, weight, lung displacement (*capacité vitale*), thoracic volume, and muscular strength. Amar argued that in general "the shape of the body . . . provides a guide for the worker's choice of one form of work over another. . . . Normally, men are organized and constructed to work in a certain way because this is the way their work is most economical." Amar argued that as a general rule physical proportions determined professional aptitudes and he attempted to classify men as well according to the morphology or "architecture of their bodies."[28]

Amar's experiments on women filing and planning led him to conclude that "women's work, pushed to the physiological limits of fatigue, and without excessive force or rapidity, represents 40 to 50 percent of an adult male's work. [Moreover] the curve declines rapidly with more pronounced exhaustion."[29] Whereas numerous observers praised women's ability to give sustained attention to repetition work during the war, Amar claimed that where significant muscular effort was required, women's attention was not very sustained; women were easily distracted and "obviously, the nervous system, besieged by sensory stimulation does not constantly guide work. . . . Thus, for laborious or complicated maneuvers, or those which require initiative, decision, the patient application of the spirit, it is physiologically contraindicated to rely on women; muscular or nervous fatigue will limit their productivity and be most prejudicial to their health."[30] From these conclusions Amar built a theory of cerebral activity that reproduced age-old views of distinct male and female nervous sensibilities. Women's heightened sensitivity to external stimuli influenced their respiration and cerebral activity, whereas men were more resistant to "external excitations [that] exercise less influence on their motives, acts, ideas, and volition. This would be . . . the deep, essential reason for reserving to the male all sustained or original work [*tout travail tenace ou original*] and to the other sex, occupations that are characterized by discontinuity or are automatic."[31] Women's nervous constitution disqualified them from certain kinds of work. Moreover, "in the vast majority of work requiring great effort and sustained attention," he argued, "there is no place for women workers. They are more appropriate for office occupations."[32] Such efforts to parse the capacities of differently gendered working bodies became more complex with regard to colonial workers.

Male colonial labor was also employed in munitions work, occasionally side by side with French women, and as Tyler Stovall has shown, French authorities regarded the intermingling of genders and races on the job as potentially dangerous. Such intermixing threatened to weaken the boundaries that normally separated differently gendered and raced workers and reflected the sexual anxieties of a colonial state.[33] Despite the fact that the category "race" only entered work scientists' lexicon when they investigated male colonial workers, their observations of these men threw into relief how the working-class European body was also a racialized body and simultaneously illustrated how colonial workers' race could shift their gender and hence the perceptions of the kinds of work they could perform.[34]

During the war, the French government coordinated the hiring of some 222,000 colonial and foreign men from Tunisia, Morocco, Algeria, Indo-China, Madagascar, and China on fixed-term contracts of up to a year, with the provision that they return to their countries of origin at the expiration of their contracts. Most of them were employed in munitions work; colonial women did not tend to migrate to France as a reserve army of labor. Industrial physiologists paid close attention to colonial workers' resistance to fatigue, and the experience revealed assumptions about how differently racialized bodies governed perceptions of productive work.[35] According to Bertrand Nogaro's and Lucien Weil's report on the wartime use of colonial and foreign labor, workers' productivity differed according to the "unequal value and different aptitudes of the diverse races."[36] The report found Moroccans, Kabyles, and Berbers to be "sturdy" and "energetic" and suitable for industrial work (munitions), whereas Arabs were more appropriate for agricultural work. The Indochinese (who included Cambodians, Cochin-Chinese, Annamites, and Tonkinois), on the other hand, tended to be "soft and submissive" and made good unskilled workers for powder factories or agriculture. In feminizing the body of the colonial male subject, Nogaro and Weil illustrated how knowledge of the body created the meanings of gender and could dictate the deployment of workers. Designations of racial difference also altered the gender characteristics of bodies. To the feminine characteristics of softness and submissiveness supposedly characteristic of Indo-

Chinese workers the report's authors added that the Indo-Chinese were especially suitable for work "requiring dexterity as opposed to physical force" —the very characteristics most often claimed for work gendered female and associated with beliefs about women's superior fine motor coordination and their "nimble fingers." "The Indo-Chinese," it concluded, "[have] no more strength than women."[37] The feminization of East Asian workers conveniently fit within the framework of an imperial system that relied on the domination of foreign bodies—although as we see below not all colonial workers were so femininzed. Nogaro and Weil also observed physical differences among white Europeans: Greeks tended to be hardy and strong, but resisted working outdoors; Portuguese peasants, on the other hand, had considerable strength and made good agricultural workers. In contrast to relative stability and normative meanings attached to the gender of European workers, the gender of colonial workers appeared less stable and marked their potential employability.[38]

Gendered and Raced Working Bodies between the Wars

The experience of employing women and colonial workers in wartime cast a shadow over scientists' analyses of the working body during the following two decades, as the intersecting meanings of masculinity, femininity, and racial difference entered the study of the working body. Jean-Marie Lahy's critique of Taylor incorporated assumptions about the link between fatherhood and citizenship that were also embedded in the new model of the citizen-worker: "One cannot abstract the worker from the man who takes part in social activities in which he occupies a more elevated position than in the factory. Head of the family, he assumes all the moral responsibilities that the direction of a household and the education of children imply; as a citizen, he participates in political life among the most active individuals."[39] Although Lahy recognized that work science should treat the body of the worker in relation to the worker's social and political identities, he assumed that gender shaped those identities.

Likewise, Jules Amar, in studies published after the war, incorporated assumptions about the female body that ignored women's continued presence in industrial work and their increasing numbers in the ranks of public-service workers after World War I. These discourses about gendered bodies lent the legitimacy of science to the practices of reconfiguring the French economy in the 1920s and 1930s. In his *Physiology of Industrial Organization,* published at the end of the war, Amar again distinguished between the physical and psychological attributes of male and female workers. In studying the cranial capacities of French men's and women's brains, for instance, Amar insisted that although he could discover no difference between men and women in the "quantity of energy produced" by their brains, he did see a difference in quality. "In the case of the woman, sensibility holds the first place. . . . In man on the contrary, abstract thought and reason come first."[40] Amar's next logical step was to insist that such characteristics produced the aptitudes that would allow employers to assess the fit between workers and jobs and could be used as a basis of professional aptitude testing.[41] Whereas men could work for up to forty years (between the ages of twenty and sixty), women could hope to work for no more than thirty years, from nineteen to fifty, at which point menopause would diminish their physical capacity. His work on the human motor consolidated gender as a category defining the white French worker: the maleness or femaleness of French workers was unambiguous.

Marcel Frois's research on work accidents among male and female mechanical press operators mirrored Amar's conclusions. Frois believed that the most frequent cause of work accidents was the lack of coordination between the hands (directing the material) and the feet (that controlled the press pedal). This lack of coordination could be due to visual or cardiac difficulties, bad lighting, or psychological problems. Among the latter, Frois pointed to the problems of mixing the sexes at work. It was distracting: " . . . this is why it is not judicious to place men and young girls side by side at work on metal presses." Moreover, Frois argued that "with women we have noticed that accidents are more frequent during stormy weather, which makes women more nervous."[42] Once again, women's nerves potentially made them unreliable workers. Frois's arguments advanced in 1930 differed only superficially from those of nineteenth-century doctors such as Louis René Villermé who studied the effects of industrial work on women and children. Whereas nineteenth-century observers emphasized the sexual tension produced by placing men and women workers in close proximity and condemned it on moral grounds, twentieth-century work scientists couched their anxieties about working-class sexuality as observations about "psychology" and workers' productivity. However, the meanings of gender when applied to colonial workers were more complex, as Amar's research on the uses of colonial labor demonstrated.

In his studies of the endurance and fatigue of North African men, Amar attempted to classify workers, introducing race as a category applicable to colonial subjects.[43] Recruiting his subjects from petty criminals housed in the Algerian prison of Biskra, Amar conducted experiments on men carrying weights while walking and climbing; his results illustrated how class, alongside gender, operated in establishing racial and ethnic distinctions. Amar's work also showed how male colonial subjects could be mobilized—not only as a reserve army of labor (or as a reserve army *tout court*) but in the service of European "science" as well. In North Africa he could find men presenting "the physical and moral temperament of beasts of burden [*le tempérament physique et moral du boeuf*]."[44] Indeed, Amar believed that well-trained French workers should travel to the colonies to train native craftsmen: " . . . it is the duty of the European worker to direct native labor which is *naturally adapted to fatiguing kinds of work which would not tax the native's endurance as greatly as it would ours.*"[45] Although he argued that examination of the brain did not enable him to arrive at firm conclusions about racial difference between Europeans and non-Europeans and that there was no firm relationship between physiological characteristics and the capacities of colonial male workers, he also claimed that "the brain of the negro . . . is less massive and less dense [than that of the European]," implying that this racial marker had consequences for the kinds of work African subjects could perform.[46] At the same time, reflecting almost a century of scholarship devoted to establishing the superiority of Kabyles over Arabs, he concluded that

> Kabyles are superior to all the Arabs in respect of the amount of daily labor of which they are capable, and the rapidity of their movements. More nervously constituted, they instinctively tend to work rapidly, and it is difficult to moderate the swiftness of their [motions].
>
> In industry and in the army, speed is a valuable factor, and presupposes a . . . neuromuscular system that reacts without delay. The Berbers appeared to display the vivacious reaction of the French workmen, while the other Arabs displayed the slowness of our peasants without possessing their tenacity.[47]

Although Amar's North African subjects allegedly showed no difference from French men when carrying weights on a flat surface, he judged Arabs to be less powerful than Europeans or North African Berbers when it came to climbing. Kabyles, however, seemed especially well suited to industrial work and physical exertion—true beasts of burden:

> The Kabyle alone is adapted to industrial work and to swift exertion . . . one may reckon that five Kabyles are equivalent to six good Arab workers.

The Muslims and the Negroes are in the same category. Their endurance appeared to be very great and their output is . . . the highest. This endurance was more particularly displayed by the way in which they resumed the same labor several days in a row without appearing to suffer. . . . But if we take into account the intelligence and dexterity of Kabyle workers, it is to them that our industries should apply in order to constitute their staffs. . . . The Muslim and still more, the Negro, should be employed only as laborers.[48]

At the same time, although racial and ethnic differences were essential in distinguishing the labor power of Europeans and non-Europeans, despite their common racial affinity even Europeans differed in their physical aptitudes for work. In a characteristic display of ethnocentrism, Amar distinguished Italian from French workers, arguing that Italians "lacked energy" and did not seem capable of "the continuity of effort which our modern industries require."[49] Thus, "science" legitimated and naturalized national as well as racial differences.

Amar's research also incorporated two issues central to the science of labor in the 1920s and 1930s when the rationalization and regulation of the working body promised to help resolve French labor shortages and answer concerns about postwar productivity. One was the application of physiology to the rational selection of workers by measuring workers' physical aptitudes in order to match the individual to the most appropriate job. Amar believed, along with many nineteenth-century solidarists, that scientific selection would create social harmony between capital and labor; work could become a form of social integration and an instrument of social progress. These ideas received attention in the 1920s in the research of Henri Laugier, Henri Piéron, Edouard Toulouse, Julien Fontègne, and Jean-Marie Lahy, who worked in state-funded laboratories and institutes such as the Conservatoire des arts et métiers, the Henri Rousselle Hospital, the National Institute for Vocational Guidance, and research laboratories of the Ecole pratique des hautes études.[50] A second set of issues concerned social and industrial hygiene and particularly the improvement of occupational health and safety and the prevention of work accidents.[51] Both sets of issues caught the attention of entrepreneurs and late Third Republic governments in their efforts to modernize industry and public services in the 1920s and 1930s. The applications of this research reproduced the gender and racial distinctions already embedded in scientists' investigations of the working body.

Science and the Working Body in Industry

In the 1920s, French industrialists' applications of industrial physiology alongside Taylorism were limited and confined largely to a few key industries such as metalworking, especially the automobile industry, electrical construction, and textiles, and to the service sector, particularly the telephone exchange. Many older firms were reluctant to set up services or laboratories to measure the physical capacities of workers prior to hiring. Although employers hardly needed scientists' assessments of immigrant workers' laboring capacities to deploy them in low-paid, unskilled labor; scientific research legitimized the racial and gender distinctions that employers already assumed. Its applications show how employers paid attention to the gender and racial characteristics of working bodies in selecting and deploying labor: industrial physiology and psychophysiology refined already existing gender divisions of labor by creating new criteria for classifying workers, rather than investigating all workers' abilities for all jobs.

In 1924 Société des transports en commun de la région parisienne (STCRP), for example, hired Jean-Marie Lahy to apply his research to the selection of male tramway conductors in order to reduce accidents. He measured men's resistance to fatigue, their capacities for distraction, their motor coordination, and their reactions to visual and auditory stimuli. Although women had worked as tramway conductors in many countries, including France, during the war, most employers believed that they replaced men only temporarily; the job of the conductor (*machiniste*) was already gendered male. Lahy did not even attempt to test women for the job, even though, as he pointed out, "The job of the conductor does not demand muscular effort, so it is not essential to measure strength as one of the basic tests for selection."[52] Lahy believed that with the aid of an apparatus called a "dynamograph" he could test future conductors for their fatigue potential and would allow the service to eliminate candidates even before they entered an apprenticeship. Indeed, the director general of the STCRP praised the virtues of these efforts and pointed to the enormous financial savings that psychophysiological testing had permitted the Society to realize. Lahy used this example to argue that factory superintendents could contribute to applying science to the selection of personnel by learning how to administer the tests that would match workers effectively to their jobs.[53] In this way factory superintendents would help to maintain the gender division of labor.

Metalworking employers also became increasingly attentive to problems of health, hygiene, and the fatigue of the male working body in the late 1920s in an effort to prevent work accidents. Indeed, one of the most important branches of work science, with the most widespread industrial applications, was research on how excessive fatigue led to accidents on the job, and problems of unprotected machinery, toxicity, and poor hygiene. Between 1929 and 1931, for example, the Comité des forges de France (French Forge Committee) and the Caisse syndicale d'assurance mutuelle des forges de France contre les accidents au travail (French Forges Mutual Assistance Fund against Work Accidents) published a series of technical bulletins devoted to preventing accidents that drew on the research of the ergonomists Armand Imbert and Marcel Frois.[54] Metalworking employers' attention to the male body at work could be seen in other areas as well that fit with their practices of social regulation and industrial welfare. Thus the Association pour le développement des oeuvres sociales dans les industries métallurgiques et mécaniques de la région parisienne (Association for the Development of Social Programs in the Metallurgical and Mechanical Industries of the Paris Region) founded a kind of scout camp, the Centre de camping André Paty, for young male workers aged thirteen to twenty who were employed in the factories attached to the Groupe des industries métallurgiques, méchaniques, et connexes de la région parisienne (GIMM). The camp functioned as a site at which masculine work culture was developed and nurtured. Adolescent boys could spend ten days at a time in the fresh air of the French countryside during the summer. Photographs of the camp reproduced in the journal *Mon métier* addressed to young male metal workers showed them living in tents and happily swimming and practicing archery, cooking over a campfire, and observing demonstrations of machines. The camp was designed to provide "moral as well as physical education" and aimed to "place young workers in healthy conditions with advice about living according to the rules of "rational hygiene.""[55]

In the context of concern about the physical health of industrial workers, metalworking employers also scrutinized women's night work. A January 1925 law had modified the French labor code to exclude women from night work between 10 p.m. and 5 a.m., so that they would benefit from a minimum of eleven consecutive hours of rest. But the law also established that temporary exceptions could be granted for adult women in the case of industries in which either the raw or manufactured materials might be perishable or undergo rapid changes—namely, in the food industries—if it was necessary to employ them at night.[56] Textile employers insisted that the manufacture of certain types of textiles required the employment of women on rotating teams, some of which worked at night. By 1931, however, during the Depression, when employers fired workers or put them on slack time, efforts were under way to extend the period considered as "night," to the period from 7 p.m. to 6 a.m. Women and children under fifteen could in theory no longer be employed on the system of double teams typical of some textile firms during these hours.[57] Although the proposal was never incorporated into the labor code, it is indicative of the increasing attention to the intersecting problems of fatigue, work accidents, and family life on the parts of both workers and employers. In some cases, those interests also intersected with employers' hiring and personnel strategies.

Automobile manufacturers Citroën, Renault, and Peugeot, however, proved to be the most eager to make use of industrial physiology and were the first to create their own "psychotechnical" services (*services psychotechniques*) in the 1930s. From its founding in 1915, the Citroën automobile firm's personnel service selected and hired skilled workers in addition to administering the firm's social services, resolving disputes, and overseeing the labor force. Unskilled workers generally did not undergo sophisticated psychophysiological testing.[58] Citroën's firm belief in science's capacity to modernize industry led him to argue that knowledge about "physical effort and the psychological qualities demanded by each form of labor" would enable scientists to place each worker in a specific line of work. "For each individual we can evaluate the dynometric coefficient of the muscles, resistance to various forms of fatigue, sensory acuity, and the rapidity of reactions to peripheral stimuli."[59] The science of the working body appeared to be the wave of the future and symbolized the modern firm.

Under the direction of Ernest Mattern in the early 1920s, Citroën's personnel officers established a technical form for each skilled job in the factory, listing the job requirements, and created similar forms for prospective employees so that the requirements of the job could be perfectly matched to the workers' aptitudes. A personnel officer then directed them to the appropriate sections of the factory "which best suited their aptitudes, according to demand."[60] In 1930, Citroën refined his selection apparatus, instituting a new psychotechnical service responsible for testing both men and women. New hires underwent a battery of aptitude and physical endurance tests. A male worker described one of the tests: "They give you an apparatus with two springs. You press on one each time the woman who is testing you makes a noise with two pieces of iron hitting against one another. Each time you press the spring, it marks on dial how quickly you respond to the noise."[61] The examination included testing of eye-hand coordination, using a perforated roll of paper rotated by a machine and encased in a box so that only five centimeters of paper were visible at a time. "With an electrified steel pointer [the subject] has to touch each hole that reveals a piece of iron which is also electrified. . . . For two minutes, over 200 holes rolled by and had to be hit."[62] Finally, the personnel officers tested the subject's muscular force by requiring her or him to squeeze a rubber bulb. A dial measured the force exerted.

> For each successful applicant the personnel service filled out a blue form containing four sections: physical assessment, work, accidents, and "various." The qualifiers [used to describe the applicant] were directly related to the efforts to rationalize production: thus for the physical assessment, the applicant was judged weak, rather weak, medium, vigorous, very vigorous. For work [in the category] rapidity: cannot maintain the rhythm, keeps up with the rhythm, goes beyond the rhythm, a little, a lot; after how long does he maintain the rhythm? Quality: number of flawed pieces.[63]

The subject's enthusiasm for work and productivity were also noted and the subject was finally scored. In addition to physical characteristics and aptitudes, the personnel service also paid attention to age. In 1926, Citroën tried to weed out men over sixty at his Javel plant. "The personnel director came in to ascertain their physical and mental condition. 'I lined them up at one end of a large room and had them walk eight or ten meters to the other end of the room to respond to [the] questions [of the personnel committee]. The way in which they covered the distance constituted . . . an important means of assessing their activity.'" Those who failed the test were fired, and the following year the company hired no one over fifty-five.[64]

The scientific selection of workers according to their physical capacities and resistance to fatigue also justified the reproduction of gender and racial divisions inside the factory. At a February 1919 conference of government officials and representatives of organized labor, a resolution called for the application of scientific methods of testing and classifying foreign male workers so that they could be placed in jobs without competing with French men, while others argued that foreign workers could replace women.[65] But work scientists' observations showed that women and colonial workers were not interchangeable. As Paul Razous noted in his 1924 study on the selection of workers, "The woman's ergographic force [the ergograph was designed to measure sustained application of effort] is proportionately more developed than the man's . . . therefore, women are more able to repeat a moderate effort than to give a maximal effort once."[66] This observation, justifying women's employment in unskilled assembly line work, found its parallel in the employment of colonial labor, even though colonial workers were not subjected to sophisticated psychomotor tests. At the same time, Jules Amar's experiments on North Africans, as well as already established ideas about the superiority of Kabyle workers, arguably influenced the employment of some 7,000 Kabyle men at Citroën and some 3,000 at Renault. Both manufacturers hired them as unskilled laborers, valued for their strength and ability to work rapidly over a sustained period. The sugar refineries of Say and Lebaudy likewise employed large numbers of Kabyle men for the same reason.[67] But even if employers' cultural assumptions about the gender and race of colonial workers influenced hiring of colonial workers in these industries more than employers' scrupulous attention to Amar's experiments, industrial physiology and psychology lent scientific credibility and legitimacy to those assumptions about how race and gender marked capacities for work.

In the textile industry as well, scientists systematically studied the working body in the process of designing apprenticeships. As in other areas, their aim was to reduce wasted motions that cost time and compromised productivity. Observers such as Charles Labriffe saw apprenticeship in certain trades in the textile industry as a natural outgrowth of the psychology and science of work. His work on apprenticeship, published in 1945, reflected the influence of nearly half a century of industrial physiology.[68] Labriffe believed that whereas certain jobs in the industry could be performed by unskilled labor, others—specifically jobs in spinning and weaving—required the mastery of certain skills that only a proper apprenticeship could impart. Apprenticeship involved testing of workers' physical capacities, particularly their general health and constitution, the strength of their heart, legs, arms, hands, stomach, and lungs, as well as sight, hearing, sense of smell, and intellectual and moral qualities, by a physician with a specialization in "social medicine" (médicine sociale).[69] Labriffe believed that the methodical collection of data about the physical and mental capacities of each individual would permit the medical-social and psychotechnical services of firms to reevaluate certain jobs that had been undervalued. Interestingly, it was men's jobs that Labriffe chose to illustrate this situation, not women's, suggesting how industrial physiology could be used in supporting certain forms of male skill and wage superiority. "This documentation will permit us . . . to re-evaluate certain professions which have been left by the wayside for lack of high wages. . . . Don't we often see common laboring men earning more than a good weaver or a roofer earning more than some foremen in weaving?"[70]

Labriffe proposed scientifically rationalizing the apprenticeship of male weavers (men constituted about 75 percent of all weavers) through a series of exercises designed to train the body and develop the physical aptitudes necessary for weaving. Learning the job involved above all educating the body to master gestures and movements that would allow the "human motor" to move optimally in conjunction with the automatic loom. Ideally, the apprentice weaver would become so sensitive to the movement of the loom that his own gestures would be automatically inscribed on his motor memory and he would execute those gestures practically without thinking. Although training and apprenticeship incorporated intellectual and moral dimensions, the emphasis on adapting the human body to the machine meant that the efficiently trained weaver would become a kind of automaton.[71] Whereas metalworking employers naturalized women's apparent synchronization with the machines, Labriffe believed that male weavers had to be taught to adapt themselves to the rhythm of the automatic loom.

Although he believed firmly in the gender division of labor, Labriffe foresaw the possibility of apprenticeship training in textiles for women and in this regard appeared as the exception among those who wrote about the gender dimensions of job training. Aptitude testing of women workers in textiles involved the evaluation and assessment of physical aptitudes as well as the intellectual and moral qualities of the workers and was the prelude to an apprenticeship. Once the physical capacities of women workers had been ascertained and their aptitudes tested, they could receive training on the appropriate machines. Time and motion studies measured the time it took to inspect, start, and set up the spinning machines, including the motions of each hand in attaching the bobbin to the mechanism and in repairing broken threads. Monitors timed the motions of women positioning and replacing bobbins on spinning machines. Aptitude tests evaluated general health and constitution and the flexibility of the legs, arms, and hands; they measured auditory memory in the midst of noise and vision—the ability to distinguish different colored threads. Employers favored tall women because of their reach and especially valued the "moral" qualities of attention, conscientiousness, ambition, and perseverance.[72] Labriffe recognized employers' concern with fatigue—the new problem of the twentieth-century workplace—and he proposed the standardization of equipment and studies of human anatomy to determine how various motions could be performed with the least fatigue.[73] The collaboration of medical and technical services in the firm could result in greater specialization of labor and more efficient productivity, such that "the woman worker will only have to think about . . . her own work . . ."[74] But observers also saw the limits to specialization and proposed that women be trained on more than one machine so that during periods of intense work employers could move them around the factory. Studies of workers' motions led observers to conclude that those who could work with two hands simultaneously were most efficient, and they even proposed that children in primary school learn exercises designed to make them ambidextrous. In addition to developing their manual coordination, women workers' auditory memory also had to be developed so that they could distinguish normal and abnormal sounds of the machine. Their visual memory and acuity had to be trained to enable them to distinguish normal or abnormal motions of the equipment.

Labriffe also proposed that women's apprenticeship in textile manufacture include training in the delicate mechanisms of the machines on which they would be working—the gear and clutch systems, the parts to grease, and maintain in good working order. Yet, although he acknowledged women's need for greater technical knowledge, he stopped short of recommending that women *use* that knowledge: the actual regulation and precision adjustment of the mechanism remained the work of men. "Even though the woman worker will never . . . touch . . . the machine, since regulation is the overseer's job, it is a good idea that she learn . . . how it works."[75] Indeed, the textile industry is a good example of how industrial physiology and Taylorism collaborated in maintaining the gender division of labor. Rationalization, even if it involved giving women new knowledge, simultaneously reinscribed masculine "property in skill" that protected men's higher-paying supervisory and technical repair jobs.

Women factory superintendents, whom employers hired to oversee the health and working conditions of women employees, could be key players in implementing the scientific selection of workers. Jean-Marie Lahy argued that superintendents should be trained in industrial psychology and psychological testing, enabling them to collaborate with psychotechnicians in the selection of workers.[76] At Michelin and Renault they assisted personnel officers by administering the tests that permitted employers to select the appropriate worker for the job.[77] Gabrielle Mounier, during her internship as a factory superintendent-in-training at the Michelin tire factory in Clermont-Ferrand, reported that the superintendent had the responsibility of hiring the women workers who counted for some 40 percent of the employees.[78] The personnel office was strategically located near the medical clinic on the factory grounds and hiring took place with the collaboration of the factory doctor. Although Michelin did not perform psychophysiological tests on its women workers, the superintendent closely monitored the body of the female employee. She regularly weighed women employees and those who lost weight were directed to see the doctor and might even be sent off to a rest home that Michelin maintained. At Renault, women superintendents supervised the psychotechnical testing service for both men and women into the 1950s.[79] But at Peugeot's psychotechnical office, established in 1938, male engineers and managers displaced the women factory superintendents in the process of worker selection.[80]

Manufacturers such as the food-processing firm Géo also used factory superintendents to supervise psychophysiological tests in the selection of prospective female employees. Carried out by a team of specialists, the tests measured physical resistance, tendency to muscular and nervous fatigue, visual acuity, the senses of touch and hearing, reaction times, manual dexterity, memory, attention span, emotivity, and suggestibility. As Mademoiselle Catalet, who worked with Jean-Marie Lahy on experiments at Géo, reported at the 1928 meeting of the Association des surintendantes, whenever employers used psychophysiological testing, production increased and training costs, as well as work accidents, decreased. As an example, she cited the Paris transport system (STCRP). Since the company had implemented psychophysiological testing in 1924, it had saved 150,000 francs on the training of tramway and bus conductors and the number of deficient workers had declined from 20 percent to 3.4 percent.[81] Catelet indeed approached the question with the same utopian outlook with which many had regarded other forms of rationalization. "Industry, instead of becoming more deadly, will fulfill a social role by permitting each [worker] to develop his or her personality instead of using up his physical and moral strength on work that is incompatible with his or her constitution."[82] At the same time, for some employers, women's working bodies could barely be distinguished from their maternal bodies. Louis Amieux, manager of another food-processing firm, reminded superintendents of their special responsibility to pay special attention to workers' fatigue, implicitly distinguishing the effects of fatigue on men (lower productivity) from women (poor mothering). He warned, "Women who have created industrial and commercial prosperity can also engender the debility of the race if they are left without protection. We mustn't forget that to the fatigue of her work she adds the fatigue that is the result of her role as a woman." Employers therefore had a responsibility to place women in the least tiring kinds of work.[83] This was the same message that Lahy brought to the annual meeting of the Association des surintendantes in 1930, when he proposed that factory superintendents' training include the study of industrial psychology.[84] But the applications of work science were not confined to industry; the measurement and supervision of the working body extended to the modernizing public-service telephone exchange.

Although most rationalization occurred in industrial work, employers also applied the findings of industrial physiology alongside Taylorist organization to service-sector work. Office, clerical, and secretarial work saw the distillation and implementation of these two forms of regulation and management in the 1920s, when Gaston Lavisse promoted William Henry Leffinwell's applications of Taylorism to the organization of office work.[85] Operating under the assumption that "the organization of the office should be inspired by methods of industrial organization," a small number of French managers applied time and motion studies to evaluate the efficiency of office work, reorganize tasks, and replace skilled male workers with young men and girls. In the late nineteenth century, just as in the United States and Britain, women typists in France, prized for their "nimble fingers," replaced men, previously hired as office accountants because of their alleged skill with numbers and fine penmanship. The modernization of the public-service sector in postwar France likewise involved the rationalization of the telephone exchange and illustrates the convergence of discourses about gendered bodies and workplace practices.[86]

The aggressive feminization of the telephone service in the 1880s occurred as the number of telephone customers dramatically expanded at the same time as a "crisis of advancement" for male workers waiting to move up in the ranks of the public service. Reluctant to hire more men as telephone operators, a strategy that would only aggravate the bottleneck of men awaiting promotion, the Administration of the Postes, Télégraphes et Téléphones (PTT) created a distinct division or grade of public sector worker, the "*dame employée.*"[87] With this distinct category of female functionary the state bureaucracy modernized the public-sector service along gender lines that paralleled private-sector industrial work. By the turn of the twentieth century, the PTT employed large numbers of women, especially as postmistresses in small village post offices in the provinces as well as in urban post offices.

Whereas the PTT hired women as specialized employees from the very beginning, the Postal Administration was reluctant to oblige men to specialize so that they could move more easily from job to job as need arose. The number of women operators soared from 812 in 1891 to over 3,300 just after the turn of the century (1905). After the war (1921), about 46,000 women worked in all services of the PTT, the vast majority as telephone operators; by 1936 the service employed over 56,000 women.[88] As in most forms of public-sector employment, the French civil service hierarchy grew more refined after World War I and men also became increasingly specialized. By the mid-1920s, women counted for three of some twenty-seven different categories of postal and telegraph employee: *dames employées* (some as *rédacteurs*, chief editorial clerks), supervisors, and principal supervisors. Men, on the other hand, constituted the corps of mail carriers, supervisors, sorters, and the majority of chief editorial clerks, and they worked exclusively as line agents, team heads, and work leaders in the category linemen and installation agents.[89]

Much as in industrial work, complex salary scales accompanied the gender segregation of public-sector job categories that had already been defined as male or female, and much as in industrial employment, family and gender influenced salary scales. Although organized women postal employees pressured the government for the adoption of equal pay when the work arguably demanded the same levels of education, skill, and training, the postal employees union, the Syndicat national des Agents, refused to support equal pay in postwar negotiations with the state. In their view, women's inextricable link with motherhood made them inherently unequal to men. Their argument that "the woman who is a mother will think more about her progeny than her administrative work" may have influenced the government's reluctance to set equitable salary scales for *dames employées* as they had done for schoolteachers in 1919.[90] At the same time, women's salaries rose steadily throughout the 1920s and early 1930s, and the Postal Administration promoted women as supervisors. In 1926, they could earn a maximum of 12,500 francs a year as principal supervisors and could become fourth class postmistresses, earning as much as fourth class postmasters, 14,000 francs a year. But the majority of *dames employées*, even if they earned 1,500 francs more than the base salary of a mail carrier, could hope to earn no more than the highest level of the lowest-paid postmaster, 9,200 francs a year.[91] Even after a series of strikes that interrupted telephone service and mail delivery in 1930, the highest salary of a *dame employée* (now 4,500 francs higher than a mail carrier) was 80 percent of the highest level of the lowest-paid postmaster.

Family and gender also influenced the salaries of male PTT employee, just as they induced private industrial employers to support prolific family men with family wage bonuses as an inducement to procreate. A lowly mail carrier who, by 1929, had reached the maximum salary after twenty-five years of service earned 10,990 francs per year: 8,000 francs of base salary, 600 francs "responsibility" compensation, a 2,240-franc housing allowance, and a 150-franc shoe allowance. But dependents' allowances could increase his salary, since he stood to earn 680 francs for one child, 806 francs for two, 1,209 francs for three, and 1,411 francs for four. Postal workers who had completed military service also enjoyed a cash benefit that would allow them to move to a higher level. Thus, a married Parisian postman with one child would earn 11, 670 francs a year.[92]

Differently gendered and sexed bodies dictated the deployment of labor in public-service work just as they dictated the employment of industrial labor. The Postal Administration believed that women's distinctive physical attributes made them good operators, although as we will see, the same characteristics could subvert the efficient operation of the system. The rationalizing impulses of Taylorism and industrial physiology came together in the 1920s and 1930s in the management of telephone operators in four areas: in attention to the gendered and raced body in the selection of candidates for the telephone service; in the scientific study of the working body of operators; in the regulation of operators' physical space and surveillance; and in concern about the health of the worker in the modern telephone exchange.

Selection

Selection of the telephone operator involved the application of extensive aptitude testing in the process of creating a new kind of postwar public-service worker. It was well known that state public-sector work could be a means of upward social mobility. Most young operators came from the lower middle class, armed with at least an elementary school certificate. Education ranked among the important criteria for selection and the Postal Administration favored women candidates who already possessed teaching certificates.[93] All candidates took a battery of tests that included writing, spelling, arithmetic, physical and political geography of France and the colonies, physics, and chemistry. They could also take an optional exam in English, German, Spanish, or Italian. Following a training period in telephone communication, successful candidates passed a practical test that included techniques of transmission and reception. The Administration gave priority to women already employed in the postal service or who were the wives, widows, daughters, or sisters of retired (or deceased) male employees.[94] Although there was no marriage bar, about half of the women entering postal work were single and tended to remain so over the course of their employment.[95] Just after World War I, regulations stipulated that candidates had to be between seventeen and twenty-five years of age, except for widows or orphans of men who had been killed in the war or who had died as a result of war-related injuries, who could be as old as thirty. By 1930, the lower age limit had been raised to twenty-one years, presumably following the shift in the legal age of majority.[96] The future operator was required to submit a certificate attesting to her good moral character signed by the mayor or the police commissioner of her town of residence. Significantly enough, the Administration did not require character references for male candidates.[97]

Nationality and race or ethnicity also influenced selection. The future telephone operator had to be "française," living as she did in the "shadow of colonialism."[98] Public-service jobs were closed to foreigners.[99] Race did not, of course, appear as a formal category in the published requirements, and it is unlikely that the Administration would have employed the category between the world wars. Yet racial difference was already inscribed in her Frenchness, a term that by definition did not apply to colonial workers. As a public-sector worker and representative of the French state she could not by definition be a colonial subject or have an accent not clearly French, a reminder of how public-sector work could serve as a privileged if not racialized enclave and that racial difference is in part about cultural competence.[100] The integration of male colonial workers in industrial work was not paralleled by the integration of either colonial men or women into the public telephone service. Colonial women—especially North African Muslim women—would not have passed the tests of cultural competence as the French administration had defined them, even if cultural constraints on public-sector service work in the metropole did not exist. The post–World War I reconfiguration of sexual politics in the African colonies that gave French women a specific role as the bearers of Frenchness contained within it an unmistakable subtext against which Frenchness was defined. Observers of colonial life called attention to the Muslim women's dissimulation in wearing the veil, suggesting that they were untrustworthy; others criticized the "debauchery" of Arab cultural practices and remarked on the poor hygiene of colonial subjects who allegedly failed to meet French standards. French colonial authorities, moreover, believed that colonial women were "the primary bearers of archaic cultures [and] . . . impediments to genuine male acculturation to metropolitan values."[101] But the male colonial workers who had been gendered female by work scientists were not admitted to the competitive entrance examination. After World War I, residents of the provinces of Alsace and Lorraine could take the examination in either French or German, but if they were unable to take the exam in French they could only hope to work in the departments of the Haut-Rhin, the Bas-Rhin, and the Moselle.[102] Constructing the modern public-service worker, then, incorporated a certain representation of Frenchness and a nationally, if not racially, marked femininity.

Beyond these formal requirements, selection criteria focused on physical attributes that theoretically could be verified during the course of an obligatory medical examination but most of which had been already presumed as cultural and racial characteristics of the working body. The voice and body of the worker constituted the crucial sites of skill and qualification. Women's pleasant voices, their allegedly inherent patience and politeness, self-control, even-temperedness, amiability, and "malleable character" all figured among the attributes that made women desirable as operators, much as these same characteristics had been used for decades to justify the employment of women in other contexts.[103] But the industrial physiologists and vocational guidance experts Julien Fontègne and his collaborator Emilio Solari also gave serious attention to physical aptitudes for the work, and in their research the cultural meanings of gendered bodies underpinned their vision of science and modernity.[104] Unlike the work scientist Jules Amar, who rarely left his laboratory, Fontègne and Solari studied their subjects at work in an effort to develop the specific criteria that would determine the requisite physical aptitudes of an operator. They measured the rapidity and precision of the operator's repetitive movements in response to lights flashing on a switchboard. As soon as a caller picked up the telephone at home, a light appeared. The operator put a pin (*fiche*) attached to a cord into the jack, flicked a switch or pressed a button into the speaking position, and immediately said "*j'écoute*" (I hear you). She then attempted to secure the number by touching the end of another pin to the jack of the corresponding number and putting the switch into the listening position to ascertain if the number was free. If it was, she introduced the pin into the jack and flicked another switch to signal the caller that the number was free. Once the person being called picked up the phone and the connection was made, the lights went out. At the end of the conversation, the lights corresponding to caller and recipient went on and the operator registered the call with another switch and removed the pins. The operator repeated these mechanical movements hundreds of times in the course of an hour—the operators whom Fontègne and Solari studied placed between 160 and 180 calls an hour; during busy periods they had to handle up to 350 calls an hour.[105]

From these observations, Fontègne and Solari developed a list of the physical and psychological aptitudes of the ideal operator. She had to be tall, with long arms and a supple upper body. She needed good eyesight and hearing, a strong back, clear respiratory passages, and a normal digestive apparatus. In addition, she needed a good auditory memory for numbers; she had to be capable of sustained attention and be ready to respond at any moment. As Fontègne and Solari noted, this activity was very different from that of the office worker "who could put off work from one day to the next." The telephone operator needed to be able to react instantly to a variety of simultaneously occurring stimuli, including differently colored flashing lights and the sounds of callers; a good operator needed good nerves—a quality that men did not possess and which made them less desirable as operators.[106] So, whereas some observers believed that women were unsuited for jobs because of their "nervous qualities," these scientists argued that women's physical difference from men—their allegedly greater nervousness, their ability to move rapidly and react quickly to external stimuli, their capacity to give sustained attention to work—made them especially well qualified for the job.[107] However, good nerves alone were insufficient. Amar judged the Kabyle men he tested to have good neuromuscular systems and to display a capacity for quick reactions to stimuli, but they were never considered for this kind of work in France. Gender and racial difference indelibly marked the working body in spite of claims to the scientific determination of aptitude. An experiment that placed men as operators on peak daytime shifts, for example, failed miserably. Men already worked the slower night shifts because labor legislation prohibited the employment of women at night. But observers in the Postal Administration noted that men couldn't sustain the pace on the busiest day shifts. They simply didn't have the nerves for it.[108] Indeed, the perceived utility of women's alleged "nervousness" (which supposedly made them unsuited for certain jobs in defense industries during the war) illustrated the malleability of gendered aptitudes.

Educating and Regulating the Operator

The handbook issued to young operators, the *Vade-mecum de la téléphoniste*, incorporated the rationalizing aims of the scientific study of work in an effort to regulate and discipline the operator.[109] This guide instructed new operators in the basic techniques of the job. It reminded operators to instill confidence in and maintain the confidentiality of the customer, guided them in dealing with irate or impatient callers, and it instructed them in the correct placement of the heavy headsets and adjustments of the microphone, which had to be kept at a few centimeters from the mouth so as to alleviate unnecessary stretching and straining of the neck.[110] The operator's dress was also important. Metallic necklaces, bracelets, or wristwatches were forbidden because of the possibility of accidents from electric shocks or because they could inhibit movement. The rationalized work of the operator involved the meshing of body and machine: she was literally linked to the switchboard by the headset. The left hand operated the keys or switches, the right hand the pins. Even the voice was regulated, especially its timbre: one shouldn't speak too loudly; it was sufficient that the voice was clear and articulate. "The syllables must be rhythmically separated so that they can be easily heard. One must not force the voice, but seek to fill the microphone with its volume . . . one must shape one's words into the microphone. . . . Pronounce not a single extraneous word." The motions of the hands had to be supple and precise and the operator had to avoid all stray motions.[111] Despite the handbook's claim that unless workers understood the reasons for each task, "unconscious Taylorism would transform them into robots, deprived of thought and initiative," the body of the operator became a human motor in the interests of modern telephone exchange.[112]

The desire to build a modern and efficient communications network also dictated the rational organization of space: the twentieth-century telephone exchange proved to be a model of rational discipline and control.[113] In an enormous, long room whose walls were covered with switchboards, women sat in straight-backed chairs close to a horizontal board of buttons and switches (the "table") and had to reach up to fit the pins into the appropriate jacks on the board. Discipline and regulation in addition to dictating the spatial rationalization of the body also involved intense competition between operators, while supervisors tracked their performance in order to provide rapid and efficient service for customers and facilitate the promotion of the most efficient operators.[114] Stationed at regular intervals in the hall, women supervisors (one supervisor for every ten to twelve operators) oversaw the smooth operation of the system, walking up and down the hall behind the operators, armed with clipboard and stopwatch, to check periodically on the number of calls operators put through, keep records of errors, and "grade" the women on their performance. Another group of supervisors randomly listened in on the operators, monitoring the quality of their calls. Operators found themselves under constant pressure to speed up the placement of calls since grades constituted the basis of promotion. Absences from one's post, even to go to the restroom, were frowned upon. An operator couldn't simply get up to leave; she had to raise her hand and wait for the supervisor to give her permission to vacate her post. Although the Administration had women work in shifts during the course of the day (from 7 o'clock to noon and from noon to seven, with another shift from seven to nine at night) and established rooms where women could lie down and relax periodically for fifteen minutes every two hours, managers attempted to extract as much effective labor as possible from the operator. Thus, women who worked a shift from seven to noon had to return in the evening to put in another two hours from seven to nine. Women who took sick leave were obliged to put in extra hours (known as a "return," *retour*), upon returning to work, or lost the rest period. As Jeanne Bouvier, labor organizer for the CGT in the 1930s, remarked in her study of operators, "[They lost] one franc a day during [an] absence and invariably [saw] their grades drop, thereby interfering with . . . possibilities for promotion."[115]

The regulation of the operator also extended from the workplace into the arena of private life. As Antonio Gramsci wrote of the Fordist regulation of sexuality in the modern twentieth-century firm, "It is worth drawing attention to the way in which industrialists . . . have been concerned with the sexual affairs of their employees and with their family arrangements in general. . . . The truth is that the new type of man demanded for the rationalization of production and war cannot be developed until the sexual instinct has been suitably regulated and until it has been rationalized."[116] The marriage, housing, and leisure of these state employees all fell within the purview of the Postal Administration. Despite the absence of the marriage bar, women who wished to marry had to make a formal request by furnishing the Administration with information about the person whom they intended to marry.[117] This requirement remained in effect through the 1930s and was based on the principle of incompatibility of certain public services (operators couldn't obtain authorization to marry policemen or mayors or assistant mayors, for example). The Administration also closely scrutinized operators' marriages to foreigners. Finally, to house the large numbers of young employees who came to Paris from the provinces, the Administration built dormitories, complete with "company" restaurants, such as the Maison des Dames on the rue de Lille, just behind the former Gare d'Orsay (now the Musée d'Orsay). This dormitory regulated the operator's off-work hours and by means of a restaurant it provided some control over operators' health. In addition, the Administration provided artistic, musical, and sports clubs designed "to combine grace with dexterity," in an attempt to fill the leisure time of the young worker with rational, self-improving activities.[118]

Although the operator's work seemed to be a model of regulation and control of the human motor, work in the telephone exchange constantly undermined that model and the very physical aptitudes that scientists and employers believed made women especially well suited for the job also made them vulnerable to a range of neurological and psychological problems. Doctors coined the term *névrose de la téléphoniste* (the operator's neurosis), a general diagnosis for the nervous exhaustion and multiple auditory and psychological problems that operators experienced. Women sought medical help for electric shocks, acute ringing in the ears, or facial neuralgia brought on by defective headsets; some presented symptoms of depression, irritability, and personality disturbances verging on hysteria. One doctor reported, "The suggestion that the patient return to work is met with cries, sobs, and convulsions." He observed that "women are naturally more exposed to this illness [*la névrose de la téléphoniste*] than men."[119] But he added that what most disturbed the "fragile brains of the Parisienne" were defective headsets and overwork. All the frustration of customers fell upon the operator. His solution was to perfect the headsets and recruit only young women with perfect hearing and healthy nervous systems.[120] Other doctors also noted nervousness and headaches, stomachaches, insomnia, and back pain, all of which contributed to this professional illness, "nervous fatigue." The very qualities of the body that made women desirable operators—their "nerves"— threatened to destabilize what otherwise appeared to be a highly rational system.[121] As repetitive work ate away at young women's health, vocational guidance experts were busy developing methods of recruitment and selection to steer young men and women to occupations for which they were deemed fit, in an effort to avoid problems such as nervous fatigue and work accidents.

Vocational Guidance and Gender

Scientists' measurements of professional aptitude and their administration of aptitude tests underpinned the new field of vocational guidance, which emerged with particular force in the interwar years and constituted another level of rationalization and labor classification.[122] Vocational guidance brought together both the rationalizing impulse of Taylorism and the belief that working bodies displayed specific characteristics that were scientifically measurable and could be used to predict job performance. A voluminous literature on *orientation professionnelle* (professional orientation or vocational guidance) detailed the measurements of muscular force, fatigue, memory, moral and physical aptitudes; other works directed specifically at women dealt with appropriate feminine careers.[123] Vocational guidance experts appeared to agree that job skills were somehow innate—a question of physiology and aptitude—rather than learned.[124] As Mary Louise Roberts has argued, the development of vocational guidance must be seen as part of the broad context of modernization, rationalization, and technocracy that permeated French society in the decade after the war and that gave rise to groups such as Ernest Mercier's and Lucien Romier's organization Redressement français.[125] Some greeted vocation guidance with the same optimism as rationalization and ergonomics at the end of World War I. Mlle Thompson, a factory superintendent interviewed by Léon Abensour in 1919, believed that better selection would remove the difference between male and female jobs. Each individual would be able to "freely choose the trades to which their tastes and aptitudes incline them without making artificial distinctions between male and female trades."[126] Yet, as with much of French elementary education and technical training, cultural perceptions of gender difference profoundly marked the practice of guiding young French men and women to "appropriate" careers. Roberts has viewed vocational guidance in the context of efforts to deal with the "problem" of the working woman in postwar France. Yet vocational guidance experts did not only promote "feminine" careers for women and mark the boundaries of gender difference in the labor market; they also participated in reinforcing and reproducing ideas about workers' masculinity. Given how science incorporated social assumptions about gender difference present in French society at large, unsurprisingly, vocational guidance reproduced many of the same ideas about gender-based aptitudes and abilities. In this sense, it reinforced other forms of rationalization. At the same time, vocational guidance experts recognized and accepted the inevitability of women's labor-force participation; their goal was to *regulate,* not to *destabilize* gender boundaries.

At the very end of the war, as vocational guidance experts dealt with the compelling need to restore productivity in a period of labor shortage, L. Dugé de Bernonville chronicled the major findings of research on the physiology of work and suggested how they could be used in vocational guidance. He argued for adopting the models of vocational guidance already used in the United States, Britain, and Germany.[127] In 1919 Jules Amar developed a method for the analysis of professional aptitudes and urged that individual employers set up a physiological testing service (*service physiologique du travail*) in their firms to measure workers' physical, psychological, and professional aptitudes.[128] But as Roberts observes, Julien Fontègne and Fernand and Louise Mauzevin made the truly critical interventions in the field by classifying the aptitudes required for literally hundreds of occupations so that once a young man or woman was tested he or she could be matched to the appropriate job.[129] Gender difference was fundamental to their classification systems. Fontègne, writing in 1921, believed that vocational guidance could help to create the future citizen-workers that France needed and asserted that in a democratic society such as France the doors to "higher positions" (*des fonctions supérieurs*) had to be open to individuals of all social classes.[130] At the same time, within social classes, men and women constituted separate categories whose differences were irreconcilable, even in a republican, democratic society. Fontègne implied that women had only recently entered the labor force and suggested that young men simply needed to be pointed to the right school; women, however, as "newcomers to modern economic life, will be employed at jobs that best respond to [their] special aptitudes."[131] He implied that finding women's appropriate vocational orientation was a more complex process: "It will require the study of the different physical, physiological, and psychological differences between the sexes, economic and social considerations of the role of women in modern life, and a methodical classification of every sort of work that is appropriate to her."[132] Fernand Mauzevin's *Rose des métiers* (1922) also illustrated how vocational guidance incorporated and normalized gender difference. This compendium listed some 250 occupations as diverse as typographers, bakers, barrel makers, mechanics, woodworkers, electricians, and conductors. Mauzevin classified the majority as male jobs; a separate section of his classificatory schema listed twenty-one "trades specific to women," including embroiderer, lace maker, stocking weaver, chamber maid, seamstress, and lingerie maker. The elaboration of a separate category of "women's trades" underscored the embeddedness of the gender division of labor in the French economy but also contributed to naturalizing it.

Mauzevin's important intervention, however, was not only to refine the schema according to which jobs were classified but to elaborate the physical and psychological characteristics of male and female bodies that were required for the job. For example, a specifically "female trade" such as millinery required that a woman be of at least average height, with good vision and hearing, that her hands not perspire or have chilblains. Mauzevin's notes recommended that she have a "chic and agreeable physique." She had to have a good sense of observation, a quick eye, good manual dexterity, and a good sense of form and color, good manners, and good grades in school. A milliner could begin her two-year apprenticeship at the age of thirteen or fourteen.[133] To enter a "male trade" as a lathe operator, however, required a very different set of physical characteristics and aptitudes. A young man had to be of at least average height and strength, with good health and vision, and free of varicose veins. Physical appearance was of no consequence. He had to be capable of concentrated attention and prudence and display a strong sense of observation and a good eye. Good manual dexterity and arm movement were also essential, as was a sense of order and care. Mauzevin recommended that for this job a young man should have one year of school beyond the *certificat d'études,* the diploma of those who did not take the *baccalauréat.* He needed good grades in mathematics, geometry, and linear design and could begin a three-year apprenticeship at the age of thirteen or, after an extra year of schooling, at fifteen—an expectation of educational attainment that appeared more often for men than for women.[134]

In addition to spelling out the specific characteristics, all job listings in the *Rose des métiers* were annotated with an aphorism or a supplementary bit of wisdom from the author that clearly communicated the gender expectations of working women and men. Aphorisms for trades identified as exclusively female included statements such as "La femme est l'âme et l'ornement du foyer" (Woman is the soul and ornament of the home); "Dans un ménage le mari doit être le moteur, la femme le régulateur" (In a household the husband is the motor; the wife is the regulator); and "Dans la plupart de ménages où la femme travaille au dehors, on tient compte de l'argent qu'elle gagne, mais on néglige celui qui se perd par suite de son absence du foyer" (In most of the households where women work outside the home, one takes into account the money she earns, but neglects what she loses by virtue of her absence from home).[135] Similar comments on the relationship between work and family were absent from the descriptions of men's jobs, where the notations focused much more on the virtues of hard work and working-class morality. Among the typical models of advice for men were "Travail et sobriété sont les deux piliers de la santé" (Work and sobriety are the two pillars of health) and "Aide ton patron à gagner davantage et il pourra te payer plus largement" (Help your employer to earn more and he'll be able to pay you more) or "Apprenez votre métier à fond, la pratique à l'atelier, la technique dans les cours, en suivant ceux qui ont des rapports étroits avec votre métier" (Learn your trade well: practice in the workshop the techniques in your courses, by following those who are directly related to your trade).[136]

Yet gender differences were not irrevocably set in stone. Mauzevin listed another 104 industrial, agricultural, and service-sector jobs as accessible to women, including jobs in metalworking, textiles, and the chemical industry. Moreover, important areas of ambiguity suggested that Mauzevin did not always neatly match gender characteristics with jobs. The jobs that he listed as "accessible to women" included engraving, an "industrial art." The trade involved engraving designs on glass or on gold jewelry and required "aware-ness of details and precision." It didn't require any special strength and the physical characteristics required for the job were limited to good vision. Sweaty hands could be a problem but were not disqualifying. The engraver had to have tenacity, perseverance, and be capable of sustained attention to the task (all characteristics that observers praised in women's industrial repetition work). He or she needed a good eye, good memory for shapes, and artistic inclinations. Good grades in linear design and ornamental de-sign classes were indispensable. All were characteristics required for women in other jobs, but although women could become engravers, Mauzevin noted that they were "not very welcome" (*peu acceuillie*) in the trade.[137] Here was a case in which social relations trumped science. In the case of soldering, the ambiguities were even more striking. Women were not only admitted to the trade but it was listed among those "specifically female trades." The male solderer should be of average height and strength, have good vision, and a good deal of sang-froid. He needed attention to the task, perseverance, pru-dence, and a sure eye, along with plenty of manual dexterity. In addition to order, care, and method, he should have good grades in mathematics, geom-etry, and linear design courses.[138] Women need not be of any particular height or strength; but they should not have sweaty hands or varicose veins. They needed agility and dexterity, but Mauzevin did not list good grades in mathematics, geometry, or linear design as qualifications.[139] Thus alongside the effort to create clear, scientifically based vocational categories, areas of gray illustrated the arbitrariness underlying a supposedly stable system of gender-based occupations.

As the effects of the 1930s Depression touched the French economy, voca-tional guidance experts further refined the masculine and feminine charac-teristics that would facilitate matching individuals to jobs. Efforts to guide women into "feminine" occupations intensified in the context of growing unemployment in France. Works like the *Guide général pour la jeunesse carus: Renseignements complets sur toutes les études, toutes les écoles ainsi que toutes les carrières et la façon d'y préparer* (1930) acknowledged the possibility that women had careers but listed "feminine careers" as an entirely separate category. This list, much more extensive than Mauzevin's, included positions such as administrative school inspectors in elementary schools and "*écoles maternelles*" (a position women had held since the nineteenth century), public assistance nurses, midwives, factory superintendents, clerks, secre-taries, and elementary school teachers (in girls' schools). Nonetheless, as Linda Clark's extensive examination of women labor inspectors has shown, despite women's ability to penetrate the ranks of labor and school inspectors, well into the twentieth century their ability to obtain positions of authority in these professions remained quite limited, despite the fact that job requirements were the same as those for men. And in the legal profession, where women had begun to make inroads, gender was never absent from the designation of appropriate feminine domains. As the *Guide* pointed out, women could now find their place in law following the creation of special juvenile courts, assuming women's inevitable association with children.[140]

The French state supported these efforts to mark out the gender boundaries of jobs. In the same year that Mauzevin published his taxonomy of occupational orientation (1922), convinced that vocational guidance would speed postwar economic recovery, the French government established vocational guidance offices under the Ministry of Public Education, designed to work in conjunction with schools.[141] In 1930, Edouard Mouvet, "psychotechnician" and assistant to the Inspection générale de l'enseignement industriel du Hainaut pour l'étude de l'orientation professionnelle (the General Inspection for Industrial Teaching in Hainaut for the Study of Vocational Guidance), produced his own taxonomy of 220 "professional monographs" with instructions on how to use them.[142] His descriptions of the aptitudes required of the male and female decorators in the pottery industry also illustrate how entrenched ideas of gender difference persisted in tandem with claims to science. They include identical physical and mental characteristics for men and women: "*tolérance et motilité*" of the limbs, strong capacities of observation, auditory and visual acuity, care, method, rudimentary primary school education, and an apprenticeship of one week. Yet the guide required women to display "the capacity for monotonous work," which was not required of male employees.[143] Men were not required to be of particularly robust constitution for this work, although Mouvet noted that they were often asked to carry heavy objects in this trade and suggested that employers inquire if an employee would be able to do so. If women, on the other hand, were expected to have a "sense of method" and "exercise care," men were supposed to be endowed with a sense of order, probity, and *taste*. Almost three-quarters of a century after Jules Simon's proclamation, Mouvet implied that men held a monopoly on "taste," demonstrating how vocational guidance experts could easily abandon "science" in favor of "nature" as a criterion for jobs. Suzanne Cordelier's *Femmes au travail: étude pratique sur 17 carrières féminines* (1935) likewise overtly relied on "la nature féminine" to direct her readers to specifically women's jobs in social work, nursing, and secretarial employment. Social work, she argued, was ideal for women because it relied on "finesse, forthrightness, a sense of nuance, and the psychological sensitivity that one immediately recognizes in women. The delicate role of conciliator and soother that women have displayed in family life . . . is now in demand more than ever given how social life has become more complex and difficult."[144] One could hardly find a more forthright statement of the alleged gender characteristics that matched women to specific jobs. Indeed, Cordelier's study demonstrated yet again the limits of science's influence in the vocational guidance movement.

Foreign and colonial workers, although they figured in scientists' experiments, did not appear in vocational guidance manuals; colonial bodies, whose capacities had already been established by industrial physiologists and naturalized even more than French female bodies, did not require special testing or characteristics to perform the menial, laborious tasks to which the majority were assigned as common industrial laborers, agricultural workers, or domestic servants. On the contrary, the effort of vocational guidance experts such as Julien Fontègne to promote vocational guidance in the formation of democratic republican elites de facto excluded immigrants from its orbit. As Fontègne's colleague E. Claparède suggested, vocational guidance could help in the formation of a new citizen-worker; "democracy, more than any other form of political organization, [needed] an élite" as an "antidote to mediocrity."[145] The claim to advance democracy implicit in the vocational guidance project underscored the idealism with which rationalization experts and particularly industrial physiologists approached the project of managing the human motor and selecting the right workers for the job, but it was not an idealism that extended to integrating foreigners into the Republic.

The optimistic belief in science's capacity to regulate and manage the body at work, while creating a new citizen-worker, inspired employers' efforts to rationalize both industry and the service sector between the wars. At the same time, science offered new legitimacy to what had already been defined as the "natural" characteristics of bodies and offered a new rationale for gender and racial divisions of labor. It justified employers' strategy of placing workers bearing different physical and social characteristics into distinct types of jobs. Refining gender divisions at work had implications for women's position in society more broadly in the context of state and employer supports for families in the emerging French welfare state, for relegating women to less remunerative "women's" industrial jobs made women secondary breadwinners, just as it did foreign and colonial workers. Women in the public-service sector arguably fared better than their industrial counterparts. Armed with education and a skill in high demand, they enjoyed higher status and better pay. *Rédactrices* won equal pay with men in the early 1920s and by the end of the decade *dames employées* won equal pay scales with male *agents*. Yet the gender discourses that informed industrial physiology and vocational guidance also helped to reproduce age-old practices of treating women as a secondary category of worker and denying women full economic citizenship. Although they acknowledged women's place in the labor market, by promoting gender and racial divisions at work French physiologists, scientists, and employers indirectly (and sometimes directly) supported a male breadwinner ideal. Organized labor reproduced this ambivalence about the gender of breadwinners so fundamental to French welfare policy in the 1920s and 1930s as it criticized the effects of rationalization and likewise lent support to men's status as breadwinners, while giving lip service to women's economic citizenship.

CHAPTER FOUR

ORGANIZED LABOR, RATIONALIZATION,

AND BREADWINNERS

Organized labor's reaction to rationalization during the 1920s and 1930s illustrated its profound ambivalence about questions of economic citizenship for women. The "scientific organization of labor," or OST (*organisation scientifique du travail*), a term that for French workers encapsulated scientific management, industrial physiology, and initiatives such as aptitude testing, provoked enormous debate and controversy in labor confederations and unions but elicited no massive resistance from French workers. The leadership of the major labor confederations supported labor rationalization as potentially beneficial, but even if it had not, organized labor was too divided and weak in these years to resist effectively new technologies and management methods. At the same time, even if rank and file workers did not all experience rationalization in the same fashion, it is far from clear that they saw these new ways of managing labor in the same positive light that many labor leaders did. Workers protested against employers' failure to respect the eight-hour day, assembly line speedups, overwork and fatigue, and low wages, all the inevitable consequences of the reorganization of labor in a setting of postwar inflation and employers' efforts to restore prewar levels of production. What is of interest here is how rationalization served as a target of worker anxiety about the shifting gender and racial boundaries of labor in the 1920s and 1930s and led to a double discourse on gender and work. Although male workers rhetorically defended the rights of women and foreigners to work and protested against the exploitation of both, their simultaneous defense of a male breadwinner norm dominated organized labor's reaction to rationalization. Labor's discussions and debates along with employers' efforts to streamline the labor process took place in a period of economic instability marked by rampant inflation.

As Alfred Sauvy's classic work on the interwar economy showed, France's economic health fluctuated wildly throughout the 1920s, with inflation reaching 44 percent between 1919 and 1920. With the occupation of the Rhur and the monetary crisis of 1923, prices soared by close to 30 percent between 1925 and 1926.[1] According to one estimate, by 1924 the price of a beef filet had increased four and a half times per kilo since 1914; the price of mutton chops increased by five times. A kilo of coffee that cost 4 francs 40 in 1914 cost 19 francs 80 in 1924, and the cost of a kilo of potatoes had almost quadrupled.[2] Although wages also rose significantly during the period, working people experienced significant disparities between wages and living costs. These changes constituted one set of concerns for working people and for organized labor in the 1920s and 1930s. Employer strategies of transforming the labor process constituted another set of issues that organized labor confronted. This chapter examines organized labor's response to postwar job fragmentation, rationalization, and the science of the working body. It argues that organized labor's concerns about family and gender mirrored employers' and the state's efforts to promote family and population growth and privilege fathers' rights in families. Workers' responses to rationalization and scientific management contributed to the discursive framework and practices that sustained the privileged position of the male breadwinner between the wars. If organized labor's opposition to women's "invasion" of the male workplace softened in the early 1920s, that opposition reemerged as French male workers experienced rationalization as a threat to their monopoly of skilled jobs and high wages.

On the one hand, many male labor activists seemed to have accepted the inevitability of women on the shop floor and expressed concern about the consequences of mechanization and speedups on women's health and fatigue. The absence of apprenticeships for women and women's relegation to on-the-job-training, the reinforcement of gender and racial divisions, and the creation of new forms of gender segmentation accompanying wage stratification may have calmed men's fears of competition. Working at different jobs, French men and women and foreign men were increasingly segregated not only in the labor market overall but within factories and offices. Even colonial workers, from whom French male workers might have had more to fear, *in theory* posed less of a threat because of their tendency to find jobs at the very bottom of the employment ladder and at the lowest wages. But because employers *did* pay them less than French men, they continued to be a source of concern. Metalworkers and others persisted in their belief in the male breadwinner norm as an ideal of working-class life. Although it is doubtful that organized labor had enough leverage to shape decisively the question of the male breadwinner, workers' discussions contributed to the larger climate of ambivalence surrounding women's economic citizenship that underscored employers' and policymakers' visions of society.

Gender and the Meanings of Rationalization

In principle, the two major wings of the French labor movement, the CGT and the CGTU, supported rationalization as a potentially progressive force for workers but differed on the details of who would control technological innovation and toward what ends. The leadership of the CGTU promoted the positive potential of "socialist rationalization" as an antidote to the new management techniques and methods of calculating wages that characterized the French economy of the 1920s. CGTU leaders relentlessly criticized employers for using rationalization to exploit workers and attacked the CGT for collaborating with employers and the government on the National Economic Council. In contrast, resuming its campaign in favor of rationalization from the prewar years, the CGT officially promoted a utopian vision of scientific management that could benefit workers by simplifying work, reducing fatigue, providing higher wages, increasing workers' buying power, and providing full employment.[3] The goal of improving living standards also fit with their view of rationalization as the best defense of the eight-hour day. Within the CGT strong advocates of rationalization emerged such as Hyacinthe Dubreuil, metalworker and head of the CGT in the Seine department, who became an idealistic defender of the ability of "American methods" to improve the lives and living standards of French workers.[4] As Gary Cross has argued, in collective bargaining agreements the CGT metalworking, clothing, and construction federations all agreed to step up production in return for employers' agreement to respect the eight-hour law passed in 1919.[5] Rank and file workers, however, were far less convinced of the benefits of scientific management than labor leaders' pronouncements would lead one to believe.

Before World War I some employers' attempts to rationalize production had elicited immediate opposition from workers, as in 1912–13, when Berliet and Renault automobile workers staged massive strikes to protest management's implementation of time and motion studies (*chronométrage*).[6] During 1922–25, and again in 1927, metalworkers in the mechanical construction industry and automobile manufacture struck against time-measurement personnel (*chronométreurs*) who were brought in from outside the firm to conduct such studies. As in the prewar strikes, workers protested that the *chronométreurs* did not allow enough time for the completion of tasks and skilled workers argued that individuals from outside the factory did not have sufficient knowledge of the work.[7] But as Aimée Moutet notes, workers "not only defended their pay, but also their professional knowledge. They could not accept taking orders from men who had no knowledge of their trade."[8] This was more or less the case at Citroën, where strikes in 1924 and 1927 against *chronométrage* attacked Citroën's attempts to reorganize production and payment methods in order to increase output in an inflationary period when employers resisted wage increases.

Although *chronométrage* affected both male and female workers, it did so asymmetrically. Whereas skilled male workers successfully demanded that they be consulted, that the *chronométreur* be knowledgeable about skilled work and come from within the factory, women's status as unskilled assembly line workers deprived them of leverage to win promises of consultation from employers. Even the language that journalists used to describe the strikes reflected the gender biases that kept women in an inferior position within the power relations of the shop floor. A strike in February 1924 occurred following the installation of new assembly lines in two workshops and a projected wage reduction that Citroën hoped would be compensated by increased productivity. "*Workers* [in these workshops]," wrote one observer, "are paid by the piece, and can make as much as 45 francs a day; *women,* on the other hand, are employed mostly in the paint shops and earn around 350 francs every two weeks."[9] This observer's language suggested how sexual difference governed the perception of who would be named as a worker: men could be workers, but women were women. As employers looked to new methods to cut costs following the brief depression that accompanied the revaluation of the franc in 1926–27, organized labor stepped up its resistance to rationalization. Another strike in December 1927 illustrated how female *manoeuvres spécialisées,* unskilled assembly line workers, resisted successfully Citroën's decision to step up mass production of lower-priced cars and reduce labor costs in the midst of monetary stabilization and partial unemployment in the metalworking industries of the Paris region.[10] In this case, workers refused to accept a speedup and new payment system. Citroën had introduced a new system of team wages calculated for two teams on rotating shifts (ensuring that no time would be lost with the shift change), and performed new time and output studies that forced workers to speed up production. The systems of payment changed so often with each new study that workers never knew exactly how much they earned until payday. Women actually found their wages to be less than what they earned previously.[11] The CGT Metalworkers' Federation protested that according to the system of team wages, work was no longer an individual matter but a collective effort and argued that the speedup didn't allow enough time to complete orders. To resolve the strike, Citroën agreed to increase women's piece rate and modify the team payment system for those who agreed to return to work, so that he could meet his goal of stepping up automobile production. In this case workers' successful resistance owed much to Citroën's overriding objective of increasing output. Eventually both women and men accepted the inevitability of time and motion studies, lured by employers' promises of productivity bonuses. At the same time, workers repeatedly attacked employers' use of scientific methods in ways that revealed the multiple meanings of rationalization.[12]

Organized workers in the metalworking and textile trades repeatedly protested the repetitious and fragmented work that resulted from the application of "scientific methods." Some used the term "rationalization" as a code-word for speedups and low piecework wages that forced workers to accelerate their work pace. In the textile industry, for example, "rationalization" meant mechanization, as well as speedups in combing (*peignage*) and the addition of extensions to machines so that they could handle more fabric, without increasing the number of women who supervised the machines. Likewise, the dangerous practice of requiring that workers clean carding machines while they were running in order to minimize slack time came under attack as a form of "rationalization."[13] In metalworking, the term meant the breakdown of the labor process, the organization of production on assembly lines, and the complex methods of wage calculation that were designed to push the limits of production. It is undoubtedly true that relatively few employers adopted rationalization wholesale: the implementation of assembly line production, psychotechnical testing, the standardization of manufacturing norms, and aggressive measurement of work time and output that characterized the large automobile manufacturers was more the exception than the rule. Yet "rationalization" occupied an important symbolic place in the minds of workers. The term became invested with all that workers hated about the modern workplace, which Charles Chaplin satirized so effectively in his classic film *Modern Times*. At the same time, labor leaders' perception of the encroachment of the scientific organization of work put the question of the gender division of skill on organized labor's agenda in two ways. First, workers criticized rationalization as a problem for the family and as both an opportunity and a problem for women; second, they criticized rationalization as an attack on male work identities. Embedded in both critiques was a defense of the male breadwinner.

Gender, the Family, and Male Worker Identities

Workers' critiques called attention to the effects of rationalization on family life, and they argued for special treatment of women and youths. In the highly mechanized textile industry, "rationalization" meant not thoroughgoing reorganization of factories according to the principles of scientific management but mechanization, increasing the number of looms workers supervised, and employing women and youths on rotating shift work. These practices allowed textile factories to run continuously and increase output and not surprisingly elicited the most vehement protests from workers as attacks on the humanity of the worker and the quality of family life. At the 1928 Textile Federation National Congress (CGTU), in the context of calling for respect of the eight-hour day and forty-four-hour week, workers called for the abolition of rotating shifts, declaring that they were "harmful to workers' health and to the life of the family . . . because family members often work in several different teams, and have to get up very early in the morning and go to sleep very late at night."[14] Under these conditions, in which entire families worked in the mills, family members barely saw each other during the week. Revealing their vision of the organization of the household in relation to gender and wage work, they protested that "double shifts make it impossible for women to prepare even one of two family meals."[15] Textile workers demanded that although in principle teamwork should be outlawed wherever it was used, workers should not have to work for more than seven hours a day. Moreover, they demanded that women and children (adolescents over thirteen) be forbidden from working earlier than six o'clock in the morning and later than seven o'clock at night and ideally should be prevented from performing shift work. But textile workers also expressed ambivalence about the *idea* of rationalization; they approved of technological and scientific progress "on the condition that it profit the collectivity and that it occur within the framework of the eight-hour day" and would make it possible for workers to consume more. Moreover, they condemned "capitalist rationalization . . . whose goal was the organization of production on the assembly line and which would put more pressure on all workers."[16]

Men charged that rationalization led to wage cuts and protested against the decline of technical training and apprenticeships. Metalworkers feared that the application of scientific management would lead to unemployment, and one activist cited the example of a German chemical manufacturer who succeeded in increasing production by 200 percent by the application of scientific management, and at the same time reduced his labor force by a third.[17] The communist-led Federation of Metalworkers attacked both the problem of overwork and unemployment and charged that men had become veritable machines, devoid of the creativity, initiative, and control once a part of the work identity of skilled workingmen.[18] Male activists at the first congress of the CGTU-affiliated Federation of Metalworkers in 1922 criticized the deskilling and dehumanizing aspects of scientific management and defended men's property in skill as the foundation of their work identity. As labor activist Chevalier stated, "[We] cannot be satisfied as workers who are always asking something of the employer. We must be conscious of our professional value and of our social value as producers. We believe that as metalworkers who love our trade that we have every interest in being good professionals. [Moreover] employers need [good professionals] because they have real abilities, and they hesitate to let them go."[19]

In the process of resisting job deskilling, metalworkers stressed the development of professional aptitudes and skills that would make them indispensable to employers. Delegates to the 1922 CGTU Metalworkers' congress agreed to create a technical review, "[for] . . . work is the basis of everything and should be accomplished with taste; consequently we must develop our professional aptitudes as much as possible. We must also consider the future role of the modern production chief and understand that if we want to control production, we have to know perfectly all its mechanisms." The proposed review would be devoted to technical education, particularly the study of the mechanisms of everyday machines, as well as common economic concepts and studies of the functioning of factories.[20] Metalworkers' emphasis on the importance of skill and professional competence accompanied the new emphasis on professional training embodied in the Astier Law. Taste and a sense of design and an ability to understand the functioning of complex machines were fundamental to male metalworkers' work identities. Indeed, some believed that the spread of vocational guidance and employers' selection were good reasons to reinforce apprenticeship. As Bouyer pointed out in the 1927 Metalworkers' Federation (CGT) congress, "Vocational guidance and professional selection require rational apprenticeship which not only consists in teaching the best method to execute work, but which calls upon film, design, and photography for purposes of demonstration."[21]

Organized labor also criticized the failure of apprenticeship programs to teach young men trade skills. Their critiques illustrated how concerns about training incorporated ideas about fatherhood and showed how adult men feared being displaced by untrained younger workers. Metalworkers implied that inadequate training for their sons was an insult to fatherhood and to the trade because employers failed to educate young men to be anything more than unskilled piece workers. Adolescents constituted an "inexperienced mass" in the hands of employers who facilitated the forward march of rationalization. "Young men who enter factories are extremely unskilled. They receive only a very weak apprenticeship; they are . . . for the most part unskilled laborers who, at 13, 14 or 15 years of age, often replace skilled workers, but of course, they earn much lower wages."[22] Fathers argued for serious technical training for their sons: "We are not simply machines."[23] Men's concerns about the dehumanizing and emasculating effects of rationalization also surfaced. As one delegate to the 1927 Metalworkers' Federation (CGT) congress put it, the assembly line threatened to "destroy the spiritual faculties of the worker." Another protested, "What we cannot accept, will not accept, is that the scientific organization of labor attacks the worker in his dignity as a man."[24] The perceived vulnerability of male workers' dignity in the face of scientific management indeed drew much stronger opposition to rationalization from rank and file activists than CGT leadership's pronouncements made visible. The Mechanics' Union of the Paris region's strongly worded anti-rationalization resolution recognized that the "intelligent principles of the [scientific] organization of labor were well founded" but declared that mechanics must energetically fight against the way employers applied it in the mechanical construction industry of the Paris region. "[In] order for the scientific organization of labor to be considered as progress for the working class . . . it must respect the human factor, that is to say the dignity of men and the right[s] . . . of the workers to whom it is applied."[25] The final resolution passed at this congress condemned "industrial reorganization as envisioned by employers" which led to the "intensification of human effort and to lowering workers' intellectual level." Industrial reorganization that was guided by the desire to improve production in order to increase consumption and worker's leisure, however, was acceptable. If workers had control of the labor process, rationalization would benefit everyone.[26] Male metalworkers continued to appeal for respect for the dignity of the workingman under rationalization through the 1930s. As one worker stated in 1933, "Mechanization has forced us to play a secondary, complementary role. [Our comrades] today feel that they are no longer indispensable." "Only a few years ago workers had a sense of their professional worth."[27] New machines had caused workers' intellectual level to decline because work no longer demanded thought or creativity.

An additional gender dimension of apprenticeship also emerged in workers' debates. Blanche Artère, leather worker and representative to the CGTU Women's Commission, protested against the absence of apprenticeships for women and confirmed the observations of factory superintendents about the lack of formal training for women. "When we start work at a factory, they immediately put us on a machine and that's it; they just leave us there for years." Untrained women, moreover, faced competition from untrained, unskilled youths.[28] And Madeleine Charpentier, speaking before the 1927 CGTU Women's Commission, noted with alarm how women furriers protested cutbacks in apprenticeship in the workshops of the fur manufacturer Révillon in the midst of the depression that followed the stabilization of the franc.[29] Indeed, the failure to train or train adequately certain categories of women underscored how employers cut costs while maintaining a reserve army of unskilled labor as the counterpart to more sophisticated methods of management. At the same time, alongside their efforts to retain control over apprenticeship and training, labor activists called for "equal wages for equal work" with respect not only to French women but to adolescents and immigrant labor as well.

Rationalization, Nationality, and Gender

Labor activists were perfectly aware of how employers manipulated gender and nationality in the process of rationalization, protested against the increasing employment of women, youths, "colonial workers, and foreigners" as specialized (unskilled) laborers, and criticized the practice of paying them less than French men.[30] As John Horne and others have shown, during World War I the deployment of colonial labor had already provoked resistance on the part of French male workers, who feared the elimination of skilled jobs.[31] In this sense it would be a mistake to exaggerate the extent to which labor stratification—in both industrial and service-sector employment—and the redefinition of jobs after the war alleviated men's anxieties about women and foreigners invading their terrain. Although many French male workers seem to have largely (if begrudgingly) accepted women's presence in the labor force and the "scientific organization of labor," evidence from labor congresses suggests considerable anxiety about competition from women, colonial, and foreign European workers. Unlike some social observers in the immediate postwar period, male labor activists did not see women as an alternative to foreign or colonial men but rather conflated them in discussions of how deskilling and the scientific organization of work created competition for French men.

Gender and racial or ethnic identities, although they were not always articulated explicitly, were clearly at stake in workers' assessments of the consequences of rationalization. In December 1924, at a CGTU-sponsored meeting for North African workers in the Paris region, labor organizers evoked the deplorable position of colonial workers regulated by the *code de l'indigénat*. This law code, under which the French government placed all colonial subjects, effectively deprived them of the freedom of association, speech, and the press that French citizens enjoyed, in addition to forbidding them from unionizing.[32] At the same time French workers criticized the fact that employers used colonial and foreign workers as a reserve army of labor to undercut French men's wages. A few months earlier, in the National Committee of the CGTU, Julien Racamond, the CGTU head of the section on foreign labor (Commission de la main d'oeuvre étrangère), called attention to the dangers foreigners posed to French male workers and demanded restrictions on immigration. With 450,000 immigrant workers in the Paris region alone, he argued, employers could and easily did use them to resist French workers' demands.[33] At the 1925 Congress of the Union des syndicats de la Seine, one delegate pointed to how employers hired women, foreigners, and youths to compete with French men and drive down their (French men's) wages.[34] In the same year, at the CGTU-affiliated Metalworkers' Federation congress, male delegates discussed how unskilled women and some men had begun to supplant skilled men. During the war, mechanization had contributed to this trend; after the war, the installation of "industrial laboratories in each industry which attempted to determine the shortest time necessary for industrial production" accentuated it. Among men, the unskilled assistant replaced the skilled worker and the unskilled immigrant replaced the Frenchman.[35] Workers further denounced employers' practice of hiring immigrant workers (at lower wages) during periods when French male workers were unemployed, implying that nationality conferred the right to employment.[36] Meeting in 1925, the CGT-affiliated Metalworkers' Federation went further and called for the formation of a national council on immigrant labor. Linking the employment of foreign workers to labor reorganization and the creation of more unskilled jobs, the activist Maurice Labé argued that the Federation wasn't opposed to the immigration of skilled workers but demanded that "only foreign labor that really responds to the needs of industry [should] be recruited."[37] Textile workers also voiced opposition to immigrants—ironic, since the mills of the Nord had historically relied on Belgian immigrant workers. In 1926 French textile workers protested against the employment of immigrants in the process of rationalizing the industry with speedups and multiple shifts. Occasionally activists appealed specifically to women's sense of injustice in portraying the miserable conditions in which foreigners worked. In the summer of 1926, for instance, in the context of the revaluation of the franc, Alice Jouenne reported in the pages of *Le Peuple* on the London congress on migration that had been sponsored by the Socialist International and the International Federation of Trade Unions. Jouenne's article appeared on a page devoted to "la femme et l'enfant," most of which was filled with fashion ideas and recipes ("rognons de mouton en brochette," in this instance). Visibly seeking to attract the female readers, she bemoaned the male immigrants who left behind their tearful wives and children to find work in foreign countries. At the same time, she argued that French workers had the right to defend themselves against "the ignorance and egotism of these newcomers who threaten to compromise [French workers'] position." Not only did immigrant workers live "diminished lives in filthy slums" but they were the cause of degrading conditions of all workers because they worked for so little and put up with such terrible working conditions.[38] Later, the activist Henri Cordier proposed closing French borders to immigrant workers.[39] We have seen that French male workers in the organized labor movement often invoked the rights of fathers as breadwinners in the process of demanding higher wages, just as social observers and legislators privileged men as both wage earners and fathers. But although French male workers defended their ability to provide for their families, they did not use this argument when referring to colonial or immigrant workers. Indeed, the latter's position at the bottom of the job and wage scales may have made them seem less manly than their French counterparts.[40]

Tension between French and immigrant workers grew in the context of the depression that followed the devaluation of the franc and partial unemployment in the metalworking and textile industries. In 1927, Marthe Désrumeaux, textile worker and labor activist from the Nord, criticized Belgian women who crossed the border from Belgium every day to work in the Lille-Roubaix-Tourcoing agglomeration. These *frontalières* were reluctant to join their French comrades in striking for wage increases because with a favorable exchange rate they actually made a little more than French women.[41] Indeed, during a lengthy strike in the Nord for a wage increase (the *grève des dix sous* of September 1928–April 1929), in a move hardly designed to win the sympathy of French workers, some Belgians reported to work as strikebreakers under the protection of French police.[42] Although delegates to the 1927 CGTU Metalworkers' Federation congress protested that the increasing use of foreign labor was a result of rationalization, the Federation promised to create a special foreign worker's office and ethnic sections in their unions and to publish newspapers in foreign languages.[43]

Colonial workers posed an even greater problem for organized labor, however. Official labor movement discourse about the unity of all workers fit awkwardly with rank and file workers' concerns about how employers might replace French men with foreign. Moreover, the restrictions of the *code de l'indigénat* made foreign workers especially vulnerable to employers. But the perception of competition from colonial workers was not confined to the *métropole*. A male Algerian delegate speaking to the 1927 CGTU Conférence nationale féminine called attention to how, in the colonies, international capitalism had created a reserve army of labor ready to compete with Europeans. "With rationalization and modernization of equipment, employers can easily create competition [between colonial labor and French] on the labor market."[44] However, within the CGTU the communists' policy of organizing immigrant workers shaped the dominant discourse on immigrants and short-circuited rank and file activists' talk of excluding them. Women's employment in the rationalized factory provoked a different kind of concern.

Labor activists pointed to how women experienced the "new methods of work" differently from men and challenged the ideal of the male breadwinner. In a long intervention on rationalization at the September 1927 Conférence nationale féminine of the CGTU, Alice Brisset, member of the executive commission of the Textile and Garment Workers' Federation, noted that one of the major effects of rationalization had been to displace men by hiring women at cheaper rates. At Citroën, "the division of labor is such that five women have replaced ten men on exactly the same job." Whereas the men were paid on piece rates, the women were paid by the day and earned three times less.[45] Brisset argued that although some men continued to support the male breadwinner ideal, postwar changes in the labor process had made it an outmoded concept. The "old middle class idea that the male worker should keep his wife and children at home; [the idea] *that he was the worker* [my emphasis] and should bring bread to his family," had been displaced. Scientific methods and economic necessity made women permanent members of the labor force, dependent for their livelihoods on a full-fledged wage.[46]

Taking the term "scientific methods" to refer to new technologies, she suggested that rationalization had actually opened job opportunities for women.

> We have arrived at the state where employers have been able to replace physical strength by technical progress. There is no longer a need, as in the old days, for as robust a labor force: the machine has replaced strength. . . . Earlier, there were no women in certain industrial categories; when one spoke of a foundry worker, he was represented as an athlete. . . . The electrification of . . . factories, the modernization of machines, and the assembly line have permitted the introduction of women's labor into all industrial branches.[47]

Brisset misread the effects of postwar rationalization on gender divisions of labor. But she saw clearly the liabilities of rationalization for workers' lives. She drew attention to the negative effects of repetitive assembly line work on women's health and called upon women's labor organizations to examine "how overwork . . . produces nervous diseases and anemia, and to look at how rationalization . . . puts the physical health of mothers in danger."[48] This was even more important given that more and more women workers now combined industrial work with housework and care work; "they have kept all the responsibilities and problems of family life; they are the ones who still do the washing, who prepare the soup, who take care of the kids and the household, and aging parents." They were affected much more than men, not only in their wages and working conditions but in their "social conditions."[49] Brisset's colleague Germaine Goujon of the CGTU Textile Workers' Federation agreed. "[W]e need to . . . attenuate the effects of rationalization on the mass of women workers. In textiles for example, we should demand that a worker supervises only seven or eight machines instead of 17; or two automatic looms instead of four . . . since we know that over production leads to unemployment and under-consumption, we should demand a six-hour day."[50] Both agreed that if deskilling and task fragmentation had opened more jobs to women, these processes had also allowed employers to use women to compete with men for unskilled jobs. The same observation found an echo in the CGT Textile Federation congress of 1928, where activists charged that employers had "industrialized [women], with the aim of creating competition between male and female workers."[51] If labor activists believed that Taylorist rationalization had failed to pay sufficient attention to the human factor and had failed to render work easier, did industrial physiology do better?

Workers followed closely industrial physiologists' logic in their own critiques of Taylorism. Employers, they charged, had turned workers into automatons and now saw "in the worker a human motor rather than a man—a man who senses; a man who thinks."[52] At the same time that scientists attempted to measure the capacities of the human motor, labor activists complained that modern science and "progress" had led to overwork rather than liberating the worker from fatigue. In addition to condemning rotating shift work, textile workers attacked the practice of supervising multiple looms on the grounds of its physical effects on the human motor. Employers' requirement that workers increase the number of looms they supervised made the task of the textile worker even more exhausting and physically taxing, given the number of physical movements a worker had to execute within the space of a normal workday. According to a Belgian physician who measured the motions required to supervise two looms, a worker would execute 2,000 half turns with as many circular movements of the head, and 20,000–25,000 visual adjustments. These coordinated motions easily led to dizziness; "the worker himself has become a machine."[53] Maurice Labé of the CGT Metalworkers' Federation likewise charged that science had resulted in increasing human effort, not liberating workers from effort: "Not content to lengthen the working day and lower wages, [employers] wish to introduce methods that will . . . increase in workers' physical effort, leading to . . . overwork."[54] Others believed that in sophisticated automobile plants like those of Citroën or Renault, where employers used psychometric or psychophysiological testing, scientific selection of workers could be a way to elicit workers' collaboration in production. And collaboration should include workers' participation in profits through stockholding and representation on factory administrative boards and collaboration in improving production—in short, another way to integrate the worker into the firm and elicit consent.[55] Although Joseph Couergou, CGTU metalworking activist, criticized the scientific organization of labor, other male workers in the CGTU argued that workers' control could avoid the worst abuses of rationalization and its assault on masculine work identities.[56]

Often organized workers criticized how scientific management and industrial physiology reduced the male body to its simplest physical attributes. A speaker at the 1927 Metalworker's Federation congress gave the famous example of Taylor's description of selecting men for the job of loading pig iron from *The Principles of Scientific Management*. Taylor observed eight men and selected one who was able to load forty-seven and a half tons of pig iron in one day. This "beast of burden," a strong, muscular Dutch man, willing to overexert himself in return for Taylor's promise of a high wage, constituted Taylor's ideal unskilled male worker, valued for his strength and ability to move pig iron rapidly and continuously with a minimum of fatigue. The other men, underdeveloped ninety-eight-pound weaklings, could load a mere twelve and a half tons per day. Taylor rejected them out of hand. Taylor's example, the delegate charged, was a clear case of "organized overwork."[57] Or, in the words of Couergou, the "reduction of work time by the reduction of existence ('la diminution du temps du travail par la reduction de l'existence')."[58] Taylor's description was an example of how scientific management and industrial physiology together enforced a set of physical and gender-based meanings of competence; employers viewed immigrant male workers as "beasts of burden" at least as often as "maids of all work."

Yet organized labor was divided over the merits of industrial physiology. Whereas industrial workers condemned the new forms of overwork, service-sector workers, if not always sympathetic to scientific management, saw some promise in its complementary technologies of organizing and selecting workers. Women telephone operators' delegates to the 1922 congress of the National Postal Workers' Union (the Syndicat national des Agents des PTT [CGT]) favored work scientists' and doctors' recommendations for aptitude testing. Calling attention to the physical effort, the weight of the operator's headset, mental exhaustion, and the large number of sick leaves operators took, they proposed more careful screening of the body—a more serious medical examination that "would focus on the overall physical constitution [of the candidate] and included a scrupulous auscultation and examination of the respiratory passages . . . [to determine] the physical aptitudes for the work."[59] Some delegates' claim that "[organizing] our working conditions in the most scientific and rational way" would allow workers to obtain "superior productivity with less effort" echoed other delegates' insistence that good selection would permit employers to find the right person for the right job and ultimately benefit all workers.[60] Employees accepted the notion of the postal service as a "highly rationalized machine" whose "social body" assured its smooth operation. But the "social body" of the service was only as good as the methods of selection that governed workers' recruitment. "It is not sufficient to distribute jobs to men," they argued, "it is necessary to know how to assign the organism to the needs of the service; how to find the right men and put each one in his place where he can render the best service."[61] For both men and women, selection required not only testing the aptitudes of future employees but also inquiring into their family honor, their background, and the moral conduct of the candidate. All candidates had to undergo a "serious medical examination."[62] Men who occupied positions of authority should be required to meet an especially long list of qualifications. They should be required to display "good health, hygiene, and physical vigor; intelligence and intellectual vigor, understanding, good judgment, ability to rapidly absorb knowledge of different subjects, breadth of vision and flexibility of spirit; moral qualities: energy, firmness, honesty, initiative, decisiveness, sense of duty, and concern about the general interest," as well as knowledge of administration and ability to command and control.[63] Insisting on these qualifications, the congress delegates believed, was the surest way to maintain professional status.

When the postal workers' union national took up the issue of professional training for men and women in 1925, workers blamed the engineers of the PTT for problems with the telephone service and proposed using the research of Lahy, Fontègne, and Solari for guidance to end operators' overwork. This would allow the Administration to introduce "more humanity in the length of rotations, breaks, and regulation." Lashing out at the "Taylor system" as "devoid of any humanitarian concern," workers condemned Taylorism as "coming from the cold brain of an engineer who is only concerned with the output of human material" and asked that the PTT Administration establish a psychotechnical laboratory on the model of similar German laboratories to investigate scientifically the problem of operators' fatigue.[64] For postal employees, industrial science promised an antidote to the worst abuses of Taylorism. However, employers (and in this case, the state) tended to be more interested in organizing and disciplining the female body at work than addressing the problem of fatigue in more than a perfunctory manner. A detailed report published in 1958 on work and fatigue that focused on the operators' "neurosis" expressed astonishment at how little had changed since the findings of Fontègne and Solari early in the century on operators' nervous fatigue.[65] Yet the comparatively little attention the Administration gave to the problem in the interwar years was entirely consistent with the productivist, modernizing thrust of economic policies of that period. As Georges Ribeill and others have noted, industrial physiology was expensive and time-consuming; the rational organization of labor according to Taylor's principles appeared to give better returns for a smaller investment. Moreover, many employers, including the Postal Administration, already had firm ideas about women's abilities and allegedly natural aptitudes for the job and remained committed to the ideal of the male breadwinner.

Overall, rationalization did not lead to massive protests among public-sector employees any more than it did in private industrial work. What did lead workers to take to the streets, however, were good old-fashioned conflicts over hours and wages. Gender difference profoundly marked organized labor's approach to both of these contentious issues.

Femininity, Masculinity, and the "Quest for Time"

Struggles over the eight-hour day constituted one of the largest sources of labor conflict during the 1920s. As historians have shown, the April 1919 reform instituting the eight-hour day came as a top-down initiative designed to head off labor actions planned for May Day 1919.[66] It specified an eight-hour day or a forty-eight-hour week of "effective work" and permitted exceptions for manufacturers such as foundries whose factories operated around the clock. The law assumed an "English week" (the *semaine anglaise*) with a half-day of four hours on Saturday in exchange for reduced hours during the week, but employers often bargained with workers for four nine-hour days in order to make up for lost time. Thus, the employers in the textile industry of the Lille-Roubaix-Tourcoing agglomeration in the Nord signed an agreement with the unions in June 1919, stipulating a forty-eight-hour week with eight hours on Monday, nine on Tuesday through Friday, and four hours on Saturday. Workers agreed to maintain prewar levels of productivity by adapting to new forms of mechanization and to "rational methods of work" and to include "light cleaning" of machines within the normal workday. Heavy cleaning would be done outside the normal workday and would be paid overtime.[67] In addition, the eight-hour law specified that employers could require "permanent overtime" of skilled workers whose expertise employers deemed necessary to the operation of factories; special emergencies could also allow employers to require overtime. The law was intended to produce no reduction in wages. Taking account of temporary shutdowns to repair machinery and the like meant that in order to do "effective work" workers could actually put in a nine- to twelve-hour day. Consultative committees made up of representatives of labor and employers hammered out the agreements in each industry.[68] Despite giving lip service to the need for a shorter workday and superficial attention to the problem of fatigue, however, employers flagrantly violated the law and, even when no exceptions had been previously worked out, forced unskilled French and immigrant workers to put in longer hours to suit production demands. These practices violated the implicit (and sometimes explicit) agreements with labor according to which workers would accept higher rates of production in return for shorter hours. Yet, given how inflation had eaten away at wages and how employers "readjusted" women's wages in the process of postwar industrial restructuring, many workers willingly worked overtime. Here we are concerned not with labor conflicts over these issues but with the centrality of the relationship between work, family, and the "social body" to organized labor's discussions of the eight-hour day.

Prior to World War I, demands for the eight-hour day and the "English week" incorporated ideals of feminine and masculine roles both at work and in the family. Within the CGT, for example, activists called upon discourses of feminine domesticity, arguing that women should work only a half-day on Saturday in order to be able to take care of household chores. This would ensure that workers would be able to benefit from a restorative day of rest on Sunday.[69] For men, "Sunday rest was to provide [them] with the wholesome influence of family life."[70] As Gary Cross has pointed out, proponents of a shorter workweek believed that family life would keep men out of cafés and reduce alcoholism.[71] Discussions of the application of the eight-hour day in the 1920s followed this model of leisure and contributed to reproducing gender ideals associated with the balance of family and work as well. At a conference of industrialists in 1923, for instance, M. de la Plasse painted a dismal picture of the fate of women who did not benefit from the Saturday half-holiday. Housework piled up during the week and on Sunday they had to do the washing and mending and clean house. "The poor overworked housewife simply doesn't have the energy to take care of herself. She abandons all thought of dressing up and stays at home. Her husband, bored with this life, leaves and goes out drinking while the kids roam around. Sunday, which should be a day of rest, of God, of family, is nothing more than a day of exhaustion, boredom, and the bar."[72] This observation, ignoring women's "heroic efforts" during the war, incorporated rather well-entrenched ideas about the domestic division of labor, but most employers cared less about the quality of workers' family lives than about restoring production after the war. Although workers tried to use the presence of women and youths to encourage employers to respect the eight-hour law, labor inspectors turned a blind eye to repeated extensions of the working day. In addition, in some industries like textiles women voluntarily worked ten-hour days in order to earn overtime pay.[73] According to the January 24, 1924, law permitting night shifts in industries handling or producing perishable goods, women could now be employed at night for periods from sixty to ninety days. In the event of a work stoppage, any employer could require night work from adult women (in proportion to the time lost).[74]

Production demands took precedence over the idea that women needed special protection, highlighting the discrepancy between the rhetoric of gender difference and economic practices. And yet the memory of the war's violent assault on the male body, the appeal of scientifically reducing effort at work, and the promise of leisure also called attention to the vulnerability of male working bodies. The issue of "usure au travail," the wear and tear of work, and the limits to which the working body should or could be pushed stood in stark contrast to the image of the burly workingmen who emblazoned the mastheads of the labor press. Considerations like this emerged during a major coal miners' strike during the summer of 1919, when the labor activist Georges Dumoulin addressed then Minister of National Reconstruction Louis Loucheur and criticized the government's failure to invest in more efficient methods of extracting coal:. "During the war, pulling as much as you could on the muscles and health of miners, you did nothing and your industrialists did nothing to improve equipment, or modify the pits. . . . You went to the point of draining men, and material. . . . Today at the very moment that the eight-hour day is being applied, you still operate on the basis of depletion and exhaustion."[75] Others linked a shorter workday to the new model of the male citizen-worker, as did Radical deputy Justin Godart, who proclaimed that more leisure would permit men to "fulfill their duties and exercise the rights of man and citizen."[76]

Simultaneously, a new vision of the citizen-worker as a family man, already assumed in postwar debates over fatherhood, emerged in organized labor's discussions of the eight-hour day and the importance of leisure in the 1920s. One CGT activist linked the question of shorter hours for men and the need for time to spend with their families to the problem of cramped housing and the postwar housing crisis: "Where will the man go, once his eight hours of work are finished? Back home to his wife and children in his cramped apartment, aerated by a filthy well? Will he stay in his filthy shack with its bare walls and miserable furnishings? No! He'll go out to the cabaret to seek the company of other idlers like himself."[77] Only the construction of healthy and agreeable housing would permit men to remain at home during their leisure hours and reconstitute family life. The writer's moral message was entirely consistent with the larger effort to entrust breadwinning men with reconstructing the family in the 1920s.

In 1922, organized labor stepped up its campaign for shorter hours as some employers, eager to maintain flexibility, attempted to get workers to agree to work a maximum number of hours over the course of a year in order to be able to weather economic fluctuations. In the city of Lyon, for example, this meant that some workers could work as much as a fifty-three-hour week, whereas in periods of economic slowdown, they would work less. Lyonnais metallurgical employers wanted to be able to prolong the workday for certain skilled workers to ten hours a day, as the 1919 law allowed. But labor leaders opposed this proposal. Alphonse Merrheim, head of the CGT Metalworkers' Federation, protested that these skilled workers sometimes lived a certain distance from the factory and couldn't get home for lunch with their families. This meant that they were away from home for as long as fifteen hours a day. "This is . . . a huge attack on family spirit. The working-man who is absent from his home can neither take care of his children's education nor give himself over to working in the garden or even acquire the extra professional training that he might need."[78] Indeed, a 1922 petition argued that men needed the eight-hour day in order to educate themselves and their families and the labor activist Maurice Guérin argued that a work-day longer than eight hours couldn't possibly leave enough time for men to fulfill their responsibilities as fathers and citizens. "How do you expect him to . . . be worthy of his multiple tasks, to think and vote well, and to live as a complete man with a fully human life?"[79] Arthur Fontaine, president of the Administrative Council of the International Labor Organization, echoed the idea that leisure was essential to working-class men because it could permit them to develop as fathers and citizens. In the fall of 1926, following the devaluation of the franc and the resulting industrial depression, as employers launched an attack against the shorter workday, the left-wing paper *Le Peuple* ran a series of articles in which writers called special attention to the significance of the eight-hour day for men's family lives. Fontaine argued that at last the workingman could develop his intellectual pursuits. The reform promised "sufficient leisure to permit the worker to be a man, that is, a spirit and a heart to which nothing human is foreign."[80] Work identities for these men included the ability to escape from work as much as the ability to preserve dignity in the face of enormous changes on the shop floor.

Organized labor's claims for respect of the eight-hour day based on fatherhood and citizenship may have influenced employer practices as much as employers' recognition that rest might make the human motor more productive.[81] But there was a fine balance to be achieved between postwar restoration of production and the inevitable adjustments required by economic cycles thereafter. Employers generally dealt with the question of work time by speeding up production and introducing methods of payment that would compensate for "lost" time. Yet the notion that physical needs for a reduced workday differed according to gender contributed to sustaining the larger cultural climate of ambivalence surrounding women's economic citizenship that surfaced in arguments for the family wage.

Gender and the Wage

The increasing differentiation of the labor force between men and women and within different categories of work in the twentieth-century factory resulted in ever more complex wage scales and systems of payment. Indeed, automobile employers' use of time and motion studies marked the height of employers' efforts to render the calculation of wages as precise and scientific as possible. This was exactly what systems of payment such as the Bedaux system aimed to do, by calculating wages up to the minute of production time. In the inflationary French economy of the 1920s, employers' efforts to step up production and reduce costs produced major conflicts with workers over wages and systems of payment. At the end of the war, industrial employers throughout France cut wages by an average of 15 percent and in the metalworking industries wage cuts increased the male-female wage gap from 18 percent during the war to 30 percent after the war.[82] Gender was always implicated in conflicts over wages, even if gender difference was not explicitly articulated, by virtue of the different positions that men and women occupied in the wage structure of firms.

Strikes at Citroën over time measurement showed how labor reacted to changes in the payment practices linked to rationalization. Workers protested against the increasingly complex systems of payment and differentiation of job categories, with variable working hours that made the negotiation of uniform wage scales all but impossible.[83] But the system of collective payment, designed so that productive workers would urge the less productive members of their team to speed up, was the real object of workers' ire: the wage, once a matter of remunerating an individual for a job, had been transformed into a collective payment. In these strikes, organized labor did not raise the male breadwinner norm. Rather, in discussing competition from women and immigrants or colonial subjects, French male workers repeatedly called attention to the problem of unequal pay and called for "equal wages for equal work" to eliminate the threat from both forms of labor. Labor activists pointed the finger at employers who underpaid immigrant laborers so that they could more easily resist the wage demands of

French men. Indeed, calls for equal wages were designed to preserve men's jobs in the face of perceived competition from women and foreign workers.

Gender inequalities also extended beyond the wage to social benefits, illustrating further how the ideas about gender difference that later underpinned the French social model began to influence policies in the 1920s. In 1925, for example, labor activists called attention to how women employees of the privately run public transportation company in the Paris region, the Société des transports en commun de la région parisienne (STCRP) earned 450 francs for exactly the same work for which men earned 525 francs.[84] Although this was hardly unusual, the practice of employing men and women at the same jobs at different wages in certain kinds of service-sector employment threw into relief just how much the gender of the worker (as opposed to the nature of the work) determined pay scales. Even when the performance of work was not a specific criterion for remuneration, social benefits paid by employers such as sickness compensation and cost of living allowances were based on gender. Thus, male workers at the STCRP were eligible for sickness compensation in the amount of their full wage after four days of illness, whereas women received only half of their wages for a period of up to ninety days.[85] These inequalities reflected assumptions about not only the value of work but also the value of the worker and assumed that even if men were not paid a family wage, they were responsible as breadwinners. At the same time, the ideal of the family wage surfaced among men within the ranks of organized labor and reinforced beliefs about the inferior value of women's work. Support of the family wage or the male breadwinner ideal suggested that quite apart from state policies that tended to privilege men's authority in the family, men's relationship to their families was also an important part of working-class male identity.[86]

The ideal of a male breadwinner figured prominently in the construction of working-class masculinity in nineteenth- and early-twentieth-century Europe. Workingmen used this idea as a code for maintaining power and authority in the private sphere, even in an economy like that of France, where women's labor force participation was relatively high.[87] Despite male workers' rhetorical defense of women's work in the immediate postwar years, the ideal of the male breadwinner continued to be part of the discursive framework of French workingmen between the wars. The majority of French male workers supported women's right to work under conditions of a highly stratified gender division of labor. While some labor activists like the Citroën strikers protested against gender differences in wages, for example, others in the trade continued to support the ideal of the male breadwinner. Indeed, men's demand for equal pay for equal work could be the complement of the demand for a male breadwinner wage. Both positions envisioned an end to women's "competition." Even when workers did not explicitly uphold the ideal of the male breadwinner, some workers demanded that "employers pay a supplement out of their profits to fathers who bear the responsibility of young children."[88] But in the context of enormous attention to the family on the part of the French state, social observers, and employers, combined with the valorization of men's position in the family in legal and cultural terms, arguments for the male breadwinner appeared frequently in the mid-1920s as employers adopted new payment systems and attempted to cut wages while simultaneously offering workers family bonuses. Although I examine workers' reactions to family allowances and the nascent French welfare state in the next chapter, it is worth considering here how gender and family were embedded in workers' concept of a living wage and their notion of economic citizenship.

Many workers expressed the desire for domestic order through the ideal of the male breadwinner. In the inflationary early 1920s when metalworkers in Le Havre struck to protest a 10 percent wage cut, they linked fathers' family and reproductive responsibilities to national duty in arguing for a male breadwinner wage. "What we ask is to have wages that are sufficient to live and to permit fathers to raise their children, to create real men and not scrofulous and scrawny men. . . . it is in these deplorable conditions that workers are asked to procreate for a healthier and stronger nation !"[89] The problem of the wage was arguably more complex in postwar France than earlier, given the numerous additions to the wage which themselves increasingly linked the wage not only to the worker as an individual but to his . or her membership in the family. As delegates pointed out in the 1925 CGT Metalworker's Federation congress, the actual effort of the worker was now only one part of the wage. Family and productivity bonuses and cost of living allowances became ever more important.[90] Speaking at the CGTU Commission on Wages at the Metalworkers' Federation congress in 1925, one delegate addressed the complexity of the wage under the system of family bonuses and production bonuses provided by the Wendel manufacturing company in Longwy, where wages could vary between 6 and 12 francs per day according to the worker's age and family responsibilities. The speaker showed how the gender division of labor failed to stem competition between men and women by accentuating gender differences in wages. Women working on piece rates in brick manufacture (*briqueterie d'usine*) earned 8 francs for an eight-hour day, whereas men doing the same work earned 14 francs 60.

Although Wendel provided production bonuses to its workers, the speaker argued that these supplements only showed how low actual wages were. "In fact, they don't constitute a fixed wage, properly speaking since all these bonuses can be withheld at a moment's notice."[91] Moreover, he protested that in some regions where family allowance funds existed, although some employers considered them as a part of the wage, "they in no way are part of the wage and cannot be considered as such!" Rabaté, an activist representing unions in the Nord, recognized that for the father with seven or eight children to support, a 450-franc family bonus per month constituted a significant addition: "Men who have family responsibilities should be paid sufficiently to be able to feed their families." But, he argued, "This must be done in such a way as not to alienate workers who do not actually benefit from the family bonus. There we have obviously broken with the old slogan, 'Equal pay for equal work.'"[92]

Arguments like these were repeated at labor congresses throughout the mini-depression of 1927. Men continued to debate women's ability to combine wage work and domestic responsibilities but never raised the same question for men. Indeed, the woman worker was still defined as a "problem." Labor's concerns about the ability of working men to support their families were also reflected in their demands for a minimum wage, a concept that appeared more frequently on the labor movement's agenda between the wars. In spite of a long section devoted to the claims of the Women's Commission on the importance of equal pay for women and attention to the health problems that rationalization imposed, the action program adopted at the 1927 Metalworkers' Federation (CGTU) congress called upon "every union to . . . engage in incessant agitation for a minimum wage for every metalworker, sufficient for him to meet his and his family's needs."[93] At the CGTU 1927 congress, Leveneur, a metalworker, criticized men for accepting women's presence in factories as normal. "A single woman must have the right to work in industry; a married woman, to take care of her household, must stay at home. We must demand high wages for men so that they can keep their wives at home."[94] Metalworkers were perhaps most extreme in their view of women's work in this highly male trade but they were not the only ones to support a male breadwinner ideal; Catholic textile employers who promoted fertility with family wage bonuses also feared that women's wage work would harm the family.

In the course of an investigation into the problem of women's work on double shifts in the textile industry, the Department Labor Commission of the Arrondissement of Lille (Commission départmentale du travail de l'arrondissement de Lille) called attention to the domestic disorder that double shifts engendered: "In effect, the double shift of eight consecutive hours has terrible repercussions for the physical, moral, and family lives of adolescents and women. The disorganization of meal times and family gatherings, the fatigue that results from so many hours at work, the entries and exits from the factory at odd hours . . . [ruins] the life of the families that supply industry with labor."[95] The solution proposed by the Commission was that married women work part-time for no more than four hours a day, as a "necessary step towards the complete suppression of married women's work."[96] In this argument, whereas augmenting the wage could bolster men's authority in the family, women needed *time* to resolve the conflict between work and domestic obligations.

Public service workers experienced seemingly greater opportunities for equity—teachers won pay equity in 1919 and PTT workers achieved wage parity in 1927, yet male public-service workers bolstered the Postal Administration's resistance to wage equality throughout the early 1920s. Discussions of the wage among PTT workers illustrated deep ambivalence about women's work and gender differences in wages, made worse by how underpaid PTT public service workers were by comparison to industrial workers.[97] Whereas the purchasing power of industrial workers in 1928 stood at 142 (based on an index of 100 in 1913), that of public service workers stood at 128 [98] The French government paid public-sector employees yearly salaries according to a complex scale that reflected not only different jobs but also four and sometimes six different levels, with differential scales within job categories. Advancement from one level to another was more a question of seniority than of skill and thus distinguished industrial workers from public-service workers. But the arguments for the male breadwinner in the public sector paralleled those in industry in the context of two parallel campaigns for wage increases. In the early 1920s, male postal employees began a campaign for a minimum wage, "le minimum d'éxistence assuré," enough to permit "education, leisure, hygiene, provision for old age and a special allowance for the maintenance of a family." Women in the PTT agitated for equal pay.[99] The demand that fathers be accorded supplements for their children implied a relationship between fatherhood, work, and wages that differed from the relationship between motherhood, work, and wages and privileged the responsibility of fathers over mothers to provide for families. In 1923 PTT workers, responding to the inability of wages to keep pace with inflation raised the demand for a minimum wage "to insure an honest subsistence to workers." This idea drew instant criticism from Mme Stanko, an ardent defender of women's rights within the PTT, who attacked the proposal for assuming that all workers had children and argued that such an assumption raised the broader question of women's role in society. What should be the relationship of the wage, remuneration for productive work, to the family, she asked, and how should one define the minimum wage in terms of the family? And how many children does one have to bear in order to constitute a family? If wages are linked to the family (as opposed to production alone) what about single men and women? Linking work, family, and citizenship, Stanko voiced skepticism about workingmen's ability to fulfill the demands of prolific manly citizenship. "The father who wishes to fulfill his duty as the perfect citizen [and patriot] who has five or six children will have a hard time getting an honest subsistence wage."[100]

Although some male PTT workers affirmed the principle of wage equity between men and women, and women agitated for equal pay throughout the 1920s, it was far from clear that rank and file activists accepted the *practice*. By the 1920s women worked in numerous areas of the postal service alongside men, at post office counters, in accounting and administrative work, in addition to occupying gender-segregated positions as telephone operators, but within the complex system of public-sector salaries they were paid considerably less than men. Women's wages had increased substantially since before the war: in 1914, they earned between 1,500 and 2,700 francs, two-thirds of what men made; in 1919, they earned between 3,800 and 7,200 francs, seven-eighths of what men made. But although the most recent wage adjustment had brought the maximum salary of women postal workers to 9,200 francs, the government increased male wages such that women now earned 20 percent less than their male counterparts.[101] Some men continued to believe that wage parity could lead to *more* competition between men and women because, with the exception of counter jobs that were reserved for the war wounded and women, and "men's jobs" of night work and mail delivery, men would have an advantage since they were physically stronger.[102] The discussion of equal wages among these public-sector workers, moreover, was complicated by recruitment practices and by the question of whether it made sense to talk about "equal work" or "similar work." As long as the recruitment exams were different for men and women (women had been fighting for a single entrance exam and similar recruitment for both men and women since 1921), the government could more easily continue to pay men and women differently. Moreover, not all work was exactly alike; men who worked the telegraph machines did not do exactly the same work as those of the same public-service grade who sorted and delivered mail. The system of advancement through the ranks of the public service (and hence to positions of higher salary) complicated the issue: older men worried that women and talented younger men might move up more quickly than they could.[103] Acknowledging men's and women's physiological differences, Mlle d'Harcourt from the Paris-Nord telephone exchange argued that it was impossible to compare the work of a telephone operator to that of a mail carrier; Stanko proposed using the concept of "work of the same importance," or "work of the same type," closer to modern concepts of "comparable worth," on the grounds that there were qualities specific to women, like patience, that made women more appropriate than men for some kinds of work. In 1923, the National Union of Postal, Telephone, and Telegraph Employees agreed to the phrase, "Equal pay for similar recruitment and work of the same order," instead of "Equal wages for equal work."[104] At the same time, in debating the family wage, organized labor's tremendous ambivalence about women's full-fledged economic citizenship emerged. Stating that "the material necessities of life obligate women to seek a supplemental wage indispensable to the subsistence of the family; . . . that [women's] presence at home is necessary for at least part of the day for family needs and for the education of her children; . . . that the work that women are obliged to perform outside of the home does not relieve them of domestic tasks, but only increases their labor; . . . [the Congress] stands in favor of part-time work for married women employees . . ."[105]

Arguments about gender roles in the family and claims on the part of men for a male breadwinner wage repeatedly emerged throughout the 1920s. The assumption that maternity made women made less productive than men and women employees who were also mothers would be much more interested in their children than in their work for the PTT underscored men's arguments. As one male labor activist stated in 1924,

> Normally, a male worker is proud and loves his profession; he experiences joy when he is hitched to his daily labors. Too often [work], for the mother, is a . . . constraint, because her true place is in the home. This state of things will cease once the male worker's wage permits him to take care of the subsistence of his family on his own and when his family responsibilities will be supported by society.[106]

Ideas about men's privileged place at work recurred again and again when postal workers debated women's advancement in the ranks and their access to supervisory positions in 1924. They acknowledged that although women could rise to the position of supervisor, principal supervisor, 4th degree postmistresses, and chief editorial clerks, they could not yet be admitted into the higher 3rd degree, to which only men had access. Although male delegates thought that this might happen in the future, at the moment it was premature. Asserting the inevitability of men's power over women, one male delegate argued,

> Whether one likes it or not, the spirit of force predominates over right or reason. . . . This brutal reality gives to men the pride of superiority or natural authority over women and to [women] fearful and instinctual submission to men. Without doubt there are exceptions, but our conviction rests on impartial analysis of the human economic and political scene, which proves that in life's order, the point to which we have evolved, men will not yet accept—at least officially—to be commanded or directed by women. If he no longer sees in her an inferior being, he still perceives her as the weaker of the sexes, whose essential social role is to be the vestal of the household and not as a directing element within the machinery of production.[107]

Finally, interventions at the 1926 PTT congress illustrated postal workers' recognition of how family and private life influenced work and wages. As one delegate noted, the idea that the wage was simply remuneration for work rendered was in the process of disappearing. The contemporary concept of the wage incorporated the idea that the male worker with family responsibilities "has the right to demand a supplement that will allow him to provide a decent living for his children. . . . The new way of remunerating the worker . . . takes account of the diverse, constitutive elements of the wage: the value of work, regional differences in the cost of living, and social expenses [*les charges sociales*]."[108] This was only reasonable, he believed, since children should not be a burden and, after all, the family is the foundation of society. But it was too risky for the congress to support the family wage "including a percentage to enable the wife to stay at home"; there were still too many households in France without children, and a family wage would disadvantage childless male workers.

Rank and file activists vigorously debated the principle of equal pay. Many believed that women *should* earn less since they couldn't legally work after 10 p.m., because they allegedly took more sick leave, and because men did heavier work. "From both the physiological and moral perspective, women's place is in the home and not in the workshop, because the true cell upon which the family rests is the family."[109] Others trotted out the old chestnut that women's work led to birth defects, stillbirths, and miscarriages. Women should work less than eight hours; married women should be able to leave work after fifteen years, with a pension proportional to their service. Rather than seek wage equality, women should be paid equal "real" wages, by which he meant a nominal wage less than men's and a significant package of social benefits.[110] Women's physical embodiment thus continued to shape the gendered meanings of work and social bodies. Moreover, this proposal effectively suggested that the state should recognize the male breadwinner norm by providing women with social supports.

Organized labor's reaction to the broad application of industrial physiology and scientific management across the economy demonstrated how rationalization legitimated and cemented gender and racial differences in employment. The divisions that these differences produced contributed to a gendered and occasionally racial model of work and economic citizenship that restricted women's economic choices and limited their wage-earning capacity. Debates within the ranks of organized labor throughout the 1920s, moreover, revealed the centrality of family and gender to labor's view of "new methods" of scientific management. Skilled industrial workers argued that rationalization threatened masculine work identities and removed initiative, control, and taste from the hands of skilled men. Women and men both protested against overwork that robbed them of the energy to devote to their families and criticized the racial or ethnic and gender dynamics of employers' implementation of rationalization. French male workers voiced their anxieties about displacement by women and foreign workers. Indeed, the application of "scientific methods" in the context of economic growth but also instability arguably accentuated men's defense of their more privileged position in the labor force and their efforts to prevent further encroachments on their terrain. At the same time, despite variation in organized labor's reactions to new ways of organizing work and methods of payment, common themes emerged across the economy even in such diverse and highly differentiated arenas as metalworking, the textile industry, and the postal, telegraph, and telephone service. Debates over work showed that masculine work identities were bound to workingmen's private-sphere interests of fatherhood and family. Concerns about the family and population, the duties of the male citizen-worker, rising living costs, and the meaning of a living wage occupied a central place in workers' discussions of rationalization. How organized labor dealt with these concerns and the primacy male workers gave to the male breadwinner norm contributed to sustaining the larger cultural ambivalence surrounding women's economic citizenship. Not surprisingly, the French social model whose broad outlines emerged in the 1920s incorporated the same set of concerns about the intersection of family, gender, and work. Employers and the state acknowledged the links between work, family, and "social citizenship" by providing welfare benefits to families, linked to employment. Organized labor simultaneously brought its claims to bear on the nascent French welfare state within a context of reframing the nature of citizenship and rights for both French and foreigners. Labor contributed to shaping the emerging social model of state-society relations of the 1920s and 1930s.

CHAPTER FIVE

TOWARD THE SOCIAL MODEL:

CITIZENSHIP, RIGHTS, AND SOCIAL PROVISION

Conservative familialists' and pronatalists' attempts to shift the foundations of rights from the individual to the family in appeals for the family vote, employers' promotion of fertility and the male breadwinner, and organized labor's support for gendered norms of economic citizenship all exerted a powerful influence on emerging notions of political and social rights in post–World War I France. During the 1920s, state policies on citizenship and the family expanded in two important domains, both profoundly influenced by France's pervasive sense of population crisis and both with significant implications for policies addressing the class and gender foundations of rights. The first concerned broadening the category of those who could be included as citizens and extending political rights by facilitating the naturalization of thousands of immigrants, overwhelmingly male, who entered the French labor market in the 1920s. The second concerned the extension of social provisions for families, designed to encourage fertility in postwar France that marked France as a leader in the formation of the European welfare state. Both sets of initiatives underscored how the meanings of gender, family, and Frenchness, along with the male breadwinner ideal, influenced political and social policies between the wars.

Historical discussions of citizenship and social provision in Western Europe have tended to emphasize either class or gender as the focus of emerging welfare states but have underplayed their interaction. They have often left working-class men and women out of the story of struggles for citizenship rights and social protections or have viewed them as the recipients of social policy or have included only their reactions to it. Much has been written about what social reformers and employers thought about workers, but relatively little work has explored working-class subjectivity in interventions on the politics of social citizenship.[1] Yet workers' debates about the accumulating array of social provisions in the 1920s showed both the persistence of ideas that priviliged the male breadwinner and a new vision of economic justice. Although government officials' and male labor activists' discussions of family policies revealed the normative assumption that women are primarily or only mothers, working women's claims for social protection in the interwar years demonstrated how they spelled out their rights to both wage work and social provisions and resisted the prevailing male breadwinner ideal. Gender and class interests converged in the process of developing and extending both economic and social dimensions of citizenship.

Feminist scholars have criticized T. H. Marshall's model of citizenship for its failure to take account of gender difference and inequality. They have argued that men and women do not experience political citizenship or the civil aspects of citizenship in the same way and that men and women experience differently the social entitlements that presumably flow from these first two levels of citizenship.[2] They have also suggested that women's lack of economic citizenship had profound implications for the gendering of social and political rights. As Alice Kessler-Harris has pointed out, the very concept of "economic citizenship captures the full complexity of [women's] exclusion, not merely from jobs, but from the range of access routes to citizenship prohibited by real or imagined cultural locations."[3] I have suggested above that the Marshallian model of citizenship and rights is not clearly applicable to France, where the universalism of republican discourses masked the exclusionary foundations of citizenship's inception and practices from 1789. Indeed, until 1944, in France, women's status as political citizens was ambiguous: prior to that year, they could not vote and were denied a panoply of civil rights within the framework of the French Civil Code.[4] At the same time, French women also lacked full economic citizenship. During the years in which the first elements of the welfare state were put into place, women enjoyed a certain degree of civil and social "citizenship" without enjoying full political or economic rights. Moreover, women's social rights devolved not from political or their (as yet incomplete) civil citizenship (as in Marshall's model) but followed from their physical embodiment—their real or potential motherhood—and their role in social reproduction. There was a certain irony to this situation inasmuch as women's sexual embodiment also provided the rationale for the impossibility of their full political citizenship.[5] Women could be mother-citizens or republican mothers but not exercise full political rights. Yet this imperfect concept, "social citizenship," nonetheless invites reflection on the way in which social policies were established on the basis of a presumed relationship between an embodied, gendered citizen and the state, even where the practice of citizenship was incomplete.

This chapter examines women labor activists' subjectivity in debates over the politics of social citizenship and social provisions. As many women saw, the granting of social provisions had important implications for their ability to exercise economic rights.[6] It considers some theoretical foundations of pre–World War I discussions about membership in the political community and looks at how these paradigms began to shift in the interwar years, first with respect to the broadening of citizen status for immigrant men, and second, with regard to the expansion of social rights designed to support the family and reproduction. Struggles over the application of an emerging package of social rights for French workers showed how gendered work identities influenced perceptions of rights and how women linked economic citizenship to social rights. Examining women's claims for social protection further suggests that citizenship was not only a status but also a practice through which individuals shaped the subjective meanings of belonging to political communities.[7] I argue that the logic of certain kinds of arguments for social protection based on gendered norms of work and family responsibilities had negative as well as positive outcomes for working women that further influenced employment-based rights.

The Body, Property, and Rights

Within the framework of classic liberal political theory two paradigms dominated discussions of citizenship, democracy, and political participation, both of them marked by gender. The first was the assumption that sexual difference automatically translated into political difference and hence inequality between men's and women's location in the polity and civil society. The belief that men were naturally guided by reason, which enabled them to operate according to the rules of law and justice, justified the association of men with the public realm and men's exercise of political rights. As we have seen, men's ability to father children could be seen as a foundation of rights as well, although political commentators never reduced men to their essential physical embodiment. Moreover, in France, unlike many other states, from the late eighteenth century, the Republic conferred rights on male citizens regardless of race.[8] Political theorists, however, assumed women to be naturally guided by the passions and their bodies, deprived of reason and a sense of justice. Their sexual embodiment determined their public, legal incapacity and their association with the private sphere.[9]

The reduction of the female body to a maternal body that tied women to the private sphere had a powerful impact on the thinking and practices of legislators, reformers, and male labor activists throughout the nineteenth and most of the twentieth centuries.[10] Women's sexual embodiment and their essentialized "natural" role in the private realm became an important foundation on which employers denied women access to certain kinds of jobs, but it also served as a justification for denying women the vote and control over their earnings, preventing them from serving as witnesses and as jurors, making contracts, testifying in court, and limiting the grounds on which they could sue for divorce. When viewed with respect to the interests of the state or nation, the maternal body became the basis of a fictitious citizenship for women called "republican motherhood" that framed women's membership in the political community by proxy, via the reproduction and nurturance of future male citizens.[11] Some reformers and suffrage advocates, bent on overturning the legal subjugation of wives to husbands and obtaining political rights for women, turned this logic around and argued that women's essential physicality, their allegedly superior connection with nature, and their role in the private sphere, especially motherhood, justified their inclusion in the polity as full-fledged citizens and would make them better mothers.[12]

A second paradigm governing rights rested on the idea that property and work conferred citizenship rights. From French revolutionaries' definition in 1789 of "active" citizens as those men who paid a tax equal to the value of three day's labor, through subsequent revolutionary moments, male workers insisted on the importance of their property in their labor as a condition of citizenship. Fathers' ability to support their families through their honest labor, they argued, gave men the right to citizenship, illustrating how men viewed the recognition of their status as workers and breadwinners as providing access to political and civil citizenship.[13] Neither revolutionaries nor government officials recognized women's status as workers or as having property in their labor and hence did not recognize the possibility of women's full citizenship on these grounds. Indeed, French law excluded women from virtually all rights to property ownership unless they were widowed or single women of the age of majority ("*filles majeures*").[14] For most of the nineteenth and early twentieth centuries, legislators and social reformers viewed the working woman as ambiguous, deviant, and precarious. They viewed women as needing state intervention and protection rather than the civic and political rights that would establish at once their right to work and their status as full-fledged citizens.[15]

Despite their exclusion from the definition of the citizen or citizen-worker, in the course of citizenship's repeated redefinition during the revolutionary movements of the nineteenth century, working-class women also claimed political rights on the grounds of their status as workers.[16] When the suffrage activist Hubertine Auclert presented a radical motion for women's right to vote at the 1879 French Socialist Workers' congress, some delegates argued for women's complete political and civil equality with men on the grounds that, like men, they had to work.[17] At the beginning of the twentieth century, the state began to recognize women's legal status as independent workers and their rights as wage earners: in 1903 women public-sector employees won the right to fully paid maternity leaves for almost five weeks after the birth of a child; from 1907 the state acknowledged married women's right to control their own wages; and the 1913 law on maternity leaves recognized working women's right to protection as mothers, even if the real object of the law was to protect infants.[18] These small steps in the direction of economic citizenship were important. At the same time, the ambiguity of French women's formal juridical status by no means prevented them from participating in public, associational life, but it unquestionably marginalized them within the formal political realm.[19] Similar arguments appeared just before and during the decades following World War I when Aline Valette, socialist, labor activist, and feminist, argued that work should be considered the basis of women's enfranchisement.[20] But women's economic citizenship received no widespread recognition, and no formal connection between women's political and economic rights could stand up.

Although left wing parties, reconstituted in the 1920s, failed to organize working women, and the male workers who dominated organized labor scarcely hid their ambivalence about women's status as workers, the labor movement nevertheless offered women a platform from which to make claims for social rights. Chapter 1 examined how the destabilization of gender relations during the war contributed to the blurring of distinctions between public and private spheres in both discourse and practice. Women's massive public presence in the labor force during World War I politicized their work and made it a matter of national interest.[21] During the war, the theoretical and legal grounds on which citizenship was denied to women were further undermined when the state recognized women's position as legal persons by providing women with the capacity to make contracts and engage in other legal operations in the absence of their husbands.[22] But by the end of the war, French women's status as "citizens" remained as ambiguous as ever in the eyes of government officials. Although women's participation in the war effort alongside men tipped the balance in favor of women's suffrage throughout Europe and the United States, in France women's citizenship ensured only their exercise of a number of civic rights, their right to the protection of the law, and social rights including protective labor legislation, as well as in the duty to pay taxes.[23] In 1920 married women won the right to unionize without the consent of their husbands (single women already had this right by virtue of the 1884 law legalizing labor unions). Later in the 1920s, women teachers active in the Union française pour le suffrage des femmes argued for full citizenship rights on the basis of their roles as both workers and as taxpayers.[24] The dual anxieties over reconstituting the labor force after the war and regenerating French population in the interwar years contributed to a shift in the two concepts of citizenship discussed earlier.

Nationality Law, Population, and Gender

The first shift concerned the relationship between citizenship rights, bodies, and fertility. Proposals for the family vote to reward prolific fathers implied a new definition of citizenship that incorporated fatherhood as a foundation of rights, suggesting that the provision of healthy children was as much a social contribution to the nation as military service. Although the family vote never became law, the implications of this effort to redefine the exercise of citizenship were striking. Women's embodiment as mothers or potential mothers still prevented them from exercising the full panoply of political citizenship rights; fertile male bodies, however, could potentially enjoy additional rights. The important link between male fertility and the duties of citizenship did lead legislators to consider expanding political rights. Some observers believed that the need to increase the number of French men and women was critical enough that France might well benefit from the fertility of foreign male workers. Ardent pronatalists set aside the "problem" of racial and ethnic difference in favor of population growth.

Nationality and class complicated the gendered meanings of rights in discussions of the potential citizenship of immigrant workers residing in France. Since the immediate postwar years, some pronatalist activists who debated the implications of immigration for the French population argued that immigrants could indeed meet the need for able-bodied workers but that French naturalization policy made it difficult for immigrants to put roots into French soil.[25] These themes came together in the campaign of the Alliance nationale pour l'accroissement de la population française (National Alliance for French Population Growth) to reduce the 1,000-franc naturalization fee, which many thought too onerous for foreign workers. An unsigned article that appeared in the Alliance's monthly journal, *Revue de l'alliance nationale pour l'accroissement de la population française*, addressed the problem of naturalization. The author observed that foreign workers could become French citizens but claimed that the majority of such workers were old men or those "beyond the normal age of marriage"; young men made up only a small proportion of those seeking naturalization. While the author believed that it made sense to reject foreigners who had criminal convictions or moral defects, or those who came to France in order to benefit from social assistance, he argued that the government should facilitate the naturalization of young men who were "worthwhile," that is, of an age when they could procreate and raise large families.[26]

In 1927, French legislators addressed this issue, reducing from ten years to three the residency period after which foreigners could apply for naturalization. In cases where a foreign national had rendered important services to France or had brought forth distinguished talents or inventions, served in the French army, or obtained French university degrees, the residency period could be reduced to a year.[27] The new nationality law also expanded the *droit du sol* rule of French nationality, specifying that any child of a foreign mother born in France or born of a French mother would be considered French. In the former case, a child could repudiate French nationality upon reaching ther age of majority; in the latter case, where the mother was French, French nationality could not be repudiated. The law further permitted French women marrying foreigners to retain their French nationality, alongside granting French nationality to children born of such unions. As the debate surrounding this important legislation made clear, in easing the requirements for both naturalization and the citizenship status of foreigners' children, legislators were less motivated by the desire to give hard-working immigrant men access to active citizenship than they were by creating potential fathers of French children. Pronatalists who lobbied for this legislation at least since 1923, particularly the members of the Alliance nationale pour l'accroissement de la population française, had already pointed to what they considered immigrants' prodigious fertility and argued that foreigners with large families or with the potential to create large families should be given preference in naturalization.[28]

Some supporters of the August 1927 law such as the theorist Jean Pluyette believed it would mitigate the potentially negative impact of foreign bodies on French soil by transforming foreigner workers into Frenchmen. But Pluyette was not willing to allow just anyone to become French and his eugenic as well as his pronatalist inclinations emerged quite clearly when he stipulated that "it is important to choose for this transfusion of new blood only robust and vigorous subjects, capable of perpetuating a healthy race."[29] Ultimately, however, for Pluyette, as for others who favored reforming naturalization law, expanding the conditions of male citizenship could both increase "French" population and assimilate foreign male workers within the orbit of French nationality, producing potential military recruits.[30] French women married to foreigners and who retained French nationality could now benefit from the family allowances and birth bonuses for French citizens, which became available in the 1920s, as could naturalized men. Such women could obtain maternity leave as well, a provision not available to a French woman marrying a foreigner before 1927.[31] In allowing a French woman to retain her nationality, the law also considered the children of a French woman to be French. While depriving immigrant men of the authority to confer automatically their citizenship on their French wives, it also acknowledged the Gallicizing influence that many believed French wives could exert on their foreign husbands. It assumed that republican mothers would remain fully attached to the Republic and could help their foreign husbands acculturate. Faced with the prospect that marriage to a foreigner could deprive France of national subjects, legislators could acknowledge the possibility that citizenship passed through the mother. Thus, state policies did not always mirror, in lock step fashion, the racial distinctions recommended by eugenics experts and some conservative politicians; the case of the 1927 naturalization law is a good illustration of how the French state admitted the possibility of racial and ethnic hybridity in specific contexts, in the service of larger social objectives.[32]

As Elisa Camiscioli has argued, although some feminists viewed the new nationality code's provision that allowed French women to retain their nationality as a step toward women's civil equality, it was a limited victory. Legislators' motives were populationist—to reverse France's demographic decline—rather than egalitarian.[33] Like proponents of the eighteenth- and nineteenth-century idea of "republican motherhood" that allowed mothers to educate future male citizens, twentieth-century lawmakers believed that women could pass citizenship on to their children and save them from the grasp of foreigners, but women still could not exercise citizenship fully. Thus the law confirmed the gendered bases of citizenship already in practice and evident in debates over the family vote and once more privileged an exercise of citizenship rooted in collective interests of the family as opposed to individual rights.[34]

Here gender played a different role than in the case of the family vote. Charles Lambert, deputy and former high commissioner of immigration and naturalization who introduced the bill into parliament wrote that this particular disposition of the law was especially important given the heavy immigration of working-class men. The law made clear that the rules governing the citizenship of women married to French men would not determine the citizenship of French women married to foreign men. As Lambert pointed out, "in the Nord, in the foreign population of 244,649 individuals, there are 70,081 women and 111,881 men. With unions becoming increasingly numerous between immigrants and French women, we see the exceptional importance of this article that not only will prevent French women *from becoming foreigners* [my emphasis], but will keep for our country all children who are French from birth, even if their fathers reside abroad."[35] Thus, the shifting racial and national composition of the French working class forced a re-evaluation of the terms of citizenship in ways that preserved its gendered foundations.

Work, the Family, and Social Policy

A second arena in which the meanings of citizenship began to shift concerned women's status as workers and the social meanings attached to women's work. Some feminists argued for women's exercise of full citizenship rights on the basis of their service to the nation as workers during the war. At the same time, women's bodies and health arguably became matters of increasing public, political concern and of increasing national interest in the interwar years. Discussions of reproduction and the control of sexuality following the war marked the entry of the state into the private domain—not for the first time, but with a purpose and under conditions that foreshadowed the continuing role of the state in France's fertility crisis throughout the 1920s and 1930s.[36] During the war, the establishment of state-mandated nursing rooms and day care centers in war factories enabled women to combine motherhood and wage work while lowering infant mortality. These initiatives demonstrated how the state regulated private life in public settings and politicized the reproductive female working-class body. The politicization of the masculine body also occurred during and after the war, although in ways that differed from the state's attention to women. In the former case, the state focused on the mutilation of men's bodies in service to their countries, and gave public assistance to the injured following the war. The industrial physiologist Jules Amar and others worked on the rehabilitation of damaged male bodies for productive labor. But for women, the regulation of reproduction rather than repair of the body or rewarding reproduction with votes took precedence. The coalescence of "public" national/nationalist concerns and "private" activities like childbearing and social reproduction was obvious in the employment of women factory superintendents to oversee the health and reproductive potential of women industrial workers. In a climate in which citizens' duty to the state as mothers and fathers was repeatedly proclaimed in different forms, it would be difficult to disaggregate both paternity and maternity from membership in the political community. The politicization of women's and men's bodies in the context of France's anxiety over its demographic deficit placed the question of gender difference squarely on the agenda of France's emerging welfare state, appeared in ideas about economic and social citizenship in the 1920s, and illustrated the tension between economic and social rights.[37]

As scholars have noted, modern French social policy began in the early decades of the twentieth century with the private intitiatives of pronatalist entrepreneurs who provided financial supports to prolific workers and laid the foundation of social citizenship. During the war, conservative Catholic textile entrepreneurs in Grenoble and in Roubaix-Tourcoing established a system of family bonuses (*sursalaires familiales*) paid to workers with dependent children, according to the number of children in their care. Men or women employees who had worked for a month could receive the allowance and families stood to receive a larger supplement if both parents and adolescents over thirteen worked for the firm. Families could add as much as 25 percent to their wages; those with six children effectively doubled the amount of their wage with a family bonus.[38] These supplements required continuity of employment—workers who struck or lost time at work forfeited the allowance—and required home visits by women welfare supervisors or visiting nurses who provided home economics education for mothers and taught them about childcare.[39] Following the war these supplements continued and employers in the metals indutries applied them as well. In 1923, the Mining and Metallurgical Industries Consortium (GIMM) substantially increased the allowances for prolific fathers, so that a father of four who made 400 francs plus an additional 40-franc family allowance experienced a 30 percent rise in aggregate wage to 570 francs a month. A father of nine children could bring home 970 francs a month, a 98 percent increase from his previous 490 francs a month.[40] From the employers' perspective these allowances encouraged the reproduction of the labor force and served as a form of wage restraint (since only workers with children received the allowance), and a means of regulating labor. Although they provided families with children significant increases in income during the inflationary postwar years, they also reflected a conservative vision of the family as an economic unit and underscored how social benefits reproduced a normative view of women as primarily mothers rather than workers.

Some employers viewed the family wage bonus as a form of male breadwinner wage or an unwaged mother's allowance which would free working-class wives to remain in the home to care for children. Immediately after the war, the administrators of the family allowance fund (*caisse de compensation*) of the metallurgical employers of the Dauphine region argued for the individualization of labor contracts that took into account the worker's family situation. Of their four family allowance initiatives, two incorporated an unwaged mother's allowance. According to the first of these programs, a married male employee whose wife did not work would receive 125 francs per month in addition to his wages, "this sum being due to each woman who works at no other occupation other than of the care of her household, even if she is able to. We seek in this way to encourage women to take exclusive care of their households and we think it opportune to encourage them to do so even if they have no children."[41] The second concerned the married worker whose wife was unable to earn wages because of illness, pregnancy, or care of one or more children under age thirteen. In this case the man received a 25-franc wage supplement per month. "[A] woman who has a single child less than thirteen years of age has the right to devote herself entirely to her household and to be relieved from wage work." Beneficiaries had to be married; widows, widowers, divorced persons, or unmarried partners had no right to this allowance.[42]

The Textile Consortium of Lille, Roubaix, Tourcoing also provided a form of unwaged mother's allowance in addition to a generous program of health and sickness benefits, paying birth bonuses of 240 francs to its employees for each child, as long as the mother didn't work. In its annual report in 1923, the Consortium noted that 61 percent of mothers stayed at home with their children; the number had dropped to 56 percent in 1927 but remained at that level through 1930. The authors of the 1928 annual report on the Consortium's social services noted with satisfaction that "mothers who benefit from family allowances stay home to care for their children. Among the 41,281 families working for the Consortium in December, 1927, 23,140 mothers remain at home . . . a happy result of family allowances . . . the entire household and each of its members profits by returning mothers to their normal functions."[43] While ostensibly designed to reduce infant mortality, these social benefits were also based upon and helped to reproduce already existing gender inequalities in the labor market. While providing families with income, they encouraged the very discontinuity in women's employment that male employers argued made women unreliable workers.

Other employers' policies also incorporated a male breadwinner or unwaged mother's allowance model. The Creusot metallurgical company, for instance, one of the most paternalistic firms, long provided a variety of social services such as retirement plans, accident insurance, medical services, and company housing. The Schneider family, owners of the firm, built a hospital and maternity clinic for workers, as well as a family center (*maison de famille*) designed to welcome and raise the children of widows and widowers. Creusot avoided hiring married women for factory work and prided itself on paying a form of male breadwinner wage to men with children: wages plus dependents' allowances that were high enough so that male workers could provide for their wives and children.[44] The Michelin Rubber Company also distributed a generous birth bonus of 400 francs for the first child, with 250 francs for each additional child for women workers with one year of service who stayed at home with their children. The bonus also required employee loyalty. A woman who worked for Michelin could receive it only if her husband did not work for a competing firm.[45] These social benefits, even if they were not generalized among firms, further demonstrated how employment-based social provisions incorporated assumptions about gender roles, notably assuming a male breadwinner norm, while ignoring women's economic rights.

A male breadwinner norm also informed the state's allowance system for public-sector workers. A woman state employee received a dependent's allowance for her children only if she was a widow, divorced, or her husband was unable to support his family. In the latter case, a wife could receive an allowance equal to that of a male state employee.[46] Companies to whom the state subcontracted public utilities like gas, electricity, and water explicitly targeted male workers and family men for such allowances. Since 1922, the state had required companies like the Paris Electricity Distribution Company and the Société de gaz de Paris to provide dependents' allowances to fathers. Lawyer René Siau suggested that these companies owed men more than a wage; they also had a moral obligation to bring about "social reconciliation." "After assuring working fathers the funds sufficient to enable them to decently support their families, the family allowance fund (*caisse de compensation*) will follow the worker in his life and contribute to . . . giving him security and confidence in the future."[47] Not only did workers for the gas, electric, and water companies receive allowances provided by the City of Paris; by 1929 their employees benefited from company allowances of 660 francs for the first child and up to 1,920 francs for four or more children. These sums were payable to fathers up to each child's sixteenth year. But the company allowance system also encouraged the training of a future male labor force. If their children became apprentices in a trade, fathers would continue to receive the allowance until their child was eighteen (or twenty-one, if the child went to university). "We note that prolonging the bonus beyond a child's 16th year is designed to favor the father who gives his children . . . the possibility of exercising a skilled trade, or an education that will permit him to have a worthwhile position in life."[48] Women who received 400-franc birth bonuses were required to stop work for a month before and after the birth of their child. In January 1928, the Paris Electricity Distribution Company began giving its women employees a substantial nursing bonus of 600 francs for the first four months that doubled as a form of unemployment allowance. Beneficiaries were required to devote themselves exclusively to their children and were forbidden to engage in any income-earning activity, even at home. Here was a case in which the company displayed its ambivalence about male behavior. The sum was paid directly to the wife so that "the husband will not be able to keep it for his private expenditures—which has been known to happen."[49]

These private and state initiatives, then, served multiple objectives in addition to the overt goal of increasing the French population and reproducing the labor force. Beyond allowing employers to contain wages in a period of substantial inflation and to regulate workers, the allowance regime aimed to secure workers' loyalty to the firm through the "manufacture of consent." Family bonuses and allowances also served as a form of employment policy that allowed employers to regulate the labor market, by encouraging women to withdraw from work before and after the birth of their children. Based on a male breadwinner norm, these policies privileged the economic rights of the French male citizen-worker.

It is worth noting that colonial workers, who were neither citizens nor completely foreigners, could not benefit from the provisions of this fledgling social model. The majority of them were single men, and although they could well have been family providers, French employers did not recognize them as breadwinners. The government discouraged the immigration (or migration) of colonial families and those who emigrated to France were exluded from private family allowances. Only the department of the Seine developed social services for immigrants, within the Surveillance, Protection, and Assistance Services for North Africans (Services de surveillance, protection, et assistance des indigènes Nord Africains, SAINA) in 1925.[50] The SAINA provided dormitory housing, medical services (the Franco-Muslim hospital in Bobigny, a working-class industrial suburb of Paris,) and a social services office, and as Clifford Rosenberg has noted, these programs not only served as a form of social assistance; they also served as a form of surveillance.[51]

Over the course of the 1920s and early 1930s, family allowances for French workers were gradually expanded and by 1930 some 32,000 companies were involved in this system.[52] In 1923 the first state-sponsored family allowance system for families with at least three children was put in place, providing 350 francs per child. Two years later a law generalized the system of paid maternity leaves for all French women and a landmark social insurance bill, in the making for eight years, was finally passed in 1928, set to go into effect in 1930. Ultimately the entire allowance system was brought under state control, extended to all families in 1932 (although until 1936 employers were permitted to administer it), and then universalized in the 1939 Family Code. Although a male breadwinner model influenced how some employers and state agencies interpreted these laws, the state did not explicitly use family policy to promote the family wage; once the state took control of the system, both men and women were entitled to receive payments. At the same time, debates over these initiatives within the ranks of organized labor illustrated the remarkable resilience of the male breadwinner norm.

Organized Labor, Social Policy, and the Male Breadwinner Ideal

Private social benefits proved tremendously complex and divisive for working people. On the one hand employers' family bonuses offered welcome income supplements that arguably assisted workers in inflationary times; some demanded increases in such provisions during labor disputes, and those not already covered pressured employers to provide family bonuses. When metalworkers in the Isère struck for application of the eight-hour day and a wage increase in June 1919, they simultaneously demanded an increase in family allowances.[53] Metalworkers in Chateau-Regnault struck for nine months in 1926 to force employers to provide them with an hourly cost of living allowance and a monthly family allowance of 12 to 16 francs per child.[54]

During strikes in the Nord in 1928, textile workers likewise demanded an increase in family allowances alongside wage increases.[55] In the midst of the Depression of the 1930s, women and men again struck to protest cuts in the employer-administered allowance scheme.[56]

At the same time, labor leaders bitterly resented how employers used the family bonus system to avoid raising wages, to the detriment of "the real wage that a working father must earn," and pointed to the compression of the wages of unmarried men and "sterile husbands."[57] In 1919, striking metalworkers in the Isère department argued that low wages forced fathers to send their sons into the factory long before they had finished school, because this was the only way to support a household. Higher family bonuses enabled fathers to support their families but were no substitute for higher wages for everyone. Their strike failed to produce a wage increase, but in a typical move to avoid raising wages more broadly, employers granted an increase in family allowances to married men with children whose wives did not work, effectively establishing a male breadwinner wage.[58] During strikes for wage increases by shoemakers in Valence in 1924 and metal-workers in Vienne in 1926, employers likewise refused to raise wages to the level strikers demanded and instead accorded a substantial increase in the family bonus.[59]

Organized labor also resented employers' use of the bonus to punish workers for labor activism, since the bonuses required continuity of employ-ment, and the home inspections by women welfare workers who investigated the childcare practices, health, and hygiene of workers' families. Some ac-tivists also voiced concerns that working-class women, usually the targets of home visits, were more susceptible to employer pressure and would pre-vent their husbands from engaging in labor activites such as strikes. Margue-rite Routier, speaking at the 1925 CGTU Metalworkers' Federation congress, pointed to how fear of losing the family bonus made women less willing to risk strike action. "When you talk about going on strike, a wife, who serves as the finance minister of the household says, ' . . . what if I lose my family bonus? . . . So much the worse; I won't strike.' " Routier argued that em-ployers should pay the family bonus regardless of workers' absences.[60] Like-wise, the activist Alice Brisset in her report to the 1926 CGTU Textile Workers' Federation congress warned against the dangers of employer paternalism implicit in allowances such as birth and nursing bonuses and the multiple social services that textile employers mounted in order to win workers' loyalty. Brisset demanded the establishment of a national family allowance fund administered by the state to replace privately admininstered employers' funds.[61] But the most visible and prolonged critique of the social policies of the nascent French welfare state came in the form of massive strikes against the application of a new social insurance law that went into effect in 1930.

Social Insurance, Masculinity, and Wages

Protests against the application of broad social insurance legislation focused not on the benefits themselves, which included illness, disability, retirement, maternity, death, and unemployment benefits, but on the law's provision that required workers to participate in financing the program. Over the seven years of parliamentary debate on the legislation, first introduced in 1921, organized labor debated the law. Although the CGT supported it as a major social reform, the CGTU categorically rejected the provision that workers should help finance the new law through wage deductions.[62] This requirement proved to be one of the law's most controversial features, especially because it went into effect just as workers in some industries began to experience the shock waves of the Depression. Although some employers raised wages to compensate for the social insurance deduction, many did not. Between July and September 1930, the Ministry of Labor counted some 505 strikes, the vast majority of which specifically targeted the requirement of the wage deduction. Workers in the *haute couture* fashion houses of the Paris region walked off the job to protest the deductions, resulting in the capitulation of Lanvin, Vionnet, Patou, and Chanel, who all quickly agreed to pay the full contribution. Metalworkers were less fortunate; strikes at the Contin Souza mechanical construction factory outside Paris resulted in a lockout.[63]

The largest protests against the 1928 law occurred in the Nord, where employers routinely refused to provide compensatory wage increases and instead established a "*prime de fidelité*," a loyalty bonus for employees with a year of uninterrupted service who had no absences for illness, a strike, or any other reason. Those who met this condition would receive a reimbursement of their wage deductions for social insurance at the end of the year. From July to September 1930, as many as 150,000 workers struck textile employers throughout the department of the Nord, demanding that the loyalty bonus be transformed into a "*prime de présence*."[64] This new bonus, effectively reimbursing the wage deduction, would be awarded for a year of service but would not require absolute continuity of employment and would remove the requirement that the worker have no absences for labor activity or illness. Moreover, after a year, the bonus would be incorporated into the wage.[65] Ultimately the protests demonstrated how the question of financing social insurance threatened to disrupt the relationship between masculine work identities and the wage. Socialist Deputy Leon Blum defended workers' demands and agreed that striking workers had grounds for protest; the bonus should directly reward work, rather than reward "workers' docility or punish their independence. This is a vital demand which their dignity as men and their sense of honor as workers prevents them from ever relinquishing."[66]

The ways that masculine dignity remained tightly bound to men's ability to earn a living wage appeared in the ways that organized labor reacted to social policy by defending the ideal of the male breadwinner. Postal workers, for instance, in debating pension legislation, argued for women's early retirement. According to 1924 legislation, mothers were given an "anticipatory retirement," by which a year of extra service would be counted for each child they had. Mothers of at least three children were accorded immediate reimbursement if they left work before retirement age.[67] Other workers explicitly linked the family bonus and fatherhood to their status as wageearners, distinguishing the production of working men from the unwaged reproduction of "non-working" women. In the same year, metalworkers protested against some employers' practice of paying the allowance directly to workers' wives. "How can we accept [this] insult to producers who are family men, when [employers] pay the family allowance to the woman and don't give it directly to the producer?"[68] The language of protest embodied an obvious assumption about the gender basis of economic rights. Metalworkers also believed that even if wives were employed, the allowance should go to the male head of household. Finally, in 1925 some postal workers demanded an unwaged mother's allowance payable directly to mothers, to enable them to remain at home. Striking textile workers affiliated with the Catholic Confédération française des travailleurs chrétiens (CFTC; French Confederation of Christian Workers) likewise demanded in 1928 that family bonuses be increased from the second child on so that the mothers could stay home. Family bonuses, they argued, should not be regarded as a gift but as a right: a remuneration due the male worker for family expenses.[69] Such claims showed how gender and family influenced organized male workers' thinking about the economic and social dimensions of citizenship.

Shifting Definitions and Arguments for Citizenship

The arguments of working men who claimed social and economic rights on the basis of their status as citizen-workers illustrate the enormous shifts in the relationships between work and family in the 1920s, as workers, employers, and state attempted to reconcile wage labor and demographic renewal. Easing requirements for the naturalization of foreigners and the private and public social policies designed to support fertility also involved redefining male citizenship in social and economic terms, as the right of working men.[70] At the same time, perceptions of women's relationship to family, work, and the state were also changing, loosening the definition of women's citzenship as a social practice.

Scholars have long noted that some women who made claims for political and civic rights did so from the perspective of maternalist politics, supporting the idea that motherhood constituted a vital service to the nation and prepared women for contributions in the political realm. Additionally, they claimed that women's abilities to be good mothers would be enhanced if they could exercise political rights.[71] Bourgeois feminists made claims for state support of maternity and housework on the grounds that maternity is a "social act" and that housework is "productive labor." In 1907 Nelly Roussel argued for protections for women based on the social function of motherhood; delegates to the 1908 Congrès des droits civils et du suffrage des femmes had also argued on these grounds, adding that pregnancy should be recognized as a form of labor: "The pregnant woman works physiologically and psychologically for the nation."[72] The 1921 decree establishing the Medal of the French Family, for instance, pointed to women's social mission and used the language of citizenship in calling upon women's duty to the nation.

Mothers should be honored as they ought to be; they should feel surrounded by the pious respect and deferential solicitude of their *co-citizens*. . . . the importance and grandeur of her social role should be apparent to everyone's eyes. The Republic ought to testify in a striking manner to her gratitude and respect toward those who contribute the most to maintaining, through their descendents, the genius and civilization, the influence and radiance of France.[73]

Unlike those who merely wanted to reward maternity, however, women's rights advocates took the occasion of renewed interest in the politics of motherhood after World War I to argue for women's rights on the grounds of their duty to their country. Women's sexual embodiment could be considered as a foundation of demographic regeneration and potentially as a ground for social rights. Now, however, working women in post–World War I France asserted their claim to both economic and social rights on the basis of their status as both mothers *and* workers. Teachers active in feminist political organizations such as Union française pour le suffrage des femmes

(French Union for Women's Suffrage) argued that postwar changes in women's position constituted a foundation for women's full citizenship rights. As Marcelle Bravey stated,

> In our times, women no longer remain at home, but each morning run off to the factory, office, or workshop. . . . The old ideas about women as "inferior . . . [or] fragile beings,"are now outmoded and the enemies of women's suffrage don't even dare to drag them out any more. At the same time, if our senators don't think that we have enough qualifications to permit us to vote, they seem to believe that we are qualified to pay taxes (1/3 of taxes are paid by women). . . . [W]e pay taxes, yet we do not have the right to control how our money is used.[74]

Although Bravey argued for full citizenship rights on the basis of women's roles as workers and as taxpayers, she didn't think that suffrage would solve all social problems, even if it was a means to improving women's position at work and in private life. War, prostitution, alcoholism, and poverty would only disappear, she believed, with a radical change of the economic system.[75] But in addition to arguing for citizenship rights *as workers,* working women also used the labor movement as a platform to claim social rights on the basis of motherhood as a social function. At the very end of World War I, women in the highly feminized Garment Workers' Federation (whose members had been mobilized to produce military uniforms during the war) had already argued for state-supported childcare services and paid maternity leaves on the grounds that pregnancy was "a function that [a woman] fulfills for her country [and] for humanity."[76] Unlike advocates of republican motherhood, these women did not claim that enjoying social rights could substitute for full-fledged political citizenship. The flurry of postwar family policy initiatives provided an opening for working women to appropriate and transform the concepts of both economic and social citizenship.

Women Claim Social Protection

Following World War I, the two major labor confederations in France, the communist-affiliated CGTU and the non-communist CGT, established women's committees in 1923 and 1929 respectively, in an effort to draw women back to the labor movement. These groups effectively gave women a political voice within the labor movement at the national level and also stimulated their engagement at the level of local unions and trade federations. In the context of private and public policy making during the 1920s and 1930s, working women in both labor confederations debated family policies and used this moment of national attention to women's bodies to claim social rights. Their articulation of rights as members of the political community reflected the different positions of the major labor confederations on the relationship between work and motherhood. CGT women largely followed the organization's pronatalist and nationalist position and privileged maternity "as a social function" from which the collectivity benefits and whose charges should therefore be borne by the collectivity.[77] In 1925, in the context of debates over the revision of maternity leave legislation, a CGT activist, Germaine Jouhaux, supported the position that "in the interests of French fertility and in order to insure the revival of the force of our race and our movement, it is essential that women raise their children themselves and remain at home, at the very least while they are nursing."[78] Jeanne Chevenard, CGT organizer responsible for women, member of the Women's Committee, and head of the Lyon Garment Workers' Union, also argued for improved maternity benefits for working mothers so that they could afford to spend more time at home with their children. These women viewed social supports as based on women's sexual embodiment and focused on the protection of infants, privileging motherhood over work.[79]

Women affiliated with the CGTU took a different approach that reflected the Communist Party's distance from the pronatalist imperative of the period—at least until 1935—and reflected its overall discourse on women's right to work. As we saw in chapter 4, in 1923 Mme Stanko, delegate to the fifth congress of the Syndicat national des Postes, Télégraphes, et Téléphones, evoked the duty of citizens to create large families for the Republic and pointed to the links between the family and the wage. During a debate on the family wage, she rejected appeals for an unwaged mother's allowance and family subsistence wage, opening the thorny question of whether there should be any relationship at all between the wage and the individual worker's family responsibilities. "If one wants to fulfill the duties of a good citizen and a good patriot," she ironized, "then you need big families, so much the better to prepare for the next 'last war,' that will make France even more victorious than [in] the war of 1914." But how many children do you need to constitute a family, and how would one define "family subsistance," she asked. Stanko rejected her fellow delegates' proposals for increasing family allowances on the grounds that doing so would lead to overpopulation and a glutted labor market.[80]

The CGTU Women's Committee also appealed to the social function of motherhood, but they did so by insisting on the responsibility of the state and employers to provide women with institutional supports in order to combine wage work and motherhood. Througout the 1920s and early 1930s they argued that women would not respond to the pronatalist appeals of the state until the state enacted policies that made maternity "respected and rewarded, that protected children, and that supported equal wages for women and men."[81] In 1925, the Union des syndicats de la Seine (Coalition of Seine Department Labor Unions) set forth a program of "Working Women's Demands" that began by asserting the need to give "women the possibility of reconciling their roles as mothers of families with their work."[82] Their program for a comprehensive state-administered social policy included obligatory paid maternity leave for all workers, guaranteed paid vacations, and state-supported nursing rooms and day care centers at work. Thus, women represented themselves in nuanced ways against the hegemonic discourse of motherhood by demanding economic citizenship alongside social rights. In contrast to the vision of social provision promoted by the CGT that saw women primarily as citizen-mothers reproducing for the nation, CGTU women's view of social provision emphasized women's interests as citizen-workers as well as mothers. Marthe Bigot, a Parisian teacher, feminist, and labor activist, took a position even more extreme than her CGTU colleagues, arguing for the primacy of women's work and criticizing maternity as an obstacle to women's larger public role. In a position that foreshadowed late-twentieth-century feminists' efforts to link rights to needs as the basis of social provision, Bigot argued that the state should recognize both women's economic and social rights through the socialization of domestic work and social reproduction, with collective housekeeping, birthing homes, and nursing homes. Political rights, she claimed, are meaningless unless material conditions permit one to exercise them. In order for women to *enjoy* full citizenship, the state must provide women with the economic and social infrastructure that makes possible the *exercise* of full citizenship.[83] Policies that recognized women's rights as social citizens but did not also include women's right to economic citizenship would merely reproduce historical inequalities.

These different positions on women's economic rights in relation to their social rights illustrated one set of dominant discourses on the French welfare state before World War II. One position defended women's right to work while simultaneously providing support for maternity. The other, based on women's withdrawal from wage labor, would compensate women for their "motherly duties," denying women's economic citizenship while making women's sexual embodiment a foundation for social policy and reinforcing the maternalist essentialism that had been used to deny women full political citizenship rights for almost a century and a half.

Few French working women in the 1920s and 1930s would have accepted the paradigmatic gendered division of public and private spheres that shaped the thinking of nineteenth-century liberal political theorists. But the assumptions that historically entitled men to citizenship on the basis of their position in the economy and denied it to women on the same grounds persisted. Men received not only political citizenship but social benefits by virtue of their economic roles; women received benefits by virtue of their dependent position in the family and on the grounds of motherhood. Gender profoundly influenced the discursive frameworks within which social policies were discussed and elaborated and the same policies in turn reinforced the meanings of gender.[84] Women's claims for social protection did not by themselves generate or allow women to shape policies. French family policy was established "from the top down" rather than in response to popular mobilization. Women lacked the political resources to influence social provisions, even though a certain number of their claims were incorporated into the Family Code of 1939 and expanded in the post–World War II welfare state. At the same time, by defining themselves as social citizens in the process of claiming rights, they challenged assumptions about political participation that had been used earlier to exclude them from rights. Whereas political theorists had argued that women's physical embodiment justified the denial of citizenship, twentieth-century women resisted the reduction of their role in society to their physical embodiment and claimed social rights on the basis of their status as both mothers and workers. However, women's contribution to demographic recovery alone was not enough to grant women full political citizenship, as the 1927 nationality law showed. By the interwar years the French state recognized women's legal status as workers, their control over their own wages, and their right to unionize without authorization from husbands or male guardians. By then working women did "own property in their labor," but this was not sufficient to accord them either full economic or political citizenship.[85]

Debates over women's social roles and the gender of breadwinners pointed to the problem of claiming inclusion in the political and social order on the basis of their sexual embodiment alone (or on the normative view of women as mothers), without also taking account of their economic citizenship and the need for economic rights alongside social rights.[86] As the state increasingly intervened in private life in the years between the wars, providing French citizens with one of the most advanced systems of welfare state benefits prior to World War II, the logic of social provision on the grounds of maternity and dependence proved to be a double-edged sword. Women could claim recognition as mothers but the assumed link between the maternal body and the nation was also used to maintain gender difference as an underlying principle of "social citizenship." Employer and state practices during the Depression demonstrated the practical effects of the tensions between these two forms of rights, economic and social.

CHAPTER SIX

ECONOMIC RIGHTS AND THE GENDER OF BREADWINNERS:

THE DEPRESSION OF THE 1930S

The debates over social rights and women's—especially married women's—economic rights that filled the late 1920s acquired new vigor once the worldwide Depression of the 1930s reached France. Sexual difference profoundly shaped unemployment's effects on social life and the policies that attempted to alleviate them.[1] The Depression pushed to the foreground the question of who counted as a family provider and exposed afresh the tension between the rights of breadwinners and the duties of mothers. This chapter examines how the French state's management of the Depression contributed to a gender-based model of economic citizenship that underscored the social model. It shows how employers, the state, and organized labor, in a manner consistent with postwar reconstruction policies, threw into question women's rights as wage earners and the rights of foreign workers.

Historians of women and gender in Britain and the United States have long noted how the worldwide Depression of the 1930s challenged men's ability to support a family and the deeply rooted historically based, symbolic linkages between masculinity and work.[2] In France as well, the Depression disrupted the prevailing model of male breadwinning and tested the limits of the gendered meanings of work and citizenship that had been elaborated over the preceding decade. The Depression constituted a historical moment in which the deep ambiguity about women and immigrant men in the labor force, alongside state policymakers' and labor leaders' defense of fathers' rights and privileges, emerged in the foreground of French social and cultural life. Unsurprisingly, the strongest challenges to women's right to work came from the same conservative groups that supported the unwaged mothers' allowances and argued for the primacy of women's maternal roles in formulating the social policies of the 1920s. Although organized labor hardly spoke with one voice about the gender of breadwinners, questions about *married* women's employment and assertions of men's privileged position as family providers were raised from across the political spectrum. Whereas many countries saw signs of economic revival after 1935 and the French economy experienced a brief and weak reprise in 1936, the Depression's effects in France lasted well into 1937 and 1938. At the same time, the Depression affected the French economy unevenly and with subtle fluctuations over the 1930s that made its effects far more complex than many scholars have assumed. This unevenness and inconsistency across the economy was reflected in the gender and racial/ethnic dimensions of the crisis.

In examining the effect of gender and racial divisions of labor on the experience of the Depression in France, this chapter looks first at the pace of slowdowns and shutdowns in French industry, the sector most severely affected by the world crisis, and in the beleaguered, yet protected service sector, and examines the complex gender inequalities of the Depression. Gender segregation protected the jobs of some men and women while hurting others. Next the chapter examines how the Depression pushed to the foreground a major debate over the gender of breadwinners. As I have argued in preceding chapters, during the 1920s the ideal of the male breadwinner remained a part of the discursive landscape of gender and work, influenced occupational opportunities open to both men and women, and influenced employer-based social policies. As *discourse* the family wage/male breadwinner ideal contributed to maintaining gender relations of power in the labor market and workplace.[3] This ideal continued to shape the gendered meanings of work under conditions where the very existence of work—as central mechanism of social insertion and, some would argue, of citizenship—was threatened.[4] Finally, the chapter shows how the state contributed to perpetuating the male breadwinner ideal and maintaining inequality through social policies designed to mitigate the effects of economic slowdown. As students of contemporary European welfare states have recently pointed out, the male breadwinner model has had long-term policy implications for some welfare regimes. Indeed, implicit in the history of the male breadwinner ideal is a story about how the family and assumptions about the right to work and the formal right to be considered a family provider became imbedded in state policies.[5] Although scholars have argued that France had a weaker breadwinner model than other states, in the 1930s social observers and state officials deployed family wage arguments vigorously, albeit with different political referents and different implications for social policy than earlier.[6] Just as gender shaped the practices of many employers who used unwaged mothers' allowances to ensure labor market flexibility, during the crisis of the 1930s the ideas about masculinity and femininity and the relationship between family and work embedded in the policies and positions explored in the preceding chapters profoundly influenced how the state managed unemployment.

Contraction and Rationalization

Although Britain, Germany, and the United States experienced economic devastation within weeks if not days of the American stock market crash of 1929, in the same year many areas of the French economy experienced record-breaking levels of production, imports, and exports. With nearly full employment, a mere 1,700 unemployed appeared in the official French registers of 1930.[7] Wages continued to rise: the nominal wage of a Parisian industrial worker, indexed at 100 in 1929, rose to 114 by 1931, and public-service-sector employees benefited from wage increases in 1928 and 1930.[8] Yet slowly but inexorably, dark clouds troubled the otherwise sunny economic horizon. Industries that had failed to modernize significantly since the war felt the brunt of the economic downturn: heavy metallurgy, steel, coal, and textiles, and industries that were oriented to France's export economy. More heavily rationalized sectors of the economy such as automobile production experienced difficulty as well, but less drastically. From the fall of 1931 the pace of layoffs accelerated, affecting men and women alike. In Montreuil, outside Paris, officials registered 464 unemployed in November 1931; but by November 1933, 1,847 workers were unemployed, and by 1935, 4,395 workers appeared in the unemployment rolls.[9] By the time the Depression reached its peak in France, February 1935, over a million were out of work, and 426, 500 received unemployment benefits. By 1936, 4.5 percent of the *active population* was unemployed nationally.[10] Recent estimates suggest that if total and partial unemployment are aggregated, the figure rises to 10.1 percent of the wage-earning population in 1936, comparable to that of Germany (10.3 percent), Britain (12.5 percent), and the United States (13 percent).[11] These figures were even higher in areas such as the manufacturing suburbs of the Paris region and in the Nord, where the textile industry suffered exceptionally. In Lille cotton mills, for example, which employed 35,000 to 40,000 workers, cotton cloth production had declined by 60 or 65 percent by 1934. In the nearby Roubaix-Tourcoing agglomeration, 22 percent of the work force was unemployed and many more were put on slack time. Some employers compensated for loss of productive capacity by cutting wages. Some simply closed their factories, as wool manufacturers did in Roubaix, where thousands found themselves out of work.[12] Others laid off workers for portions of the day or for weeks at a time, producing "partial unemployment." Spurred by the CGTU, workers in the Nord organized committees of the unemployed (*comités des chômeurs*) that marched to Paris to bring their plight to national attention in November 1933.[13] Unemployment in the textile industry nationwide increased by 565 percent between November 1931 and April 1932.[14]

In France overall, industrial slowdown had predictable effects on wages. Between 1929 and 1935, industrial wages declined by 25 to 28.5 percent on average as many workers found their working hours cut (the average working week fell from 48 hours in 1929 to 43.9 in 1936).[15] As Serge Berstein has pointed out, these aggregate figures mask the fall in prices that accompanied declining wages between 1931 and 1935. Between 1929 and 1935, the purchasing power of hourly wages for those workers who remained employed full time increased (see below).[16]

Service workers in the public sector fared better than industrial workers in that fewer of them lost jobs: teachers, postal workers, and telephone operators remained employed for the most part throughout the crisis, despite freezes of hiring and promotions.[17] But the average wages of "petits fonctionnaires" declined by almost 14 percent over the course of the crisis.[18] In February 1933 under Prime Minister Edouard Daladier the government made all public-sector service workers subject to wage reductions in the form of surtaxes graded according to income on all those earning more than 20,000 francs per year (a primary school teacher made between 10,000 and 16,000 francs; a chief editorial clerk made between 12,000 to 20,000 francs), resulting in a 2 percent wage cut for those at the lowest level of the civil service ladder and as much as 8 percent for the highest paid.[19] Several months later parliament voted to apply a surtax of between 1.5 percent and 6 percent on all civil service incomes above 12,000 francs and in April 1934, under Gaston Doumergue, the surtaxes were raised to a minimum of 5 percent on all civil servants' salaries, with a progressive imposition between 6 and 10 percent on all salaries above 20,000 francs.[20] At the same time, a decline in the cost of living of 21.4 percent between 1930 and 1935 meant that civil servants sustained their purchasing power throughout much of the Depression.[21] Because full-time work increasingly became an exception in industry, many viewed public-service-sector workers as privileged.

Over the course of the Depression, chronic instability—"partial unemployment" or slack time—increasingly characterized the working lives of both men and women in most areas of manufacturing. Even before the crash, in the summer of 1929, Renault laid off employees for several days a week at one of its workshops. Summer, always a slow time in automobile manufacture, brought further layoffs and closures the following year, and workers were given ten days off without wages in August and a week off at the end of the year. By the summer of 1931, at the Chenard and Walker automobile factory in Gennevilliers outside Paris men were being laid off every other day or, as it was popularly known, "put out to go fishing" (*mis à la pêche*).[22] Renault sometimes laid off workers for part of the week and rehired them the following week at lower wages: in August 1932 the company put two-thirds of its labor force on a seventeen-day "forced vacation."[23] Consistent with company regulations, Renault gave only an hour's notice. One man recalled the practice of slack time: "Some days, at 8:30 [in the morning], the overseer would announce to his workers, 'we've had to stop because we're missing parts in such and such a workshop; come back after lunch.' So the guys would pass the time in the café and come back at 1:30 only to hear, 'we still don't have the parts; come back tomorrow morning.' We lost our wages for the day. No one complained—it was normal."[24]

Employment instability combined with a highly refined division of labor in the automobile industry also meant that at Renault as at Citroën and other large factories, while some men could be out of work for several days or more, others worked overtime.[25] But although partial and irregular unemployment affected everyone, employers protected French men's access to certain higher-paying jobs such as night work. Extra hours that stretched into the night were available to men but not to women, who were "protected" by the 1892 law banning them from working at night; immigrants who had previously worked on night shifts were laid off and French men hired in their place. One man employed in Renault's military material division between 1925 and 1938 recounted, "An hour before the end of the day, the team head would pass: 'You, you stay this evening; you too.' The majority of men were eager to work overtime—there were even some who slept in the workshop. When we started up in the morning, they had already been there for an hour. When we left at the end of the day, they left an hour later. We asked them, 'Did your wife kick you out?' "[26]

Workers at the telephone manufacturing firm of Thomson-Houston in Paris also experienced increasing "partial unemployment" and high turnover. Government cutbacks in the funds allocated to the PTT for telephone equipment translated into reduced production and layoffs at least to the end of 1935 and then again from 1937 when the demands of national defense likewise affected the government funds available to the PTT. Gender differences also shaped men's and women's employment opportunities during the Depression. At Thompson-Houston, between 1930 and 1936, the average number of women working per month fell by almost 50 percent, as did the total annual hours worked by women personnel.[27] One-quarter of the women worked for less than a month; half of the women remained less than three months. The numbers of semi-skilled women working full time shrank over the period so that in 1934, among the 389 women who passed through the company doors, only 73 remained employed for the entire year.[28] Although men also experienced employment instability—45 percent of male workers hired by Thompson between 1930 and 1939 remained for no longer than a year—overall turnover among skilled men was lower, because the company made more of an effort to keep them employed.[29] Some employers also attempted to compensate for a reduced labor force by adopting or further developing methods of rationalization.

Although employers had rationalized industries such as automobile manufacture, light metalworking, food processing, electrical assembly, and government services such as post offices and telephone exchanges, between 1925 and 1930 high employment persisted in these areas in spite of organized labor's dire predictions to the contrary.[30] From 1930 on, however, industrial employers fired workers or put them on slack time while trying to maintain production levels, using scientific management techniques to reorganize existing workers more effectively. Just as in postwar rationalization, Depression rationalization mirrored the already present gender divisions of the labor force and also led to new gender differences based on deskilling men's work, the employment of women at newly unskilled tasks, and the intensification of work. Employers used several principal strategies. First, some substituted women for male workers in trades where the process of deskilling men's jobs that began during the war continued into the 1930s. In light metalworking in 1932, for example, employers replaced male workers whom they had paid 7 francs 50 an hour with women whom they paid at 4 or 4 francs 75 an hour.[31] One woman at Renault remarked sardonically in 1935 that "only two years ago, unskilled laborers (*manoeuvres spécialisées*) [working] on two machines earned 6 francs 50 an hour; we [work on four and] earn only 3 francs 50 an hour. So is it the case that women are stronger than men if they can do double the amount of work?"[32] The same gender divisions that shaped women's low wages also shaped employers' Depression-era wage policy. For example, announcing a wage cut in the winter of 1934, Lille textile employers cut men's wages by 6 percent and women's by 8 percent.[33]

Employers also used piece rates more aggressively, deploying systems of payment such as the Bedaux system, based on draconian calculation of estimated productivity as a basis for payment.[34] Simone Weil's account of her work under this system in the Alsthom metal factory during the Depression, described in chapter 2, provides a poignant example. The practice was also used increasingly not only in industry, in mines and steel mills, but also in the service sector, in banks and department stores. Berthe Albrecht, who served as a superintendent-in-training at the Galeries Lafayette department store in 1937, reported that the Planus system, like the Bedaux system, sped up women's work in the packaging and shipping department, so that her co-workers found themselves "incapable of doing anything at a normal rhythm, even their housework."[35] Finally, increasing use of time measurement (*chronométrage*) alongside new methods of calculating wages allowed firms across industries to increase production and simultaneously to lower wage costs.[36] The Bedaux Society, devoted to convincing employers of the cost-saving benefits of the system, lent its expertise to time measurement in textile production. "By increasing the speed of purely manual tasks like reattaching broken threads on looms, Bedaux time measurement allowed increasing the number of looms that a woman supervised, without adding mechanical enhancements."[37] Similar methods were used by Schlumberger in Mulhouse to refine the task specialization of women in its weaving workshops. In the process of intensifying and speeding up the labor process, textile employers also multiplied the number of looms that workers supervised at the silk mills in the region around Lyon, where the Gillet company employed some 1,500 women and colonial workers on the Bedaux system. The Grand Pré Textile mills in Besançon, for instance, required that workers supervise thirty-two or thirty-four looms at a time, provoking a strike in August 1935 to reduce the number of looms to no more than twenty-four.[38] In the Nord linen industry, employers required both male and female workers to supervise twice the number of looms they had in the pre-Depression years, a practice that local officials feared would lead to more unemployment. This practice had not been uncommon before the Depression, but it intensified in the 1930s, as did the practice of double and triple shifts.[39]

Although organized labor opposed multiple shifts as interfering with family life, employers insisted that the practice was necessary during the Depression in order for the mills to operate continuously and to maintain the industry's internationally competitive position. In the wool industry in 1933, employers also justified the employment of women on double day shifts of seven hours each and men on a single night shift on the grounds that continuous employment was vital to certain stages of the production process. They argued that the necessity of treating soaked and washed wool immediately while it was still warm meant that the wool industry should be given the same exceptions in labor agreements as other industries that operated round the clock (such as forges that relied on continuously operating blast furnaces). Otherwise they would be forced to cut production and lay off workers.[40] Workers' resistance to these techniques provoked some twenty-eight strikes in the textile industry between 1931 and 1935 and led the CGT to shift its position on the potential benefits of rationalization. The Bedaux system also provoked strikes, usually when wages failed to keep pace with accelerated production norms. In 1931, 50 women struck Jaeger in protest against the use of Bedaux production norms, bringing with them 440 male employees. In order to end the strike, although Jaeger refused to grant a wage increase, the company instead created a family allowance fund incorporating a birth bonus and installed a vacuum system to remove dust in the workshops.[41] The settlement illustrates employers' preference for using family policy to compensate workers during the Depression, targeting mothers in need of support, rather than implementing more expensive across-the-board wage increases for all workers.

In some cases employers' efforts to speed up production backfired and forced them to stabilize employment. Women at Jaeger, for instance, found it impossible to meet the production norms set by the Bedaux system until they had worked for the company for some time. Mlle Nick, a factory superintendent working on the production of gauges, found it impossible to produce more than 70 pieces an hour, whereas the Bedaux norms required 150 pieces per hour. Male adjusters and regulators, likewise found it impossible to keep up, even on familiar machines.[42] The result was that some employers, Peugeot and Renault notably, began to work toward stabilizing at least a portion of their labor force from 1933 or 1934 by retaining more skilled and semi-skilled workers full time. But as Aimée Moutet also notes with reference to Simone Weil's experience, women's fear of losing part of their wages in the midst of the Depression if they were unable to keep up with production norms also served as a form of stabilization among women in electrical or mechanical construction. "Fear and forced submission as subaltern workers . . . dominated. The fear of not meeting the production norms constituted a permanent source of shame."[43] According to Moutet, women's integration into industrial work required that to a certain extent they accept their position as subordinate workers whose value was judged and fixed by the employer, even if seemingly arbitrarily. If it took courage to challenge these conditions under normal circumstances, it was even more difficult to challenge them during the Depression, when one considered oneself lucky to have a job at all. Weil reported on the resulting power relations between women and male foremen at Alsthom, illustrated by the case of a woman who protested that the time measurement expert (*chronométreur*) gave her insufficient time to complete her work: "She had apparently been given a very low paying job . . . [so] she complained. [The *chronométreur*] yelled at her as though she were a rotten fish, using a lot of vulgar language. . . . She said nothing, but bit her lip, consumed by humiliation, visibly holding back tears, and undoubtedly, an even stronger desire to respond violently."[44] The woman returned to work, defeated and humiliated at the interaction.

Within a small number of firms, efforts to stabilize the labor force involved implementing new techniques designed to "manufacture consent," such as the establishment of the suggestion box, born of Depression-era employers' effort to integrate workers into the firm, promote "company spirit," and even to benefit from workers' expertise to improve production. This initiative also accompanied cutbacks in employer-financed social programs for employees under the pressure of the Depression. At the Géo food processing firm, for instance, the suggestion box varied according to the gender of the personnel. For skilled men and salaried male employees, the company explicitly solicited technical suggestions about efficiency and marketing. But from unskilled women and male laborers, the company elicited suggestions about the details of the organizing work—how to best expedite orders or avoid wasting water. As Moutet points out, "As a form of discipline, all the more strict in its application to women, the system of suggestions was only designed to get them to accept more easily management's orders."[45]

A few manufacturers invested in new equipment during the Depression to raise output. Food processing employers Géo and Olida, shoe manufacturers, the telephone equipment assembly division of Thomson-Houston, and the Lip foundry in Besançon all built assembly lines in the early 1930s that permitted them to employ women in a greater range of tasks.[46] Renault built a new 220-meter assembly line at his Ile Seguin factory between 1930 and 1935, the longest continuous assembly line in the French auto industry, to facilitate the employment of unskilled men.[47] The number of skilled men at Renault, who represented over 46 percent of the workforce in 1925, fell to just over 32 percent by 1939.[48] But Depression rationalization more commonly involved the reorganization of labor rather than investment in new equipment. Even the attention to fatigue and the application of psychotechnical testing that had preoccupied a certain number of employers before the Depression fell by the wayside. Exceptionally, Renault and Citroën, who had established psychotechnical testing services in the 1920s, and the Paris Transport Company (Société des transports en commun de la région parisienne, STCRP) continued to use these services to select male apprentices, and the Compagnie du Nord railway company created a new a psychotechnical laboratory in the 1930s, following the guidelines of Jean-Marie Lahy. Their main goals were stabilizing a small cadre of skilled workers, increasing production, and reducing work accidents.[49]

Overall, Depression rationalization did not generally involve massive substitution of women for men. Nor did it lead to the substitution of immigrant men for either French women or for French men. Rather, the intensification of scientific organization already underway permitted the employment of women and unskilled men on a wider range of already existing processes. These included more aggressive application of the Bedaux system along with more scrupulous time measurement and assembly line speedups. However, techniques of increasing production at lower costs had predictable effects on the gender division of unemployment.

Unemployment, Gender, and Difference

Although few people in France were untouched by the Depression, working people did not experience its effects equally. Employment patterns and wages varied enormously according to gender and race or nationality, and within as well as between different job categories. Although some historians have been quick to assume that women were among the first fired, this does not appear to have been the case in the majority of industries.[50] France was no different from other countries where gender segregation made some workers vulnerable to layoffs and protected others. Throughout the period, women's unemployment rates remained lower than men's. At the height of the Depression, men made up the vast majority of the unemployed nationally, over 70 percent. Women's unemployment, as a proportion of all who lost jobs, peaked in August and September 1932 at 27 percent and declined thereafter to 24 percent in the summer of 1933 and to 23 percent in the summer of 1936.[51] These shifts are confirmed by data showing that in the manufacturing industries of the Paris region, women's share of unemployment declined from 36.4 percent in 1931 to 28.8 percent in 1936 and 23 percent in 1938.[52] Gender differences in unemployment figures, moreover, appeared consistent despite important regional and departmental variations. For example, although the Nord and the Vosges were both highly industrialized departments with extensive textile industries employing large numbers of women, in 1936 they experienced very different unemployment rates. The Nord, much more highly urbanized, saw relatively high unemployment: 9.3 percent for men and 4.7 percent for women; the Vosges on the other hand, saw much lower rates, 2.9 percent for men and 2.2 percent for women.[53]

Women's status as unskilled, low-paid workers allowed them to remain employed to a greater degree than men, but the feminization of certain sectors like textiles was not a predictable safeguard against unemployment— like men, women experienced layoffs and slack time. In the civil service, in the context of a rising debate about women's employment, government ministries imposed quotas on the number of women who could be hired as chief editorial clerks, and some imposed restrictions on women's eligibility to participate in the competitive examinations (*concours*) that could lead to admission to such jobs.[54] Well before the impact of the Depression on French industry became visible, highly feminized sectors such as textiles and the garment trades, where women made up between 60 to 70 percent of employees nationally, began to experience the effects of contraction and competition. In the textile towns and cities of the Nord and Normandy, for example, slack time was common from 1927 on, reaching eight to twelve hours per week in cotton spinning and weaving (both of which employed large numbers of women) and by 1930 in Lille some companies worked at 60 percent of capacity; the cotton industry overall ran at only 55 percent of capacity. The practice of employing workers on multiple looms also accounted for the devastating unemployment in this industry and provoked strikes. In the Parisian garment industry women experienced massive layoffs from 1929. Workers of both sexes struck to protest cuts in the working week.[55] As Catherine Omnès has shown, the pace of gender-differentiated unemployment varied over the course of the Depression. Women experienced higher unemployment than men early on: 9.5 percent (of the labor force) as opposed to 7.4 percent for men in 1931 in the heavy industries of the department of the Seine. But as the effects of the downturn deepened, men's unemployment rose to 17.3 percent by 1936, whereas women's rose to 16.3 percent in some industries. Male building workers and carpenters experienced relatively high unemployment in the thirties—10 percent for the industry.[56] Metalworkers constituted one of the largest groups of the unemployed—a group in which women constituted 11.7 percent of workers in 1931. Between the fall of 1931 and the spring of 1932, unemployment in this industry increased by six times, from 5,973 to 44, 012. Despite brief improvements at the end of 1932 and 1933, unemployment in metalworking rose to

90,430 by February of 1935; 6.4 percent of workers in the trade were out of work. By February of the following year, some four months before the Popular Front government of Léon Blum came to power, the number of declared unemployed had dropped to 76,577.[57]

Overall, the gender division of labor, along with skill and age, shaped patterns of work and joblessness. Skilled male workers tended to be more protected from the worst effects of the Depression than unskilled, and most experienced relatively short layoffs. In fact, male turners, adjusters, and sheet metal workers were in such high demand in the defense industry that the government created a special school (l'Ecole Rachel) designed to select and train unemployed male workers for rapid deployment in defense plants. Skilled male lathe operators were also in demand in the automobile industry, as were mechanics. At Thomson-Houston although men suffered relatively high turnover, they generally stayed on the job longer because of company policies designed to stabilize the skilled male labor force.[58] Seniority and professional expertise sheltered skilled male carpenters, plumbers, and masons from massive unemployment and age also protected men from layoffs. Younger men suffered less unemployment in certain trades than older men, whereas age and physical condition combined to produce prolonged periods of joblessness for unskilled laborers.

At the same time, Depression-era industrial rationalization facilitated women's ability to retain some jobs. The creation of unskilled work and improvements to machines that had created dozens of jobs for women in metalworking in the 1920s meant that women's unemployment rates remained almost twice as low as men's. In 1936, in the Paris region, women made up 6.4 percent of the unemployed in light metalworking, whereas men counted for 11.4 percent of unemployed in metalworking.[59] In textiles, manufacturers "rationalized" production by forcing women to run multiple spinning and weaving machines and in some cases women's employment increased as they were shifted to automatic shearing and weaving machines that men had run earlier. By the last years of the Depression, stocking manufacturers hired women to operate machines that men had run at the beginning of the downturn. Occasionally, women substituted for men in sales, but generally in inferior or badly paid jobs.[60] Yet apart from these cases, overall few women replaced men, suggesting that men had little to fear from women's "competition" for scarce jobs.[61] In fact, the opposite just as often occurred: employment strategies not infrequently incorporated a male breadwinner model consistent with the more general practice of privileging work as a male right on the assumption that men and especially fathers (rather than women or mothers) should be responsible for providing for families.[62] In metalworking, employers often fired married women piercers, molders, and assembly line workers and replaced them with men in order to limit the number of unemployed men. In foundries in which women were sometimes employed as borers (*noyauteuses*) or even as molders, as soon as it became necessary to lay off workers, employers did their best to ensure jobs for men, especially heads of families, rather than women.

In the food industries as well, it was rare for women to substitute for men; women continued to be employed primarily at packaging, labeling, and in the arrangement and presentation of products, even if the first two of these processes were now performed on an assembly line. The highly refined gender division of labor in telephone equipment assembly meant that men and women each constituted about 50 percent of employees at Thomson-Houston, despite the pressure of the Groupement des industries métal-lurgiques to repress the accumulation of jobs ("*cumul des fonctions*"). By the "accumulation of jobs" the conservative metalworker's organization meant women's "dual functions" as wage earners and mothers. These employers believed that women must choose between the two. But the very gender divisions that had been refined through rationalization also made it difficult for employers to lay off women in this industry and these divisions remained intact, with men working as machine adjusters, turners, polishers, and ma-sons, for instance, and women as bobbin winders (of telephone wire), cable connectors, assemblers, turners, and cutters, for example.[63]

In package manufacture, where women made up a sizable number of employees, men who made wax-lined boxes destined for the relatively shel-tered pharmaceutical and food processing industries held onto jobs. Women, on the other hand, who worked with finer packaging materials destined for luxury goods like perfumes and candy, whose market declined during the Depression, lost jobs. Indeed, the most serious female job losses occurred among women who worked in the luxury and high export trades: garment manufacture and textiles, perfumes, leather goods and the fashion industry. These professions made up between 39 and 46 percent of the female unem-ployed between 1931 and 1938. In some luxury trades as many as 50 percent of the female labor force was out of work. The same was true in textiles, where women concentrated in the luxury branches experienced significantly higher unemployment than men, who worked in skilled jobs—bleaching, dying, and finishing.[64] In the food industry, on the other hand, less affected by the Depression since it served a stable internal market, women "had a privileged position: minimal unemployment (3.1 percent in 1936), increasing numbers, and a rising rate of feminization (37.3 percent in 1931 and 38.8 percent in 1936)."[65] Overall, the gender division of labor and women's segregation in low-paid and unskilled repetition jobs in industry helps to explain their apparently lower numbers among the ranks of the unemployed. It may also be that women's increasing numbers among the ranks of public-service-sector workers and private-sector service occupations, relatively untouched by the crisis, help to account for their apparently lower aggregate unemployment rates. But unemployment was a complex condition that shifted over the course of the Depression. Moreover, contemporaries' measurement of unemployment may have underestimated the joblessness of both women and men.

Counting the Unemployed

Unemployment varied with the peaks and valleys of business cycles even in the Depression years. Women's employment patterns, like men's, differed for different trades and skill levels and included periods of relatively long, but temporary, inactivity. In the department of the Seine, despite several periods of recovery in metalworking and the garment trades, the numbers of women seeking unemployment assistance—one of the principal means of assessing joblessness—increased dramatically from a low of 13,577 in August, 1933 to 23,776 by February 1935. Although the numbers of these women declined in 1936, they rose again the following year and reached a peak of 24,602 in the winter of 1938.[66] Moreover, the influence of gender on the gathering of statistics may have obscured the real extent of female joblessness.

Gender divisions within the labor force influenced the collection of data and shaped the representation of women's unemployment. As Robert Salais, Nicolas Baverez, and Bénédicte Reynaud have pointed out, the Depression of the 1930s threw into relief the inadequacy of definitions of unemployment that had been elaborated in the 1890s and that had served as the foundation for statistical representations of work and inactivity well into the twentieth century. These definitions may also have resulted in the underenumeration of unemployment prior to and during the Depression. For example, the definition of unemployment in the 1896 census recognized but did not decisively include the joblessness of industrial homeworkers or "*travailleurs isolés*" (literally "isolated workers"), the majority of whom, historians have suggested, were women. Unemployment for late-nineteenth-century statisticians was linked to work *in an establishment,* whether workshop or factory. Thus, the statistical model of unemployment excluded a form of work well known to be typical of women, whether they were French or foreigners: industrial homework. Here, gender divisions already embedded in the labor force influenced the practice of counting workers.[67]

Moreover, women's heavy presence in the domestic garment industry also ultimately bore on their eligibility for unemployment benefits because officials treated this occupation as "half-way between a domestic occupation and work that was institutionally recognized as such. Women garment workers performing industrial homework were designated as '*isolées*,' isolated workers, and beginning with the 1896 census, were designated as 'an intermediary category composed of individuals who are neither employers nor someone's employees.' "[68] Despite the undercounting of such workers nationally, they made up some 41 percent of all garment workers counted in the department of the Seine in the 1931 census.[69] Their status as workers arguably confounded state statisticians, for whom they defied easy categorization—both on the grounds of their gender and on the grounds of the location of their wage-earning activity. The slippery boundaries between paid labor and unpaid domestic labor in the minds of statisticians and the fact that seamstresses doing home work appeared to have no stable institutional link with an employer seemingly disqualified them as real workers. Such women, as home workers, often had trouble obtaining from their employer the job certificate that was necessary to demonstrate to municipal unemployment assistance bureaus that they had become unemployed. Work and nonwork merged imperceptibly in a manner that historians of home workers have noted elsewhere.[70] These definitions were not by themselves based on gender difference. Immigrant and French men also performed industrial home work and hence were also classified as "*isolés.*" However, the fact that proportionately more women performed industrial home work meant that fewer of them would appear in official statistics as unemployed. As I suggest later, methods of defining the very category "unemployed" and of counting them had serious consequences for whether or not workers could obtain unemployment assistance.

Historians' estimation of unemployment has also incorporated another problem associated with the ways in which the data was collected: the problem of basing statistics on self-declaration. Because historians have relied on statistics from unemployment assistance bureaus—established piecemeal by municipalities, as there was no national system of assistance—to estimate unemployment, women's joblessness was almost certainly undercounted because of the problem of women's underdeclaration. For instance, the Office départemental de placement et l'organisation des secours de *chômage* de la

Seine (Department of the Seine Unemployment Assistance and Placement Office) only recorded data for those workers who officially declared themselves as unemployed in order to receive assistance. Moreover, women encountered difficulties reinserting themselves into the labor market when jobs became available. Although about a quarter of the women who became temporarily unemployed between 1929 and 1938 found jobs within the next few months, with each new period of layoffs, they experienced longer periods of joblessness.[71]

The gender division of labor in industrial work likely allowed women to experience less overall unemployment than men, even if the real extent of their unemployment has very likely been underestimated. Indeed, their joblessness fluctuated: the Depression's effects in some trades could be devastating, while those in more "protected" jobs (notable public-sector service workers, such as teachers or telephone operators) were not the inevitable victims of structural unemployment. Those who kept full-time jobs experienced relative stability and in a period of falling prices saw their purchasing power improve.[72] Racial and ethnic difference also shaped workers' experience of the Depression and social protection.

"Taking Bread from the Mouths of the French"

As scholars such as Gary Cross, Gérard Noiriel, and Ralph Schor have pointed out, immigrant workers disproportionately suffered the effects of the Depression, not least of all from an unprecedented wave of xenophobia spanning the political spectrum. Conservative deputies such as Pierre Amidieu du Clos decried the "invasion of foreigners," and some blamed immigrants for taking bread from the mouths of Frenchmen.[73] A tract published by the ultra-right-wing Action française in April 1934 in the industrial port city of Toulon illustrated this sentiment, denouncing internationalism and charging that immigrant workers had reduced French workers to poverty. The tract contrasted the numbers of French unemployed starkly with the numbers of foreigners still employed, even though the categories were not exactly comparable: "In the Seine, 160,000 French unemployed; 230,000 wage-earning foreigners; in the provinces, 184,000 French unemployed; 460,000 wage earning foreigners. Who is to blame?"[74] Xenophobic attacks on immigrants were of course a transnational phenomenon, occurring within the larger context of resurgent nationalism, fascism, and Nazism abroad and the rise of fascist mass organizations in France. Alongside these attacks pronatalists supported selective immigration in the service of increasing population, and the French colonial empire "came home" in the Colonial Exposition of 1931. Hostility to immigrant workers became more overt than ever before. Numerous voices within and outside government argued that employment should be the privilege of French nationals—especially French fathers—and foreigners should be denied work permits. These same voices encouraged the government to pursue the repatriation of immigrants and migrants that some employers had already begun and spoke in favor of closing borders to newcomers.[75]

The debate over the relationship between immigration and unemployment also came from left-wing deputies and politicians and from members of organized labor who, although they avoided blatant xenophobia, nonetheless called for measures to reduce the size of the foreign labor force and for giving priority to French men. Within the ranks of organized labor, many of these appeals came from trades, such as construction and metalworking, that had long supported the ideal of the French male breadwinner.[76] Beginning in 1930, men in these trades in the CGT regional group in the Seine and Seine-et-Oise protested against immigrants for undercutting French workers and blamed unemployment on foreigners, arguing that employers should limit foreigners to no more than 10 percent of the labor force.[77] Generally the CGTU unions gave at least rhetorical support to foreigners and protested against expelling them, as they did in the Nord in 1933, insisted on equal wages and equal rights for foreigners, in contrast to the CGT's overt promotion of the protection of "national labor."[78] The government took the opportunity to regulate immigrants more aggressively than ever.

Responding to widespread pressure, the Ministry of Labor organized trains to return foreign workers to their countries of origin and engineered the passage of the Law for the Protection of National Labor in August 1932, which established that immigrant labor could constitute no more than 5 percent of the labor force in public-sector jobs. Defining "national" labor as a category apart from "foreign" labor, French policymakers deployed a nationalist rationale with the aim of protecting French workers. The law stipulated that separate decrees would fix limits on the number of immigrants employable in the private sector, and by 1936 employers had signed 553 decrees.[79] Transport requisitions permitted the transportation of foreign workers to French borders. The 1932 law also reinforced foreigners' obligation to obtain ministerial authorization prior to setting foot on French soil, facilitating the regulation of foreign workers in both private and public employment.[80] According to one estimate, the law led to layoffs of a third of immigrant workers in the most industrialized departments by 1936.[81] The mining companies of the Nord-Pas de Calais, whose labor force included over 40 percent immigrant men in 1930, fired 15 percent of their French labor force and 39 percent of their foreign workers (the national figure for the mining industry was 24 percent).[82] Nationally, the foreign labor force accounted for in the censuses of 1931 and 1936 dropped by 36 percent; the French labor force, by comparison, dropped by 12.8 percent. Men were in the majority in both cases but constituted the vast majority of the foreign unemployed.[83] In 1934, the government mounted an even more aggressive campaign to restrict foreign labor and appointed the Interministerial Committee for the Protection of French Labor, with the charge of drafting new legislation with additional controls on immigration.[84]

As Cross argued, the reaction to immigrant workers during the Depression revealed tremendous ambiguity. Alongside xenophobia, many recognized the necessity of foreign labor to the French economy.[85] In spite of how government officials and many observers on both the right and the left linked immigration to Depression unemployment, many employers resisted restrictions, illustrating how essential a racially and ethnically diverse labor force had become to certain sectors of the French economy. They pointed to the same attributes that industrial physiologists believed they had uncovered in their studies of foreign bodies' resistance to fatigue and tolerance for hard labor to justify their continued employment of foreign workers. In protests against the 1932 law and against the government's failure to renew Belgians' work permits, textile employers in the Nord argued that the 60,000 Belgian "frontaliers" (border residents) they employed were essential for their ability to perform unskilled "difficult" labor in various sectors of the industry. If they could no longer employ these workers, factories would be forced to close and create even more unemployment. The labor inspector in charge of the Lille arrondissement concurred. He noted, "The Belgians are especially in demand for their courage, their physical endurance, and their modest pretensions. They willingly accept work that our compatriots reject or work that the latter are incapable of executing for a long period of time." At the same time as noting the differences in the laboring capacities of French and Belgian bodies, he also maintained that alongside their differences, Belgians and French shared a certain fundamental similarity; those who settled in France wound up "assimilating to our race and melting into it."[86] Textile employers in the south of France likewise protested that whereas the French specialized in jobs that were not particularly taxing, Spanish adults—men and women alike—were well suited to difficult preparatory work in spinning and carding. Their sons and daughters specialized as *rattacheurs,* attaching broken threads on looms—a task for which they couldn't find French workers.[87] The racial or ethnic division of labor meant that in spite of support for restrictions on immigration, limits were applied unevenly. At the same time, women's labor and especially married women's work came under scrutiny. Whether or not women's unemployment was higher than men's and irrespective of the tenacity of the gender division of labor, conservative social observers blamed women, as they did immigrants, for men's joblessness. The meanings attached to sexual difference already embedded in workers' and employers' concepts of skill, the wage, the body, and nationality of the worker buttressed the reproduction of the male breadwinner ideal that underscored French social policy.

Economic Rights and Motherhood

Given how state officials, organized labor, and employers repeatedly invoked French men's duty as family providers during the 1920s, it is hardly surprising that women's economic rights should be contested during the Depression. French women's abilities to hold on to jobs while French men stood on line at public assistance offices to receive their unemployment benefits unquestionably rankled among those who saw work as inextricably tied to male duty and French fatherhood. Like attacks on foreign "invaders," attacks on women's rights as economic citizens from the political right and ultra right, especially in the 1930s, accompanied the glorification of women's domestic and family roles.[88] At the same time, public opinion divided on women's labor force participation and women's claim to economic rights. On balance, the strongest attacks on women's rights as workers and demands to give priority to hiring men over women (or to laying off women rather than men) came less from organized labor than from industry and from pronatalist and Catholic organizations such as the Union féminine civique et sociale.

In 1934, at the height of the Depression, Charlotte Bonnin, activist in the Syndicat des Postes, Téléphones et Télégraphes, visited the department of the Nord:

> I observed, with pleasure, numerous women still employed in the foundries . . . at jobs where one is used to seeing men; they have been there for a long time, the male workers acknowledge this and don't believe that women should cede their jobs to unemployed, skilled men. This fact deserves recognition, because it suggests a clear evolution in the thinking of male workers in the direction of justice as far as women are concerned.[89]

Bonnin's optimism about the recognition of women's economic citizenship stood in stark contrast to historical evidence of how women's right to work was contested during the Depression. Organized labor spoke with multiple voices on the matter, however.

Male activists in the CGTU metalworking unions of the Paris region in 1931 remarked on the fact that women, youths, and immigrant workers made up almost 53 percent of metalworkers in all phases of "ordinary metalworking" (appliances, machine parts, and tools), heavy foundry work, automobile production, and aviation. Yet these activists respected the official party line; they refrained from arguing for the family wage and the exclusion of women, youths, and immigrant workers from these jobs but at the same time called attention to the high proportion of workers other than adult French men as a challenge to French men's employment.[90] As in earlier years, organized labor continued to identify women's work in small metalworking shops as a problem, but now they rejected the idea that eliminating women from the factory floor would eliminate wage competition and/or unemployment. Acknowledging the definitive presence of women in metalworking, they resolved that the Metalworkers' Federation should resist women's industrial exploitation by campaigning for equal unemployment benefits, equal pay for equal work, banning night work and work in dangerous jobs, and better maternity leave and family policies.[91] Although metalworking labor activists continued to address the "problem of the woman worker" in the 1930s as they did earlier, they now seemed prepared to acknowledge the inevitability of women's work in these trades rather than invoke the rights of male breadwinners.

Similarly, although male textile workers during the First World War had resisted women's work on heavy Jacquard looms, by the later 1920s and into the 1930s male labor activists supported the treatment of women as equal partners. This position owed much to women's presence in the textile labor force. In 1931 women made up 59 percent of the labor force in textiles nationally, and 52 percent of the labor force in the department of the Nord (by 1936 their proportion had dropped off slightly to 57 percent and 51 percent respectively).[92] But even in the Nord, which next to the Seine suffered the second highest unemployment rates in France, it was hardly possible for textile activists to defend the male breadwinner. Alongside immigrant workers, women had become integral to textile manufacture since the expansion and rationalization of the industry in the 1920s.[93] Rather than proclaim the rights of male breadwinners, textile workers leveled their protests against rationalization and particularly the supervision of multiple looms. They demanded equal access to unemployment benefits for all workers, regardless of age, sex, and nationality, and improved benefits for all workers.[94] Labor leaders' and feminists' defense of women's right to work during the Depression was consistent with their defense of women's economic rights more broadly but also reflected broad divisions within the ranks of organized labor. Whereas the socialist Germaine Fauchère defended an allowance for stay-at-home mothers in 1934, the communist Jeanne Buland roundly condemned such implicit encouragement that married women leave the labor force.[95] Women in the CGTU, echoing the official communist position, condemned efforts to return working women to the home as "demagogic" and divisive and opposed unwaged mothers' allowances as an effort to confine women to the family and servitude to their husbands and children. They argued that the problem was not with women's productive (by which they meant wage) labor but with the fact that "they become the exploited who work for the profit of their employers." To return women to the home, "to let them make do with the meagre wages of their husbands, to let their children go hungry, is this . . . re-establishing the family?"[96] Dockworkers, on the other hand, held fast to the male breadwinner ideal. Men in this exclusively male trade in the port city of Dunkerque protested that "renters, who have nothing to feed their wives and children, can hardly pay their rent . . . let us rise to defend bread for our wives and children."[97] The official position of the CGT during the Depression privileged the male breadwinner.

At its 1933 congress CGT activists openly supported the primacy of a domestic vocation for women. Alongside an official discourse that proclaimed the right to work for all stood the assertion that women had the right to work only "if necessary." The CGT women's organizer, Jeanne Chevenard, argued that the CGT should support family allowances large enough to allow women to remain at home—effectively an unwaged mother's allowance.[98] But not all CGT-affiliated unions accepted this position. Members of the Union fédérale des employés (business employees, clerks, and shop workers), who proposed limiting married women's work at their 1933 congress, recognized the impossibility of such a measure.[99] Just before the reunification of communist and non-communist labor confederations in 1936, CGT activists' position shifted. Delegates to the 1935 CGT congress from the garment workers,' postal workers,' teachers,' tobacco workers,' railway workers,' and hat makers' federations all protested against women's withdrawal from the labor force, even in the context of job scarcity. Condemning the unwaged mother's allowance, they proposed instead a reduction in the working hours of all workers as a solution to the problem of Depression unemployment.[100] Indeed, a 1938 poll conducted by the Fédération nationale des syndicats des employés (National Federation of Unions of Office and Shopworkers), which included numerous saleswomen, clerks, and secretaries, demonstrated a firm rejection of the unwaged mother's allowance and a defense of women's right to work.[101]

Within the ranks of organized labor, only the Catholic CFTC consistently maintained a vision of the family based on women's dependence on a male breadwinner in their "natural role" as wives and mothers. The secretary of the Syndicat féminin de Lille (CFTC), Mlle Vion, defended the return of working women to the home and argued that raising men's wages would permit women to fulfill their "natural mission." Although she recognized the need for single women and widows to work, she proposed that women be encouraged to work only part time for no more than four hours per day, as a first step toward the total suppression of married women's work. Women who remained at home, she argued, deserved to receive the same nursing bonuses as factory or shop workers.[102]

Employer organizations and some policymakers argued the most strenuously for removing married women from the labor force in order to protect men's jobs. The conservative Société d'études et d'informations économiques promoted reducing the size of the female labor force overall as a measure of "economic and social progress" in 1931. Women's entry into professional careers had taken them away from their "natural sphere" and had transported them into a sphere "which is congruent neither with reason, nor with their *natural instincts.*"[103] The Society's *Bulletin* quoted the work of the Italian sociologist Gina Lombroso, daughter of the well-known criminologist Cesare Lombroso, who had written extensively on women's industrial work, protective labor legislation, and women's suffrage. Lombroso criticized the rampant gender confusion that resulted from women taking on "men's jobs" and argued that women's labor force participation was responsible for high taxation in industrialized countries. Now the state had to pay for all the unpaid care work that women formerly performed in their homes: caring for children and the sick, economizing to see families through hard times, making clothing for the family, educating children, and caring for unemployed men.[104] In a similar vein, but with more concrete proposals, Maurice Olivier, representing employers' organizations in the Nord, launched the recommendation that women with three or more children be barred from employment and receive instead an allowance equal to two-thirds of the average wage they would have made. This use of family benefits to restrict women's labor force participation would give a mother of four children three-quarters of the wages she would have made, and the mother of five children would receive the equivalent of her entire wage in the form of an unwaged mother's allowance.[105] This recommendation incorporated the conviction that women's unpaid household labor would compensate for any loss of their monetary contribution to the family. In similar fashion, the Union des industries métallurgiques et minières, de la construction mécanique, électrique, et métallique (UIMM), reporting on the condition of metalworking in the winter of 1932, illustrated how employers incorporated beliefs about the right of male breadwinners to priority in employment. They claimed that in layoffs the companies had taken account of the worker's family situation. Bachelors and those "without roots in the local community" (by which they meant immigrant workers) were discharged first. Married women were laid off rather than their husbands because "the unemployment of a married woman is in no real sense total unemployment; she can compensate for the loss of her income with economies to insure the survival of her household."[106] These assertions about married women's work constituted moral positions on the distribution of resources in times of scarcity, but the implication that married women should be dependents supported by their husbands also incorporated an unmistakable judgment about gender privilege in the labor force and in the family. Moreover, some employers matched the discourse of the "femme au foyer" (woman at home) with policies designed to encourage women to stay at home.

I have discussed in the previous chapter how many employers' implementation of family policies incorporated the expectation that mothers who received allowances would remain at home to care for children. Such initiatives multiplied during the Depression. Writing in 1938, Madeleine Caunes, a lawyer, spoke *against* the liberal concept of the individual wage based on work alone and *for* the notion of the social wage as incorporating the worker's family needs. As Caunes stated, "Nature imposes a sacred duty on the father to feed and care for his children."[107] The broad distribution of an unwaged mother's allowance would enable fathers to perform that sacred function and would moreover constitute a good policy in conditions of high unemployment. Caunes listed employer initiatives in this direction in 1931 by the Maison Simonet-Godard in Paris, which gave an extra 40 francs a month to wives who had been employed by the company and agreed to remain at home after the birth of their first child. In Roubaix, the "Mère au Foyer" Fund (Mother at Home Fund), established in 1933, grouped twenty textile and metals employers independent of the *Caisses de Compensation* that distributed family allowances. The Fund gave allowances to the wives of men who worked for member companies and had at least one child under school age. In order to receive them they had to live under the same roof as their husbands and children and had to agree not to work at any paying job. Although this system privileged the male wage earner, it also permitted women some measure of control over resources by paying the allowance directly to the mother. In a 1937 judgment in a conflict involving the Chemical Industries of the department of the Maine, Maître de Requêtes au Conseil d'Etat (Master of Requests in the Council of State), M. Blondel, argued in favor of an unwaged mother's allowance in this industry where women's numbers had increased dramatically in the 1920s. According to Blondel, women who remained at home with their children would henceforth receive 125 francs per month benefit. "The maintenance of the woman at home constitutes one of the essential elements of a stable and fertile family life and is designed to insure the education and care of children in the best conditions at the least cost. This [unwaged mother's] benefit must be regarded as one of the normal functions of the family allowance system."[108] By the height of the Depression, employers in Lille, Lyon, Vienne (Isère), St. Etienne, and St.Chamond had all increased family allowances to enable women to remain at home.[109] By 1938, twenty-two companies provided such allowances.[110]

It is unclear how effective these measures proved in convincing women to remain at home, at least during the Depression. Women's lower unemployment rates suggest that women accepted neither the rhetoric of the *femme au foyer* nor employers' financial incentives to remain out of the labor force en masse. Moreover, apparently not all families were equal. Under the terms of reciprocal agreements between France and other countries designed to facilitate the employment of immigrant workers in France in the 1920s, and consistent with the economic logic of French employers eager to encourage the reproduction of the labor force, foreigners such as Belgians working in the Nord could be eligible for family allowances. In November 1938, however, as rising nationalism accompanied talk of war and a center-right government returned to France, a decree law made family allowances available only to French nationals. This legislation was further developed by decree laws of 1939 through 1943, under the Vichy government, making the allowance available only to families with one income.[111] In the meantime, pronatalist and Catholic women's organizations added their voices to the chorus demanding the withdrawal of women from the labor force.

Contesting the Right to Work

In early November 1931, the pronatalist physician Charles Richet published an inflammatory condemnation of women's work in the Parisian daily *Le Matin*, blaming women for unemployment and infant mortality. Women's labor had increased production beyond the capacity of French consumers to absorb it, he argued. Reducing women's employment and returning them to hearth and home could prevent the Depression from taking a further toll. Richet's article produced a flurry of indignant responses from middle-class feminists as well as from workingwomen across the economic spectrum.[112] But some social scientists and economists regarded his views favorably. Paul Pic, writing in the *Revue politique et parlementaire,* argued in favor of an international convention under review by the International Labor Office that would privilege hiring adult men and severely restrict women's and adolescents' employment. Pic proposed additional restrictions on women's night work, work considered to be "dangerous to women's health," and the reinforcement of laws protecting maternity.[113] But even before Richet had launched his salvo, women on the political right and social Catholic organizations had begun to organize a vigorous campaign against working women, especially working mothers, in a defense of the male breadwinner ideal.

The most vehement attacks on women's right to work and defenses of the male breadwinner came from the Union féminine civique et social, UFCS (Feminine Civil and Social Union), whose Ligue de la mère au foyer (Women's Housewives' League), founded in 1933, vigorously promoted women's domestic vocation and campaigned to encourage married women to leave paid employment.[114] Supporting a family wage paid to the male head of household and recognizing that financial incentives would be needed to get women to give up wage work, they proposed an unwaged mother's allowance, the development of industrial homework and part-time work, a special allowance for newlyweds, and preference in hiring male household heads.[115] Together, the Ligue de la mère au foyer and the Union féminine civique et sociale played a prominent role in attempting not only to influence public opinion but to promote legislative initiatives that would encourage married women to withdraw from the workforce.[116] As the effects of the Depression worsened in 1935, the rhetorical opposition to women's work and legislative initiatives gained momentum. In February of that year, Minister of Labor Paul Jacquier declared in the Chamber of Deputies that women's place was in the home, not in the factory, and that all workers over sixty should retire.

Several days later he retracted these words in the Senate and claimed that the government would not force women to leave their jobs.[117] But Jacquier's initial pronouncement legitimated further conservative attacks on married women's labor force participation. In March 1935, two Catholic deputies, in collaboration with Butillard, drafted a proposal for a law that would eliminate family allowances for the first child in order to fund the payment of an unwaged mother's allowance.[118] Although the law did not pass, it was reintroduced during the following two legislative sessions in a modified form. Ultimately, these proposals failed in the face of a Popular Front wage policy that sought to raise all workers' wages rather than pay some workers to stay at home.[119]

Other pronatalists echoed Jacquier's proposals with appeals addressed specifically to men. Working women, they charged, not only caused the unemployment of honest workingmen but were to blame for France's depopulation crisis. Allowing women to work had ruined thousands of homes; it also gave women the habits of luxury and earning, tastes that would take forever to eliminate. Men had a duty to pay attention to their homes "as the sacred source of human life."[120] Henri Roulleaux-Dugage, promoter of the family vote for fathers, writing in the official organ of the Fédération nationale des associations de familles nombreuses (National Federation of Large Family Associations), condemned selfish bachelors. He promoted the superiority of the fecund working man, "the married father . . . holds [in his hands] the guarantee of social order and is far superior to the isolated, nomadic bachelor who is responsible only to himself."[121]

Attacks on women that blamed them for unemployment and employer initiatives to encourage women's withdrawal from the labor force predictably drew fire from feminists. Marguerite Thibert, employed by the International Labor Organization (ILO) defended women's right to work in the pages of the *Revue internationale du travail,* arguing that restricting women's right to work would only hurt working-class families' standard of living, reduce already diminished consumption even further, and impose new burdens on society.[122] The feminist paper *La Française* ran countless articles supporting women's right to work throughout the 1930s.[123] Andrée Jack, a feminist lawyer on the Court of Appeals, protested measures such as the Laval decree of 1935 that deprived women public employees who were married to other public employees from receiving the housing allowance normally given to public-sector workers.[124] Responding to the polemic over married women's work, the Association des surintendantes d'usine (Women's Factory Superintendents' Association) conducted a survey among industrial workers all over France. The results, published in the proceedings of the Association's annual meeting for 1934, revealed overwhelming support for the view that married women needed and wanted to work and attempted to counter accusations that women had contributed to rising unemployment. The Association recommended home economics education that would enable working mothers to combine their roles as mothers and workers and also argued in favor of educating young men about their family responsibilities.[125] But surveys of public opinion such as this did little to alter the popular perception that women did not belong in the workplace as long as men were unemployed. Deep questions about the legitimacy of women's employment and support for employer policies that consciously privileged men's position as breadwinners dominated public discussions of Depression-era unemployment. State policy also contributed to maintaining the notion of gender privilege in work and confirmed underlying support for a family model based on women's dependence on male providers.

State Policy and the Male Breadwinner

Attacks on women's right to work, blaming women for men's unemployment, and defending a male breadwinner norm raised anew serious and age-old questions about women's economic citizenship that simmered close to the surface for over a decade of postwar reconstruction. What was new about these attacks, however, was the way in which the gendered meanings of economic rights affected social policy in the 1930s. Politics was undoubtedly important: with the exception of the brief period of the Popular Front left-wing coalition from 1936 to 1937, France weathered the Depression under conservative governments known for their support of the male breadwinner ideal. In two key areas the gendered meanings of employment and unemployment proved critical: in the legislative initiatives and legal measures adopted in the mid-1930s designed to reduce state expenses and in practices governing the distribution of unemployment assistance.

Although, as I have noted, public-sector employees, including teachers, postal and telephone workers, and women editorial clerks (*rédacteurs*), arguably suffered the effects of the Depression differently from industrial workers, they were not immune to state efforts to reduce expenses while simultaneously responding to the public debate over women's employment. In 1929, for example, the Prefecture of the Seine imposed a quota on the numbers of women who would be admitted to the state examination for admission to the post of *rédacteur* at the Paris city hall. The Paris Public Assistance office likewise imposed quotas on the number of women who would be hired for this position and the government decreed a graduated cut in the salaries of public employees, beginning with the mid-level ranks of the public service (which included the *rédacteurs*).[126] Additional restrictions limited the number of women who could be hired by the ministries of Labor, Health, Interior, and War. By 1934, War Minister Philippe Pétain blocked women's access to the position of *rédacteur* in his ministry, making military service a requirement for the job.[127] Even teachers suffered the effects of government cutbacks. In 1933 the government laid off teachers and suspended further recruitment for a year.[128] In July 1935, center-right Prime Minister Pierre Laval issued a series of decrees (*décrets-lois*) designed to trim state expenses, imposing pay cuts of 5 to 10 percent for public employees and including a measure that would reduce the residency allowance provided to married state employees. In practice this meant that a woman public-service-sector employee whose husband was also a public employee would no longer receive a separate residency allowance and would suffer a reduction of approximately 25 percent of her income.[129] The laws also changed pension legislation that had allowed women public-service-sector employees who were widows of public employees to receive two-thirds of their husbands' pension, limiting the amount that the widow could receive from both her pension and her husband's combined.[130]

The management of unemployment benefits also showed how the state supported the rights of French men as breadwinners. The French state was slow to establish a formal policy on unemployment. Christine Daniel and Carole Tuchszirer have chronicled the nineteenth- and twentieth-century debates between legislators and between organized labor and state policy makers over *assistance* (which assumed temporary need for relief) versus *insurance* (a more durable commitment to compensating workers). As they note, legislators preferred to leave the responsibility of providing unemployment assistance to the labor movement rather than create a state program of unemployment insurance.[131] Gradually, however, the state began to implement piecemeal unemployment compensation. In November 1914, for example, the government created a special fund to help those who had lost jobs because of the war, and this fund extended after the war to assist soldiers returning from the front. An April 1918 decree defined the eligibility of beneficiaries who could demonstrate that they had worked for "a long enough period preceding their unemployment" in a job "for which they earned a regular wage." In 1926, following the revaluation of the franc and resulting spike in unemployment, the government further revised the conditions under which the unemployed could draw benefits, imposing a residency requirement of at least three months. But these measures were designed to supplement not replace labor union funds. During the Depression, however, the fact that only a small number of women belonged to labor unions meant that few benefited from organized labors' unemployment assistance funds. Those who were unionized received less assistance than men because they paid lower membership fees.[132] Non-unionized women as well as men relied on municipal unemployment assistance funds, supported by the state. The government gave subsidies to towns and cities of over 10,000 inhabitants and the local municipalities were left to disburse them. But there was enormous variation in how funds were distributed. Communes held the right to determine the period of previous employment required for eligibility; some localities (Paris and Lyon, for example) took into account the family situation of the unemployed, whereas others did not. In Lyon and other cities, recipients of benefits had to sign in daily at the unemployment assistance bureau during working hours, and anyone who failed to do so for four consecutive days was presumed to have found work. But if this level of variation made assistance uneven, gender also shaped definitions of eligibility and the distribution of benefits.

Determining entitlement to benefits and the administration of benefits stemmed from how the government counted unemployment; women's plausibly lower rates of self-declaration and statisticians' probable underestimation of women's unemployment influenced the distribution of benefits and underscored how state policy operated on the basis of and reproduced the male breadwinner norm. Even if women registered less often than men,

> the unemployment benefits given to a male head of household are no different, whether his wife was a housewife or unemployed. . . . The result is that often she [the wife] simply doesn't bother registering for benefits. Moreover, when the husband works and his wife becomes unemployed, the husband's wages might well be higher than the ceiling below which unemployment benefits would be accorded to the household. In this case, the wife has no interest in declaring herself as unemployed.[133]

As Maryse Marpsat points out, married women, as well as youths living with their parents or co-residing older relatives, were only recognized by the unemployment assistance bureaus as entitled to receive payments if the male head of household was himself unemployed. And even if that was the case, they did not always receive benefits as individuals. "The male head of household's allowance was increased according to a system of coefficients reflecting a certain idea of the family hierarchy and for married women did not take into account whether or not they had actually been employed outside the home."[134] Although the unemployment offices not only provided a monetary payment but theoretically also helped workers find new jobs, not only did they fail to recognize women as independent wage earners in the distribution of benefits but they offered jobs more often to the worker who corresponded to the "model" unemployed worker: the middle-aged French married man and head of household. It was to these workers that the bureaus gave priority when jobs became available. Finally, women who did apply for benefits received proportionately less assistance than men in the form of direct payments because unemployment compensation was based on a proportion of the wage; women's lower wages translated into lower unemployment compensation. Thus, the rules governing the distribution of assistance reinforced the gendered effects of counting the unemployed and in practice reinforced the male breadwinner model, even in a highly feminized area such as industrial homework.[135] Women's dependence on men was the standard underlying the distribution of benefits.

The same practice of giving priority to the male breadwinner appeared in a government circular spelling out the conditions of benefits in August 1933. Again, the government singled out the male head of household as the recipient of unemployment assistance, specifying that "to the main allowance accorded to the head of household (*chef de ménage*) may be added allowances to other members of the family living in the same household." The Minister of Labor added, "If the head of household is not unemployed and does not receive the principal allowance, he cannot receive supplementary allowances [for unemployed family members]. Notably, he has no right to an allowance for his spouse, whether or not she is unemployed."[136] Only if the resources of the male head of household were utterly insufficient could he receive a supplemental allowance for his dependents. But this was an exceptional situation. "In particular, when the head of household has no dependent children or relatives, we see no reason why he should receive his spouse's allowance. According to article 214 of the Civil Code, the husband is responsible for furnishing his wife with all that she needs, according to his abilities [*selon ses facultés et son état*]."[137] Thus, the state linked a family's entitlement to benefits to the employment status of the male head of household and incorporated the assumption of women's dependence on a male breadwinner, an assumption that followed directly from the ambiguity of women's legal personhood within French law and their incomplete economic citizenship.[138]

If the government assumed women's dependence on a male breadwinner in distributing benefits, the case of foreign workers showed how national difference could destabilize the male breadwinner ideal that underpinned policy directed at French workers. By the early 1930s, foreign workers counted for about 10 percent of the working population, but their ability to benefit from public assistance was ambiguous.[139] Nationally, although immigrants counted for between 11 and 12 percent of the recipients of assistance (12.7 percent of the total number of unemployed foreigners received assistance) they could only be given unemployment compensation if they came from a country that had made a reciprocity agreement with France.[140] But even this was no guarantee of assistance. In 1932 the city of Roubaix, where textile factories employed large numbers of Belgian workers, refused unemployment benefits to foreign workers, despite the Franco-Belgian reciprocity agreement.[141] Moreover, because the administration of benefits was left to the discretion of local authorities, rules could be modified to deny benefits.[142] Some municipalities imposed residency requirements for the receipt of assistance. Foreigners' eligibility in the department of the Seine, for instance, was restricted according to a prefect's circular of 1935 that limited the attribution of benefits to those residing in the Seine since at least July 1, 1934.[143] Finally, although a February 15, 1935, decree promised a state subvention to workers employed as part of public works unemployment assistance programs, the recipients had to be French and had to have been registered for at least a month with a local unemployment assistance fund.[144] In the context of Depression xenophobia, pleas from largely communist groups that organized the unemployed *comités de chômeurs* pressed for equal benefits for French and immigrant workers, as well as for men and women. But these fell on deaf ears.[145] In the view of many local governments, immigrant workers had no fundamental claim on unemployment assistance. Moreover, although gender marked the policies governing unemployment assistance for French workers, gender norms linking work and fatherhood did not prevail in the case of immigrant workers, whose status as breadwinners figured less prominently in the minds of government officials. The notion of the male breadwinner itself proved ambiguous for those whose national or colonial status eclipsed their social rights.[146] Indeed, the state did not always consider foreign men on fixed-term labor contracts as family breadwinners—especially North Africans and Polish miners and agricultural laborers—because they often came to France as single men without their families. Although little is known about whether these men sent wages home to families or spouses in their countries of origin, what does seem clear is that the 1927 naturalization law notwithstanding, the state did not always consider foreign fatherhood in precisely the same way as French fatherhood.

A "New Deal" for Gender Equity?

The elections of May 1936 that brought the Popular Front government to power ushered in a period of heady excitement full of hope for a "New Deal" for French workers. Indeed, the Matignon Accords provided an unprecedented commitment on the part of the state and employers to protecting workers' rights to collective bargaining in addition to legislation establishing the forty-hour week, wage increases, and the first universal paid vacations in France. But in spite of Prime Minister Léon Blum's appointment of three women undersecretaries—Suzanne Lacore as Undersecretary for Child Welfare, Cécile Brunschwicq as Undersecretary of Education, and Irène Joliot Curie as Undersecretary for Scientific Research—there was no "New Deal" of gender equity for French workingmen and women.[147] In terms of the settlements that ended the massive labor unrest of 1936 and in terms of employer policies, gender inequality in the labor market and in the workplace persisted with striking tenacity. Catherine Omnès has even argued that as a result of Front populaire wage settlements, the metalworking industries of the Paris region may even have experienced a decline in women's employment. "Faced with the revalorization of low wages, that is, the majority of women's wages, many employers [in the Paris region] held off hiring women. According to the . . . Conseil général de la Seine, the abnormally low hires of women in metallurgy [in that department] were entirely due to 'the wage settlements established by collective contracts.' "[148]

Throughout the economy collective bargaining agreements that established new wage scales and categories incorporated longstanding gender divisions that the Depression only reinforced. In the stocking industry, for example, although male and female workers won wage increases and would no longer be docked for work stoppages, a gender division of labor was spelled out for the entire industry. "Tasks were divided, even subdivided, and then labeled by gender. Thus, women would be 'knitter-minders,' but not 'knitter-operators,' the distinction being that women could not intervene to fix the circular frames on which a small number of women now worked."[149]

A collective labor agreement (*convention collective*) signed in June 1936 in the metalworking industry reorganized job categories, spelled out the difference between semi-skilled workers (*ouvriers professionnels*) and skilled workers (*ouvriers qualifiés*), and adjusted wages accordingly. At Renault, unskilled women assembly line workers (*ouvrières spécialisées*, o.s.), paid at the very bottom of the wage scale, received a 20 to 30 percent wage increase, considerably more than men of the same category (14 percent). But even this increase, bringing their wages to 5 francs 30 an hour, left them earning less than the lowest-paid unskilled male worker (6 francs 10 an hour).[150] In Vierzon in the department of the Cher, another collective labor convention signed in December 1936 showed how gender difference was reproduced in service-sector work. The agreement spelled out the categories and wages of office workers in the metalworking industries of the town, specifying glaring wage inequalities in jobs performed by men and women with the same job description. Male clerks responsible for record keeping, calculating, classifying, and filing, would earn 850 francs a month; women doing exactly the same work would earn 675 francs a month, 21 percent less. Male accountants were to earn 1,000 francs a month, whereas women would earn 775 francs for virtually the same work. Employers appropriated preexisting gender norms to justify wage differentials: the companies would employ only women on office machines (typewriters and adding machines) at 750 francs; office boys, on the other hand, responsible for distributing the mail and running errands, earned 825 francs.[151] At the same time, employers used family policy strategically in order to avoid across the board wage increases beyond those established by the Matignon Accords of June 21, 1936, preferring instead to raise family allowances. During negotiations at Renault, for instance, in response to workers' demands for a wage increase after the September 1936 devaluation of the franc, management argued that increasing family allowances was a better way to fight inflation than raising wages across the board. "If these discussions are to lead to an increase in industry's expenses, this should be resolved by improving the scale of family allowances, or better yet, by adopting, when necessary, a cost of living adjustment that takes account of family expenses."[152]

This position was entirely consistent with the pronatalist policies that underscored the emergent French welfare state in the interwar years and that marked post–Popular Front social initiatives. As Europe dug itself out of the Depression and lurched toward another war, metalworking employers renewed their commitment to promoting the interests of the family, a policy pursued since the end of the last war. Denis Phan has noted how, in an internal memo of June 1938, Renault management "distinguished the purchasing power of the individual from the purchasing power of the family in striving to substitute family bonuses for wage increases. 'If sooner or later it appears necessary to adjust workers' wages to the cost of living, it should be only workers with family responsibilities.' "[153] As Phan notes, this "reasoning was justified by a moral valuation of purchasing power . . . [management argued that] 'the disproportion between the purchasing power of the individual metalworker, or the married, childless worker and the worker with family responsibilities remains scandalous.' " After all, they reasoned, encouraging reproduction of the French population was the only way to reproduce the labor force and stimulate consumption.[154] The culmination of this logic in the Family Code of 1939 illustrated how the state followed this logic and supported a new set of family-oriented policies that incorporated a male breadwinner norm.

The Family Code incorporated the family-oriented logic that governed social policy in France since the 1920s. Concern about low population growth continued unabated in the 1930s—indeed low fertility was seen as a problem serious enough for social Catholic groups and pronatalist groups such as the Congrès de natalité de Lille to propose the creation of a Ministry of Population.[155] But not until after eight years of serious unemployment did such a proposal come to fruition under the government of Edouard Daladier, in the creation by decree of the High Committee on Population and the Family Code, and resulting in the formation of a Ministry of the Family in 1940. The purpose of the High Committee was to coordinate the activities of government ministries with regard to "the development of fertility, rural repopulation, an end to urban overcrowding, and to develop French policy on the penetration, residency, and establishment of foreigners on French territory and their integration into the French population."[156] Within a few months, the Committee had elaborated the Family Code, which modified and codified all existing legislation governing the protection of the family— the entire system of family allowances and related fiscal dispositions—and laid the foundations for postwar family policy.[157] One of its major innovations was the incorporation of the unwaged mother's allowance, fixed at 10 percent of the average departmental wage, obligatory in all urban centers, and accorded to any family in which there was a single wage earner. Although in theory the wage earner could be either a man or a woman, given the fact that women's wages were so much less than men's, the allowance effectively encouraged women rather than men to stay at home. Thus, the Code effectively supported the deployment of family allowances as a way to regulate employment, by encouraging women to withdraw from work in order to care for children, implicitly calling into question women's economic citizenship.[158]

The Depression proved to be a critical historical moment in the elaboration of the French welfare state, during which debates over economic citizenship and over the legitimacy of women and foreigners as breadwinners encapsulated all the tensions surrounding these issues of the post–World War I years. It is tempting to explain the defense of the male breadwinner ideal during the Depression as a reaction to women's apparently lower rates of unemployment and the demoralization of those who saw the right to work as preeminently a male right. It does indeed appear that with the exception of initial layoffs in the garment and textile industries, overall women may have weathered the Depression somewhat more successfully than men. Women who remained employed saw their purchasing power improve.[159] But this explanation by itself is unsatisfactory. The purchasing power of men who remained employed and did not experience major wage cuts increased for the same reasons as women's. The very groups that might have protested the most vehemently against women's work—organized workingmen— momentarily refrained from doing so. On the other hand, other voices that criticized women workers and promoted the rights of male breadwinners in the years following World War I renewed their attacks, this time adding a xenophobic and nationalist thrust to their vision of the relationship between the family and economic and social rights. Alongside employers and conservative social observers, the French state also encouraged the reproduction of gender norms through its management of social policy in the 1930s, demonstrating that the state is by no means a neutral actor in producing and implementing ideology as well as social policy.[160] The practices governing entitlement to and the distribution of unemployment assistance incorporated discourses upholding the centrality of the family and related assumptions about gender and work. But these assumptions applied only to French nationals, not to immigrant workers. Ultimately, by supporting an unwaged mother's allowance, the state sought the resolution of social problems in reinforcing the private sphere of the family and in maintaining the rights of men as family providers for dependent women and children.

The trauma and devastation of war weighed heavily on France throughout the 1920s and 1930s and reinforced the effects of gender difference on economic and social policies and practices. Gender divisions and inequalities in employment mattered greatly in shaping the intimate details of economic recovery, concepts of citizenship, and the social policies that they generated, and in turn laid the foundations of the French social model: the broad package of rights and social benefits of the French welfare state. This book has shown how post–World War I attempts to reconstruct society and the labor force mobilized the meanings of masculinity and femininity in the enactment of new policies. The state's efforts to rehabilitate male authority in the family and men's privileged position in work have often been under-emphasized in historians' accounts of postwar recovery. Yet this agenda exerted a powerful influence in shaping opportunities for both men and women—and particularly the practices of economic citizenship—after 1919. Arguably, France's ongoing demographic crisis, an object of national concern before 1914 and a matter of renewed anxiety in the context of France's high wartime mortality, exerted enormous influence on the postwar reconstitution of gender norms. The revalorization of motherhood that historians have observed in the aftermath of wars and other disasters was accompanied by state efforts to give new recognition to the social value of fatherhood, with advantages to fathers that verged on radically revising the exercise of citizenship. At the same time French legislators repeatedly rejected the expansion of political rights for women. The simultaneous social critique of those who resisted maternity and paternity constituted critical armatures of the cultural foundation upon which the rebuilding of France occurred.

The economic effects of these moves to affirm the boundaries of sexual difference were manifold and visible in the maintenance of job segregation, gender divisions of skill and wages, and employers' regulation of the labor force. Maintaining these forms of difference not only flowed from cultural discourses but fit with the productivist and rationalizing imperatives of employers, who were eager to restore postwar levels of production, and the state, which supported and mobilized those discourses. The fact that reconstruction was accomplished with the help of thousands of largely male non-French and colonial workers, moreover, complicated the cultural landscape while facilitating economic recovery and the sustained prosperity of the 1920s. Immigration supplied workers and also potential husbands and fathers to a country starved of young men, but the social status of most immigrants at the very lowest rungs of the social ladder was never very much in doubt.

Economic recovery, accomplished with the aid of rationalization in a few key industrial areas as well as in public service, took place in part through the refinement of gender divisions but also through racial and ethnic divisions of labor in areas as diverse as automobile manufacture, textiles, the post office and telephone exchange. Age-old ideas about women's and men's natural abilities as workers prevailed, reproduced ideas about the gender of skill, and maintained gender relations of power in the labor force. Industrial physiology shifted observers' focus from the body as a unit of reproduction to the working body as a human motor, but clearly the latter did not displace the former. The creation of new forms of "women's work" accompanied new forms of "men's work," although in multiple instances men and women worked side by side on assembly lines, conveyor belts, and in supervising textile machinery. But geographic proximity on the shop floor did not mean equality for industrial workers. French male industrial workers benefited from training and skills to which few women or immigrants had access. Science confirmed and reinforced sexual and racial difference and the inequalities to which they led. Although it held forth the promise of making orderly and rational a world irrevocably marked by the irrationality of war, it incorporated its own biases in matters of gender and race and reinscribed "natural" differences on the bodies of both male and female, immigrant and colonial workers, legitimizing employers' deployment of women, French men, and foreigners.

Working for the state as an employer, public-sector workers fared somewhat better. The historian Linda Clark has illuminated how gender influenced employment in state administrations and has noted that women made progress moving up the ranks of public administration *because* of discourses

of gender specificity: their allegedly "natural" maternal and nurturing qualities and their supposedly innate sense of justice and moral superiority.[1]
Women in public-service jobs like the telephone service or teaching likewise
had more opportunities for advancement than industrial workers in the
private sector and achieved wage parity with men by the end of the 1920s. In
this sense the state as an employer could be a progressive force for equality.
Yet if gender difference opened opportunities for women in the public sector,
it also closed off avenues of advancement at the higher levels. With the
exception of primary school teaching, where the qualifications and requirements for men and women were the same, gender segregation prevailed. As
Clark has shown, women's jobs in state administration continued to be
defined by gender; women labor inspectors focused on the protection of
mothers; women in the Ministry of Hygiene, Assistance, and Social Protection focused on the needs of children. During the Depression the state implemented gender-specific policies designed to protect men's public-sector
employment. That telephone operators managed to win access to the same
competitive examinations as men in the postal service owed much to the fact
that their job had never been defined as a male job. Indeed, the example of
public-sector employment shows how the state reinforced gender-based inequalities just as industrial employers did.

Family also shaped individuals' relationship to work, but in contradictory
ways. Persistent beliefs in women's "essential" ties to family and motherhood
served as a rationale for maintaining their secondary position in the labor
market and even led some legislators and social observers to propose that
they be paid to withdraw from the labor force altogether. Men's roles as
fathers, on the other hand, privileged their position in the labor market and
reinforced their claims to preferential treatment. These divergent effects of
one's relation to the family illustrate the power of gender to shape men's and
women's opportunities in daily life. The result was that state and employers
supported a male breadwinner norm and downplayed women's economic
citizenship. I have suggested that employment data alone as an indicator of
the presence of a strong or weak male breadwinner norm says little about the
practical and cultural dimensions of breadwinning. Yet how social actors
think about economic rights and economic citizenship is crucial to understanding how welfare policies have developed historically. Male breadwinner
discourse, although not decisive in limiting women's employment in France,
had remarkable durability and exerted considerable influence. Efforts to
bolster the authority of fathers in the family after World War I accompanied
employers' rewards for mothers who left work to bear and care for children.

Employment-based inequalities also governed thinking about the foundations of citizenship and the nature of social citizenship and influenced family allowances, citizen's rights to assistance in economic crisis, and the unequal distribution of unemployment compensation during the Depression. Women's right to work at the occupation of their choice at wages equal to those of men remained contested and relatively insecure.

Organized labor in France contributed to sustaining the deep ambivalence about women's economic rights in the interwar period. Labor's rhetoric of equality for all led to unprecedented efforts to organize women and immigrant workers and gave French women a unique platform from which to voice demands and attempt to influence labor strategy. At the same time as they gave lip service to "equal pay for equal work," many male labor activists upheld the male breadwinner ideal. Officially, they continued to view both women and immigrants as separate categories of labor, much as employers did, and never succeeded in bringing large numbers of either under the umbrella of unions. Even the numbers of organized French male workers dwindled steadily throughout the interwar years until the heroic moment of the Front populaire. The fact that throughout almost the entire period labor suffered from multiple internal political fractures did not make this task any easier. For many in the ranks of organized labor, rationalization and science held forth the promise of a better world with rising living standards, leisure, and participation in a fledgling consumer culture—a far cry indeed from the brash proclamations of the prewar revolutionary syndicalists. For others, the new "scientific methods" led to overwork, sapped workers of their energy, and proved damaging to family life.

The pressing need for labor between the wars and concern about family and population as prominent keystones of national security brought together gender, nationality, and class in developing the framework of the interwar liberal democratic state. Broadening citizenship was one way to do this. French policymakers, desperate to increase French population, facilitated the naturalization of foreigners, the vast majority of them working-class men who had settled on French soil, allowed French women to retain their nationality, and proclaimed the irrevocable Frenchness of their children. In spite of the ways that doctors and social observers developed new varieties of racial thinking and new taxonomies of race in the interwar years, questions of race or nationality arguably paled before the larger goal of resolving the French demographic crisis.

Employment-based inequalities also governed thinking about the gender foundations of citizenship and social rights. Protecting motherhood and the family was another way in which the liberal state expanded its reach, long before Marshall articulated his notion of social citizenship. Although the development of the French welfare state occurred outside of workers' control, social protection became a site at which working-class women articulated their identities as *both* workers and mothers, as *both* economic and social citizens. But the shadow of the male breadwinner ideal could be seen in the background in the gendered logics of private regimes of social provision and state support for mothers' withdrawal from paid employment. During the Depression, the male breadwinner ideal did not drive women from the labor force but reinforced both the discourse and practice of women's dependence within the family. The Depression simultaneously confirmed the extent to which women were solidly embedded within the French economy *and* the durability of gender inequalities. State reinforcement of a male breadwinner norm through policies designed to manage Depression-era unemployment contributed to the picture.

The 1939 Family Code, with its provision for an unwaged mother's allowance, gave state sanction to the male breadwinner ideal. That moment was quickly followed by an authoritarian regime that attempted to return women to the home once and for all and provide concrete rewards to the prolific male breadwinner and father in ways that went much further than efforts to reward republican fatherhood of the preceding two decades. However, the experience of the Occupation almost guaranteed that gender would be in the forefront of questions of equity in the post-1944 era—beginning with granting suffrage to women—and that gender equality would become part of the founding myth of the Fourth Republic. The first economic planning document (the first *Plan*) issued in 1945 called upon women (alongside immigrants) to do their part in the economic reconstruction of France by returning to work. As the Preamble to the 1946 Fourth Republic Constitution as well as that of the Fifth Republic (1958) proclaimed, "The law guarantees to women rights equal to those of men in all domains," and affirmed that "Everyone has the duty to work and the right to obtain employment."[2] Yet the extent to which that founding myth had the capacity to engender economic citizenship for women in the late twentieth and early twenty-first centuries was another matter.

If it is the case that French policies on the family and employment during the 1920s and 1930s that incorporated fundamental inequalities of gender, race, and ethnicity laid the foundation for the French social model of the later twentieth century, then what were the effects of gender-based (and occasionally racial) foundations of work and rights on the post–World War II welfare state? The existence of prewar forms of social protection—family allowances, social insurance, and provisions for unwaged mothers' allowances, among others, all incorporated into the social policies of Vichy—facilitated the rapid restoration of postwar measures designed to boost population growth. Indeed, during the war, in an apartment on St. James Square in London, a group of French social reformers officially known as the Section sociale de la commission pour l'étude des problèmes d'après guerre économique et social (Social Section of the Commission for the Study of Postwar Economic and Social Problems) sketched out the contours of the postwar French welfare state.[3] Immediately after the war, the broad features of the social model were solidified though a series of laws establishing the social security system and extending its protections to all French citizens residing in France (October 5 and 19, 1945, and May 22, 1946), providing coverage for illness, injury, old age, death and work accidents, and reimbursement up to 80 percent of medical expenses. Additional legislation reinforced the prewar system of family allowances available to all working people (August 22, 1946) and spelled out the terms of maternity and prenatal allowances.[4]

At the same time, postwar social policy incorporated astonishing ambivalence about the gender dimensions of breadwinning. Although the first *Plan* of 1945 called upon women to work, following DeGaulle's declaration in the same year that "We need twelve million beautiful babies in twelve years," in 1955 the government put in place an allowance for unwaged mothers who stayed at home to care for dependent children.[5] This element of continuity in social policy under the Provisional Government and its incorporation into the Fourth Republic welfare state reflected a growing pronatalist consensus on the political center and right and simultaneously incorporated flexibility for employers in regulating women's postwar employment.

Likewise, important gender inequalities within the labor force stood out in sharp relief against the egalitarian rhetoric of Liberation leaders. In this regard, patterns of postwar employment demonstrated strong continuities with the prewar period. Women's aggregate labor-force participation (as a percentage of women in the total population) declined until the 1960s (from 32 percent in 1946 to 27.9 percent in 1962).[6] Women remained confined to unskilled, low-paid work, as of 1970 making up some 67 percent of all unskilled workers (*ouvriers specialisés*) and 76 percent of laborers (*manoeuvres*), and only 10 percent of those in administrative positions. Women in private and semi-public-sector employment earned 66 percent of their male counterparts.[7] Women's economic citizenship was still not fully recognized and although they won full political citizenship with the April 1944 decree that granted women the right to vote, their access to full civil rights lagged. In spite of the equality guarantees of the Constitutions of 1946 and 1958, women labored under a host of civil constraints built into the French Civil Code, particularly within marriage, and lacked full legal personhood. Despite major reforms of the Code in 1965, husbands continued to hold the legal right to determine the household residence, to authorize their wives' employment, and to administer communal property, as well as to control their wives' earnings. The husband remained the legal head of the family and exercised authority over his children. These inequalities in employment and civil rights that maintained women's dependence within the family had implications for the social policies of the postwar years.

The expansion of family allowances and social security and the promise of day care centers and nursery schools following World War II arguably facilitated women's employment and made it possible for women to combine wage earning and childbearing. Yet these features of the French welfare state were neither immediately nor completely reflected in practices after the war. As Antoine Prost has shown, in spite of public pronouncements in favor of women's contribution to reconstructing the postwar society and economy, during the Fourth Republic the dominant paradigm governing family policy was pronatalist; women were encouraged not to work and to remain in the home, caring for children. The mother, not the state, was to take primary responsibility for children and indeed the state did little in these years to encourage women's employment, particularly in the arena of day care and nursery schools.[8] Indeed, the decline in women's labor force participation during the late 1940s and 1950s was hardly accidental, given a social consensus that promoted male breadwinning.[9] This pattern shifted when women entered the labor market en masse during the rapid economic growth and high employment of the late 1960s, and the proportion of married women in the labor force grew to 50 percent by 1968. However, the economic crisis of 1973–74 and high unemployment alongside women's continued high labor force participation forced the government of Valery Giscard d'Estaing to consider the development of a new set of family policies. These policies addressed what had been defined as the problem of reconciling work and family but what in reality amounted to the problem of the incompatibility of women's paid employment and motherhood.

We have seen that during the 1920s and 1930s French employers not infrequently used family policies—family allowances, birth bonuses, and/or unwaged mothers' allowances—to regulate the size of the labor force and to avoid generalized wage increases, especially in moments of economic slowdown, in effect using family policy to regulate employment. These initiatives, while providing employers with much-desired flexibility, incorporated assumptions about the gender of caregivers and were strongly suggestive of more widespread ambivalence—especially among employers and organized labor—about women's status as wage earners. Similar assumptions about mothers' unpaid care work were likewise embedded in state initiatives on childcare in the decades following the end of World War II in moments of economic slowdown. A parental leave law, the Congé parental d'éducation, passed in July 1977, for example, part of the Giscardian package of reforms, constituted one of several initiatives that benefited women who chose to leave the labor force.[10] Originally introduced as a "mother's leave," the law provided that a wage-earning mother of a child less than three years of age could take an unpaid leave from work for a period of up to two years to raise her child, if she had worked for at least a year and worked for a company of at least 200 employees. The law provided that she would be able to return to her job after this period. But as Jane Jenson and Mariette Sineau note, "The government, which had originally proposed [the law as a] 'mother's leave' designed to 'permit wage-earning women to more easily reconcile professional and familial obligations,'" came under sharp criticism from left-wing deputies who decried its implication that the reconciliation of work and family responsibilities was strictly a women's issue and charged that the unpaid character of the leave only perpetuated gender inequalities.[11] Although the government changed the language of the law from "mother's leave" to "parental leave," it refused to require that the leave be paid for fear of compromising the competitive position of French businesses.[12] Given the significant wage disparities between men and women, the unpaid nature of the leave virtually guaranteed that women would take the leave and men would continue to work. The position of the Senate in the debate over the law illustrates the persistence of gendered discourses of motherhood and breadwinning through the naturalization of women's care roles in postwar France among some French legislators: "'First of all, the right to a parental leave belongs naturally to the mother . . . even if the mother's wages are higher than the father's her natural aptitude for raising the young child should take precedence over her [financial] contribution to the household; financial considerations should certainly not determine the family's choice of the beneficiary of the parental leave.'"[13]

Even under the socialist presidency of François Mitterrand, notable for its remarkable record of legislation on behalf of gender equity, the persistence of important gender inequalities in employment influenced the French social model. Again, the parental leave policies and mechanisms of care established in the 1980s are a case in point. Once again, during the economic crisis of the 1980s when the bloom of "les trentes glorieuses" had begun to fade, legislators passed a law providing a *paid* leave, the Allocation parentale d'éducation (Parental Education Allowance, APE). Coming on the heels of a series of progressive measures designed to ensure greater gender equality—modifying tax law to recognize the independence of married women wage earners, eliminating the husband as the head of household in fiscal matters, and establishing gender equality in public sector jobs, among other initiatives—the APE, in contrast, replicated important dimensions of gender *in*equality.[14] The January 1984 law provided a salary-based allowance to a wage-earning parent of either sex who withdrew temporarily from full-time work (and introduced the possibility of part-time work) in order to care for a child, renewable up to the child's second year. Mitterrand, a strong advocate of the law, pointed to the value of "our most important resource: youth" and evoked the dangers of demographic decline, "a menace to the very existence of our people." Parents would now be able to fulfill their main responsibility, the education of their children.[15] Under the terms of the law, an allowance of 1,000 francs per month would be paid for two years to a parent who interrupted paid employment on the occasion of a birth of a third child (or more). Once again, the law came under sharp criticism from socialist deputies who argued that because the allowance was given only for the third child, it created a distinction between children. More important, the level of benefit made the allowance look even more like a "mother's wage" since fathers, who typically earned more than mothers, would be very unlikely to take the leave, a situation that appeared to introduce a form of gender discrimination. Finally, only parents who had been employed were eligible for the allowance; parents who were unemployed were excluded from the benefit.[16] The following year, under the premiership of Jacques Chirac and the regime of "cohabitation" with the socialists, an amended law passed that extended the period of the APE to three years but restricted the allowance to parents who had worked for two consecutive years over the preceding ten years. As Jenson and Sineau point out, this meant that "mothers who were at home while they awaited their third child could claim the APE." In addition, this amended version of the allowance permitted no wage-earning activity whatsoever. "Return to part-time work (or to a part-time paid training program) was only possible for a maximum of one year prior to the child's third birthday. These dispositions of the law were largely interpreted as an effort to get women to leave the labor force and reduce unemployment."[17] In this version, the allowance really took on the character of a mother's wage (or as some have called it, "a model of temporary homemaking") not unlike that introduced in 1939, designed to encourage working mothers to withdraw from the labor market.[18] As scholars have noted, pretending that such policies are gender-neutral "ignores the prevalence of vertical and horizontal labor market segmentation."[19] Presenting what is essentially a home child-care allowance "as a choice, predicated on renouncing. . . . paid work . . . also obscured the effective division of labor in families (liable to be reinforced by temporary homemaking), which will persist as long as fathers do not claim this right."[20]

This book has suggested that racial and ethnic difference alongside and sometimes intersecting with gender also influenced state and employer policies on family and employment. Just as women's questionable economic citizenship influenced policies of the French welfare state and simultaneously reproduced women's inferior status in the labor market, colonial workers' ambiguous status as citizens had parallel effects. Gender also shaped their place in the social model. The numbers of colonial subjects in France rose significantly in the post–World War II years, as numerous North Africans migrated to the metropole in search of work.[21] The vast majority were Algerians. Before World War II, the status of North African men, as colonial subjects rather than full-fledged citizens, had excluded them from mainstream social security and welfare state provisions. However, following the war, the granting of citizenship to Algerian colonial subjects meant that in theory they had the same rights to welfare state provision as other French citizens. Amelia Lyons has argued that few Algerian migrants took advantage of these entitlements, either because they were unaware of their eligibility or had little understanding of the process of dealing with state bureaucracy. Ultimately the state provided special services for them in the 1950s but, following the gender-based logics of the French welfare state in the interwar years, established a gender-differentiated system of benefits.[22]

Newly minted citizens from the French colonies received social benefits that corresponded to the assumption on the part of the state and policymakers that men would be breadwinners and women would be homemakers. Single male workers received language and job training and job placement as well as limited dormitory housing. Women and families, on the other hand, benefited from social services distinct from men's. As Lyons shows, after World War II and in a major departure from the practices of the interwar years, the French state supported Algerian family settlement in

France in preference to the migration of single men. In the context of heightened nationalist agitation in Algeria and among Algerians in France in the 1950s, the French believed that expanded social services would stabilize the migrant population in France. Women in particular became the instruments of stabilization, charged with providing a comfortable family life that would keep men away from Algerian nationalist organizations. As Lyons writes, "If women could internalize proper French homemaking skills they would influence their husbands and the next generation. Surrounded by the trappings of a modern consumer household, and with ties to their communities through schools and other institutions, Algerian men would no longer fall under the spell of the FLN."[23] In a manner consistent with the pronatalist thrust of policies directed at French women, Algerian women now became eligible for the Medal of the French Family, established after the war to reward prolific motherhood.[24] In addition to helping families find housing and providing language training, social benefits for women focused on housekeeping and childcare and lessons in French cooking. No courses attempted to integrate them into the labor market.[25] While these services may have improved migrants' living standards and attempted to integrate them into French society in a limited way, their gender specificity and cultural assumptions about the gender of breadwinners reproduced precisely the assumptions of the interwar years about the scope and limits of the social model.

Postwar social policies that addressed French families and the colonial migrants illustrate how the foundations of social initiatives established in the interwar years persisted in the French social model following World War II. The tremendous ambiguity surrounding women's status as full-fledged economic citizens and the persistence of a pronatalist agenda that together informed the policies and practices of the emerging welfare state in the 1920s and 1930s exerted a powerful influence on the French social model of the postwar years and beyond. The use of family policy as an instrument to regulate employment of French workers was unmistakable. Not only did gender influence the shape of social policy; social policies that implicitly (or explicitly) incorporated a male breadwinner norm—even as other policies supported women's labor force participation—in return informed the contours of women's economic and social rights and also shaped the scope of opportunities available to immigrant men and women. French women who withdrew from the labor market temporarily to care for children lost wages and seniority, despite assurance that they could resume their former employment following a leave. Colonial migrants likewise experienced the effects of the gender and racial contours of the welfare state that in their case were designed to meet both social and political agendas. In both cases the resulting social model incorporated perceptions of gender and racial or ethnic difference that underscored the ambiguities of French citizenship and their consequences for rights in the late twentieth century and the early twenty-first.

Introduction

1 See, for example, "M. Chirac et M. Schröder défendent 'le modèle social européen' à côté du président polonais," *Le Monde,* May 21, 2005; "Verbatim: 'Je m'engage à faire vivre et progresser le modèle français,'" *Le Monde,* June 2, 2005; Guelaud, "Les ressorts du non, 3. Promotion sociale—le modèle social français est à bout de souffle," *Le Monde,* June 3, 2005. As scholars have noted, the concept of the "European model of society" is at least in part an abstraction, inasmuch as the model varies tremendously from country to country according to employment levels and forms of social protection. See, for instance, Ross, "The EU Crisis in a Different Light."

2 Marshall, *Citizenship and Social Class and Other Essays.*

3 Recently feminist scholars have begun to consider supplanting Marshall's three stages / categories of citizenship with an additional category of "economic citizenship," lifting the rights to work and subsistence from the civil and social categories of citizenship, in the interest of framing policies that address economic justice. See Kessler-Harris, "In Pursuit of Economic Citizenship"; Kessler-Harris, *In Pursuit of Equity;* and Lewis, "Economic Citizenship."

4 Siim, "Welfare State, Gender Politics, and Equality Policies," 179.

5 See Rosanvallon, *Le sacre du citoyen.* French women only achieved the important civil right to bodily integrity in 1975, when they won reproductive rights.

6 Nord points to both the importance and the limits of pre-1914 state-sponsored initiatives in "The Welfare State in France: 1870–1914." Janet Horne discussed the importance of the Musée social in the rise of the French welfare state in the nineteenth century in *A Social Laboratory for Modern France.*

7 See, for example, Ewald, *Histoire de l'état-providence;* Stewart, *Women, Work and the French State, 1878–1919;* and Baldwin, *The Politics of Social Solidarity.* Pedersen, *Family, Dependence, and the Welfare State in France and Britain, 1914–1945,* discusses how the state assumed control of family allowances that began as private

employer initiatives. See also Clark, *The Rise of Professional Women in France,* on women's roles as the agents of state reform. Dutton, *Origins of the French Welfare State,* underscores the complexities of French welfare policy formation as a combination of both state and private (employer and mutual aid) models of provision.

8 Offen, "Dépopulation, Nationalism and Feminism in Fin-de-Siècle France"; Dubesset, Thébaud, and Vincent, "Les munitionettes de la Seine"; Downs, *Manufacturing Inequality;* Roberts, *Civilization without Sexes.*

9 For a view of the comparatively slow pace of French welfare reform, see Baldwin, *The Politics of Social Solidarity,* 102. The French established a national pension fund in 1850 and an accident insurance fund in 1868. Labor legislation limited child labor in 1874; banned women from night work and imposed further regulation on child labor in 1892; and in 1898 the French passed their first accident insurance legislation. See Ewald and Stewart; Accampo, Fuchs, and Stewart, eds., *Gender and the Politics of Social Reform.* Stone examined solidarism's initiatives in *The Search for Social Peace.* See also Nord and Dutton, 3.

10 The literature on the welfare state—both on France and on France in a comparative context—is voluminous. On the family policy dimensions of welfare state measures, see, for example, Talmy, *Histoire du mouvement familial, 1896–1939;* Ceccaldi, *Histoire des prestations familiales en France;* and Cova, *Maternité et droits des femmes en France.*

11 Pedersen. See also Talmy, Cova.

12 Pedersen, 18. Jenson takes a similar view of the relative weakness of male breadwinner discourse in France in "Gender and Reproduction or, Babies and the State" and "Representations of Gender." See also Lewis, *Women and Social Policies in Europe,* and Lewis and Ostner, "Gender and the Evolution of European Social Policy," who identify a "moderate" breadwinner model in France; Siim, *Gender and Citizenship.*

13 Downs.

14 There is a substantial feminist comparative literature on the contemporary European welfare state that has analyzed the gender biases of certain forms of welfare provision. See, for example, Jenson, "Friend or Foe? Women and State Welfare in Western Europe"; Siim; Lewis; Gordon; selected essays in Koven and Michel, eds., *Mothers of a New World;* Bock and Thane, eds., *Maternity and Gender Policies.*

15 See Stewart; Auslander and Zancarini-Fournel, eds., *Différences des sexes et protection sociale;* Accampo et.al.

16 See Krémer, "Les inégalités professionelles hommes-femmes sont devenues plus injustes," 16; and Krémer, "Les inégalités hommes-femmes persistent dans le monde du travail"; Fabre, "Les députés débattent de l'égalité professionnelle hommes-femmes," and "La gauche vote sans enthousiasme le texte du PS sur l'égalité professionnelle hommes-femmes." The principal innovation of the law, presented by Catherine Génisson (Socialist deputy from the Pas-de-Calais), was that it imposed financial penalties for employers' failure to review and annually redress inequalities in male and female wages. See also, Maruani, ed., *Les nouvelles fron-*

tières de l'inégalité; Maruani, *Travail et emploi des femmes*; Hubert, "The Rocky Road of Gender Equality"; Ostner, "From Equal Pay to Equal Employability."

17 See Jenson, "Friend or Foe," on the contradictory outcomes for women of modern welfare states.

18 See, for example, Jenson and Sineau, *Qui doit garder le jeune enfant?*; Mahon, "Child Care"; Olson, "Recognizing Gender, Redistributing Labor"; Morgan and Zippel, "The Origins and Effects of Care Leave Policies in Western Europe."

19 Kessler-Harris, *In Pursuit of Equity*, 10.

20 Ibid., 11.

21 Although I argued in earlier work ("Engendering Work and Wages") that in France, defense of the male breadwinner ideal seemed to disappear in the 1920s, further research into the rhetoric and practices of employers, the state, and organized labor suggests that this was not the case.

22 See Downs; Thébaud, *La femme au temps de la guerre de quatorze*; Dubesset, Thébaud and Vincent; Grayzel, *Women's Identities at War*.

23 Roberts has argued for the importance of these challenges to traditional gender norms in *Civilization without Sexes*. See also Desanti, *La femme au temps des années folles*.

24 Childers explores some of these ideas from a different perspective in the first chapter of *Fathers, Families, and the French State, 1919–1945*.

25 Landes, *Women and the Public Sphere in the Age of the French Revolution*; Clark, "Manhood, Womanhood, and the Politics of Class in Britain 1790–1845"; and McClelland, "Rational and Respectable Men." Riot-Sarcey, *La démocratie à l'épreuve des femmes*; Scott, *Only Paradoxes to Offer*; Frader, "Social Citizens without Citizenship"; Canning and Rose, eds., *Citizenships and Subjectivities*.

26 See Stoval, "Color Blind France," *Paris Noir*, and "The Color Line behind the Lines."

27 Cross, *Immigrant Workers in Industrial France*; Lequin, ed., *La mosaïque de la France*; Milza, *Les Italiens en France de 1914 à 1940*; Schor, *L'opinion française et les étrangers,1919–1939*. Noiriel, *Le creuset français*; Noiriel, *Population, immigration, et identité nationale en France*. See essays by Dubois, Rosenberg, Camiscioli, and Beriss in Chapman and Frader, eds., *Race in France*, that address the problems of race and ethnicity in French immigration.

28 Stovall, *Paris Noir*, "Color-Blind France," and "The Color Line behind the Lines" are notable exceptions.

29 Noiriel, *Les ouvriers dans la société française*, 123.

30 Ibid., 121–25.

31 Fourcaut, *Femmes à l'usine en France dans l'entre-deux guerres*; Reynolds, *France between the Wars*, chapters 4 and 5; and Macmillan, *Housewife or Harlot?*, 157–92. Omnès, *Ouvrières parisiennes*, has also relied on internship reports of factory superintendents in training and the retirement dossiers of the Institution de retraite nationale interprofessionelle des salariés to tease out women's experiences of work. More generally on the history of French women in the 1920s, see Desanti;

and Bard, *Les filles de marianne;* Dubesset and Zancarini, *Parcours des femmes;* and Chenut, *The Fabric of Gender.*

32 Bouvier, *Mes mémoires;* Colin, *Ce n'est pas d'aujourd'hui;* Blum, "Féminisme et syndicalisme"; Sohn, "Féminisme et syndicalisme," and Sohn, "Exemplarité et limites de la participation féminine à la vie syndicale"; Chenut, *The Fabric of Gender.*

33 Reynolds, chapter 5, and Omnès, *Ouvrières parisiennes.*

34 On the political history of the period, see, for example, Becker and Berstein, *Victoire et frustrations 1914–1929,* and Borne and Dubief, *La crise des anneés trentes.*

35 Albistur and Armogathe, *Histoire du féminisme français,* 392. Cova, 304–20.

36 See Becker and Berstein on these developments, especially the significance of the devaluation of the franc. See also Jeannenay, *François de Wendel et la république.*

37 Cross; Green, *Ready-to-Wear and Ready-to-Work.*

38 Reynolds's *France between the Wars* and Omnès's *Ouvrières parisiennes* are notable exceptions.

1. Reconstruction and Regeneration

1 Winter, *The Great War and the Twentieth Century.*

2 Cross, *Immigrant Workers in Industrial France,* 55.

3 Robert, "Women and Work in France during the First World War," 262.

4 Downs, *Manufacturing Inequality;* Thébaud, *La Femme au temps de la guerre de quatorze.* McMillan, *Housewife or Harlot;* Darrow, *French Women and the First World War.* Whereas in some scholars' eyes the war reproduced an already familiar gender division with men at the front and women behind the lines, more recent scholarship has emphasized the ways that women became participants in the war, as bombing erased the distinction between "home" and "the war front." See Grayzel, *Women's Identities at War.*

5 On this debate, see Stovall, "The Color Line behind the Lines." On colonial workers in France more generally, see Stovall, "Color Blind France?"

6 See Perrot, "The New Eve and the Old Adam." Perrot emphasizes how the crisis of masculine identity manifested itself in antifeminism and fear of women's increasingly visible economic independence before the war as well as after. There is, of course, a considerable literature written by men on the sheer terror of war beginning with Henri Barbusse's well-known *Le feu.* Equally poignant expressions of the full range of men's experiences at the front are to be found in the trench press discussed by Audoin-Rouzeau, *Men at War 1914–1918.*

7 This critique of women has been well described by Roberts in *Civilization without Sexes,* chapter 1.

8 Quoted by Thébaud, 296, from Rageot, *La natalité.* My translation.

9 From *L'Horizon* (December 1918), cited by Audoin-Rouzeau, *Men at War,* 124.

10 Perochon, *Les gardiennes,* 38.

11 See also Audoin-Rouzeau's more widely ranging discussion of soldiers' reactions to the home front in chapters 4 and 5 of *Men at War.*

12 Barthas, *Les carnets de guerre de Louis Barthas*, 539. My translation. Barthas, a cooper from Peyriac-en-Minervois, a small village in the Corbières mountains of southern France, may also have been expressing his surprise at Parisian life in general.

13 Roberts claims that "[soldiers] exaggerated female wartime independence as a need to dominate men," *Civilization without Sexes*, 25. Roberts emphasizes men's critique of women's lives of pleasure and leisure during the war, women's sexual betrayal and "spiritual sovereignty," as reflected in the literature of the war and postwar years. See also Gilbert, "Soldier's Heart," and Higonnet and Higonnet, "The Double Helix." On Britain, see Elaine Showalter, "Rivers and Sassoon," 61–69.

14 Roberts touches on the destabilizing effects of the war on masculine identity, 26– 27, 33, 138–43, and analyses the threat to male identity in this period as linked to men's concerns about sexual potency and their ability to bear children in the face of women's alleged rejection of motherhood and claims for independence (the so-called *crise de mariage*). See also Sherman's insightful *The Construction of Memory in Interwar France* and "Monuments, Memory, and Masculinity in France after World War I"; and Childers, "Paternity and the Politics of Citizenship in Interwar France" and *Fathers, Families, and the French State*.

15 George L. Mosse's *Nationalism and Sexuality* is a classic statement. See also Offen, "Depopulation, Nationalism and Feminism in Fin de Siècle France"; Quine, *Population Politics in Twentieth Century Europe;* Parker, Russo, Sommer, and Yaeger, eds., *Nationalisms and Sexualities;* McClintock, " 'No Longer in a Future Heaven' "; and Stoler, "Sexual Affronts and Racial Frontiers."

16 The French birthrate was 18.1 per thousand in 1914. See Ronsin, *La grève des ventres*, 197; Thébaud, *Quand nos grand-mères donnaient la vie*, 295; Mitchell, *European Historical Statistics 1750–1970*, table A-3.

17 Zola, *La fécondité* (1899), and see the excellent discussion in Pedersen, chapter 1, and Roberts, 100.

18 See Thébaud, *Quand nos grand-mères donnaient la vie; Les femmes au temps de la guerre de quatorze;* and Dubesset, Thébaud, and Vincent, "Les munitionnettes de la Seine"; Cova, chapter 4; Stewart, *Women, Work, and the French State*.

19 There is by now an abundant literature on the importance of family and reproduction in the making of the French welfare state. See, for example, Talmy, *Histoire du mouvement familial en France, 1896–1939;* McLaren, *Sexuality and the Social Order;* Thébaud, *Quand nos grand-mères donnaient la vie;* Cova, *Maternité et droits des femmes en France;* Spengler, *France Faces Depopulation;* Pedersen, *Family, Dependence, and the Origins of the Welfare State;* Quine; and Offen. See also the forum "Population and the State" in *French Historical Studies* 19 (Spring 1996): 633–754; and Accampo, Fuchs, and Stewart, eds., *Gender and the Politics of Social Reform in France, 1870–1914*.

20 Once considered the stuff of propaganda and panic journalism, the atrocities of war, including the rape of French women in the occupied territories, have been

shown to be more extensive than previously imagined. See Horne and Kramer, *German Atrocities 1914.*

21 The experience of rape also threw into relief the blurred boundaries between the home front and the war front and the position of French women as targets of war–particularly as they were subject to aerial bombing. See Grayzel, 39–48, and Becker, "To Remember and to Forget?"

22 The first set of questions is addressed by Wishnia, "Natalisme et nationalisme pendant la première guerre mondiale"; the second set by Harris, "The 'Child of the Barbarian.'" Grayzel addresses both issues in chapter 2 and points to the way rape underscored the image of women as defenseless victims and also made motherhood another battlefield. On the rape of French women in wartime, see also Darrow, *French Women and the First World War,* 114–25.

23 This is Grayzel's general argument, 52–63; on French mother's milk conferring nationality, see Wishnia.

24 Harris, "The 'Child of the Barbarian,'" 186–88; Audoin-Rouzeau, *L'enfant de l'enemi (1914–1918),* 69–72 et seq. Audoin-Rouzeau argues that gang rape functioned as an instrument of male solidarity for German soldiers: "Groups [of men] united around the bodies of humiliated and brutalized women, who became the objects of solidarity and communication between soldiers. . . . rape . . . became a privileged manifestation of 'masculine connivance,' a rite of admission [into the group] and of virilization" (76, my translation). As George Mosse has observed, war itself was an invitation to the performance of manliness (*Fallen Soldiers,* 61). "Manliness" in war was arguably linked to displays of sexual prowess and nationality, as well as whether one was victorious or among the defeated.

25 See Harris, "The 'Child of the Barbarian,'" 180–83. Audoin-Rouzeau points to how wartime novels that represented rape challenged the foundations of French masculine identity in portraying men, as well as women, as victims. "Within a system of representations that made the protection of women one of the anchors of French national feeling, rape was translated as anxiety about the failure of men, their impotence and their powerlessness" (96, my translation). Audoin-Rouzeau calls attention to the "masculine fascination with rape, a fascination undoubtedly exacerbated by the primacy of virility at the heart of this society of men at the front" (82). He also points out the complicity of the masculine gaze evoked by the visual as well as literary representation of rape: "Belles, denudées, les victimes sont finalement offertes au regard du lecteur masculin, amené de la sorte à une trouble connivance avec les auteurs du viol" (81).

26 Grazel, 66.

27 Quoted by Audoin-Rouzeau, 145–46 (my translation). Audoin-Rouzeau argues persuasively that the war and confrontation with the Germans gave French racial thinking a hitherto unknown legitimacy.

28 Harris, 196. In Harris's words, "barbarian sperm seemed of amazing tenacity and potency."

29 Dr. Variot, chief physician of the Hospice dépositaire des enfants assistés à Paris

(public assistance children's hospital) and president of the Société d'anthropologie de Paris, in a speech given to the Society, in *Extraits des Bulletins et Mémoires de la Société d'Anthropologie de Paris,* Séance du 8 février 1915, quoted by Audoin-Rouzeau, 144. See Audoin-Rouzeau's discussion of the views of Dr. Paul Rabier and Dr. Hamonic, 144–45. Audoin-Rouzeau argues persuasively that these views became widespread outside medical circles. As he points out, national anxieties about "degeneration" and moral decadence, seen in the prewar writing of Vacher de Lapouge, Gustave Le Bon, Jules Soury, Maurice Barrès, and others, influenced the wartime debate over the fate of these children.

30 Harris, 198–200. German accounts of rapes by French colonial (Senegalese) troops also made racial discourse a feature of anti-French propaganda. As Audoin-Rouzeau writes, "on est ici au sources de l'indignation allemande, très largement orchestrée comme on le sait, mais immense néanmoins, suscitée par les violences sexuelles attribuées aux 'Sénégalais' dans la Rhénanie occupée en 1919, puis dans le Ruhr dans 1923, violences solidement adossées à l'imaginaire coloniale du début du siècle sur la sexualité africaine" (35–36).

31 See, for example, J. Laumonier, "Les batârds de la guerre dans la population française," *La Gazette des Hôpitaux* February 20, 1919, cited by Grayzel, 259, note 52; Schneider, *Quality and Quantity,* especially 116–207. Schneider shows how these concerns were transported into the 1920s and 1930s.

32 Mitchell.

33 Schneider, 121. Cova (31–32) distinguishes natalists, who argued for state initiatives in support of population growth, from familialists, who were suspicious of state intervention and preferred that private associations promote the family as a moral institution.

34 Virtually all the literature cited in note 19 above has focused on women, with the exception of Pedersen. See especially the introduction and chapter 1. Pedersen argues that in France issues of gender were less significant in shaping French family policy than in Britain, and that France's history of low population growth made children and the family (rather than individuals) the focus of welfare state policy. Jane Jenson argues similarly, while noting that French welfare state policy did much to facilitate the employment of women. See Jenson, "Gender and Reproduction, or Babies and the State."

35 Schneider, 122; Clark, *Schooling the Daughters of Marianne.*

36 The first maternity-leave law, the Engerand Law, passed before the war in 1909, specified that women who took maternity leaves could resume their previous employment after the leave. The Strauss Law of 1913 required employers to allow pregnant, French working women four weeks off of work before and after delivery and accorded women a small allowance during the time they remained at home. Cova, 152–69.

37 Thébaud, *Quand nos grand-mères donnaient la vie.*

38 Offen, "Women, Work, and the Politics of Motherhood in France, 1920–1950," 138.

39 Thébaud, *Quand nos grand-mères donnaient la vie,* 21.

40 See especially Cova, 16, and chapter 3. Offen argues in "Population, Nationalism, Feminism" that feminists supported the promotion of motherhood in the service of national population renewal at the end of the nineteenth century.

41 On the UFCS, see Pedersen, "Catholicism, Feminism, and the Politics of the Family during the Late Third Republic."

42 On the UFCS campaign for the unwaged mother's allowance, see Pedersen, "Catholicism, Feminism, and the Politics of the Family," 253–60. Theirs was not a position supported by feminists.

43 The term "maternal feminist" is Karen Offen's; see her "Contextualizing the Theory and Practice of Feminism in Nineteenth Century Europe."

44 Cova, 222.

45 Ibid., 226.

46 Ibid., chapter 5, provides a particularly good summary of feminist defense of motherhood. See especially 241, 265–69, and 274–79.

47 I discuss in the next chapter how employers appropriated this theme.

48 On Bernège and the Taylorization of the household, see Martine Martin, "Femmes et société: le travail ménager (1919–1939)"; and Martin, "Ménagère: une profession? Les dilemmes de l'entre-deux-guerres." Françoise Thébaud points out that during the war, L. Baudry de Saunier began this process of rationalizing the household with practical cooking guides directed to saving energy. Thébaud, *Les femmes au temps de la guerre de quatorze.*

49 Werner, "Du ménage à l'art ménager."

50 On Germany, for example, see Bridenthal, "Professional Housewives."

51 Keranflech-Kernezne, *La vie et les oeuvres à la campagne*, 261; Moll-Weiss, *Les écoles ménagers à l'étranger et en France*; Le Blanc, *Enseignement ménager*; Vimont, *Un cours ménager volant.*

52 This campaign was entirely consistent with social Catholics' critique of women's industrial labor in the interwar years. For examples of manuals of domestic economy both prewar and postwar, see Bussard, *Le livre de la fermière*; Aurain, *L'école ménagère agricole chrétienne à la campagne*; Darcy, *Petit cours d'enseignement ménager*; Ecole ménagère ambulant de la Sarthe, *Quelques recettes pratiques appliqués à l'école ménager*; Ecole ménagère Les Fontenelles (Doubs), *Résumé des cours d'économie domestique*; Chenelette, *La journée ménagère à l'école.*

53 Ganay, "Pour la formation d'une élite rurale"; Keranflech-Kernezne, *La femme à la campagne*, 215–28. See also Keranflech-Kernezne, *Trois semaines rurales féminines.* Participating in these initiatives, groups like the Ligue patriotique des françaises and the Jeunesse agricole catholique féminine likewise attempted to combine religious appeals to women with home economics education.

54 See Duvergier, *Collection complète des lois, décrets, ordonnances, et règlements*, 460–62; and Archives nationales [hereafter AN] F10 2631, Enseignement agricole ménager.

55 Keranflech-Kernezne, *La femme à la campagne*, 167, 182–86.

56 See Talmy, vol. 2, 14–21. Talmy provides an extremely detailed examination of the

relevant legislation of the 1920s and 1930s and argues that financial constraints resulted in only minimal applications of the laws.

57 Schneider, 121–22; Thébaud, *Quand nos grand-mères donnaient la vie*, 20–21. Some of these prizes incorporated nationalist and moral objectives. The Prix Lamy and the Cognacq Jay prizes both required that the recipients be French and the Prix Lamy required that they be both French and Catholic; one of the Cognacq-Jay awards required that the mayor of the commune where the potential recipients lived testify about the family's reputation and morals.

58 Ronsin, 198.

59 Bertillon echoed arguments made by Frédéric Le Play thirty years earlier. Bertillon, "Le problème de la dépopulation"; Quine, 64–65. See also Bertillon, *La dépopulation de la France, ses conséquences, ses causes, et mesures à prendre pour le combattre*. Fernand Boverat, secretary general of the Alliance in the late 1920s, linked masculinity and patriotism in *Patriotisme et paternité*.

60 Bertillon, "Le problème de la dépopulation," 358–62.

61 On the application of the law in the colonies, see Boverat, "Il faut à la France une politique d'immigration." As Roberts points out (160), Radical opponents of the surtax argued that it amounted to a punitive measure tantamount to "procreation by constraint."

62 Roberts emphasizes the debate over whether or not single women or widows should pay the tax, 160–65. See also 298, note 63.

63 Talmy, vol. 2, 30–31 and 97; Ronsin, 199; see also Roberts, 160–65.

64 France, *Journal Officiel de la République française. Chambre. Débats parlementaires.* [hereafter cited as *J.O. Chambre. Débats parlementaires*] April 17, 1920, 1053.

65 *J.O. Chambre. Débats parlementaires*, April 17, 1920, 1072.

66 *J.O. Chambre. Débats parlementaires*, March 11, 1921, 1185.

67 Ibid.

68 Ibid.

69 Ibid. As Pedersen shows, debates over who should receive allowances carried into the 1930s after the government generalized the allowance system. Pedersen, "Catholicism, Feminism, and the Politics of the Family," 261–63.

70 *J.O. Chambre. Débats parlementaires*, March 11, 1921, 1192. The Ministry of Hygiene was created in 1920 as the first cabinet-level health ministry; and its first minister, A. Breton, was a leading natalist. As William H. Schneider points out, this was a logical step in state intervention in matters of social hygiene and population issues. See Schneider, 120.

71 *J.O. Chambre. Débats parlementaires*, March 11, 1921, 1193.

72 *J.O. Chambre. Débats parlementaires*, March 23, 1921, 1365.

73 Talmy, vol. 2, 24.

74 *J.O. Chambre. Débats parlementaires*, March 23, 1921, 1362.

75 Ibid., 1362–64.

76 Ibid., 1364.

77 Talmy, vol. 2, 25–29.

78 Ibid., 93.

79 Ibid., 97.

80 Fernand Boverat, "La dénatalité, ses dangers et les mesures à prendre pour l'enrayer," 2. Boverat argued that low fertility led to male unemployment because without children to keep women at home, women would work and take away men's jobs (7).

81 On the promotion of maternity and motherly childrearing, see Klaus, *Every Child a Lion;* Koven and Michel; Cova. On advice to fathers as well as to mothers, see Viollet, *Les devoirs du mariage;* Viollet, *La bonne entente conjugale;* Viollet, *Le Mariage;* Viollet, *La loi chrétienne du mariage;* Sevegrand, *Les enfants du bon dieu.* I am grateful to Judith Surkis for calling my attention to Viollet's work and his promotion of Christian paternity.

82 Letters written to the Abbé Viollet by Catholics during the 1920s and 1930s on sexuality and marriage offer vivid testimony of this tension, even if they came from elites. See Sevegrand, *L'amour en toutes lettres.*

83 See Schneider, 146–69. As Schneider points out, the proposal foundered on disagreement over whether only men or women and men should be examined and subsequently became entangled with proposals for a personal national health card. The latter was adopted in 1939 and in 1942 the Vichy regime made this information subject to government scrutiny (Schneider, 172). On eugenics in France more generally, see Carol, *Histoire de l'eugénisme en France,* chapter 6 on racial selection.

84 Schneider, 212–15. For an excellent discussion of the intersecting concerns about immigration, racial mixing, and gender, see Camiscioli, "Producing Citizens, Reproducing the 'French Race.' "

85 Boverat, "Il faut à la France une politique d'immigration," 119.

86 Lambert, *La France et les étrangers,* 74–78.

87 Literature on the "rural exodus" in the 1920s also focused on the problem of "racial decline" and the writers Lucien Romier, Emmanuel Labat, Charles Heyraud, and Jean Yole raised the specter of racial degeneration due to the low rural birthrate. These writers argued that by repopulating the countryside, men and women could stem demographic decline and maintain the vigor of the race. See Romier, *L'explication de nôtre temps;* Labat, *L'âme paysan;* Heyraud, *Vouloir vivre;* Yole *La malaise paysanne.* Right-wing writers pursued these themes in the 1930s. See Goussault, *Syndicats paysans,* 11–12; Marescal, *L'exode rural et l'école rurale.*

88 Schneider, 214–15. As Schneider points out, contemporaries assumed, rather than sought to define, the meaning of "race."

89 Quoted by Schneider, 236.

90 Martial, *Traité d'immigration et de la greffe interraciale.* Gérard Noiriel, *Le Creuset français,* 35, argued that Martial's physical anthropology was a minority current. However, his voluminous works on the topic gave him a prominent voice on the general theme of racial selection. Others included Pluyette, *La doctrine des races et la selection de l'immigration en France;* Muret, *La crépuscule des nations blanches;* Pairault, *L'immigration organisée et l'emploi de la main d'oeuvre en France.*

91 See Schneider's discussion of Martial, 235–55. Schneider stresses the shift in Martial's ideas from toleration of immigrant workers to biological eugenics by the late 1930s. As Elisa Camiscioli remarks ("Producing Citizens, Reproducing the 'French Race,'" 595), "Participants in the immigration debate conceived of the 'French race' as a dynamic construct with the ability to incorporate select elements into its fold. In consequence, the dominant racial metaphor was one of judicious mixing rather than an appeal to 'racial purity.'"

92 On the civilizing or Gallicizing capacities of French women in marriages with foreigners, see Camiscioli, "Producing Citizens," 614–15; and Camiscioli, "Intermarriage, Independent Nationality, and the Individual Rights of French Women."

93 Martial, 209, 224.

94 See, for example, Hause, with Kenney, *Women's Suffrage and Social Politics in the French Third Republic;* Smith, *Women's Political and Civil Rights in France, 1918–1945;* Biddleman, *Pariahs Stand Up!;* Landes, *Women and the Public Sphere in the Age of the French Revolution;* Fraisse, *Muse de la raison;* Klejman and Rochefort, *L'égalité en marche;* Bard, *Les filles de Marianne;* Pateman, *The Disorder of Women.* See also Offen, "Women, Work, and the Politics of Motherhood in France"; and Cova. Talmy provides a meticulous account of the legislative battles surrounding the slow death of family suffrage proposals, 38–52 and 99–119. See also Childers, "Paternity and the Politics of Citizenship in Interwar France."

95 Smith, 232. Some family vote advocates eventually admitted the possibility of a vote for mothers as well as for fathers as a strategy to win over feminists, but they were unsuccessful.

96 Quoted by Smith, 227.

97 See the discussion in Smith, 226–34; and Talmy, vol. 2, 38–52.

98 Talmy, vol. 2, 49.

99 Abbé Lemire opposed giving men additional votes based on the number of their children and argued that doing so would fall into "precisely the anarchic individualism to which the family is opposed. The goal of our project on the family vote is to recognize the place of the family in the state, by giving it a political right corresponding to its fundamental form" (my translation). Talmy, vol. 2, 47.

100 Talmy, vol. 2, 99.

101 Ibid., 101.

102 See Enfière, *Le vote familial.* Enfière linked men's exercise of citizenship to childbearing and hoped that the family vote would produce legislative initiatives designed to favor the family rather than promote individualism. Enfière also proposed dividing the family vote so that mothers would get as many votes as they had girls and fathers would get as many votes as they had boys. This would presumably stimulate as well as reward procreation.

103 Pernot, preface to Toulemon, *Le suffrage familial ou suffrage universel intégral.*

104 Toulemon, 86.

105 Ibid., 121–22.

106 Abensour, "Le problème de la démobilisation féminine," 492. Downs, 204.

107　*L'Union des métaux,* September–December 1916, 4–5; Robert, "Ouvriers et mouvement ouvrier parisiens pendant la grande guerre et l'immédiat après guerre," 514; Robert, "La CGT et la famille ouvrière."

108　Perrot, "Préface," 8.

109　*L'Union des métaux,* May 1916, 8–10. Downs has of course documented well this dynamic in the French metalworking industries.

110　*L'Union des métaux,* September–December 1916, 4–5. Robert, "Ouvriers et mouvement ouvrier parisiens," 514.

111　Thébaud, *La femme au temps de la guerre de quatorze,* 187–88.

112　Robert, "Ouvriers et mouvement ouvrier parisiens," 524.

113　*L'Union des métaux,* September–December 1916, 2.

114　Ibid., 3.

115　Robert, "Women and Work in France during the First World War," 261.

116　AN F7 13367, Rapport de police (Sureté générale) au Ministère de l'Intérieur, April 9, 1919.

117　Robert, "La CGT et la famille ouvrière," 59. My translation.

118　AN F7 13812, Tract issued by the Syndicat général des industries chimiques. See additional examples in Robert, "La CGT et la famille ouvrière."

119　Abensour, "Le problème de la démobilization féminine," 493. See Downs, 202–25, on the reclassification of metal workers.

120　On the prewar discourse on women and the incompatibility of work and motherhood, see Frader, "Engendering Work and Wages." On hiring women at their prewar "women's jobs," see, for example, anonymous article in *Débats,* December 1918.

121　Abensour, 493.

122　Ibid., 494.

123　Ibid., 495.

124　Ibid., 500.

125　This view differs substantially from the picture painted by Mary Louise Roberts of unremitting blame cast on women for the marriage crisis of the 1920s. See Roberts's discussion of the "marriage crisis" in chapter 5 of *Civilization without Sexes.* Juquelier, "Le travail féminine dans l'industrie après la guerre," 485. On the same theme, see Magnier de Maisonneuve, *Les institutions sociales en faveur des ouvrières d'usine.*

126　Valdour, *Ouvrières parisiennes d'après guerre,* 118, 142, 146.

127　Abensour, 498, quoting from an article published by Jouhaux in *Europe nouvelle,* December 7, 1918.

128　See Fédération française des travailleurs du livre, *Onzième congrès national tenu à Nancy du 8 au 13 septembre 1919,* 252–80; see further discussion of women in the trade, 281 ff.

129　Fédération unitaire des ouvriers et ouvrières sur métaux, *4e Congrès national à Paris les 12–14 décembre 1927,* 269.

130　AN F7 13367, Police report of January 4, 1919, on unemployment in the Paris region.

131 AN F7 13367, Police report of January 3, 1919 on meeting of unemployed women in the metal, chemical, and garment industries.

132 AN F7 13367, Police report of January 10, 1919, on January 9 meeting at the Bourse du Travail, Paris; *Information ouvrière et sociale* no. 88 (January 12, 1919). After 1919 the name of this journal changed to *Information sociale.*

133 AN F7 13367, Police reports of January 25, 1919; January 27, 1919; February 4, 1919; March 2, 1919, and March 10, 1919. See also newspaper articles in this file, "Le Chômage à Paris," *La France libre,* January 19, 1919; "La Réunion d'hier après-midi," *La Bataille,* January 19, 1919; "Les Chômeuses parisiennes," *La Bataille,* February 4, 1919; "L'indemnité de licenciement des chômeuses des usines de guerre," *La Vérité,* February 4, 1919; "Par la démobilization féminine, 17,000 employées d'administration sont menacées de chômage," *Le Petit Parisien,* February 6, 1919. On Couergou, see Maitron and Pennetier, "Joseph Couergou."

134 The government policy of reimbursing employers some portion of severance pay had been in place since the end of the war. See "Pour les ouvrières en chômage: La nouvelle circulaire," *La Bataille,* March 2, 1919.

135 "Le chômage dans les industries de guerre," *Information ouvrière et sociale* no. 91 (January 23, 1919), 2–3.

136 "Conférence des offices de placement," *Information ouvrière et sociale* no. 94 (February 2, 1919), 1–2.

137 Ministère du Travail. Statistique générale de la France et observation des prix. Comité permanent d'études relatives à la prévision des chômages industriels, *Compte-rendu des travaux. Années 1917–1920.*

138 Cross, 46–52. Figures come fom Viet, *La France immigrée,* 36.

139 Lewis, "The Company of Strangers," 36.

140 Cross, 35–36.

141 Noiriel, *Le creuset français,* 142, Annexes statistiques, 408, 411. These figures are for 1931.

142 Cross, 161.

143 See Stovall, "Color-Blind France?" and "The Color Line Behind the Lines"; Vidalenc, "La main-d'oeuvre étrangère en France et la première guerre mondiale (1901–1926)." On wartime conflicts between French and foreign workers and between foreign groups, see Schor, *Histoire de l'immigration en France,* 42.

144 Toulouse, *La question sexuelle et la femme,* 147.

145 Hamp, *Les métiers blessés,* 217, 225. As I suggest below, the comparison between Asians and women was not accidental, as Asian men were not infrequently described as "soft" and "feminine."

146 Juquelier.

147 Morel, "Action politique et sociale."

148 Valdour, 35–37.

149 Cross, 50.

150 Ibid., 49–50.

151 Fédération nationale ouvrier de l'industrie textile, *XVIIe Congrès national tenu à Mulhouse les 13, 14, 15 août 1922,* 118–19.

152 CGTU, *Congrès national ordinaire. 3ième Congrès de la CGTU, Paris, 26 au 31 août 1925,* 392–418. The CGTU paid particular attention to colonial workers who, under the *régime de l'indigénat,* were denied the right to assume leadership positions in unions or to engage in union propaganda. Foreign workers could be expelled for helping to translate union tracts into their native languages.

153 AN F7 13618, Union des Syndicats de la Seine. Notes et presse, 1920–1923, "Rapport de la Commission féminine," sent to the Ministry of Interior, March 27, 1922; see also "Appel aux femmes" of the Commission de propagande et de recrutement syndical de la main d'oeuvre féminine, sent to the Ministry of Interior, March 29, 1922.

154 CGTU, *3ième Congrès de la CGTU,* 152–53.

155 These were the words of CGTU teacher-activists Adrienne Montégudet and Marie Guillot. See "La conférence sur l'organisation des femmes," 2. See also "conférence féminine," in CGTU, *2ième Congrès de la CGTU, 1923,* 615–16.

156 CGTU, *3ième Congrès de la CGTU,* 522–23, 529.

157 In chapter 5 I examine how working-class women envisioned reorganizing social reproduction in the 1920s.

158 AN F7 13618, Union des Syndicats de la Seine, notes et presse, 1920–1923. See, for example, broadsides "Appel à toutes les femmes, à toutes les mères," "Aux ménagères, aux femmes."

159 Some of this had to do with the explicit terms under which immigrant men were recruited, for construction work, heavy agricultural labor, masonry, mining, and filling in trenches.

160 Figures on agricultural employment from Daric, *L'activité professionnelle des femmes en France,* 30. Percentages of women's aggregate labor force participation are from Robert, "Women and Work in France," 262. Robert argued that the economic demands of war had little permanent impact on women's industrial labor and that the war marked the beginning of a long-term decline in women's overall labor force participation. Growth occurred in women's service sector employment, especially in banking and insurance and in public service sector jobs (communications and teaching). If one takes wage labor as the definition of an activity rate, then there is a strong argument for leaving aside agriculture when calculating women's activity rates, for women's agricultural wage labor could often not be separated from women's nonwage labor on family farms. At the same time, there are good reasons to treat census figures with caution. As Sylvie Schweitzer has argued, the 1926 census reevaluated the categories according to which women's work was counted and did not count women working at home as wage earners, even if they performed income-earning activity; nor did it count women who were "farmers/housewives" as economically active. Schweitzer, *Les femmes ont toujours travaillé,* 80.

161 Daric. Women's labor nonagricultural labor force participation declined by 1.5 percent between 1921 and 1926, rose thereafter by 1.2 percent to 1931, and fell off by

1 percent by 1936 under the impact of the Depression. See Zerner, 10. See also Toutain, *La population de la France de 1700 à 1959.*

162 Zerner, 12.

163 République française, Ministère du Travail, Statistique générale de la France, *Résultats statistiques du recensement générale de la population. 1921. 1926;* Gueland-Léridon, *Le travail des femmes en France,* 26. See also Downs.

164 Delatour, "Le Travail de la femme pendant la première guerre mondiale et ses conséquences sur l'évolution de leur rôle dans la société."

165 See Robert, "Women and Work in France," 262.

166 See Deldyke, Gelders, and Limbor, *La population active et sa structure,* 167.

2. Gender Division and the Family

1 Eugénie Rey, "Rapport de stage [de surintendante] fait aux usines de la compagnie "Thomson-Houston," du 17 au 30 juin 1921, 1, 3–4, in Archives de l'école des surintendantes d'usine. My translation. On factory superintendents in the interwar years, see below and Downs, chapter 7. Rey spent three weeks as a worker at Thomson-Houston on an internship as part of her training as a future factory superintendent. This experience gave the future superintendent a glimpse of work inside the factory and a better awareness of the concerns of the workingwomen whom she would eventually supervise. The reports were often surprisingly candid about work, health, and hygiene on the job, despite the fact that they were written to show how factory superintendents could ameliorate women's working conditions.

2 See, for example, Kuisel, *Capitalism and the State in Modern France.*

3 For an overview of this research, see Bradley, *Men's Work, Women's Work;* Frader, "La division sexuelle du travail à la lumière des recherches historiques." Most of the theoretical literature has addressed Britain and has constituted a historiographical debate in feminist scholarship on the economy. For explanations that stressed "patriarchy," see Barrett, *Women's Oppression Today;* for those that stressed the primacy of capitalist relations, see Beechy, *Unequal Work,* and Gucksmann, *Women Assemble.* Heidi Hartmann examined the intersections in "Capitalism, Patriarchy and Job Segregation by Sex"; Zillah Eisenstein developed the idea of "capitalist patriarchy" to examine the intersection of the two systems in *Capitalist Patriarchy and the Case for Socialist Feminism.* Many scholars in Western Europe and North America have by now abandoned the term "patriarchy" as a fundamental element of all social systems as too broad to account for the multiple forms gender inequality has taken historically.

4 Philips and Taylor, "Sex and Skill."

5 Tilly, *Durable Inequality,* 135.

6 Ibid., 8.

7 Ibid., 135.

8 Ibid.

9 Rose, "Gender Segregation in the Transition to the Factory"; and Rose, *Limited Livelihoods*, chapter 5, on the English carpet industry.

10 The term "opportunity hoarding" is Tilly's.

11 Downs, *Manufacturing Inequality*. On France, see also Chenut, *The Fabric of Gender*. Some of the pioneering work on Britain includes Walby, *Patriarchy at Work;* Cockburn, *Brothers;* and Cockburn, *Machinery of Dominance.* Miriam Glucksmann's work examined the interwar period as did Laura Downs's comparative study of French and British metalworking.

12 France, Ministère du travail, *Bulletin du ministère du travail* [hereafter cited as *Bulletin*], nos. 9–11 (September–November 1916): 396; and *Bulletin*, nos. 1–3 (January–March 1917): 33.

13 *Bulletin*, nos. 1–2 (January–February 1918): 7.

14 *Bulletin*, nos. 9–11 (September–December 1916): 387–89; *Bulletin*, nos. 1–3 (January–March 1917): 20–21.

15 On the contingency of skill, see Phillips and Taylor, "Sex and Skill"; and see Rose, "Gender Segregation," on employers' use of existing gender differences to fit skill levels in industry.

16 See *Bulletin*, nos. 1–2 (January–February 1919).

17 Downs.

18 Ibid., 90–94 and 100–114, 202–25, and chapter 7.

19 Phillips and Taylor, 79.

20 On the history of technical training in France, see Charlot and Figeat, *Histoire de la formation des ouvriers, 1789–1984*. On the moral implications of technical training for good citizenship expressed in the work of nineteenth-century political economists and industrialists, see 170–79.

21 Charlot and Figeat, 212–29.

22 Lahy, "Les conflits du travail."

23 "La femme et l'enfant dans l'industrie" *La Voix du peuple* [newspaper of the CGT], December 1916, 20.

24 See, for instance, Wiesner, "Guilds, Male Bonding, and Women's Work in Early Modern Germany."

25 "La femme et l'enfant dans l'industrie."

26 See Fédération française des travailleurs du livre, *Onzième congrès national tenu à Nancy du 8 au 13 septembre 1919*, 228 ff.and 289. This was as good an example as any of a form of opportunity hoarding by male workers that helped to perpetuate inequality.

27 Absensour, "Le problème de la démobilisation féminine," 501. My translation.

28 Ibid.

29 The law had been debated before the war. On the Astier Law, see Charlot and Figeat, 237–61; Moutet, *Les logiques de l'entreprise*, 145 ff.

30 Charlot and Figeat, 245.

31 Ibid., 245–46. My translation.

32 Ibid., 243–44. My translation.

33 Magnier de Maisonneuve, *Les institutions sociales en faveur des ouvrières d'usine*, 80. See also 54, 70–101. My translation.

34 Ibid. This interpretation of home economics as a form of "technical training" was not unique to France. The 1891 German labor code included housekeeping schools in its expanded definition of skilled training schools for workers. Canning, *Languages of Labor and Gender*, 140 and 305.

35 *Première conférence internationale du service social, Paris 8–13 juillet 1928*, t.III, 195–201. On the promotion of home economics training by women factory superintendents, see "Rapport de Mademoiselle Geoffroy sur ce que font et peuvent faire les surintendantes pour 'l'éducation familiale,' et l'enseignement ménager," in Association des surintendantes d'usine et des services sociaux, *Assemblée générale, 21 février 1928*, 29–34. See also AN F22 471, Supplément au *Bulletin municipal officiel [de Paris]* (February 4, 1922), discussion of the Commission administrative des comités de patronages d'apprentis on the need for apprenticeship and on initiatives that had been taken for boys and girls in the Paris region, 787–90.

36 According to Robien, home economics training was incorporated into twenty-seven of the commercial and industrial schools in Dunkerque, Lille, Roubaix, Rouen, Tourcoing, Cherbourg, and Brest under the influence of E. Labbé, director of technical education. *Première conférence internationale du service social*, 201.

37 Martin, "Ménagère: une profession?" 92.

38 AN F22 471, Supplément au *Bulletin municipal officiel [de Paris]* (February 4, 1922), 787.

39 See advertisement for the Ecole d'enseignement technique féminin on back page of Supplément au *Bulletin municipal officiel [de Paris]* (February 4, 1922) in AN F22 471.

40 Martin, "Ménagère: une profession?" 92–93.

41 Chenut, "The Gendering of Skill as Historical Process"; Chenut, *The Fabric of Gender*.

42 Chenut, "The Gendering of Skill as Historical Process," 91.

43 Brochure published by the Groupe d'études de l'industrie textile in 1921, cited by Dubesset and Zancarini-Fournel, *Parcours de femmes*, 58–59.

44 Dubesset and Zancarini Fournel, 59.

45 Downs; Omnès, *Ouvrières parisiennes;* and Moutet, *Les logiques de l'entreprise*.

46 Omnès, 118.

47 Contracts d'apprentissage, 1928–33. Archives de la Ville de Paris (AVP) (Villemoisson sur Orge) 181.

48 Omnès, "Interview with Mme. Georges (1985)," in "Jeunes provinciaux d'hier, Parisiennes d'aujourd'hui," Enquête dirigée par Françoise Cribier, Laboratoire d'analyse statistique et méthodologique appliquée à la sociologie (LASMAS), Paris. I am grateful to Françoise Cribier for giving me access to these interviews.

49 Omnès, *Ouvrières parisiennes*, 128–29.

50 Preamble to the Convention de la Couture October 23, 1923, and *Bulletin du ministère du travail* (October–December 1926), 431, both cited by Omnès, *Ouvrières parisiennes,* 121. My translation.

51 Convention de la Mode, April 10, 1924, cited by Omnès, *Ouvrières parisiennes,* 121.

52 Green, *Ready-to-Wear and Ready-to-Work,* 168.

53 Ibid., 170–71.

54 Ibid., 177.

55 Omnès, *Ouvrières parisiennes,* 123. My translation.

56 Omnès, *Ouvrières parisiennes,* 119, note 29, and 123, note 50. Green provides an excellent discussion of the instability of gendered notions of skill in chapter 6 of *Ready-to-Wear and Ready-to-Work.*

57 See Rey, "Rapport de stage."

58 Marthe Teyssot, "Rapport fait sur mon stage d'ouvrière à l'usine Forman" (July 1920), in Archives de l'école des surintendantes d'Usine.

59 Mlle. Renard, "Rapport de stage d'ouvrière à l'usine de Textilose du 12 au 15 octobre 1925," in Archives de l'école des surintendantes d'Usine. See also Hermann, "Rapport de stage à l'usine Jacob Delafond et Cie. Du 10 au 21 janvier 1921"; and Fabre, "Rapport de stage d'ouvrière du 10 au 22 janvier 1921 aux Ateliers de Construction Lavalette."

60 Fourcaut, *Femmes en usine dans la France de l'entre-deux guerres,* 52.

61 Cited by Lambérioux-Chapet, "Les ouvrières pendant l'entre-deux-guerres 1920–1936," 10–11.

62 Lambérioux-Chapet.

63 Labriffe, *L'apprentissage dans l'industrie textile.*

64 Ibid., 18–19.

65 Charlot and Figeat, 253.

66 Ibid., 254–55.

67 Ibid., 254. In 1920, the Paris city council proposed setting up a program of selection to determine which young men should be directed to professional training schools, on the assumption that the majority would not qualify and would learn a trade on the job. Thus, built into their understanding of professional training was the notion that it would serve an elite of young men. See Anonymous, "L'orientation professionnelle en matière de l'apprentissage," *Information sociale,* July 4, 1920, 6. The article made no mention of apprenticeship for women.

68 Charlot and Figeat, 256–57.

69 AN 39 AS 985, Archives du GIM, cited by Omnès, *Ouvrières parisiennes,* 120.

70 Charlot and Figeat, 256–57.

71 Moutet, 146–47.

72 Ibid., 147–48. See also Schweitzer, *Des engrenages à la chaîne,* 93.

73 Schweitzer, 93.

74 Ibid., 94.

75 Moutet, 148; Tilly.

76 Downs provides an excellent discussion of this issue with respect to women in Parisian metalworking in the 1920s.

77 See, for example, Cross, *The Quest for Time,* chapter 5.

78 Taylor's first work to appear in France in 1907, *Etude sur l'organization du travail dans les usines,* was published by the *Revue de métallurgie;* subsequent works were published in French within a year of their appearance in the United States. There is a voluminous literature on Taylorism apart from Taylor's own published work. For a sampling of the literature on the reception of Taylorism in France, see Fridenson, "Un tournant taylorien de la société, française (1904–1918)"; Cohen, "Ernest Mattern chez Peugeot (1906–1918) ou comment peut-on être taylorien?"; Moutet, *Les logiques de l'entreprise;* Christin, "Les enjeux de la rationalisation industrielle (1901–1929)." See also Maier, "Between Taylorism and Technocracy," on the cultural and political appeal of Taylorism; and Rabinbach, "The European Science of Work," 475, note 1; Cross, "Redefining Workers' Control"; Moutet, "Patrons du progrès ou patrons de combat?"; Ribeill, "Les organisations du mouvement ouvrier en France face à la rationalisation (1926–1932)."

79 See Braverman, *Labor and Monopoly Capital,* chapter 4.

80 "Notre enquête sur le système Taylor: Les observations de M. Henri Le Chatelier," *Information ouvrière et sociale,* September 14, 1919, 2.

81 Schweitzer, 57.

82 Ibid., 34 and 57–59.

83 AN 39 AS 914 Groupement des industries métallurgiques de la région parisienne (GIM) Archives, Typewritten list "Catégories professionnelles et salaires demandés par le comité d'entente des ouvriers en Métaux [1919]."

84 Schweitzer, 40.

85 Ibid., 76.

86 I have relied upon and paraphrased (my translation) Schweitzer's description of this transformation, 76.

87 By comparison, women made up 12.6 percent of metalworkers in Britain in 1930. Omnès, 133, note 91.

88 Report of Mlle. N., superintendent in training interned at Jaeger, September 9–23, 1931, cited by Omnès, 136; Moutet, 165.

89 Weil's factory journal, along with several essays and letters, was published as *La Condition ouvrière.*

90 Weil, 40.

91 Moutet, 167.

92 This is Moutet's term. It is not clear that this was a term used by contemporaries, although it is tempting to speculate about the feminization of immigrant workers whom employers deployed at a range of unskilled jobs throughout the factory.

93 Moutet, 168–69. Moutet relies principally on the reports of factory superintendents in training to argue that the situation of the unskilled woman worker improved in the 1920s. Yet the reports of the superintendents-in-training that I have

read ranged from expressions of naïve optimism about the joys of factory work to litanies of complaints about the harshness and boring monotony of the work. Both views could hardly be separated from fact that these young middle-class women entered factories for the first time and for brief periods of two to three weeks (172).

94 Ibid., 172.

95 Ibid., 173.

96 Rhein, "Jeunes femmes au travail dans le Paris de l'entre-deux-guerres," 157–58. France experienced the height of the Depression in these years; it would have been even more unlikely for women to work in highly skilled male jobs during this period.

97 Moutet, 170–71.

98 Faure, "Camille et Jeanne, ouvrières à la raffinerie Say," 51–52.

99 Delasalle, *Le travail de la femme dans l'industrie textile et du vêtement dans l'arrondissement de Lille,* 25 and 27.

100 *Bulletin,* 23ième année, nos. 9–11 (September–December 1916): 387–89; *Bulletin,* nos. 1–3 (January–March 1917): 20–21.

101 *Bulletin,* nos. 10–12 (October–December 1917): 456–57.

102 Delasalle, 40.

103 Labriffe, 8.

104 Ibid., 19.

105 Fourcaut, 65.

106 Labriffe, 52.

107 Pasqualini-Bieganski, "La main d'oeuvre féminine textile dans l'arrondissement de Lille, 1919–1939," 41. See also 114–30 on the gender division of labor.

108 Chenut, "The Gendering of Skill," 93.

109 Delasalle, 41.

110 Ibid., 42–49.

111 Ibid., 51.

112 On men's demands that they alone be allowed to work on certain "male" machines, see Rose, *Limited Livelihoods.*

113 Simon, *L'ouvrière* (Paris: Hachette, 1861), 25, cited by Dubesset and Zancarini-Fournel, 63. My translation.

114 Dubesset and Zancarini-Fournel, 64.

115 Ibid., 132–34.

116 Omnès, "La politique de l'emploi de la Compagnie française des téléphones Thomson-Houston face à la crise des années 1930," 50. My translation.

117 Downs, 216.

118 See Moutet, 165–70 and 173. On gender and sex segregation and wage discrimination, see for example, Bradley; Kessler-Harris, *A Woman's Wage;* Jenson, Hagen, and Reddy, eds., *The Feminization of the Labor Force,* especially "Women's Employment in Comparative Perspective," 17–44.

119 See also Schweitzer, 98. This system of payment could not work on an assembly

line where production norms were set by the speed of the line. On assembly line work, the "*boni*" was collective and was divided by the members of the work team. Under the leadership of Ernest Mattern, who served as director of Citroën's labor service from 1925 to 1927, Citroën introduced a new form of "*boni*" based on minute-points (0.02 centimes per minute or 1 fr. 20 per hour) to reward output per minute. Schweitzer, 98.

120 Fourcaut, 103–4. The Bedaux system was a form of rationalization where team leaders monitored the efficient expenditure of motion and energy with a minimum of rest breaks. It was first introduced in mining in France before the war.

121 See Downs, 214–15.

122 Quoted by Fourcaut, 52. See also Downs, 214, quoting the director of the Loire iron works after the war. This view of women's drive to be productive on repetitive piecework is strikingly similar to that found in the Hawthorne study of men and women workers at the Hawthorne Works of the Western Electric Company in Chicago in the 1920s. See Kessler-Harris's discussion in *In Pursuit of Equity,* 50.

123 AN 39 AS 914 Groupement des industries métallurgiques de la région parisienne (GIM) Archives, Typewritten list "Catégories professionnelles et salaires demandés par le Comité d'entente des ouvriers en Métaux [1919]."

124 Downs, 223.

125 Moutet, 307.

126 Pasqualini-Bieganski, 32–35.

127 Union des syndicats de la région parisienne, *Ve Congrès de syndicats de la Seine et Ier Congrès des unions des syndicats de la Seine et Seine-et-Oise fusionées tenu des 25 janvier, 1er et 22 février 1925,* 246.

128 Pedersen, 245. See also Pedersen's discussion of the administration of these funds through the *caisses de compensation.*

129 On earlier concepts of the family wage, see Frader, "Engendering Work and Wages."

130 See Siau, *La fonction sociale d'une grande entreprise,* 21–22, and 50–94. Thébaud, "Le mouvement nataliste dans la France de l'entre-deux-guerres."

131 See Pinot, *Les oeuvres sociales dans les industries métallurgiques,* 151–56.

132 "Les Grèves lyonnaise," *Information sociale,* March 21, 1920, 4.

133 Paraf, "Budgets d'ouvriers, de fonctionnaires et de techniciens."

134 Dutton, *Origins of the French Welfare State,* 16, 18.

135 Cited by Dutton, 26.

136 Cited by Magnier de Maisonneuve, 8.

137 Magnier de Maisonneuve, 8.

138 Ibid.

139 Henri-Collot, "Rapport de stage d'ouvrière fait à la manufacture de chaussures 'Incroyable' (Maison Dressoir) du 6 au 21 janvier [1921]," in Archives de l'école des surintendantes d'usine.

140 Noiriel, *Population, immigration, et identité nationale en France,* 66–67. See also Schor, 103.

141 Noiriel, *Le creuset français,* 142; Mauco, 304.

142 Cross, *Immigrant Workers in Industrial France*, 130.

143 Le Guillou, "L'émigration russe en France, Boulogne-Billancourt et les usines Renault, 231.

144 Mauco, *Les étrangers en France*, 265–66. Cross, *Immigrant Workers* (132), points out that 18 percent of foreign workers in the Nord worked in textiles. See also Bruyneel, *L'industrie textile de Roubaix-Tourcoing.*

145 Bruyneel, 45.

146 Pasqualini-Bieganski, 3. The 12 percent national figure comes from Mauco, 268.

147 Bruyneel, 61–63. The agreement also stipulated that each of the contracting countries was obligated to warn the other of restrictions on foreign labor that might be enforced "to disencumber the labor market, if necessary" (62). On the history of international contractual agreements facilitating immigrant workers, see Cross, *Immigrant Workers.*

148 Bruyneel, 63.

149 Mauco, 266.

150 Pasqualini-Bieganski, 56.

151 Cross, *Immigrant Workers*, 258, note 11.

152 Sirot, "Les conditions de travail et les grèves des ouvriers coloniaux à Paris," 77, citing articles in *L'Humanité* (June 20, 1923) and (May 8, 1929).

153 Mauco, 310.

154 Schweitzer, 80. On the importance of North African colonial workers in the Paris region and the number of Kabyles, see Sirot, 70 ff.

155 Cited by Le Guillou, 235. My translation.

156 Le Guillou, 255. Cross, *Immigrant Workers*, 133, table 13 "Comparison of Economic Status Profiles by Department, 1931."

157 Cross, *Immigrant Workers;* Green.

158 Sirot, 74.

159 Cited by Schweitzer, 70–71.

160 Schweitzer, 108.

161 Gomar, *L'émigration algérienne en France*, 63–64. In the following passage, Gomar's designation of Algerians as different from "foreigners" reflected the Algerians' special status as colonial subjects with limited rights in France under the *code de l'indigénat.*

162 AN 39 AS 914 "Observations présentées par le groupe des industries métallurgiques, mécaniques et connexes de la région parisienne au sujet de la fixation des pourcentages de main d'oeuvre étrangère dans les industries des métaux de la région parisienne, January, 1935."

163 Sirot discusses this point in his examination of strikes by Algerian workers in Paris during the 1920s, 90–91.

164 Mauco, 270. Mauco seems to have overlooked that "excessive parsimony" could have been poverty.

165 Ibid., 272–73.

166 Ibid.

167 Union patronale de la région d'Halluin, *Salaires et conditions du travail, 1929,* 7.

168 See Henri-Collot, "Rapport de stage."

169 de la Gorce, "Interview with Mme. D. (1985)," in "Jeune provinciaux d'hier, vieux parisiens d'aujourd'hui," Survey directed by Françoise Cribier, LASMAS. I am grateful to Françoise Cribier for giving me access to the transcriptions of the interviews.

170 Omnès, *Ouvrières parisiennes,* 155 and 158–65.

171 Ibid., 159.

172 Ibid., 163.

173 Cited by Omnès, *Ouvrières parisiennes,* 163. Omnès shows how, during the Depression, women regularly migrated from job to job within a single factory. Although Omnès regards this "internal flexibilization" as a form of labor force stabilization, willingness to move from service to service within a factory was also a strategy that allowed women to remain employed (197–98).

174 Schweitzer, 81.

175 Ibid., 106. Schweitzer also calls attention to the use of the *Bulletin Citroën,* distributed to workers free of charge to "build the collectivity of producers and introduce a spirit of unity and sense of 'household' " (107) as well as palliate the negative consequences of rationalization.

176 See especially Downs, chapters 5 and 7. The reports of these young middle-class superintendents-in-training written during their factory internships provide valuable insights into factory life and particularly the relations between women workers, supervisors, and employers. Yet these reflections were also shaped by the class position of superintendents-in-training. Their observations ranged from tremendous idealism to pity for workers. The opening of factory superintendent jobs to women represented a new opportunity for bourgeois women in the 1920s. See Verdès-Leroux, "Pouvoir et assistance."

177 See Association des surintendantes, *Compte rendu annuel de l'assemblée générale du 13 février 1923,* 2; Association des surintendantes, *Assemblée générale du 21 février 1928,* 4; Fourcaut, 20.

178 On the employment of factory superintendents in other industries, see Rapports de stages des surintendantes, in Archives de l'école des surintendantes d'usine. See also Fourcault, 21; and Association des surintendantes, *Assemblée générale du 21 février 1928,* 4.

179 On the *caisses de compensation,* see Pedersen.

180 On solidarism, see Stone, *The Search for Social Peace.* The aim of solidarists to bring about a peaceful *entente* between capital and labor was repeated numerous times in the writings of *surintendantes* and the Association leadership. For example, Mlle Delagrange, factory inspector and superintendent, wrote in 1929 about the importance of providing leisure activities for workers: "If the worker doesn't know that the employer takes an interest in his life outside of the factory, the large family composed of employers and employees will never come into being." Delagrange praised the example of worker housing complete with library, theater,

sports fields, musical societies, home economics, and professional schools provided by the railroad companies for its workers. See also Depret, *Etude sur l'oeuvre sociale de la Compagnie des Chemins de Fer de l'Est*, especially 179 ff. On solidarism and the work of superintendents, see also Downs, 247–48.

181 "Rapport de M. Michalon," in Association des surintendantes, *Assemblée générale du 21 février 1928*, 16. My translation.

182 Ibid., 16. My translation.

183 "Rapport de M. Amieux," in Association des surintendantes, *Assemblée générale du 21 février 1928*, 8. My translation.

184 "Rapport de M. Amieux." On the work of the *surintendante* as a moral force, see, for instance, report of J. Buclier, "Stage d'ouvrière du 4 au 15 avril 1927," 6; "Report of M. Decré," Association des surintendantes," *Assemblée générale du 4 mars 1930*, 15–16; Legoux, *La surintendante d'usine;* Gerrand and Rupp, *Brève histoire du service social en France,* 50; and Downs, chapter 7.

185 "Rapport de M. Amieux," 10.

186 Ibid., 11–12.

187 "Rapport de M. Michalon," Association des surintendantes. *Assemblée générale du 21 février 1928*, 18.

188 "Rapport de M. Peugeot," Association des surintendantes, *XVe Assemblée générale de l'Association des surintendantes d'usines et des services sociaux,* 27–28.

189 Schweitzer, 103–5.

190 "Rapport de Mlle. Javel," in Association des surintendantes, *Compte rendu de l'assemblée générale du 13 février 1923*, 6.

191 Downs discusses how superintendents deployed class differences in this way, 256 and 259.

192 "Rapport de Mlle. Javel."

193 "Exposé de Madame Brunschvicg," Association des surintendantes, *Assemblée générale [1931]*, 16.

194 Ibid.

195 Letter from Mme Fromentin, Association des surintendantes, *Assemblée générale [1931]*, 17–18. See also Mme Fromentin, "Le service social aux colonies," in Association des surintendantes, *XVIe Assemblée générale,* 27–30. The superintendent's colonial civilizing mission as described by Brunschvicq and Fromentin spoke to the ambiguities and complexities of their goals. As one of France's leading feminist activists, Brunschvicq encouraged the development of social service as a professional career for women that would enable them to bring their feminine skills to the resolution of social problems. Their colonial vocation was similar to that of certain British feminists in the late nineteenth and early twentieth centuries, as described by Burton, *Burdens of History.*

196 "Rapport de Mme. Fromentin," Association des surintendantes, *Compte rendu de l'assemblée générale du 13 février 1923*, 8.

197 "Rapport de M. Peugeot," Association des surintendantes, *XVe Assemblée générale de l'Association des surintendantes d'usines et des services sociaux,* 28.

198 "Rapport de M. Michalon," 17.

199 "Rapport de Mlle. Javel," 7.

200 "Rapport de M. le Général Appert. L'action d'une surintendante dans une grande usine de la banlieue parisienne," Association des surintendantes, *Assemblée générale [1931]*, 11–13.

201 "Rapport de M. Decré," Association des surintendantes, *Assemblée générale du 4 mars 1930*, 15.

202 Ibid., 16.

203 See Downs, 259 ff.

204 Downs uses the term "command," 181, 259–64. See Gramsci, *The Prison Notebooks of Antonio Gramsci*, 279–318, especially 310.

205 Lequin, "La rationalisation du capitalisme française, a-t-elle eu lieu dans les années vingt?"

3. Managing the Human Factor

1 Nineteenth-century discussions of the right to work, social and family policies, the qualifications of citizenship and the problem of male military preparedness already incorporated attention to differently gendered bodies. See, for example, Villermé, *Tableau de l'état physique et moral des ouvriers [1840]*; Nye, *Crime, Madness, and Politics in Modern France*; Mosse, *Nationalism and Sexuality*; and Rabinbach, *The Human Motor*, 224–28. Rabinbach's work is the most extensive study of the science of the working body in English, although he does not address its gender or racial dimensions. On state interventions to regulate working bodies, see Stewart, *Women, Work, and the French State*; Auslander and Zancarini-Fournel, eds. *Différence des sexes et protection sociale*; Pedersen, *Family, Dependence, and the Origins of the Welfare State*; Koven and Michel, eds., *Mothers of A New World*; Fuchs, Accampo, et al., *Family, the State, and Welfare in Modern France*; Canning, *Languages of Labor and Gender*; Downs, *Manufacturing Inequality*; and Frader, "Social Citizens without Citizenship." Maier discussed how advocates of Taylorism and industrial physiologists collaborated to construct "a new image of class relationships," in "Between Taylorism and Technocracy," 29.

2 Weil, *La condition ouvrière*.

3 See Amar, *The Physiology of Industrial Organization and the Re-employment of the Disabled*, 227–358. See also Hughes Monod, "Jules Amar," in Fontanon and Grelon, *Les professeurs du conservatoire national des arts et métiers*, vol. 2, 102–3.

4 Gardey and Löwy discuss the constitution of "nature" in the biological and human sciences in *L'invention du naturel*.

5 On the wartime use of colonial labor, see Nogaro and Weil, *La main d'oeuvre étrangère et coloniale pendant la guerre*; Stovall, "Color-blind France?," and Stovall, "The Color Line behind the Lines," which analyses the different responses of the French to North African immigrant labor and European immigrant labor. Stovall argues that the war lessened tensions between the French and European immi-

grants whereas it heightened hostility toward colonial workers of color. On immigrant workers, see Cross, *Immigrant Workers in Industrial France;* John Horne, "Immigrant Workers in France during World War I"; and John Horne, *Labour at War.*

6 See Rabinbach's discussion of cultural and social modernity with reference to the science of work in *The Human Motor.*

7 On the mutually constitutive character of these categories, see Harding, "Introduction," in Harding, *The "Racial" Economy of Science.* Harding writes, "It is clear that 'race' and gender, racism and sexism, construct and maintain each other. . . . Class and gender policies have constructed and maintained racial hierarchies just as race policies have done for class and gender hierarchies" (11). See also Turbin, Frader, Rose, and Glenn, "A Roundtable on Gender, Race, Class, Culture and Politics."

8 I am grateful to Rayna Rapp and to Ann Laura Stoler for conversations on this subject. See Stoler, "Racial Histories and Their Regimes of Truth," and Stoler and Cooper, "Between Metropole and Colony." As Stoler and Cooper write, citing George Stocking and others, "The concepts of culture and race have long served to buttress one another in crucial ways. . . . [racism] has long depended on hierarchies of civility, on cultural distinctions of breeding, character, and psychological disposition, on the relationship between the hidden essence of race and what were claimed to be its visual markers" (34). On race as a historical invention and as an ideological category, see Fields, "Ideology and Race in American History." On the problematic status of race as a marker of difference and on historians' tendency to view Europeans as raceless, see Fields, "Slavery, Race, and Ideology in the United States of America." Europeans were hardly devoid of race consciousness and often confused nationality and "race." On the links between notions of racial difference and national identity, see Malik, *The Meaning of Race,* 128–48; Lebovics, *True France.* Herrick Chapman and I explore the complexities of the term "race" in France in more detail in Chapman and Frader, "Introduction," in Chapman and Frader, eds., *Race in France.*

9 Conklin, "Redefining 'Frenchness',"67. Conklin discusses how perceptions of racial difference became more marked in France during the 1920s and 1930s. Historians have long noted the importance of eugenics and public health in nation-building. See Schneider, *Quality and Quantity,* and Weindling, *Health, Race, and German Politics.* On the cultural distinctions of "civility" and their links to concepts of the nation and to class, see Elias, *The Civilizing Process,* especially part I, chapter 2.

10 Harding points out that science is laden with conflicting tendencies: regressive collaboration with racist and Eurocentric beliefs on the one hand; and on the other hand, the progressive effects of "scientific procedures that have proved effective in identifying racist and imperialist tendencies in the sciences" (14).

11 In the words of Roy Porter, "the body must be regarded as mediated through cultural sign systems." See Porter, "History of the Body," 215.

12 Thompson, "Time, Work Discipline and Industrial Capitalism."

13 The first stage "represented the creation of a disciplined workforce; the second was characterized by the struggle over the duration and value of labor time." Rabinbach, "The European Science of Work," 506, note 111.

14 Lahy, *Le système taylor,* preface, v. On Lahy's critique of Taylor, see also Rabinbach, *The Human Motor,* 250–52.

15 Lahy, *Le système taylor,* 122. For a brief, useful discussion of Lahy and other industrial physiologists, see Moutet, *Les logiques de l'entreprise,* 49–50.

16 See Lahy, *Le système taylor,* 156–57. Taylorism and work science both shared productivist goals; Rabinbach, *The Human Motor,* 253. Industrial fatigue research was international in scope, as Rabinbach shows. In 1913, Chauveau presided over a committee charged with investigating the physiology of work, which was created by the French Minister of Labor Henri Chéron and on which physiologists Jules Amar and M. A. Imbert both sat. See Chauveau's report "Le travail professionnel."

17 As Rabinbach points out, industrial physiology took account of changes in the labor process occurring outside the laboratories in which it was first conceived. "Concern with fatigue, time, and motion reflected deep social changes in the nature of the factory and the emergence of a workforce that no longer had to be subjected to the moral economy of industrial discipline outside the workplace. Instead, workers had to be taught to internalize the regularity imposed by machine technology and adapt to newly intensified work norms" ("European Science of Work," 507). The literature on this work is voluminous. For an excellent review, see Ribeill, "Les débuts de l'ergonomie en France à la veille de la première guerre mondiale." Rabinbach, *The Human Motor,* examines its implications for national and national modernist politics, and his "The European Science of Work" provides a summary and discussion of national differences among work scientists' approaches. See also Fontanon and Grelon, eds., *Les professeurs du conservatoire national des arts et métiers.* It is quite possible that in measuring the efforts of the male body these scientists were also struggling with their own definitions of masculinity. I am grateful to Antoinette Burton for this suggestion. As Ribeill observes, there were differences in the approaches of these men. Marey, Frémont, and Amar conducted their experiments outside the laboratory, with workers on the job (14).

18 Amar, *Le moteur humain* (1914). A second edition of this was published in 1923. See also Ribeill, 11–12, 15.

19 Moutet, 29.

20 The law of January 27, 1880, required gymnastics training for boys in French *lycées* (Rabinbach, *The Human Motor,* 224). According to Amar, the physiologist Mosso wrote, "The catastrophe of Sedan will go down in history as the victory of German legs." Amar, *Le moteur humain,* 673.

21 Rabinbach, "The European Science of Work," 492; *The Human Motor,* 130–31, 224–27, 265–70. See also Ehrenberg, *Le corps militaire.*

22 Rabinbach, *The Human Motor,* 265.

23 Downs; Fridenson, "Un tournant taylorien de la société française, 1904–1918"; Foucault, *Femmes à l'usine;* Weil, *La condition ouvrière.*

24 Frois, *La santé, et le travail des femmes pendant la guerre,* 62. See Cross, *A Quest for Time,* 117.

25 Frois, 76–80.

26 Frois, 27. Henri Pinard and Alphonse Bonnaire, both physicians, investigated the conditions of workingwomen in French munitions factories during the war, with particular reference to maternity. See Dubesset, Thébaud, and Vincent, "Les munitionettes de la Seine," 202–8.

27 Dubesset, Thébaud, and Vincent, 196, note 34.

28 Amar, *Le moteur humain,* 148–78; also 323–24

29 Amar, "Les lois du travail féminine et de l'activité cérébrale," 560.

30 Ibid., 561. My translation.

31 Ibid., 562. My translation.

32 Amar, *Le moteur humain,* 606.

33 Stovall, "The Color Line." On the sexual tensions of racial intermingling in colonialism, see Stoler, "Carnal Knowledge and Imperial Power."

34 I thank Antoinette Burton for calling attention to this point. Tyler Stovall demonstrates how these intersections appeared during World War I in "The Color Line."

35 See Stovall, "The Color Line," 747.

36 Nogaro and Weil, 26. There were approximately 30,000 North African workers already in France prior to the war, most of whom worked as unskilled laborers in mining and industry (5). In 1915, the Undersecretary of State for Artillery and Munitions in the Ministry of War hired several hundred Kabyle workers for artillery manufacture and the Minister of Agriculture hired several hundred for agricultural work in the region south of Paris. A more systematic mobilization of colonial labor began in 1916. On the differences in treatment of European and colonial labor, see Stovall, "Color-Blind France?"

37 Stovall, "Color-Blind France?" 48. Stovall observes that during the war such supposed physical characteristics came to be viewed as a moral deficiency: laziness. Dexterity was the skill most often associated with women, usually because of cultural beliefs about women's superior fine-motor coordination and their "nimble fingers." See also Downs, 83–84.

38 Nogaro and Weil, 49–50, 54.

39 Lahy, *Le système taylor,* ix. My translation.

40 Amar, *The Physiology of Industrial Organization,* 43.

41 Amar, *Le moteur humain,* 2nd ed., 116.

42 Frois, *La protection des ouvriers travaillant aux presses à métaux,* 6.

43 The attention to race in the work of industrial physiologists such as Jules Amar was partly based on early anthropological attempts to evaluate and classify human abilities anthropometrically. See Amar, *Le moteur humain,* 2nd ed., 155. On Amar's study of the body at work, see also Ribeill, 14–16, and Camiscioli, "Labor Power and the Racial Economy," 4–6.

44 Henri Le Chatelier, "Introduction," in Amar, *Le moteur humain*, x.

45 Amar, *The Physiology of Industrial Organization*, 210, emphasis mine.

46 Amar, *The Physiology of Industrial Organization*, 43. On the constitution of racial categories in colonial Algeria and their deployment in the creation of the notion of the "bad Arab" and the "good Kabyle," see Lorcin, *Imperial Identities*.

47 Amar, *The Physiology of Industrial Organization*, 219–20. This observation also revealed how French workers' characteristics were defined.

48 Amar, *The Physiology of Industrial Organization*, 220. Amar presented the data of a certain Dr. Gould on the renal force of white American soldiers compared to Indians, blacks, and mulattos: "whites, 144.4 kg.; Negroes, 146.7 kg.; mulattos, 158.3 kg.; Indians 159.2 kg." Amar commented that the data showed that "civilized nations are more robust than 'savage' nations" (*Le moteur humain*, 179), leaving the reader to conclude which nations counted as "civilized" and which as "savage."

49 Amar, *The Physiology of Industrial Organization*, 204. See also Camiscioli, "Labor Power and the Racial Economy," 6. The only defect of the French laborer was that "his temperament is impulsive." Amar believed French workers needed better vocational training and better hygiene at work.

50 See Schneider, "The Scientific Study of Labor in Interwar France." On how the arguments of these men transcended solidaristic arguments for marrying the interests of labor and capital, see Cross, *A Quest for Time*, 120–22. As Cross also points out, British scientists believed that the increased leisure that would result from a shorter, more efficient work day and higher productivity would allow Britain to " 'build an improved race' " (120). This is an example of how loosely the notion of race was used to reflect both color and nationality. On the vocational guidance applications of work science, see also Roberts, *Civilization without Sexes*, 183–96, and 206–11.

51 Much of the research of these laboratories was specifically directed toward the prevention of industrial accidents and focused on male workers: railway switchmen, tramway and bus drivers, welders, and mine workers. See, for instance, Lahy, *La sélection psychophysiologique des travailleurs*, and articles in the review *Travail humain* founded by Lahy and Laugier in 1933. See also Schneider, "The Scientific Study of Labor," and below.

52 Lahy, *La séléction psychophysiologique des travailleurs*, 19. Moutet argues that the STCRP was willing to take this step because it was relatively new (the new Paris transport system was a creation of the postwar years) and therefore had fewer entrenched traditions, and work accidents could be far more serious in the public transport system. Moutet, 153.

53 Lahy, "Rapport de M. Lahy," *Xe Assemblée générale de l'association des surintendantes d'usine*, 26–27.

54 Frois, *La prévention des accidents au travail*, and AN F22 596, collection of *Bulletins techniques*.

55 Anonymous, "Centre de camping André Paty," *Mon métier* 2ième année, no. 11 (May 1929): 149–50.

56 See Anonymous, "L'emploi des femmes la nuit," *L'Usine,* January 15, 1927, clipping in AN 39 AS 988 Groupement des industries métallurgiques (GIM) Press clippings 1927–1940.

57 See Union des industries métallurgiques et mécaniques (UIMM), *Assemblée générale ordinaire du 17 février 1931,* 12. Quite possibly this proposition reflected some industrialists' attempt to reduce working hours by virtue of the ban on women's night work.

58 Moutet, 153.

59 Anonymous, "L'organisation scientifique du travail," *Information ouvrière et sociale* no. 89 (January 1919): 1–2.

60 Schweitzer, *Les engrenages à la chaîne,* 63.

61 Ibid.

62 Ibid., 64.

63 Ibid. My translation.

64 Ibid., 59–60.

65 Anonymous, "Conférence des offices de placement," *Information ouvrière et sociale* no. 94 (February 2, 1919): 1–2.

66 Cited by Downs, 255, from Paul Razous, *La sélection des travailleurs,* 11.

67 Sirot, "Les conditions de travail et les grèves des ouvriers coloniaux à Paris," 73. As Sirot notes, by 1932 once the Depression struck the automobile industry, their numbers declined dramatically.

68 Labriffe, *L'apprentissage dans l'industrie textile.*

69 Ibid., 23–26.

70 Ibid., 26. My translation.

71 As Labriffe wrote, "Dans chaque exercise l'apprenti doit retrouver au moins un des gestes du métier, le résultat est atteint quand ce geste est automatique, par la mémoire motrice. Il n'a plus alors que . . . entretenir cet automatisme en rappelant le geste au cours d'exercises complexes" (104) and "par conséquent, il importe de trouver les gestes appropriés . . . à chacune des opérations et d'arriver . . . les faire exécuter correctement jusqu'au . . . l'automatisme" (110).

72 Labriffe, "Feuille de chronométrage de temps de bobinage," and the sample "Fiche professionnelle de bobinage" et "Fiche professionnelle de tissage," 48–49 and 79.

73 Labriffe, 58–81. The section in question focused on the work of bobbin winders and the young girls who assisted them.

74 Ibid., 68.

75 Ibid., 72 and 80.

76 "Rapport de M. Lahy," Association des surintendantes, *Assemblée générale [1931],* 26–27.

77 On the use of women factory superintendents as the agents of industrial psychophysiology, see Downs, 252–55. See also Omnès, *Ouvrières parisiennes,* 152. As Omnès points out, some employers were attracted to industrial psychophysiology for selecting workers in hopes of minimizing turnover. Women factory superin-

tendents often experienced conflict with male overseers who previously had more influence than they did over hiring and firing.

78 On Renault, see Moutet, 153; on Michelin, see Moutet and Gabrielle Mounier, "Quelques notes sur mon stage près de la surintendante des usines Michelin à Clermont-Ferrand [1929]," 5 in Archives de l'école des surintendantes d'usine, Paris. M. Michelin was an honorary member of the Association des surintendantes d'usines et des services sociaux, as was Peugeot. Marie-Louise Legoux also promoted the role of the superintendent in hiring; she noted the importance evaluating the morality as well as the physical abilities of the worker and suggested that the superintendent pay attention to these factors for men as well as for women. See Legoux, "La surintendante d'usine."

79 Lefebvre, "Rapport de stage." On Michelin's social services division, see Legoux, 64. Peugeot also maintained several rest homes, as did the Paris electricity company.

80 See Cohen, "Le travail social."

81 Catalet, "Rapport de Mademoiselle Catalet sur la 'sélection professionnelle,'" 28.

82 Ibid.

83 Amieux, "Rapport de M. Louis Amieux," in Association des surintendantes d'usines et des services sociaux, Assemblée générale 21 février 1928, 8. See also Michalon, "Rapport de M. Michalon," in Assemblée générale 21 février 1928, 17.

84 Lahy, "Rapport de M. Lahy," Association des surintendantes d'usines, Assemblée générale 4 mars 1930, 26–27. Lahy was then directeur du laboratoire de psychologie appliquée à l'Ecole pratique des hautes études.

85 See Gardey, "Un monde en mutation," 824–33. See also Braverman, Labor and Monopoly Capital, 306–26.

86 See Anonymous, "L'organisation méthodique du travail et son application aux postes et télégraphes"; Anonymous, "Le téléphone en France et à l'étranger"; Anonymous, "Administration industrielle."

87 This story of the feminization of the French postal and telephone service is well told by Bachrach, Dames employées, 30–50. See also Bouvier, Histoire des dames employées; Bertinotti, "Carrières féminines et carrières masculines." The category dame employée" included all women working in the Postal, Telegraph, and Telephone (PTT) service. Bachrach, 42; Pezerat and Poublan, "Femmes sans maris."

88 Vignes, Les téléphonistes des PTT, 12; Bachrach, 69. Figures on the interwar period are not disaggregated by service. See République française, Ministère du travail, de l'hygiène, de l'assistance et de la prévoyance sociale, Statistique générale de France. Women counted for 22.5 percent of PTT workers in 1906, 30.3 percent in 1926, and 32.8 percent in 1931.

89 Many French administrative offices, beginning with the Ministry of War, allowed women to take the state entry exam for the position of chief editorial clerk (rédacteur) beginning in May 1919, due to the lack of qualified men for the position. The Administration of the Postal, Telegraph, and Telephone services, however, was not one of these. See Clark, The Rise of Professional Women in France, 145.

90 "Report de la Gironde sur le Ve congrès (1924)," in Syndicat national des agents des PTT de France et des Colonies, *Bulletin officiel*, 8–9. See also Frischmann, *Histoire de la Fédération CGT des PTT*, 260–62.

91 Frischmann, 260.

92 Anonymous, "La Grève des PTT," *Information sociale* no. 328 (June 6, 1929): 4. Somewhat predictably, during a mail carriers' strike for higher wages, the government responded that the fact that it accorded wage supplements to fathers on the basis of how many children they had was grounds not to grant a general wage increase.

93 Bachrach, 51; Bertinotti, 637.

94 République française, Ministère des PTT, *Bulletin menusel des PTT* no. 1 (January 1890): 315–16; *Bulletin mensuel des PTT* no. 18 (1922): 411–15.

95 See Pezerat and Poublan, 129–30, who report that in 1921 50 percent of all female postal workers were widowed, divorced, or unmarried. Although this figure incorporated the effects of male mortality during the war, it was consistent with low marriage rates among women postal workers before the war. The vast majority of men, on the other hand, tended to be married.

96 *Bulletin mensuel des PTT* no. 18 (1922): 411; Ministère des PTT, *Bulletin officiel du ministère des PTT* no. 17 (1930): 694.

97 This difference suggests that nineteenth-century suspicions of woman workers' sexual morality persisted after World War I. On nineteenth-century views, see Scott, " 'L'ouvrière, mot impie, sordide,' " and Scott, "A Statistical Representation of Work," in *Gender and the Politics of History*.

98 The phrase is Rayna Rapp's (personal communication to the author).

99 On the requirements for admission to the competency examinations where these criteria were spelled out, see, for example, *Bulletin mensuel des PTT* no. 18 (1922): 411–15. On the ambiguity of the Frenchness of colonial subjects, see essays by Dubois, Rosenberg, and Lewis in Chapman and Frader, eds., *Race in France;* Schor, *Histoire de l'immigration en France,* 110.

100 Cultural competence also incorporated "civility" and itself contributed to the construction of Frenchness within the public service. See Elias, *The Civilizing Process.*

101 See Conklin, 57 and 76–83; J. Pedersen, " 'Special Customs,' Paternity Suits and Citizenship in France and the Colonies, 1870–1912." Janet Horne places somewhat more emphasis on French women's "civilizing" work among Muslim women in North Africa whose wearing of the veil they considered a form of dissimulation and whose hygiene was by implication not up to French standards. Janet Horne, "In Pursuit of Greater France." Hubertine Auclert painted a somewhat different picture in her *Femmes arabes en Algérie* (1900). See Clancy-Smith, "Islam, Gender, and Identities in the Making of French Algeria, 1830–1962."

102 Thus, regional origins complicated the determination of aptitude—an employee who spoke with a thick regional accent was not acceptable unless her pronunciation could be "corrected." "Frenchness" was still a category that distinguished

among and between French women of different social, regional, and educational—as well as racial—backgrounds. See Ministère des PTT, *Bulletin menusel des PTT* no. 18 (1922): 412; *Bulletin officiel du ministère des PTT* no. 17 (1930): 695.

103 See Martin, *"Hello Central,"* 58–60; Bachrach. See Fontègne and Solari, "Le travail de la téléphoniste," 92.

104 See Fontègne and Solari. Roberts (187) argues that in debates about vocational guidance, the French attempted to "reconcile the ongoing modernization of economic and social life with time-honored cultural traditions." This certainly applies to work scientists' evaluations of women's capacities.

105 Fontègne and Solari, 85–86 and 95.

106 Ibid., 93–95. The Dutch applied industrial physiology to telephone operators even more aggressively. See Korving and Hogesteeger, "Psychotecnik bei der PTT Niederlands." On male operators, see Bouvier, 179. See also the discussion of Münsterberg's and McComas's experiments on telephone operators in Pieron, Magne, and Frois, *Physiologie du travail,* 96 ff.

107 On the problems posed by women's alleged nervousness, see Amar, *L'orientation professionnelle.*

108 Bouvier, 179.

109 Rougier, *Le Vade-mecum de la téléphoniste.*

110 Ibid., 10–11.

111 Ibid., 12–13 and 17.

112 Ibid., 7.

113 Bertho, *Histoire des télécommunications en France,* 75.

114 See Vignes, 23, and Bertinotti, *Artisans d'hier et communications d'aujourd'hui,* 14.

115 Bouvier, 182. Women resisted some of these practices, although the majority of labor struggles turned not on the constraints of rationalization and work discipline but on improving pay scales and opportunities for advancement. Women labor activists sought the elimination of the *dame employée* as a separate category and the corresponding incorporation of women into the categories reserved for men.

116 Gramsci, "Americanism and Fordism," in *The Prison Notebooks of Antonio Gramsci,* 296–97.

117 See Ministère de commerce, de l'industrie et des colonies, *Bulletin mensuel du ministère de commerce, de l'industrie et des colonies* no. 1 (January 1890): 315; Bouvier, 204–5.

118 Rougier, 24. Single women who made up the majority of telephone operators constituted the focus of these activities as well as of the housing arrangements. Telephone operators, along with other postal workers, and teachers won paid maternity leaves in 1911. See Anonymous, "La poste au féminin," 17.

119 Dr. Clapart (fils), *Maladies et accidents professionnels des téléphonistes à Paris,* 12–17. The fact that the vast majority of women operators worked on the busy daytime shifts accounted for this greater exposure.

120 Dr. Clapart (fils), 19.

121 This is probably why Alexander Millerand, Minister of Public Works and the PTT in 1910, proposed the revolving recruitment of young operators who could be encouraged to leave the Administration with a bonus at age twenty-five and who could be prohibited from working beyond age thirty-five. See Millerand, "Le nouveau recrutement des téléphonistes." Since they were considered "floating personnel," these young women could be easily laid off, permitting the Administration to save money or adopt new technologies without worrying about the seniority of public-service workers. The project was never adopted. On the concern with "nervous fatigue," see also Cross, *A Quest for Time*, 113.

122 Ribeill, 21.

123 See Roberts, 188–94 and 312, notes 26 and 27, on some of the literature that emerged in this period and the literature that was directed at women. See also Fontègne, *L'orientation professionnelle et la détermination des aptitudes;* Mauzevin, *Rose des métiers;* Clément, *Le mouvement d'orientation professionnelle;* Mouvet, *Orientation professionnelle des jeunes gens et enfants.* Roberts is correct to point to how vocational guidance experts attempted to steer women into "feminine" occupations in order to reproduce a certain model of femininity. It is also true that the same experts simultaneously participated in reproducing cultural ideals of masculinity in their descriptions of appropriate "men's jobs."

124 See, for example, Dugé de Bernonville, "Travail professionnel," 19.

125 Roberts, 187–88, 191–93.

126 Abensour, "Le problème de la démobilisation féminine," 496.

127 Dugé de Bernonville, "Travail professionnel" and "Le travail professionnelle."

128 Amar, "Méthode d'examen des aptitudes professionnelles." Amar's research on women's professional aptitudes served as a fundamental reference for the work of Fontègne and others. Amar, "Réflexions d'un physiologiste sur la femme et le féminisme," and Amar, "L'origine et les conséquences de l'émotivité féminine."

129 See Roberts, 190–91.

130 Fontègne, 211.

131 Ibid., 16.

132 Ibid., 17.

133 Mauzevin, 353.

134 Ibid., 209.

135 Ibid., 353, 355–56.

136 Ibid., 195, 257, 296.

137 Ibid., 129.

138 Ibid., 203.

139 Ibid., 362.

140 Bibliothèque d'orientation professionnelle, *Guide général pour la jeunesse carus,* 747. Race was not entirely absent from the vocational guidance movement. In a section of the book devoted to "Les situations dans les exploitations agricoles coloniales," the *Guide* pointed to the physical and moral qualities of the colonial settler: "Surrounded by natives, the European must demonstrate great moral

strength and the deepest sense of justice with regard to these *populations primitives* [my emphasis]. Demonstrations of anger can result in a notable loss of authority" (397).

141 Roberts, 184; 307 note 4.

142 Mouvet, *Orientation professionnelle des jeunes gens et enfants.* Mouvet's work had been authorized by the French government for inclusion in the Bibliothèques des conférences cantonales des instituteurs (local teachers' libraries) and in the Bibliothèques des écoles normales (normal school libraries).

143 Ibid., 112–13.

144 Cordelier, *Femmes au travail,* 53.

145 Quoted by Fontègne, 209.

4. Organized Labor and Rationalization

1 Sauvy, *Histoire économique de la France entre les deux guerres,* vol. 1., 74–81.

2 "Report on the VIIe Congrès du syndicat national des agents des PTT de France et des colonies (1924): Les traitements et les indemnités. Rapport du conseil," in *Bulletin official du congrès du syndicat national des agents des PTT de France et des colonies,* 1.

3 See Cross, *The Quest for Time,* chapter 9. See also Cross, "Redefining Workers' Control," which discusses metalworkers' prewar attacks on rationalization as an insult to the ingenuity of skilled male workers.

4 Cross, "Redefining Workers' Control," 161. See Dubreuil, *Standards* and *Nouveaux standards.*

5 Cross, "Redefining Workers' Control," 154. See also Schweitzer, *Des engrenages à la chaîne,* 126.

6 Fridenson, *Histoire des usines Renault,* 73–79.

7 On the strikes of the 1920s against time-measurement studies, see Moutet, *Les logiques de l'entreprise,* 174–82. See also, AN F7 13892, 13894 and 13895 Police reports on the CGTU, various reports on strikes, 1922–25, and Fédération unitaire des ouvriers et ouvrières sur Métaux, *IIe Congrès national fédéral* [1923], 25 on a strike at Audincourt of women protesting time and motion studies.

8 Moutet, 176.

9 Anonymous, "Le travail à la chaîne," 5; and Moutet, 177. My emphasis.

10 Moutet, 178.

11 See discussion of wages at Citroën in CGTU, *Congrès de la fédération unitaire des ouvriers et ouvrières sur métaux* [1927], 174.

12 Moutet, 83–85 and 179.

13 AN F22 190 "Grèves du textile, 1927–1928," "Pour les dix sous d'augmentation. En avant!" *L'Humanité* (September 19, 1928), 1.

14 "Le congrès national de la fédération de Paris. La semaine de 44 heures," 2.

15 "Le travail en double équipe pour les femmes et les enfants," circular from the Chambre de commerce de Lille in response to an inquiry from the Ministère

du travail et de la prévoyance sociale, in Archives départementales du Nord (ADN) 77 J 2318.

16 *L'Ouvrier textile* no. 35 (December 1928): 2.

17 Fédération des ouvriers en métaux et similaires de France (CGT), *Congrès fédérale* [1927], 175.

18 AN F7 13771 Press clipping, "Salaires, chômage, et rationalisation dans la métallurgie," *L'Humanité*, December 14, 1927.

19 Fédération unitaire des ouvriers et ouvrières sur métaux (CGTU), *Premier congrès national* [1922], 202. My translation.

20 Ibid., 203.

21 Fédération des ouvriers sur métaux et similaires de France (CGT), *Congrès fédéral* [1927], 170–73. My translation.

22 Fédération des ouvriers et ouvrières sur métaux (CGTU), *Congrès national* [1927], 256.

23 Fédération unitaire des ouvriers et ouvrières sur métaux (CGTU), *IIe Congrès national federal* [1923], 149–50.

24 Fédération des ouvriers sur métaux et similaires de France (CGT), *Congrès fédéral* [1927], 179 and 193.

25 Ibid., 200.

26 Ibid., 218.

27 See the intervention of Jeannin, in Fédération des ouvriers sur métaux et similaires de France (CGT), *Compte-rendu du XVIIIe congrès fédéral* [1933], 152–55; and also *Compte-rendu du XVIIIe Congrès fédéral* [1929], 209.

28 CGTU, *Congrès national ordinaire* [1927], 610.

29 Ibid., 626.

30 See, for example, "Les résolutions votées au congrès de Bordeaux. Les travailleurs ne feront pas les frais de la rationalisation capitaliste," *L'Humanité*, September 26–27, 1927; AN F7 13584 CGTU 1922–28, CGTU, *Bulletin d'information*, "Conférences aux cadres syndicaux"; and *La Vie syndicale. Bulletin official de la CGTU* 5ième année no. 26 (March–April–May, 1927). These critiques were also developed in Fédération des ouvriers sur métaux et similaires de France (CGT), *Congrès fédéral* [1927], 166–68.

31 Horne, *Labour at War;* Stovall, "Color-blind France?," and Stovall, "The Color Line behind the Lines."

32 On the regulation of immigrants, see Cross, *Immigrant Workers in Industrial France*, 180–85; and Lewis, *The Boundaries of the Republic;* Rosenberg, *Policing Paris.*

33 "A la CGTU. Travailleurs coloniaux," 6. "Le comité national de la CGTU," 6. The French Communist Party criticized Racamond and the Main d'oeuvre étranger section for this position as antithetical to the principles of worker internationalism and they later dropped the demand for limiting immigration. See also "La main d'oeuvre étrangère et les syndicats," 4; "Le comité national de la CGT, 12–20 septembre," 3.

34 Union des syndicats de la région parisienne, *Ve Congrès de syndicats de la Seine et Ier congrès des unions des syndicats de la Seine et Seine-et-Oise fusions* [1925], 245.

35 Fédération unitaire des ouvriers et ouvrières sur métaux (CGTU), *IIIe Congrès national* [1925], 159–60.

36 Ibid., 122–23 and 162.

37 Fédération des ouvriers sur métaux et similaires de France (CGT), *VIIe Congrès fédéral tenu à Paris* [1925], 260, 263.

38 Jouenne, "Migrations humaines."

39 Cordier, "Le congrès de migrations."

40 On the questionable manliness of immigrant workers in Britain in the interwar period, see Tabili, "Women 'of a Very Low Type,'" 176.

41 CGTU, *Congrès national ordinaire* [1927], 608–9.

42 See various reports in AN F 22 191 Grèves dans le textile. Nord, 1928–29, especially Rapport du Préfect du Nord au Ministère du Travail, September 20, 1928.

43 CGTU, *Congrès national ordinaire* [1927], 136 and 270.

44 Ibid., 635.

45 Ibid., 353.

46 Ibid., 584.

47 Ibid., 584, 586. My translation.

48 Ibid., 588.

49 Ibid., 586.

50 Ibid., 599. My translation.

51 *L'Ouvrier textile* 35 (December 1928): 3.

52 Fédération des ouvriers sur métaux (CGT), *Congrès fédérale* [1927], 162–63.

53 Anonymous, "Le machinisme et le rôle de l'ouvrier."

54 CGT Fédération des ouvriers sur métaux, *Congrès fédérale* [1927], 162–63.

55 Fédération unitaire des ouvriers et ouvrières sur métaux (CGTU), *Congrès national* [1927], 155–56.

56 Couergou, cited by Schweitzer, *Des Engrenages à la chaîne,* 128. Cross, in "Redefining Worker's Control," emphasizes that the CGTU placed great stock in worker's control as the key to realizing the benefits of scientific management.

57 CGT Fédération des ouvriers sur métaux, *Congrès federal* [1927], 175–76.

58 See *Fédération unitaire des ouvriers et ouvrières sur métaux (CGTU)* [1927], 29, 33–34, 36–41, 156–57, and 166–68.

59 Syndicat national des agents des PTT (CGT), *IVe Congrès des agents des PTT* [1922]. See especially the intervention of Mme. Stanko, delegate for the operators, 130–32. On labor's reaction to Taylorism, see Cross, "Redefining Workers' Control," and *A Quest for Time*; Ribeill, "Les organisations du mouvement ouvrier en France face à la rationalisation (1926–1932)"; Fridenson, "Un tournant taylorien."

60 Syndicat national des agents des PTT (CGT), *IVe Congrès* [1922], 107, 140. See also discussions in this congress on specialization and the scientific organization of labor.

61 Anonymous, "Le congrès du syndicat national des agents des PTT."

62 Ibid.

63 Ibid., 9.

64 Syndicat national des agents des Postes, Télégraphes et Téléphones (confédéré), *VIIième congrès national* [1925], 268–83. Delegates laughed off the suggestion that the problem of women operators' fatigue could be solved by hiring men.

65 Begoin, "Le travail et la fatigue."

66 The international campaign for the eight-hour day began in 1880. Gary Cross argues in *The Quest for Time* (159) that by 1922 the future of the eight-hour day was assured. Yet the record of strikes during the 1920s suggests that employers used multiple techniques to avoid compliance. For examples, see AN F7 13892, Grèves, on strikes for wage increases and applications of the eight-hour law; AN F7 13771, Police Report on the 1931 congress of the Fédération des ouvriers sur métaux (CGT); AN F22 181 Grèves, 1921, Reports from labor inspectors and prefects; AN F22 190, Grèves du textile 1927–28; Fédération des ouvriers en métaux (CGT), *Compte-rendu du VIIIe congrès fédéral* [1929], 210; Fédération des ouvriers sur métaux (CGT), *Xe congrès fédéral* [1931]; Fédération unitaire du Textile-Vêtement et partis similaires, *3e congrès tenu à Paris* [1926] (n.p., n.d.), 61–68. See also articles on the application of the eight hour day in *Information ouvrière et sociale,* in no. 128 (June 1, 1919); "L'éffritement des huit heures" (August 12, 1922): 3; "Les congrès ouvriers," *Le Textile* no. 121 (October 16, 1924): 4–5; and various articles in *Le textile* no. 268 (January 12, 1928).

67 "Dans l'industrie textile," 3. See also series of articles on the application of the eight-hour law, *Information ouvrière et sociale* no. 128 (June 1, 1919), especially "Un complement à l'accord du 17 avril 1919," 6–7, which spelled out the exceptions to the eight-hour day in the metallurgical industry. Women and youths could work from 5 a.m. to 10 p.m. or from 4 a.m. to 9 p.m., as long as each period was divided into two shifts of eight hours each.

68 Cross, *A Quest for Time,* 283, note 45.

69 Ibid., 94–102. See also Guilbert, *Les femmes et le syndicalisme en France,* xx.

70 Cross, *A Quest for Time,* 94.

71 Ibid., 101.

72 Cited by Lambérioux-Chapet, "Les ouvrières pendant l'entre-deux guerres 1920–1936," 53.

73 See, for example, discussion of labor inspectors' collusion with employers in Fédération nationale ouvrière de l'industrie textile de France, *XVIe Congrès nationale* [1920], 53–60; on women's tendency to work overtime, Fédération unitaire du textile de France, *Congrès constitutif de la fédération* [1922], 105–6.

74 Anonymous, "L'emploi des femmes la nuit." Women were still prohibited from working more than ten hours of work in any twenty-four-hour period. Employers could not require that adult women work at night to make up for a work stoppage for more than fifteen days a year without the prior approval of the labor inspector.

75 Anonymous, "Usure physique des mineurs," 2. My translation.

76 Cross, *A Quest for Time*, 175. See also the intervention of Maurice Labé in the debate on paid vacations, Fédération des ouvriers des métaux et similaires de France (CGT), *VIIe Congrès fédéral* [1925], 300. Labé argued that paid vacations should be considered a right of "a category of citizens," by which he meant workingmen.

77 "Les huit heures," 3. On the issue of worker housing, see also Cross, *A Quest for Time*, 298, note 14.

78 Anonymous, "La vie économique," 3.

79 See Cross, *A Quest for Time* 297, note 14; Guérin, "Les 8 heures et la vie 'humaine' des travailleurs," *La Voix sociale*, August 13, 1922, cited by Childers, "Paternity and the Politics of Citizenship in Interwar France," 95. Childers persuasively argues that workers tied demands for reduced work time to their desire to spend leisure time with their families (96–97).

80 Fontaine, "La journée de huit heures représent un progrès très important de la condition ouvrière," 1. See also Childers, 96, "[The eight-hour day] assures . . . each employee enough leisure to permit him to be in the best sense of the word, a man." As Childers points out, not all social observers and government officials agreed that work time should be reduced. But many of their arguments turned on the morality and potential alcoholism of workingmen, suggesting another view of working-class masculinity.

81 Cross argues in *Quest for Time* that employers' respect for workers' leisure developed gradually as they realized that rested workers could be more productive.

82 On the 10 to 15 percent wage cuts in 1921 and workers' responses, see diverse reports in AN F 22 181, Grèves, 1921; on the increasing gender gap in wages, see Downs, 210.

83 See, for example, discussions at the *Congrès de la fédération unitaire des ouvriers et ouvrières sur métaux (CGTU)* [1927], 174–75, 178–79.

84 Union des syndicats de la région parisienne, *Ve Congrès* [1925], 246. See also the intervention of Defiliquier, 259.

85 Union des syndicats de la région parisienne, *Ve Congrès* [1925], 246.

86 See Frader and Rose, "Introduction," 1–33; I discuss this issue further in "Engendering Work and Wages."

87 See Frader, "Engendering Work and Wages," and Rose, *Limited Livelihoods,* for examples.

88 ADN M 595/41, Textile: CGT 1919–34. Placard sent by Commissaire central, Tourcoing, to Prefect of the Nord, October 24, 1920.

89 Anonymous, "La grève des métallurgistes du Havre," 6–8. My translation.

90 Fédération des ouvriers sur métaux (CGT), *VIIe Congrès fédéral* [1925], 286.

91 Fédération unitaire des ouvriers et ouvrières sur métaux (CGTU), *IIIe Congrès national* [1925], 24.

92 Ibid., 155.

93 Fédération unitaire des ouvriers et ouvrières sur métaux (CGTU), *Ve Congrès national* [1927], 265.

94 CGTU, *Congrès national* [1927], 646.

95 ADN M 571/13 Commission départementale du travail de l'arrondissement de Lille, séance du 29 août 1930. My translation.

96 Ibid.

97 Judith Wishnia has discussed public sector workers' battles for higher wages in *The Proletarianizing of the Fonctionnaires,* chapters 8 and 9.

98 See Wishnia, 253, and Sauvy and Depoid, *Salaires et pouvoir d'achat des ouvriers et des fonctionnaires entre les deux guerres,* 58.

99 Anonymous, "Rapport sur VIIe Congrès du syndicat national des agents des PTT de France et des colonies (1924)," 4. For examples of equal pay demands, see AN F 7 13737, Protestations des fonctionnaires contre la réduction du traitement et extraits de presses sur l'activité syndicale 1926–28.

100 Syndicat national des Postes, Télégraphes et Téléphones, *Ve congrès* [1923], 238.

101 "Le congrès des PTT: traitements, indemnities, et l'échelle mobile," 10. On teachers' higher wages, see "Un meeting des dames employées des PTT," 8.

102 Syndicat national des Postes, Télégraphes et Téléphones, *Ve Congrès* [1923], 245–46.

103 Ibid., 250.

104 Ibid., 254–59.

105 Ibid., 453–54. My translation.

106 "Rapport sur le congrès du syndical national des agents des PTT [1924]," 8.

107 Ibid., 9. My translation.

108 Women teachers made a maximum of 12,000 francs. "Le congrès des PTT: traitements, indemnities, et l'échelle mobile," 9.

109 "Le congrès des PTT: traitements, indemnities, et l'échelle mobile," 10.

110 Ibid.

5. Toward the Social Model

1 Pedersen, in *Family, Dependence and the Origins of the Welfare State,* examines organized labor's reactions to social provisions. My interpretation differs from that of Alisa Del Re, *Les Femmes et l'état-providence.* Del Re emphasizes the social control dimension of social provision in France and argues that working-class men and women in the labor movement opposed social protection. I argue that working-class men and women viewed state-administered social rights as a preferable alternative to employer-administrated provisions.

2 See, for example, Hobson, "Feminist Strategies and Gendered Discourses in Welfare States"; Orloff, "Gender and the Social Rights of Citizenship"; Siim, "Gender, Power, and Citizenship"; and Siim, *Gender and Citizenship.* Orloff provides an excellent overview of recent work in "Gender and the Welfare State." Pierre Rosanvallon argues somewhat differently for the problem of applying Marshall's model to the French case in *Le Sacre du citoyen.*

3 Kessler-Harris, *In Pursuit of Equity,* 12.

4 On the exclusionary foundations of citizenship in France, see Landes, *Women and the Public Sphere in the Age of the French Revolution,* and Riot-Sarcey, *La Démocratie à l'épreuve des femmes.* See also Stone, "Republican Ideology, Gender, and Class"; Stone, "The Republican Brotherhood"; Scott, *Only Paradoxes to Offer,* chapter 1.

5 Eighteenth- and nineteenth-century opponents of women's political rights cited women's physical "incapacity," maternity, and childbirth as grounds for the denial of full citizenship rights to women. For an eighteenth-century rebuttal of these arguments, see, for example, Condorcet, "On the Admission of Women to the Rights of Citizenship [July, 1790]"; Landes's discussion of Condorcet, *Women and the Public Sphere,* 112–17, and especially 115. See also Pateman, *The Sexual Contract;* and "Equality, Difference, Subordination," 17–31.

6 Broad claims for social rights were fundamental to the thinking of the "utopian" socialists such as Babeuf, Fourier, and St. Simon and appeared in later French socialists' claims for a "a social republic" in which social and economic rights would be recognized along with political rights. See Dogliani, "Une laboratoire de socialisme municipal."

7 On citizenship's subjective meanings and on citizenship as practice, see Canning and Rose, "Introduction," 4.

8 See Dubois, "Republican Anti-Racism and Racism."

9 See Pateman, "Feminist Critiques of the Public/Private Dichotomy," especially 105–9; Pateman, "Introduction," "The Disorder of Women," "The Fraternal Social Contract," and "Feminism and Democracy," in Pateman, ed., *The Disorder of Women;* Landes. This paradigm was hardly confined to the "classical" theorists. See Fraser, "What's Critical about Critical Theory"; and Young, "Impartiality and the Civic Public."

10 A substantial literature examines nineteenth-century arguments against granting full civil and political rights to women on the grounds of natural difference in Britain and France, especially seen in debates in France over the Civil Code and in both France and Britain over suffrage. See Hollis, *Women in Public;* Biddleman, *Pariahs Stand Up!;* Hause and Kenney, *Women's Suffrage and Social Politics;* see also Pateman, "Feminist Critiques," 113. See also Mary Poovey, "The Abortion Question and the Death of Man," 243; and Foucault, *The History of Sexuality.* The English-language reference to women as "the sex" throughout much of the nineteenth century spoke volumes about the reduction of women to their sexual characteristics.

11 Landes, 138–39.

12 See Hause and Kenny; Offen, "Theory and Practice of Feminism in Nineteenth Century Europe." Offen has labeled this "maternalist feminism." See also Offen, "Defining Feminism," and responses by Nancy Cott and Ellen Carol Dubois in *Signs* 15 (Autumn, 1989): 195–209; and Moses's critique of Offen in "Debating the Present, Writing the Past." As Moses points out, working-class St. Simonian women argued for women's right to work and for civic rights as part of women's more general quest for political and sexual freedom. See also Moses, *French Femi-*

nism in the Nineteenth Century, which shows that from 1848 maternity became one among several arguments for women's civic rights. Susan Kingsley Kent, *Sex and Suffrage in Britain 1860–1914,* argues persuasively that feminists used the language of political economy to demonstrate to men the public nature of domestic, "private" life (85). The radicalism of suffrage feminism in particular, she shows, lay in its challenge to the ideal of separate spheres (207).

13 On workers' concept of property in labor as an argument for citizenship, see Sewell, *Work and Revolution in France;* see also "Le Manifeste des Soixante Ouvriers de la Seine (1864)," in Cahm, ed., *Politics and Society in Contemporary France (1789–1971),* 78; *La Revue républicaine* 11 (1834–35): 48, cited by Riot-Sarcey; Thibault and Riot-Sarcey, "La Préhistoire de la protection." On the notion of the "femme au foyer" as expressed within the French working class, see Perrot, "L'Eloge de la ménagère dans le discours des ouvriers français au XIXe siècle."

14 The legal term *"filles majeurs"* referred to adult single women or widows, who were accorded certain rights over property and contracts. The term "fille" typically only applied to adult unmarried women and was suggestive of the potential of marriage to confer gender—womanhood—on adult females.

15 On the paternalistic impulse behind French protective legislation, see Stewart, *Women Workers and the French State.* On the definition of the woman worker as a problem, see Scott, "L'Ouvrière," and Zancarini-Fournel, "Archéologie de la loi de 1892 en France."

16 For examples in the revolutions of 1830 and 1848, see Riot-Sarcey, 79, 89, 147, and 181 ff.; Scott, "Work Identities for Men and Women," 102–8. Women in 1848 argued for citizenship on the basis of motherhood. See Moses, *French Feminism,* 132–35 and 139–49.

17 See *Séances du congrès ouvrier socialiste de France. Troisième session tenue à Marseille [1879],* 184–88. For an example of a strong argument in favor of women's political and civil equality with men, see the intervention of delegate Joseph Bernard (Grenoble): "En reconnaissant à la femme le devoir de produire pour consommer, vous devez lui reconnaitre le droit de discuter les lois ou conventions qui l'intéressent dans la société. En un mot, vous devez l'égalité civile et politique, dans la société nouvelle" (185–86). Bernard was one of several delegates to make arguments for women's citizenship on the grounds of work. On Auclert's campaign for suffrage among the socialist and workers' movements, see Hause, *Hubertine Auclert, the French Suffragette,* 47–67.

18 On women's legal position, see Albistur and Armogath, *Histoire du féminisme français,* and Arnaud-Duc, "Les contradictions du droit." On protective labor legislation, see Stewart, chapter 8. Stewart argues that the main concern of legislators and reformers was not the protection of women's right to work or even women's health but the health of children.

19 See especially Sowerwine, *Sisters or Citizens?;* Hilden, *Working Women and Socialist Politics in France;* and Boxer, "Socialism Faces Feminism."

20 Zylberberg-Hocquard, *Féminisme et syndicalisme en France,* 87. This statement appeared in the newspaper *L'Harmonie sociale.*

21 See Dubesset, Thébaud, and Vincent, "Quand les femmes entrent dans l'usine"; Dubesset, Thébaud, and Vincent, "Les Munitionnettes de la Seine"; Downs, "Women's Strikes and the Politics of Popular Egalitarianism in France, 1916–1918."

22 See Albistur and Armogathe.

23 Gradually, legislators acknowledged that even if women were not full-fledged citizens, they nonetheless needed certain rights. After Republicans won control of the French legislature in 1879, legislation began to reverse some of the Civil Code's limits on women's public and private behavior. In the 1880s and 1890s they won the right to elect members to the High Council on Public Education, departmental public education councils, and business tribunals. In 1907, in addition to married women gaining control over their wages, working women became eligible to sit on the Conseils de Prud'hommes, the worker-employer arbitration councils established under the First Empire. Finally, in 1938, the government eliminated the provision of the Civil Code specifying that a husband owed his wife protection and maintenance while the wife owed her husband obedience. Women thus won the right to open a bank account, purchase or alienate property, and enroll in a university course. On the restrictions of the Code and the reforms of the Code pertinent to women, see Albistur and Armogathe, 239–45, 392–93, and 396–97; Arnaud-Duc.

24 See below. Teachers active in the Union française pour le suffrage des femmes (French Union for Women's Suffrage) made this argument. See Burle, "Le vote des femmes."

25 "Immigration et naturalization," *Revue de l'alliance nationale pour l'accroissement de la population française* no. 134 (September 1923): 279–81.

26 Ibid.

27 See text of law reproduced in Martial, *Traité de l'immigration,* 226–27.

28 See Camiscioli, "Intermarriage, Independent Nationality, and Individual Rights of French Women."

29 Pluyette, *La Doctrine des races et la selection de l'immigration,* 4.

30 As Mary Lewis has pointed out, the debate over naturalization raised questions about what it actually meant to be "French" and whether even naturalized citizens were truly French. Lewis argues that members of the Alliance and legislators were ambivalent about the assimilation of immigrants. Bearing children constituted one route to assimilation and nationality. Lewis, "Bring Us Your Labor, Your Children, Your Fecund Fathers."

31 See, for instance, the case of a French woman at the Dressoir shoe factory who married a Belgian in 1921 and was not eligible for maternity leave. Henri-Collet, "Rapport de stage ouvrière fait à la manufacture de chaussures 'Incroyable' [Dressoir]."

32 Cross argues that naturalization benefitted older migrant groups such as Italians, rather than newer groups such as Poles. *Immigrant Workers in Industrial France,* 178.

33 Camiscioli. Jane Misme, feminist and editor of *La Française,* opened a debate in 1921 on women's right to retain their citizenship after marrying a foreigner in her article "Les françaises, doivent-elles épouser des étrangers?" She advised, "Before inciting our girls to link themselves to foreigners, let us obtain . . . laws that allow them to remain French, at least. We advise not marrying foreigners unless they [foreign men] obtain French nationality for themselves and for their children."

34 I am paraphrasing Camiscioli, 57. As Camiscioli points out, lawyers and social observers argued that "marriage to a French woman simplified the assimilation of immigrant men" (62).

35 Lambert, *La France et les étrangers,* 115–16.

36 Attention to women's bodies during wartime was paralleled by the focus on the mutilation of men's bodies (and the politicization of the male body) in men's service to their country. See Gilbert, "Soldier's Heart." See also Dubesset, Thébaud, and Vincent, "Quand les femmes," and "Les munitionnettes." On the interwar years, see Fourcaut, *Les Femmes à l'usine en France dans l'entre-deux guerres;* and Downs, *Manufacturing Inequality.* As Mary Lynn Stewart argues, late-nineteenth-century exponents of industrial hygiene selectively paid attention to the relationship between industrial hygiene and birth rates for women in occupations such as match manufacture (159–61). See also Gordon, "Ouvrières et maladies professionnelles sous la troisième république"; Roberts, *Civilization without Sexes.* For the examples of a similar politicization of the female body in Germany between the 1880s and 1890s, see Canning, "Social Politics, Body Politics," and "Feminist History after the Linguistic Turn." .

37 On prewar discussions of nationalism and maternity, see Offen, "Depopulation, Nationalism, and Feminism in Fin-de-Siècle France"; on the debates over maternity leave, see Stewart, chapter 8. Pedersen provides an excellent discussion of the development of French family policy between 1919 and 1945.

38 Pedersen, 245. See also her discussion of the administration of these funds through the *caisses de compensation,* 224–88. As Pedersen shows, the number of *caisses* grew steadily from 15 in 1920 to 255 in 1932 (231). On the development of French social policy, see also Thébaud, "Le mouvement nataliste dans la France de l'entre deux guerres."

39 Pedersen, 273–74.

40 Dutton, *Origins of the French Welfare State,* 27.

41 Anonymous, "Le problème de la natalité," 4.

42 Anonymous, "Le problème de la natalité."

43 See Archives départementales du Nord, [hereafter, ADN] M619/79 "L'éffort social du Consortium de l'industrie textile en 1928," typescript. This report listed the number of beneficiaries according to the number of children by city. In addition to family allowances, the Consortium's industrial welfare program included sponsorship of associations, committees, musical, choral, sport and popular game societies, all designed to promote "social peace." See also Anonymous, "L'oeuvre

sociale de l'industrie textile en 1924"; Anonymous, "L'action des organisations patronales"; Siau, *La Fonction sociale d'une grande entreprise*, 33.

44 Pinot, *Les Oeuvres sociales des industries métallurgiques*, 198. See also Magnier de la Maisonneuve, *Les Institutions sociales en faveur des ouvrières d'usine*, 8.

45 Siau, 72.

46 Bibliothèque de l'orientation professionnelle, *Guide général pour la jeunesse carus*, 358; Siau, 20.

47 Ibid., 69.

48 Ibid., 69–70.

49 Ibid., 74.

50 Lyons, "Invisible Immigrants," 84.

51 Rosenberg, *Policing Paris*, chapter 7; Rosenberg, "Albert Sarraut and Republican Racial Thought."

52 See Talmy, *L'Histoire du mouvement familial en France*; Pedersen, "Catholicism, Feminism, and the Politics of the Family during the Late Third Republic," 254; and Pedersen, *Family, Dependence*. See also Albistur and Armogathe, 392.

53 Anonymous, "La double loi économique des salaires," 2.

54 See Archives nationales (AN) BB18 2752, Reports of Procureur général, Nancy, au Ministre de Justice, Paris, March 26, 1926, on strike at Chateaux-Regnault.

55 Rapport du Préfet du Nord au Ministre du Travail, Paris August 3, 1928 in AN F22 191, *Grèves textiles du Nord, 1928–1929*.

56 See AN BB18 2880 Rapport du Procureur général, Montpellier au Ministre de Justice, Paris, August 18, 1933, on strike of workers in Graissessac (l'Hérault) to protest against a cut in family allowances. See also AN BB18 3064, Rapport du Procureur général, Nancy au Ministre de Justice, Paris, December 28, 1937, on striking metalworkers, and Rapport du Procureur général, Nancy au Ministre de Justice, Paris, August 28, 1937, on striking construction workers. Both strikes occurred to protest cuts in family allowances.

57 Anonymous, "La double loi économique des salaires."

58 Ibid.

59 AN BB18 2706, Rapports du Juge de Paix du Canton de Romans au Procureur général de la République, Valence, on strike of shoemakers in Romans, May 12 and 15, 1924; BB 18 2752 Rapport du Procureur général, Grenoble, au Ministre de Justice, Paris October 13, 1926.

60 Fédération unitaire des ouvriers et ouvrières sur Métaux (CGTU), *IIIe Congrès national. Rapports et compte-rendu du IIIe Congrès fédéral à Paris* [1925], 207. Pedersen (*Family, Dependence*, 250) notes that a 1922 strike in Tourcoing (Nord) protested against an employer's refusal to give a family bonus to workers who missed even a day of work. See also the report of Buisson (Fédération des employées) in CGT, *XXIIIe Congrès confédéral à Paris . . . compte-rendu des travaux* [1923], 119–25, which summed up the CGT position on the family bonus system.

61 Fédération unitaire des ouvriers et ouvrières sur métaux, *IIIe Congrès national*.

Rapports et compte-rendu [1925], 154–55; CGTU. *Congrès national ordinaire. IIIe Congrès de la CGTU* [1926], 541; "Rapport sur les allocations familiales par la camarade Alice Brisset."

62 See Dutton, 99–118, for an excellent discussion of the law.

63 Figures on numbers of strikes in Dutton, 109. See AN F22 13 Application de la loi sur les assurances sociales, Rapport du Ministre du Travail on labor protests in the Paris region, July 10, 1930, and subsequent reports of labor inspectors in Paris of July 10, 1930, and August 4, 1930.

64 Figure is from Dutton. As of July 30, 1930, 17,000 workers were on strike in Lille alone. See AN F22 213, L'inspecteur divisionnaire de la 5e cironscription à M. Le Ministre du Travail, July 30, 1930, 3; AN BB18 2831 Rapport du Procureur général, Douai au Ministre du Justice, Paris, on strikes in the Nord department.

65 Bruyneel, *L'Industrie textile de Roubaix-Tourcoing,* 106.

66 Anonymous, "Grèves du Nord," 3. A year later, as the depression in the textile industry worsened, employers backed down and withdrew the bonus entirely, forcing workers to bear the 4 percent contribution. See Bruyneel, 129–48 and 166–67.

67 *Bulletin officiel du syndicat national des agents des* PTT *de France et des colonies* (May 1924), 6.

68 Fédération des ouvriers sur métaux et parties similaires de France [CGT], *VIIe Congrès fédéral tenu à Paris* [1925], 287. See also Pedersen, *Family, Dependence,* 314 ff and 360.

69 Syndicat national des agents des Postes, Télégraphes et Téléphones (Confédérés), *VIIe Congrès* [1925], 151–53. A proposal for a family wage was adopted by the 1923 congress of this organization. On Catholic support for family bonuses, see "A propos du conflit textile," *La Croix du Nord,* September 3, 1928, in ADN M619/79.

70 On the redefinition of male citizenship linked to procreation, see Pedersen, *Family, Dependence,* 361. On citizenship as practice as well as status, see Lister, "Citizenship"; and Canning and Rose, "Introduction," 4.

71 See Hause and Kenney; Offen, 327–55.

72 On Roussel, see Acampo, *Blessed Motherhood, Bitter Fruit;* Zylberberg-Hocquard, 140; on the 1908 congress, Zylberberg-Hocquard, 127. French workers had demanded municipally financed maternity allowances at least since 1892. At the Fifth National Congress of Unions and Corporative Workers' Organizations (Cinquième congrès national des syndicats et groupes corporatifs ouvriers de France) in 1892, for example, delegates adopted a resolution for obligatory maternity leave six weeks before and six weeks after the birth of a child, with an allowance equal to the number of days wages lost to be paid by the municipality. The resolution was not a defense of women's social rights as workers but part of a strategic move to regulate women's work, designed as much to ease the perceived competition between men and women as it was to diminish the exploitation of women workers. See *Ve Congrès national des syndicats et groupes corporatifs ouvriers de France* [1892], 56.

73 See Bell and Offen, eds., *Women, the Family, and Freedom,* 308. The emphasis is mine.

74 Bravey, "Le droit de vote féminin et nous."

75 See also Burle and Durand, "Notre féminisme," 6. My translation.

76 See Jeanne Bouvier's intervention in the 1919 congress of the Fédération d'industrie des travailleurs de l'habillement, cited by Blum, "Féminisme et syndicalisme," 123. " 'Women have the right to [maternity] leave—not in misery, but at the expense of the State, with a minimum [payment] based on the minimum wage established in their region' " (124).

77 Prewar supporters of "the social function of motherhood" included Paul Lafargue, socialist activist and deputy from the Guesdist *Parti ouvrier français* (French Workers' Party), who argued in 1892 for a maternity leave policy funded by taxing employers and based on the social function of motherhood and childbirth. See Stewart, 119. The demand for recognition of maternity as a *social function* performed for the state and society also appeared in the 1908 Congrès des droits civils et du suffrage des femmes (Zylberberg-Hocquard, 127).

78 Jouhaux, "Le congrès de l'internationale des travailleuses," *La Voix du peuple* 53 (July–August 1925): 332. See also *La Voix du peuple,* special issue on "Assurances sociales" (September–October 1923).

79 Blum also argues that CGT women more clearly identified with their maternal roles than did women in the CGTU (107–9, 118–27).

80 See the debate on the family wage in the context of the discussion of public-sector salaries, intervention of Mme Stanko, in Syndicat national des postes, télégraphes et téléphones, *Ve Congrès* [1923], 238–40.

81 Anonymous, "Le fascisme est là," *L'Humanité,* January 1, 1925, 5. See also Doyen, "Pourquoi un programme de revendications pour les ouvrières." Pedersen also argues in *Family, Dependence* that CGTU objections to the family wage bonus were based on "employers' stranglehold over administration of the welfare funds" (279).

82 Doyen.

83 Bigot, *La Servitude des femmes.* These views were shared by other teachers in the Groupes féministes de l'enseignement laïque. See, for example, Alquier, "La Maternité, fonction sociale"; Anonymous, "Congrès des groupes féministes de l'enseignement laïque (Marseille, 1930)." For a contemporary discussion linking rights and needs claims with respect to modern welfare states, see Fraser, "Struggle over Needs," and Fraser, *Justice Interruptus.*

84 For a different formulation, see Esping-Anderson, *The Three Worlds of Welfare Capitalism,* 11.

85 As Canning and Rose state, "Those who were excluded from all or some citizenship rights on the basis of gender, race, or ethnicity frequently took up the discourses and rhetorics of citizenship to make claims upon nation, state, or local communities" ("Introduction," 5).

86 French government and private-sector initiatives to return women with children

to the home as a form of employment policy in the 1980s and 1990s illustrate the consequences of these arguments. See Frader, "Social Citizens without Citizenship," 125.

6. Economic Rights and Gender

1 A standard analysis of the Depression in France remains Sauvy, *Histoire économique de la France*. On the emergence of the category of the unemployed, see Salais, Bavarez, and Reynaud, *L'invention du chômage*, 77–123. Topalov, *La naissance du chômeur*, places the emergence of unemployment as an analytical and statistical category at the end of the nineteenth century in Britain, France, and the United States. As Topalov points out (323), in France the recognition of unemployment as a category resulted in the first unemployment census in 1896 and the redefinition of categories of employment and wage earner. On this point, see also Salais et al., 27–76. The best contemporary study of unemployment and a most valuable source (although it is hardly unmarked by its share of assumptions about the gender of work and skill) is Letellier, Peret, Zuber, and Dauphin-Meunier, *Le chômage en France de 1930 à 1936*. See also Dubief, *Le déclin de la IIIe république*; Borne and Dubief, *La crise des années trentes 1929–1938*; Berstein, *La France des années trentes*; Marseille, "Les origines 'inopportunes' de la crise de 1929 en France"; Boyer, "Le particularisme français revisité." Reynolds, *France between the Wars*, addresses women's experience of the Depression in chapter 5.

2 See, for example, Kent, *Gender and Power in Britain*, chapter 7; Kessler-Harris, *Out to Work*, 250–72; Kessler-Harris, *In Pursuit of Equity*.

3 As Michael Hanagan has argued, workers' rhetoric about the importance of the male breadwinner did not always or accurately reflect their family experiences. Male breadwinner rhetoric coexisted with a simultaneous demand for jobs for women and a willingness to adopt family labor strategies that optimized the working capacities of all family members. Women did not withdraw from the labor force (Hanagan, "Family, Work, and Wages"). Global and comparative studies suggest, moreover, that the male breadwinner family may have been "a historical exception confined to specific countries or regions in the Western world or to certain limited periods in the historical development of these ideas. Janssens, "The Rise and Decline of the Male Breadwinner Family?," 9.

4 On work as a mechanism of social insertion and as a form of citizenship, see Castel, *Les métamorphoses de la question sociale*, 452.

5 See Jenson, "Friend nor Foe?"; Pedersen, *Family, Dependence, and the Origins of the Welfare State*; Sommestad, "Welfare State Attitudes to the Male Breadwinning System"; von Oertzen and Rietzschel, "Comparing Postwar Germanies."

6 See Jenson and Pedersen.

7 Berstein, 25–26.

8 Noriel, *Les ouvriers dans la société française*, 175; Berstein, 48.

9 Noriel, *Les ouvriers dans la société française*, 176; Berstein, 35.

10 Letellier et al., vol. 1, 37, estimate that 1,089,000 were out of work, 2.6 percent of the total French population, using the number of those seeking jobs as a basis for the calculation. For the figure of 4.5 percent unemployment as a percentage of the labor force, see Marchand and Thélot, *Le travail en France*, 77. For the figure of 426,500 receiving unemployment assistance, see Schor, *Histoire de l'immigration en France*, 128.

11 Baverez, "Chômage des années 1930, chômage des années 1980," 107.

12 See Rapport du Commissaire divisionnaire de police spéciale, Lille au Préfet du Nord March 10, 1934, in Archives départementales du Nord (ADN) M 605/21–23. On wage cuts, see Anonymous, "Une baisse de salaires est annoncée pour le 1er février dans la filature de coton." On factory closures and the depression in combing, see Anonymous, "La crise dans l'industrie lainière du Nord" ; Anonymous, "La fermeture des peignages de laine de Roubaix-Tourcoing" ; Rapport du Commissaire de police, Roubaix au Commissaire central, July 26, 1934, for example, in ADN M571/27 La crise de peignage.

13 See file on the march and the meetings of unemployed workers organized largely by the CGTU in ADN M 161/18, especially Rapport du Commissaire divisionnaire de police spéciale, Lille au Préfet du Nord, April 14, 1933, and Rapport du Commissaire divisionnaire de police spéciale, Lille au Préfet du Nord, December 12, 1933.

14 Letellier et al., 99.

15 Berstein, 48.

16 Ibid., 48; Letellier et al., 60.

17 Sohn, "Féminisme et syndicalisme," 22; Clark, *The Rise of Professional Women in France*, 148.

18 Berstein, 48.

19 Clark; Sauvy, 54–55.

20 Berstein, 44. These wage reductions produced tremendous protests on the part of unionized civil servants, but to no avail.

21 Ibid., 44; Sauvy, 133. Sauvy estimates that civil servants' purchasing power increased between 12.9 percent and 18.9 percent, depending on their level.

22 "40,000 métallos en vacances forcées. Dans les usines rationalisées à outrance depuis des mois, l'attacque contre les salaires se pursuit," *L'Humanité*, August 3, 1931, clipping in AN F7 13785 Syndicats. Activités syndicales métaux, 1930–31.

23 See Depretto and Schweitzer, *Le Communisme à l'usine*, 34; Phan, "Productivité, emploi, et salaires ouvriers chez Renault des années 1930," 67. The National Economic Council's 1936 report on unemployment in the textile industry noted that in May 1932, 88.5 percent of workers in the textile industry experienced partial unemployment or slack time (*chômage partiel*). The percentage of workers on slack time dropped subsequently and then rose again by the following January to 78.2 percent. The numbers rose and fell over the next year, reaching 71.3 percent in February 1935, and declined thereafter, illustrating the tremendous fluctuations that characterized this industry (as well as many others) in these

years. Président du Conseil. Conseil national économique, *Le Chômage dans les industries textiles,* 5.

24 Cited by Phan, 67–68. My translation.

25 On Citroën, see Schweitzer.

26 Depretto and Schweitzer, 19. My translation.

27 Omnès, "La politique d'emploi de la Compagnie française des Téléphones Thomson-Houston face à la crise des années 1930," 43.

28 Ibid., 47.

29 Ibid.

30 See, for example, Letellier et al. vol. 1, 30. On organized labor's views of rationalization as a cause of the Depression, see Anonymous, "Le congrès national de la fédération [du Textile] de Lille, Compte rendu résumé," 1; and Anonymous, "Les méthodes nouvelles de production et de chômage" ; Anonymous, "Où allons nous? La crise de la métallurgie dans la région parisienne," Union syndicale des travailleurs de la métallurgie, voiture-aviation, et similaires de la région parisienne [CGTU]," *Xe Congrès.* . . . *[les 1–13] juillet [1931],* brochure in AN F7 13771 Metalworkers, 1931, 7; and Anonymous, "L'attacque contre les conditions du travail et de vie des ouvriers," in ibid., 9. Although this position was more typical of the communist-influenced CGTU, from about 1931 the CGT likewise attacked rationalization's effect on unemployment. See police report of December 14, 1931, on the December 1931 Congrès de la Fédération des ouvriers sur métaux in AN F7 13771.

31 Lambérioux-Chapet, "Les ouvrières pendant l'entre-deux-guerres 1920–1936," 24.

32 Ibid., 24. Such substitution did not occur everywhere. At Thomson-Houston, a highly refined gender division of labor precluded hiring women to replace higher paid men. Omnès, "La politique d'emploi," 50.

33 Rapport du Commissaire de Police d'Hellemes-Lille au Préfet du Nord January 30, 1934, and Commissaire divisionnaire de Police spéciale, Lille au Préfet du Nord, March 10, 1934, in ADN M605/21–23.

34 On the use of piece rates, see Phan, 70 and 81. In 1937, 81 percent of the workers at Renault were paid according to piece rates. On Thomson-Houston, see Omnès, "La politique d'emploi," 56.

35 Berthe Albrecht, Rapport de stage aux Galeries Lafayettes, June 29, 1937, cited by Moutet, *Les logiques de l'entreprise,* 318.

36 See Moutet, *Les logiques de l'entreprise,* 209–20. For a more extensive discussion of rationalization initiatives during the Depression, see chapters 8–15.

37 Moutet, *Les logiques de l'entreprise,* 299–300.

38 On Gillet, see Moutet, *Les logiques de l'entreprise,* 299. See Procureur général, Besançon au Ministère de la Justice, August 14, 1935, on strikes of textile workers in the arrondissement of Besançon, AN BB 18 2953 Grèves 1935. On earlier strikes over the same issue in 1931, see AN F7 13921 Textile, various prefect reports. On a similar strike of women in the Frey textile firm in Mulhouse in 1934, see AN F7 13922 Rapport du Préfet du Haut-Rhin, July 23, 1934.

39 Rapport du Commissaire de Police, Ville de Lomme au Préfet du Nord, Janu-

ary 17, 1933, and Rapport du Commissaire spécial, Lille, au Préfet du Nord, June 28, 1933, on CGT protest against the increase in numbers of looms supervised in AD N M 595/41.

40 Letter and Rapport du Syndicat des peigneurs de laine [employers] du Roubaix au Préfet du Nord, June 24, 1933, practice of double shifts in ADN M 605/21–23.

41 Moutet, *Les logiques de l'entreprise*, 345. A year later women struck Jaeger again to protest wage cuts of 10 to 20 percent. In addition to protesting against the cuts that "reduce our families to misery," one striker argued that Jaeger could improve working conditions by providing the women with warm milk and work clothing. See Police report on meeting of metalworkers in support of the strike at Jaeger, October 14, 1932, in AN F7 13786.

42 Moutet, *Les logiques de l'entreprise*, 310.

43 Ibid., 319–20.

44 Weil, *La condition ouvrière*, 83, also cited by Moutet, *Les logiques de l'entreprise*, 320. My translation.

45 Moutet, *Les logiques de l'entreprise*, 331. On the use of the suggestion box more broadly, see Moutet, 324–30.

46 On Géo and Olida, see Moutet, *Les logiques de l'entreprise*, 231–32, and on shoe manufacture, 235.

47 Moutet, *Les logiques de l'entreprise*, 225–27.

48 Noriel, *Les ouvriers dans la société française*, 179.

49 Moutet, *Les logiques de l'entreprise*, 333 and 334.

50 Noriel, *Les ouvriers dans la société française* (172–73), assumed that industrial employers quickly fired women as the Depression struck. As I suggest below, this is incorrect. See also Reynolds, chapter 5. On the American case, see Milkman, "Women's Work and the Economic Crisis"; Kessler-Harris, *Out to Work*, 250–72.

51 Letellier et al., 66. I am leaving aside here the differential effects of the Depression according to age. Older workers made up a larger proportion of the unemployed than younger (ibid., 71–78).

52 See Omnès, *Ouvrières parisiennes*, 172, who relies on the Rapport Pouillot for the Seine and the 1er Circonscription de l'inspection du travail (Seine, Seine-et-Oise, Seine-et-Marne).

53 Salais, et al., 80. Unemployment rates might have also appeared lower in rural departments because industrial workers often compensated for slack time with agricultural labor or did not declare themselves as unemployed because of their ability to benefit from family agricultural production. On this point, see Marpsat, "Chômage et profession dans les années trentes," 61.

54 Clark details the position of women in public administrative jobs during the Depression in chapter 6.

55 See Letellier et al., 48–49. On strikes in the textile industries of the Nord, see AN BB18/2831, Ministry of Justice dossiers on strikes and demonstrations. Some strikes in 1930 occurred against the application of the 1928 social insurance law that required a worker contribution to social insurance as workers began to experience

the effect of the slowdown. Concerned about diminishing wages, they demanded that employers pay workers' contribution. See also AN BB18/2953 on strikes to protest wage cuts later in the 1930s as the Depression worsened in the Nord. See also Funffrock, "Les Grèves ouvrières dans le département du Nord." On unemployment in the Parisian garment industry, see Omnès, *Ouvrières parisiennes*, 172.

56 Letellier et al., 109–12. They report that women made up 1.4 percent of wage earners in the building industry in 1931. On building workers and unemployment, see also Marpsat, "Chômage et profession dans les années trentes," 60–62.

57 Letellier et al, 104. These statistics reflect the numbers of workers who applied for and received unemployment assistance through municipal public assistance organisms.

58 See Omnès, *Ouvrières parisiennes*, 193. At Thomson-Houston women experienced relatively less job stability in the face of irregular production norms. Forty-five percent of the men employed between 1930 and 1939 stayed no more than a year. In 1934, 74 percent of the women hired in the course of the year failed to remain employed for the entire year (193).

59 Omnès, *Ouvrières parisiennes*, 180.

60 Letellier, et al., 69–70.

61 Ibid., 68–69.

62 Ibid.

63 Omnès, "La politique d'emploi," 50.

64 Omnès, *Ouvrières parisiennes*, 183–84. Omnès reports that women experienced 14.3 percent unemployment in the packaging industry in 1936 in contrast to men's 5.3 percent and 17.7 percent unemployment in textiles as opposed to men's 11.1 percent in 1936.

65 Omnès, *Ouvrières parisiennes*, 179.

66 Ibid., 174–75.

67 For an excellent discussion of the problem of calculating women's unemployment, see Omnès, *Ouvrières parisiennes*, 170, note 11.

68 Marpsat, "Chômage et profession dans les années trentes,"66. My translation.

69 Ibid.

70 Ibid.

71 Omnès, *Ouvrières parisiennes*, 176.

72 On this point, see Sauvy, 403–6; Omnès, *Ouvrières parisiennes*, 213–18.

73 Schor, 121. On the xenophobic reaction, see also Cross, *Immigrant Workers in Industrial France*, 186–90; Noiriel, *Les ouvriers dans la société française;* Lewis, *The Boundaries of the Republic*.

74 Reproduced in Schor, 122.

75 Anonymous, "Comment lutter contre le chômage et atténuer ses effets?" 4.

76 This topic is explored in detail for Paris by Rosenberg, *Policing Paris;* and for Lyon and Marseille by Lewis, *The Boundaries of the Republic*.

77 Anonymous,"Le chômage et la main d'oeuvre étrangère," 3.

78 See Rapport du Préfet de Police, October 3, 1932, on Congrès de l'union syndicale

(unitaire) des travailleurs de la métallurgie in AN F 7 13786 and "Des incidents avant et après," unidentified newspaper clipping referring to the hunger marches of 1933 in ADN M161/18 Marche de faim des chômeurs, 1933. See Commission administrative de l'Union départementale des syndicats ouvriers confédérées du Nord, Report of December 10, 1934, arguing that foreign labor should be treated the same as French but also protesting that the 1932 Law on National Labor (see below) was not applied in the Nord. The Union départementale leveled a strong protest against underpaid Belgian workers who, in addition to receiving lower wages, also received lower family allowances (4).

79 Schor, 127.

80 Viêt, *La France immigrée.*

81 Noiriel, *Les ouvriers dans la société française,* 172. Yet foreigners still counted for less than a fifth of all construction workers, a quarter of workers in heavy metallurgy, and a third of all workers in mining.

82 Schor, 125–26.

83 Cross, *Immigrant Workers in French Society,* 203; Letellier et al., 132–33, report that men counted for 80 percent of unemployed foreign workers.

84 Cross, 198–99.

85 Ibid., 187–88.

86 ADN 77J 2263 Main d'oeuvre étrangère, Rapport de l'inspecteur divisionnaire de la 5ième circonscription, Ministère du Travail, au Préfet du Nord, June 23, 1932; *Annales de la Chambre de Commerce de Tourcoing,* November–December 1931, on the debate over the Law on the Protection of National Labor; and *Annales de la Chambre de Commerce de Tourcoing,* March 1933, in the same dossier. Letellier et al. (129) argue that government attempts to repatriate foreign workers and to restrict immigration actually resulted in a rather small drop in the total number of foreigners, an observation that is also supported by Schor, 124.

87 Schor, 128.

88 Similar debates took place in the United States and across Europe. See Kessler-Harris, "The Gendered Limits of Social Citizenship in the Depression Era." De Grazia, *How Fascism Ruled Women,* and Koonz, *Mothers in the Fatherland,* show how fascist and Nazi regimes condemned working women and curtailed their limited rights as workers during the Depression. On right-wing rhetoric against working women in Depression-era France, see Koos and Sarnoff, "France."

89 Bonnin, in *Le Droit des femmes* (August 1934), cited by Bard, *Les Filles de Marianne,* 316. My translation.

90 AN F7 13771, Police files on activities of the CGTU. Brochure, Union syndicale des travailleurs de la métallurgie, voiture-aviation, et similaires de la région parisienne, *Xe congrès [1931],* 11–12. See also AN F7 13771, Police report on Congrès de la Fédération des ouvriers sur métaux, September 13, 1931, where similar issues were raised.

91 See *Le Métallurgiste* 54 (January 1928): 4. The congress demanded maternity leave at full pay for eight weeks before and eight weeks after the birth of the child, regardless of the mother's nationality; nursing allowances for the duration of

nursing; employer-sponsored nursing rooms and day care centers, washing rooms and bathing facilities, and eating halls for women workers. See also articles in the same paper on women's protests against employers' failure to prevent work accidents and for the protection of maternity in the context of May 1st demonstrations in 1929, Anonymous, "Les ouvrières de la métallurgie chômeront le 1er mai"; and Anonymous, "Les travailleuses françaises participeront au Ve congrès de l'ISR," 4.

92 See Delasalle, *Le travail de la femme dans l'industrie textile et du vêtement dans l'arrondissement de Lille*, 25–27.

93 Women's presence in the textile labor force of the Nord increased steadily from 39 percent in 1901 to 52 percent in 1931 (Delasalle, 27). By the 1930s, foreign workers (mostly Belgians) represented as little as 10 percent and as much as 90 percent of the labor force in textile cities close to the Belgian border. See ADN M616/27C, Chômage 1932, Journées d'action. Rapport de l'Inspecteur divisionnaire de la 5ième circonscription au Préfet du Nord, June 23, 1932.

94 ADN 595/41 CGT 1919–34 Textiles. Rapport du Commissaire de police Préfet du Nord, January 17, 1933 and June 28, 1933; ADN M616/27C Tract issued by the Comité de chômeurs, d'Armentières, January 12, 1932. These were only a few of the demands. Others were equivalent unemployment assistance for workers of both sexes, including those who performed industrial homework; free transportation; the establishment of municipal soup kitchens; public works programs; and the right of foreign workers to receive unemployment assistance. Another tract in the same dossier issued by the Comité de chômeurs de Tourcoing showed how some workers assumed a male breadwinner model when they protested against only "seven francs per day allocated to the unemployed [male worker–*chômeur*], head of household," while at the same time it demanded "equal assistance for all, youths as well as women." See also letters from *comités de chômeurs* in 1935 defending women's right to work and unemployment benefits equal to those men received in AN F7 677 Voeux relatifs au chômage. The *comités de chômeurs* were organized by the communists and these defenses of women's rights were consistent with communists' rhetorical support for women's labor force equality.

95 Fauchère, *Le travail des femmes;* Buland, *Femme, défends-toi!*

96 Rougé "Le retour de la femme au foyer," 297. Pedersen, 404–5.

97 ADN M616/27C Tract from the Union locale unitaire de Dunkerque, announcing a day of action for November 8, 1932. My translation.

98 CGT, *Congrès confédéral national, 1933,* 48 and 308–9. See also Blum, "Féminisme et syndicalisme," 109, 110–11; Frader, "Engendering Work and Wages."

99 Union des employés et employés chômeurs de Strasbourg et environs, November 2, 1933; Anonymous, "L'emploi des femmes mariées," *La Française,* December 2, 1933.

100 See Confédération générale du travail (CGT), *Congrès confédéral de Paris* [1935], 270–71. See also Thébaud, "Le Mouvement nataliste dans la France de l'entre-deux-guerres"; Coron, "Pour une France libre, forte et heureuse" ; Raymond, "La dépopulation et la misère d'enfance."

101 Fédération nationale des syndicats des employés, *La femme au travail ou au foyer.*

102 See ADN M571/13 Commission départementale du travail de l'arrondissement de Lille, séance du 29 août 1930. In addition to her concern with the way that married women's work had led to the "disorganization of the family," Vion protested against the practice of requiring women and adolescents to work on double shifts for eight consecutive hours, a practice that she argued was dangerous for women's health and would not leave women enough time to prepare meals. See also Esther Pasqualini-Bieganski, "La main d'oeuvre féminine textile dans l'arrondissement de Lille, 1919–1939," 74–80. Louis Blain, secretary of the Fédération textile des Syndicats libres (CFTC), proposed that returning mothers to the home would help solve the unemployment crisis (Pasqualini-Bieganski, 80).

103 Anonymous, "Les variations de la main d'oeuvre en France," my emphasis. The article quoted from a recent issue of the *Bulletin de la Société d'études et d'informations économiques.*

104 Anonymous, "Les variations de la main d'oeuvre en France."

105 See Anonymous, "La lutte contre le chômage," 10.

106 *Rapport annuel de l'Union des industries métallurgiques et minières, de la construction mécanique, électrique, et métallique* (February 27, 1932), 3, in AN F7 13786 Syndicats métallurgiques.

107 Caunes, *Des mesures juridiques propre à faciliter la présence de la mère au foyer ouvrier,* 24–25.

108 Ibid., 75–79. My translation.

109 Ibid., 84–87.

110 Talmy, *Histoire du movement familial en France,* vol. 2, 199 and 202–3.

111 See Cann, *Les allocations familiales,* 71–73.

112 On Richet, see Bibliothèque Marguerite Durand (BMD), Dossier on Richet, including letters from workingwomen and others taking issue with his views; articles in *La Française,* the official paper of the Ligue française des droits des femmes (LFDF), *l'Oeuvre, le Droit des Femmes,* and *La Dame des téléphones,* among others. See also Bard, 313–18, on Richet and feminists' response to arguments against women's work. In fact, French women addressed the issue of married women's work almost two years earlier in the pages of the feminist press in response to existing debate on this issue outside France. Offen also points to the Richet controversy in "Women and the Politics of Motherhood in France, 1920–1940."

113 Pic, "Le mouvement législative ouvrier en France et à l'étranger et la crise mondiale."

114 For the full story of the work of the UFCS and the Ligue de la Mère au Foyer, see Talmy, vol. 2, 197–204; and Pedersen, 393–411.

115 See Omnès, *Les ouvrières parisiennes,* 169, citing an appeal of support for the Comité du retour des mères au foyer (Committee for the Return of Mothers to the Home), sent by the Union féminine civique et sociale to the *Revue mensuelle de l'Union des industries métallurgiques et minières* (May 1932). According to Omnès, the UFCS proposed that the *caisses de compensation* (which administered family allowances) finance the unwaged mother's allowance by abolishing the allowance

for the first child; the newlyweds' allowance would be paid to the male wage earner who had just married and whose wife remained at home. It would stop if by the end of the second year the couple had not borne any children. The UFCS maintained close links with the UIMM, but Omnès argues that this employer organization resisted these ideas in favor of a more pragmatic and flexible position on women's employment. See Omnès, *Les ouvrières parisiennes*, 169, notes 1–6, and 170.

116 Some of this story is discussed by Pedersen, 398–401, who argues that in the context of the continued low fertility in France, the UFCS found allies in the pronatalist Alliance nationale de l'accroissement de la population française, equally concerned about the effects of married women's work on the family. See also Talmy, vol. 2, 203 ff.

117 Bard, 316.

118 Talmy, vol. 2, 203. See also Pedersen, 399.

119 Talmy, vol. 2, 204.

120 Lefebvre-Dibon, "La crise économique et la femme au foyer," 86.

121 Roulleaux-Dugage, "Le vote familial." My translation.

122 On the feminist response to attacks on women's right to work, see Bard, 313–29; Thibert, "Crise économique et le travail féminin, I"; and "Crise économique et le travail féminin, II." See also Fuss, "Chômage et placement des femmes." Fuss supported Thibert's conclusions but argued for a sharper division of labor and for home economics training to professionalize domestic tasks. See also Jack's response to the press campaign denouncing women's work in "Le chômage et le travail des femmes."

123 See, for example, Brunschvicq, "L'offensive contre le travail féminin"; Brunschvicq, "A propos du travail féminin"; Brunschvicq, "Le Travail industriel et le foyer ouvrier"; Maltrait "La Femme doit-elle travailler sans une nécessité absolue?," and the debate in subsequent issues. Brunschvicq, editor of *La Française* and president of the Union française pour le suffrage des femmes, argued that the principle of women's right to work had to be defended at all costs as an individual right. She also claimed that "in times of depression, women who are working for a *salaire d'appoint* [pin money] should be the first to give up their place [at work]." However, "as soon as one steps away from the general principle and begins to examine individual situations, we realize how difficult it is to define a *salaire d'appoint*" (my translation). Brunschvicq, "A propos du travail féminin," 2.

124 Jack, "Le chômage et le travail des femmes."

125 Delagrange, "Le travail de la femme mariée," 31–48.

126 See Clark, 169–72. In chapter 6 Clark provides a detailed discussion of women's reaction to quotas and closures of the state examinations (*concours*) to women.

127 Ibid., 174–75, 179–84. Clark shows how the Conseil d'état ruled in favor of women's right to work but allowed ministries to effectively limit employees on the basis of gender according to their "special needs."

128 See Bruhat, "Où on est. Le chômage dans le second degré."

129 Bard, 317.

130 Clark, 186.

131 Daniel and Tuchszirer, *L'état face au chômeurs,* chapter 4, 99 ff.

132 Letellier et al., vol.1, 127.

133 Ibid., 70–71. My translation.

134 Marpsat, "Chômage et profession," 57. See also discussion in Reynolds, 115–17.

135 As Salais et al. note, this distinction may help to explain the relatively lower levels of unemployment in France (by comparison with other European countries) in the 1930s. However, as they also point out, during the 1930s, women's unemployment patterns more closely resembled the male model given the decline of women's industrial homework (from 541,000 in 1906 to 214,000 in 1936) (24). "Alors qu'en 1896 les déclarations des 'sans-emploi' sont pour les femmes essentiellement liées au travail à domicile, elles apparaissent en 1936 à proximité de la position de l'ouvrière dans un établissement (96).

136 Cited by Marpsat, "La Statistique des chômeurs secourus en France de 1931 à 1939," 187.

137 Cited by Marpsat, "La Statistique des chômeurs."

138 I leave aside the question of benefits to unmarried couples, but see Marpsat, "La Statistique des chômeurs."

139 Cross, 131; Letellier et al., 131. As Letellier et al. point out, the proportion of unemployed differed considerably among different national and ethnic groups.

140 Letellier, et al., 131.

141 Rapport du Commissaire spécial, Roubaix au Préfet du Nord, January 12, 1932. The charge was made by the *comité de chômeurs.*

142 Marpsat, "Chômage et profession," 57.

143 Ibid., 54.

144 See Circular, Ministère du Travail March 12, 1935, in AN F22 677 Voeux relatifs au chômage.

145 For these appeals, see, for example, "Notre charte: Les chômeurs sont résolus à lutter," in ADN M616/27c Chômage 1932: Journées d'action; and "Les armes légales du chômeur," in ADN M616/18 Marches de faim des chômeurs, 1933.

146 Cohen and Hanagan argue, "Because unemployment was less salient in France and its burden was placed disproportionately on the backs of the young, the old, and the foreign . . . it is not surprising that unemployment [policy] was a low priority among French workers." See "Politics, Industrialization and Citizenship," 104.

147 Reynolds emphasizes the symbolic politics of these appointments: *France between the Wars,* 159–62.

148 Omnès, *Ouvrières parisiennes,* 175–76. My translation.

149 Chenut, "The Gendering of Skill as a Historical Process," 100; Chenut, *The Fabric of Gender,* 382–83.

150 Phan, 86.

151 "Barèmes de salaires établis par les conventions collectives des employés, techniciens, et agents de maîtrise des industries métallurgiques et mécaniques dans le

canton de Vierzon, 15 décembre 1936," in AN F22 1702 Conventions collectives. Métallurgie. See other examples in this dossier. See also "Conventions collectives," *Revue menuselle de l'Union des industries métallurgiques et mécaniques* no. 198 Supplément (April 1937).

152 Phan, 88. Employers likewise followed these practices after the Second World War, when they attempted to compensate for pay cuts by improving social services. Moutet, 345.

153 Phan, 88. My translation.

154 Ibid., 88–89. My translation.

155 Talmy, vol. 2, 232.

156 Ibid., 233.

157 See Talmy, vol. 2, on the details of the Code, its innovations, and modifications, 234–41.

158 Ibid., 235. See also Jenson and Sineau, *Mitterrand et les Femmes,* who remark on a similar use of family policy in the Parental Education Allowance of the 1990s.

159 Omnès, *Ouvrières parisiennes,* 213–21.

160 Evans, Rueschemeyer, and Skocpol, eds., *Bringing the State Back In,* encouraged scholars to look at the importance of the state as a political and historical actor. Countless feminist studies of the state and social policy have made this point very well. For historical examples, see Stewart, *Women, Work and the French State;* Pedersen. See also Cronin, *The Politics of State Expansion.*

Conclusion

1 Clark, *The Rise of Professional Women in France.*

2 Jenson and Sineau, *Mitterrand et les françaises, un rendez-vous manqué,* 37; "The Constitution of the Fourth Republic," in Cahm, ed., *Politics and Society in Contemporary France,* 163. My translation.

3 Dutton, *The Origins of the French Welfare State,* 202.

4 Cahm, 497 and 500–503; Rioux, *La France de la IVe république* 1, 118; Rioux, *La France de la IVe république* 2, 215. According to Dutton, the self-employed were not included in the postwar regime of family allowances.

5 Rioux, *La France de la IVe république,* vol. 2, 216.

6 On women's labor force participation, see Droits de la femme, *Les femmes dans une société des inégalités,* 12.

7 Droits de la femme, *Les femmes dans une société des inégalités,* 36–37; Frader, "Women, Work and Inequality in Contemporary France"; Jenson and Sineau, 39.

8 Prost, "L'évolution de la politique familiale en France de 1938 à 1981."

9 Jenson and Sineau, *Qui doit garder le jeune enfant?,* 141.

10 Ibid., 144–48.

11 Ibid., 148.

12 Ibid.

13 Jenson and Sineau, *Qui doit garder le jeune enfant?,* 148. My translation.

14 For a full discussion, see Jenson and Sineau, *Mitterrand et les Françaises,* especially chapter 7 and annexe 5, "Droits des femmes: Bilan législatif," 360–62.

15 My discussion draws heavily on Jenson and Sineau, *Mitterrand et les françaises,* 260–67; and Jenson and Sineau, *Qui doit garder le jeune enfant?,* chapter 6.

16 Jenson and Sineau, *Mitterrand et les Françaises,* 262.

17 This agenda was criticized by the centrist senator Jean Cauchon, *rapporteur* for the Commission des Affaires sociales, who stated, "This allowance confuses two objectives: a natalist, familialist objective, which we support; and an anti-unemployment objective." Quoted by Jenson and Sineau, *Qui doit garder le jeune enfant?,* 155. My translation.

18 Jenson and Sineau, *Mitterrand et les Françaises,* 263. Feminist scholars have recently questioned the effects of European welfare regimes' care policies on women's citizenship. Trudie Knijn and Monique Kremer have argued, for example, that welfare states construct the needs and rights of caregivers "in ways that contribute to gender inequality of citizenship rights." They argue that allowances for mothers and maternity leaves have been shaped such that in the " 'modern family' . . . women were not only enabled do care, but were also condemned to do so. This new care regime made women largely dependent on their husbands." Knijn and Kremer, "Gender and the Caring Dimension of Welfare States," 328, 329. See also Ungerson, "Social Politics and the Commodification of Care," and Heinen and Martiskainen de Koenigswater, "Framing Citizenship in France and Finland in the 1990s."

19 Heinen and Martiskainen de Koenigswater, 173.

20 Ibid.

21 Between 1946 and 1962, the numbers of North African immigrants increased from 40,488 to 410,373; Algerians made up 12 percent of all migrants to France in 1954 and a little over 16 percent in 1962. Weil, *La France et ses étrangers,* 558.

22 Lyons, "Invisible Immigrants," 97 ff.

23 Ibid., 6–8. See also 120–21.

24 Sophie Lanri, "Algériennes et mères françaises exemplaires," and Lyons, 122.

25 Lyons, 125–27.

Archives

Archives de la Ville de Paris (AVP) (Villemoisson sur Orge) 181. Contrats d'apprentissage. 1928–33.

Archives de l'école des surintendantes d'usine, Ecole supérieure du travail social. Paris.

ARCHIVES DÉPARTEMENTALES DU NORD (ADN)
    ADN M 161/18 La crise de peignage. 1933.
    ADN M 571/ 13 Commission départemental du travail de l'arrondissement de Lille.
    ADN M 571/27 La crise de peignage. 1934.
    ADN M 595/41 Textile: CGT. 1919–34.
    ADN M 605/21–23 Mouvements sociaux, syndicats. 1934.
    ADN M 616/18 Marches de faim des chômeurs. 1933.
    ADN M 616/27c Chômage. 1932.
    ADN M 619/79 Grève des dix sous. 1928.
    ADN 77J 2263 Main d'oeuvre étrangère.
    ADN 77 J 2318 Textiles.

ARCHIVES NATIONALES (AN)
    AN BB18 2706 Justice. Grèves. 1924.
    AN BB18 2752 Justice. Grèves. 1926.
    AN BB18 2831 Justice. Grèves. 1930.
    AN BB18 2880 Justice. Grèves. 1933.
    AN BB 18 2953 Justice. Grèves. 1935.
    AN F7 677 Voeux relatifs au chômage.
    AN F7 13367 Police générale. 1919.
    AN F7 13584 Police générale. CGTU 1922–28.

AN F7 13812 Police générale. Tract issued by the Syndicat général des industries chimiques.

AN F7 13892 Police générale. CGTU. Strikes. 1922–23.

AN F7 13894 Police générale. CGTU. Strikes. 1923–24.

AN F7 13895 Police générale. CGTU. Strikes. 1925.

AN F7 13618 Police générale. Union des Syndicats de la Seine. Notes et presse. 1920–23.

AN F7 13771 Police générale. Presse. 1931.

AN F7 13737 Police générale. Activité syndicale. 1926–28.

AN F7 13785 Police générale. Syndicats. Activités syndicales métaux. 1930–31.

AN F7 13786 Police générale. Syndicats. Grèves métaux. 1932.

AN F7 13921 Police générale. Textile. 1934.

AN F10 2631 Enseignement agricole ménager. 1938.

AN F22 181 Travail et sécurité sociale. Grèves. 1921.

AN F22 190 Travail et sécurité sociale. Grèves du textile. 1927–28.

AN F 22 191 Travail et sécurité sociale. Grèves dans le textile. Nord. 1928–29.

AN F22 213 Travail et sécurité sociale. Application de la loi sur les assurances sociales. 1930.

AN F22 471 Travail et sécurité sociale.

AN F22 596 Travail et sécurité sociale. *Bulletins techniques.*

AN F22 1702 Travail et sécurité sociale. Conventions collectives. Métallurgie.

AN 39 AS 914 Groupement des industries métallurgiques de la région parisienne (GIM).

AN 39 AS 988 Groupement des industries métallurgiques de la région parisienne (GIM).

Printed Government Documents

France. *Journal Officiel de la République française. Chambre. Débats parlementaires* [*J. O. Chambre. Débats parlementaires*], April 17, 1920.

——. *J. O. Chambre. Débats parlementaires,* March 11, 1921.

——. *J. O. Chambre. Débats parlementaires,* March 23, 1921.

France. Ministère de commerce, de l'industrie et des colonies. *Bulletin mensuel du ministère de commerce, de l'industrie et des colonies* no.1 (January 1890).

France. Ministère des PTT. *Bulletin mensuel des PTT* no. 1 (1890).

——. *Bulletin mensuel des PTT* no. 18 (1922).

——. *Bulletin officiel du ministère des PTT* no. 17 (1930).

France. Ministère du Travail. *Bulletin du ministère du travail* nos. 9–11 (September–November 1916).

——. *Bulletin du ministère du travail* nos. 1–3 (January–March 1917).

——. *Bulletin du ministère du travail* nos. 10–12 (October–December 1917).

——. *Bulletin du ministère du travail* nos. 1–2 (January–February 1918).

——. *Bulletin du ministère du travail* nos. 1–2 (January–February 1919).

——. Statistique générale de la France. *Résultats statistiques du recensement générale de la population. 1921. 1926. Tome II. Population présent. Résultats par département.* Paris: Imprimerie nationale, 1925, 1929.

——. Statistique générale de la France et d'observation des prix. Comité permanent d'études relatives à la prévision des chômages industriels, *Compte-rendu des travaux. Années 1917–1920.* Paris: Imprimerie nationale, 1920.

France. Ministère du travail, de l'hygiène, de l'assistance et de la prévoyance sociale. *Statistiques générales de France. Résultats statistiques des recensements généraux de la population. 1921, 1926, 1936.* Paris: Imprimerie nationale, 1922, 1928, 1937.

Ville de Paris. *Bulletin Municipal Officiel.*

Newspapers and Journals

Les Cahiers du Bolchévisme
La Française
L'Humanité
Information ouvrière et sociale (after 1919, *Information sociale*)
Le Métallurgiste
Revue de l'Alliance nationale pour l'accroissement de la population française
L'Union des Métaux

Labor Congresses

Bulletin official du congrès du syndicat national des agents des PTT *de France et des colonies.* 3 bis série supplémentaire (May 1924): 1.

Confédération générale du travail (CGT). *Congrès confédéral national, 1933. Compte rendu sténographique des débats. XVIIIe Congrès national corporatif (XXII de la* CGT*) 26–29 septembre 1933.* Paris: Editions de la CGT, 1934.

——. *Congrès confédéral de Paris. Compte-rendu sténographique des débats du XXIX Congrès national corporatif (XXIIIe de la* CGT*) 24–27 septembre 1935.* Paris: Editions de la CGT, 1936.

Confédération générale du travail unitaire (CGTU). *2ième Congrès de la* CGTU*. 1923.* Paris: Maison des syndicats, 1924.

——. *Congrès national ordinaire. 3ième Congrès de la* CGTU*, Paris, 26 au 31 août 1925.* Paris: Maison des syndicats, service de l'imprimerie, 1925.

——. *Congrès national ordinaire. Bordeaux, 19–24 Septembre 1927.* Paris: Maison des syndicats, service de l'imprimerie, 1928.

Fédération des ouvriers sur métaux et similaires de France (CGT). *VIIe Congrès fédéral tenu à Paris les 23, 24, et 25 aout, 1925. Compte-rendu des travaux du congrès.* Versailles: Imprimerie cooperative Gutenberg, 1925.

——. *Xe congrès fédéral tenu à Paris les 13–14 septembre 1931. Rapport morale et administratif. Compte-rendu des travaux du congrès;* Fédération unitaire du Textile-

Vêtement et partis similaires, *3e congrès tenu à Paris les 28–30 novembre 1926* (n.p., n.d.).

——. *Congrès fédéral tenu à Paris les 24 et 25 juillet 1927. Compte-rendu.* Versailles: Imprimerie la Gutenberg, 1928.

——. *Compte-rendu du VIIIe congrès fédéral tenu à Paris les 15–16 septembre 1929.* Versailles: Imprimerie coöperative Gutenberg, 1930.

——. *Compte-rendu du XVIIIe congrès fédéral tenu à Paris les 24–25 septembre 1933.* Versailles: Imprimerie coopérative Gutenberg, 1933.

Fédération française des travailleurs du livre. *Onzième congrès national tenu à Nancy du 8 au 13 septembre 1919* (Paris: Imprimerie nouvelle, 1919).

Fédération nationale des syndicats des employés. *La femme au travail ou au foyer. Rapport présenté au 29e congrès fédéral des employés. Clermont-Ferrand, 17, 18, 19 avril 1938.* Rennes: Imprimeries réunies, 1938.

Fédération nationale ouvrière de l'industrie textile de France. *XVIe Congrès nationale tenu à Rouen les 6, 7 et 8 septembre 1920. Compte-rendu.* Paris: Imprimerie nouvelle, 1920.

——. *XVIIe Congrès national tenu à Mulhouse les 13, 14, 15 août 1922. Compte-rendu sténographique.* Paris: Imprimerie nouvelle, 1922.

Fédération unitaire des ouvriers et ouvrières sur métaux (CGTU). *Premier congrès national. Compte-rendu. St.Etienne les 23, 24, et 25 juin 1922.* Paris: Maison des syndicats, 1922.

——. *IIe Congrès national fédéral. Paris les 29, 30, 31 juillet 1923.* Paris: Maison des syndicats, 1923.

——. *IIIe Congrès national. Rapports et compte-rendu du 3e comité fédéral tenu à Paris les 1–3 septembre 1925.* Metz: La cootypographie, 1925.

——. *Congrès de la fédération unitaire des ouvriers et ouvrières sur métaux 12–14 décembre 1927.* Paris: Maison des syndicats, 1927.

——. *4e Congrès national à Paris les 12–14 décembre 1927.* Paris: Maison des syndicats, 1928.

Fédération unitaire du textile de France. *Congrès constitutif de la fédération tenu à Lyon les 22, 23, 24 juin 1922. Compte rendu sténographique des séances.* Paris: n.p., 1922.

Séances du congrès ouvrier socialiste de France. Troisième session tenue à Marseille du 20 au 31 octobre 1879 à la salle des Folies-Bergères. Marseille: Imprimerie générale J. Doucet, 1879.

Syndicat national des agents des Postes, Télégraphes et Téléphones (CGT). *IVe Congrès des agents des PTT tenu à Paris les 19–22 avril 1922.* Limoges: Imprimerie nouvelle, 1922.

——. *Ve congrès tenu à Paris les 16–19 mai 1923.* Epernay: Imprimerie sparnacienne, 1923.

——. *VIIième congrès national tenu à Toulouse les 10–13 juin 1925.* Epernay: Imprimerie sparnacienne, 1925.

Union des industries métallurgiqes et mécaniques (UIMM). *Assemblée générale ordinaire du 17 février 1931*. Vannes: Imprimerie LaFoyle et J. de Lamarzelle, 1931.

Union des syndicats de la région parisienne. *Ve Congrès de syndicats de la Seine et Ier congrès des unions des syndicats de la Seine et Seine-et-Oise fusionés tenu des 25 janvier, 1er et 22 février 1925*. Paris: Maison des syndicats, service de l'imprimerie, 1925.

Ve Congrès national des syndicats et groupes corporatifs ouvriers de France tenu à Marseille du 19 au 22 octobre 1892. Compte-rendu receuilli dans les archives de la Bourse de Travail de Marseille. Paris: Rivière, 1909.

Unpublished Interviews

Interviews conducted as part of "Jeune provinciaux d'hier, vieux parisiens d'aujourd'hui." Survey directed by Françoise Cribier, LASMAS (Laboratoire d'Analyse statistique et méthodologique appliqué à la sociologie). I am grateful to Françoise Cribier for giving me access to the transcriptions of the following interviews:

Gilles de la Gorce, Interview with Mme D., 1985.

Catherine Omnès, Interview with Mme Georges, 1985.

Published Print Sources

Abensour, Léon. "Le problème de la démobilization féminine." *La Grande revue* no. 1 (January 1919): 49.

Accampo, Elinor. *Blessed Motherhood, Bitter Fruit: Nelly Roussel and the Politics of Female Pain in Third Republic France*. Baltimore: Johns Hopkins University Press, 2006.

Accampo, Elinor, Rachel G. Fuchs, and Mary Lynn Stewart, eds. *Gender and the Politics of Social Reform*. Baltimore: Johns Hopkins University Press, 1995.

Albistur, Maïté, and Daniel Armogathe. *Histoire du féminisme français*. Paris: Des Femmes, 1977.

Alquier, Henriette. "La maternité, fonction sociale." *Bulletin des groupes féministes de l'enseignement laïque* 39 (October 1927):1–3.

Amar, Jules. "Les lois du travail féminin et de l'activité cérébrale." *Comptes rendus hebdomadaires des séances de l'Académie des Sciences* 167 (July–December 1918): 560.

——. "Méthode d'examen des aptitudes professionnelles." *L'Exportateur français*, May 15, 1919.

——. *Le moteur humain et les bases scientifiques du travail*. Paris: Dunod, 1914.

——. *Le moteur humain*. 2nd ed. Paris: Dunod, 1923.

——. *L'orientation professionnelle*. Paris: Dunod, 1920.

——. "L'origine et les conséquences de l'émotivité feminine." *Compte-rendu de l'académie des sciences*, January 4, 1919.

——. *The Physiology of Industrial Organization and the Re-employment of the Disabled.* Translated by Bernard Miall. Edited with notes and an introduction by A. F. Stanley Kent. London: Library Press Limited, 1918.

——. "Réflexions d'un physiologiste sur la femme et le féminisme." *Revue Bleue,* February 16–23, 1918.

Anonymous. "L'action des organisations patronales: Au consortium de l'industrie textile de Roubaix-Tourcoing." *Information sociale* no. 277 (March 5, 1928): 4.

Anonymous. "Administration industrielle." *Annales des PTT* II (1917): 356–86.

Anonymous. "A la CGTU. Travailleurs coloniaux." *Information sociale* no. 134 (January 22, 1925).

Anonymous. "Une baisse de salaires est annoncée pour le 1er février dans la filature de coton." *Le Grand echo,* January 13, 1934.

Anonymous. "Centre de Camping André Paty." *Mon métier. Revue de perfectionnement professionnel.* 2ième année, no. 11 (May 1929): 149–50.

Anonymous. "Le chômage dans les industries de guerre." *Information ouvrière et sociale* no. 91 (January 23, 1919): 2–3.

Anonymous. "Le chômage et la main d'oeuvre étrangère." *Information sociale* no. 390 (December 18, 1930): 3.

Anonymous. "Le comité national de la CGT, 12–20 septembre." *Information sociale* no. 119 (October 2, 1924): 3.

Anonymous. "Le comité national de la CGTU." *Information sociale* no. 122 (October 23, 1924).

Anonymous. "Comment lutter contre le chômage et attenuer ses effects?" *Information sociale* no. 394 (January 29, 1931): 4.

Anonymous. "Un complement à l'accord du 17 avril 1919." *Information ouvrière et sociale* no. 128 (June 1, 1919): 6–7.

Anonymous. "Conférence des offices de placement." *Information ouvrière et sociale* no. 94 (February 2, 1919): 1–2.

Anonymous. "La conférence sur l'organisation des femmes." *L'Humanité,* December 27, 1921, 2.

Anonymous. "Congrès des groupes fémininstes de l'enseignement laïque (Marseille, 1930)." *Bulletin des groupes féministes de l'enseignement laïque* 57 (October 1930): 1–2.

Anonymous. "Le congrès du syndicat national des agents des PTT." *Bulletin official du syndicat national des agents des PTT de France et des colonies* (March 1924): 3–4.

Anonymous. "Le congrès national de la fédération de Paris: La semaine de 44 heures." *L'Ouvrier textile* no. 35 (December 1928): 2.

Anonymous. "Le congrès national de la fédération [du Textile] de Lille, Compte rendu résumé." *L'Ouvrier textile* no. 44 (October 1931):1.

Anonymous. "Les congrès ouvriers." *Le Textile* no. 121 (October 16, 1924): 4–5.

Anonymous. "Conventions collectives." *Revue mensuelle de l'Union des industries métallurgiques et mécaniques* no. 198 Supplément (April 1937).

Anonymous. "La crise dans l'industrie lainière du Nord." *Le Nord industriel,* July 28, 1934.

Anonymous. "Dans l'industrie textile." *Information ouvrière et sociale* no. 136 (June 20, 1919): 3.

Anonymous. "La double loi économique des salaires." *Information ouvrière et sociale* No. 136 (June 20, 1919): 2.

Anonymous. "L'éffritement des huit heures." *Information ouvrière et sociale* no. 11 (August 12, 1922): 3.

Anonymous. "L'emploi des femmes la nuit." *L'Usine,* January 15, 1927, 3.

Anonymous. "L'emploi des femmes mariées." *La Française,* December 2, 1933.

Anonymous. "Le fascisme est là." *L'Humanité,* January 1, 1925, 5.

Anonymous. "La femme et l'enfant dans l'industrie." *La Voix du peuple* no. 726 (December 1916): 20.

Anonymous. "La fermeture des peignages de laine de Roubaix-Tourcoing." *Le Grand echo,* July 22, 1934.

Anonymous. "La grève des métallurgistes du Havre." *Information sociale* no. 16 (September 14, 1922): 6–8.

Anonymous. "La Grève des PTT." *Information sociale* no.328 (June 6, 1929): 4.

Anonymous. "Grèves du Nord." *Information sociale* no. 378 (September 18, 1930): 3.

Anonymous. "Les Grèves lyonnaises." *Information sociale* no. 204 (March 21, 1920): 4.

Anonymous. "Les huit heures: Les huit heures de loisirs. Comment organiser le loisir: la réforme de l'habitation." *Information ouvrière et sociale* no. 128 (June 1, 1919): 3.

Anonymous. "Immigration et naturalization." *Revue de l'Alliance nationale pour l'accroissement de la population française* no. 134 (September 1923): 279–81.

Anonymous. "La lutte contre le chômage." *Information sociale* no. 397 (February 26, 1931): 10.

Anonymous. "Le machinisme et le rôle de l'ouvrier." *L'Ouvrier textile* 35 (December 1928): 4.

Anonymous. "La main d'oeuvre étrangère et les syndicats." *Information sociale* no. 117 (September 18, 1924).

Anonymous. "Un meeting des dames employées des PTT." *Information sociale* no. 183 (February 4, 1926): 8.

Anonymous. "Les méthodes nouvelles de production et de chômage." *L'Ouvrier textile* No. 44 (October 1931).

Anonymous. "Notre enquête sur le système Taylor: Les observations de M. Henri Le Chatelier." *Information ouvrière et sociale* no. 157 (September 14, 1919): 2.

Anonymous. "Le nouveau recruitment des téléphonistes." *L'Action,* February 23, 1910.

Anonymous. "L'oeuvre sociale de l'industrie textile en 1924: La mère au foyer." *Information sociale* no. 130 (February 26, 1924): 8.

Anonymous. "L'organisation méthodique du travail et son application aux postes et télégraphes." *Annales des PTT* VIII (1923): 835–976.

Anonymous. "L'organisation scientifique du travail." *Information ouvrière et sociale* no. 89 (January 1919): 1–2.

Anonymous. "L'orientation professionnelle en matière de l'apprentissage." *Information sociale* no. 229 (July 4, 1920): 6.

Anonymous. "Les ouvrières de la métallurgie chômeront le 1er mai." *Le Métallurgiste* (May 1929).

Anonymous. "La poste au féminin." *Référence*, September 7, 1984.

Anonymous. "Pour les dix sous d'augmentation. En avant!" *L'Humanité*, September 19, 1928, 1.

Anonymous. "Pour les ouvrières en chômage: La nouvelle circulaire." *La Bataille*, March 2, 1919.

Anonymous. "Le problème de la natalité." *Information ouvrière et sociale* no. 108 (March 23, 1919): 4.

Anonymous. "40,000 métallos en vacances forcées: Dans les usines rationalisées à outrance depuis des mois, l'attacque contre les salaires se pursuit." *L'Humanité*, August 3, 1931.

Anonymous. "Rapport sur VIIe Congrès du syndicat national des agents des PTT de France et des colonies (1924): Le salaire doit assurer une vie décente." *Bulletin officiel du congrès du syndicat national des agents des PTT de France et des colonies* (May 1924): 4.

Anonymous. "Report de la Gironde sur le Ve congrès (1924)." Syndicat national des agents des PTT de France et des Colonies. *Bulletin officiel du syndicat national des agents des PTT de France et des colonies* Paris: Maison des syndicats, 1924.

Anonymous. "Les résolutions votées au congrès de Bordeaux: Les travailleurs ne feront pas les frais de la rationalisation capitaliste." *L'Humanité*, September 26–27, 1927.

Anonymous. "Le téléphone en France et à l'étranger: Progrès technique, organisation rationnelle." *Annales des PTT* VIII (1923): 565–98.

Anonymous. "Le travail à la chaine." *Information sociale* no. 89 (February 14, 1924).

Anonymous. "Les travailleuses françaises participeront au Ve congrès de l'ISR." *Le Métallurgiste* 6 (June 1930): 4.

Anonymous. "Usure physique des mineurs." *Information ouvrière et sociale* no. 134 (June 22, 1919): 2.

Anonymous. "Les variations de la main d'oeuvre en France." *Information sociale* no. 392 (January 15, 1931): 3.

Anonymous. "La vie économique: L'éffritement des huit heures." *Information sociale* no. 12 (August 17, 1922): 3.

Arnaud-Duc, Nicole. "Les contradictions du droit." In Geneviève Fraisse and Michelle Perrot, eds., *Le XIXe siècle*. Vol. 4 of *Histoire des femmes dans l'occident*, edited by Georges Duby and Michelle Perrot. Paris: Plon, 1992. 84–116.

Association des surintendantes de France. *Compte rendu annuel de l'assemblée générale du 13 février 1923*. Paris: 1923.

Association des surintendantes d'usines et de services sociaux. *Assemblée générale 21 février 1928*. Paris: Moderne imprimerie, 1928.

———. *Assemblée générale du 4 mars 1930*. Paris: A. Et. F. Debauve, 1930.

———. *Assemblée générale* [1931]. Paris: n.p., 1931.

———. *Compte rendu de l'assemblée générale du 13 février 1923*. Paris: Association des surintendantes, 1923.

———. *XVe Assemblée générale de l'Association des surintendantes d'usines et des services sociaux*. Paris: ASSUSS, 1935.

———. *XIVe Assemblée générale*. Paris: Imprimerie "Elbe," 1934.

Audoin-Rouzeau, Stéphane. *L'enfant de l'enemi (1914–1918): Viol, avortement, infanticide pendant la grande guerre*. Paris: Aubier, 1995.

———. *Men at War, 1914–1918*. Translated by Helen Phail. Oxford: Berg, 1992.

Aurain, L. *L'école ménagère agricole chrétienne à la campagne*. Paris: Emmanuel Vitte, 1909.

Auslander, Leora, and Michelle Zancarini-Fournel, eds. *Différences des sexes et protection sociale*. Saint-Denis: Presses universitaires de Vincennes, 1995.

Bachrach, Susan. *Dames employées: The Feminization of Postal Work in Nineteenth Century France*. New York: Institute for Research in History and the Haworth Press, 1983.

Baldwin, Peter. *The Politics of Social Solidarity: The Class Bases of the European Welfare State, 1875–1975*. Cambridge: Cambridge University Press, 1990.

Barbusse, Henri. *Le feu*. Paris: Flammarion, 1916.

Bard, Christine. *Les filles de Marianne: Histoire des féminismes 1914–1940*. Paris: Fayard, 1995.

Barrett, Michèle. *Women's Oppression Today*. London: Verso, 1980.

Barthas, Louis. *Les carnets de guerre de Louis Barthas, tonnelier, 1914–1918*. Paris: François Maspéro, 1979.

Baverez, Nicholas. "Chômage des années 1930, chômage des années 1980." *Mouvement social* 154 (January–March 1991).

Becker, Annette. "To Remember and to Forget: Is There a Gender Issue?" Talk given at the Center for European Studies, Harvard University, April 5, 2001.

Becker, Jean-Jacques, and Serge Berstein. *Victoire et frustrations, 1914–1929*. Paris: Seuil, 1990.

Beechy, Veronica. *Unequal Work*. London: Verso, 1987.

Begoin, Dr. D. P. "Le travail et la fatigue: La névrose des téléphonistes et des mécanographes." *La Raison* nos. 20–21 Premier trimestre, 1958.

Bell, Susan Groag, and Karen Offen, eds. *Women, the Family, and Freedom: The Debate in Documents*. Vol. 2. Stanford, Calif.: Stanford University Press, 1983.

Berstein, Serge. *La France des années trentes*. Paris: Armand Colin, 1988.

Bertho, Catherine. *Histoire des télécommunications en France*. Toulouse: Editions Erès, 1984.

Bertillon, Jacques. *La dépopulation de la France, ses conséquences, ses causes, et mesures à prendre pour le combattre.* Paris: F. Alcan, 1911.

——. "Le problème de la dépopulation: Le programme de l'Alliance nationale pour l'acroissement de la population française." *Revue politique et parlementaire* 12 (1897): 544.

Bertinotti, Dominique. *Artisans d'hier et communications d'aujourd'hui, 1850–1950.* Paris: Editions des Archives nationales, 1981.

——. "Carrières féminines et carrières masculines dans l'administration des postes et télégraphes à la fin du XIXe siècle." *Annales. E.S.C.* 3 (Mai-juin, 1985): 625–40.

Bibliothèque d'orientation professionnelle. *Guide général pour la jeunesse carus: Renseignements complètes sur toutes les études, toutes les écoles ainsi que toutes les carrières et la façon d'y préparer.* Paris: Librairie Carus, 1930.

Biddleman, Patrick Kay. *Pariahs Stand Up! The Founding of the Liberal Feminist Movement in France, 1858–1889.* Westport, Conn.: Greenwood Press, 1982.

Bigot, Marthe. *La servitude des femmes.* Paris: Librairie de l'Humanité, 1921.

Blum, Françoise. "Féminisme et syndicalisme: Les femmes dans la Fédération de l'Habillement." Mémoire de maîtrise. Université de Paris I, 1977.

Bock, Gisela, and Pat Thane, eds. *Maternity and Gender Policies.* New York: Routledge, 1991.

Borne, Dominique, and Henri Dubief. *La crise des années trente, 1929–1938.* Paris: Seuil, 1989.

Bouvier, Jeanne. *Histoire des dames employées dans les Postes, Télégraphes, et Téléphones.* Paris: PUF, 1930.

——. *Mes mémoires: Une syndicaliste féministe, 1876–1935.* Edition préparée par Danièle Armogathe avec la collaboration de Maïté Albistur. Paris: Maspero, 1983.

Boverat, Fernand. "La dénatalité, ses dangers et les mesures à prendre pour l'enrayer." *Le Musée social* XLIIIe année no. 1, nouvelle série (January 1936): 2.

——. "Il faut à la France une politique d'immigration." *Revue de l'alliance nationale pour l'accroissement de la population française* 129 (April 1923): 137–38.

——. *Patriotisme et paternité.* Paris: 1913.

Boxer, Marilyn. "Socialism Faces Feminism: The Failure of Synthesis in France, 1879–1914." In Marilyn Boxer and Jean Quataert, eds., *Socialist Women.* New York: Elsevier, 1980. 75–111.

Boyer, Robert. "Le particularisme français revisité: La Crise des années trente à la lumière des recherches récentes." *Mouvement social* no. 154 (January–March 1991): 3–40.

Bradley, Harriet. *Men's Work, Women's Work: A Sociological History of the Sexual Division of Labor in Employment.* Cambridge: Polity Press, 1989.

Braverman, Harvey. *Labor and Monopoly Capital: The Degradation of Work in the Twentieth Century.* New York: Monthly Review Press, 1974.

Bravey, Marcelle. "Le droit de vote féminin et nous." *Bulletin des groupes féministes de l'enseignement laïque* 66 (March–April 1932): 25–27.

Bridenthal, Renate. "Professional Housewives: Stepsisters of the Women's Movement." In Renate Bridenthal, Atina Grossman, and Marion Kaplan, eds., *When Biology Was Destiny*. New York: Monthly Review Press, 1984. 153–73.

Brisset, Alice. "Rapport sur les allocations familiales par la camarade Alice Brisset." Fédération unitaire du Textile-Vêtement et Partis similaires de France et des colonies. *IIIe Congrès national à Paris les 28–30 novembre 1926*. Paris: Maison des syndicats, 1926. 41–43.

Bruhat, Jean. "Où on est: Le chômage dans le second degré." *Bulletin des membres de l'enseignement du 2e et 3e degrés. Supplément à l'Ecole émancipée* [Fédération des syndicats de l'enseignement] no. 20 (February 12, 1933).

Brunschvicq, Cécile. "A propos du travail féminin." *La Française*, February 17, 1933, 2.

——. "L'offensive contre le travail féminin." *La Française*, January 28, 1933, 2.

——. "L'offensive contre le travail féminin." *La Française*, March 18, 1933, 2.

——. "Le travail industriel et le foyer ouvrier." *La Française*, June 24, 1933, 1–4.

Bruyneel, Robert. *L'industrie textile de Roubaix-Tourcoing devant la crise économique et la législation sociale*. Paris: Editions et publications contemporaines Pierre Bossuet, 1932.

Buland, Jeanne. *Femme, défends-toi!* Paris: Bureau d'éditions, 1932.

Burle, Marie "Le vote des femmes." *Bulletin des groupes féministes de l'enseignement laïque* no.52 (November–December, 1929): 7–8.

Burle, Marie, and Suzanne Durand. "Notre féminisme."*Bulletin des groupes féministes de l'enseignement laïque* 45 (October 1928): 6.

Burton, Antoinette. *Burdens of History: British Feminists, Indian Women, and Imperial Culture, 1865–1915*. Chapel Hill: University of North Carolina Press, 1994.

Bussard, Odette. *Le livre de la fermière: Economie domestique rurale*. Paris: Librairie J-B Baillière et Fils, 1906.

Cahm, Eric, ed. *Politics and Society in Contemporary France: A Documentary History (1789–1971)*. London: George G. Harrap and Co. Ltd., 1972.

Camiscioli, Elisa. "Intermarriage, Independent Nationality, and Individual Rights of French Women." *French Politics, Culture, and Society* no. 17 (Summer/Fall, 1999): 52–74.

——. "Labor Power and the Racial Economy: the Selection of Foreign Workers in France in the Late Third Republic." Presented at the conference "Blurring the Boundaries: Politics and Culture in the French Third Republic." University of Michigan, Ann Arbor, 1997.

——. "Producing Citizens, Reproducing the 'French Race': Immigration, Demography, Pronatalism in Early Twentieth Century France." *Gender and History* 13 (November 2001): 593–621.

Cann, Jeanne. *Les allocations familiales, l'allocation de la mère au foyer et l'allocation de salaire unique dans le commerce et l'industrie*. Londéac: Imprimerie Traonouil-Anger, 1944.

Canning, Kathleen. "Feminist History after the Linguistic Turn: Historicizing Discourse and Experience." *Signs: Journal of Women, Culture, and Society* 19 (1994): 368–404.

——. *Languages of Labor and Gender: Female Factory Work in Germany, 1850–1914.* Ithaca, N.Y.: Cornell University Press, 1996.

——. "Social Politics, Body Politics: Recasting the Social Question in Germany 1875–1900." In Laura L. Frader and Sonya O. Rose, eds., *Gender and Class in Modern Europe.* Ithaca, N.Y.: Cornell University Press, 1996. 210–37.

Canning, Kathleen, and Sonya O. Rose, eds. *Gender, Citizenship, and Subjectivities.* Malden, Mass: Blackwell, 2002.

Canning, Kathleen, and Sonya O. Rose. "Introduction: Gender, Citizenship, and Subjectivity: Some Historical and Theoretical Considerations." In Kathleen Canning and Sonya O. Rose, eds., *Gender, Citizenship, and Subjectivities.* Malden, Mass.: Blackwell, 2002. 4.

Carol, Anne. *Histoire de l'eugénisme en France: Les médecins et la procréation XIXe–XXe siècles.* Paris: Seuil, 1995.

Castel, Robert. *Les métamorphoses de la question sociale.* Paris: Seuil, 1994.

Caunes, Madeleine. *Des mesures juridiques propre à faciliter la présence de la mère au foyer ouvrier.* Paris: Editions A. Pedrone, 1938.

Ceccaldi, Domininque. *Histoire des prestations familiales en France.* Paris: Caisse d'allocations familiales, 1957.

Chapman, Herrick, and Laura L. Frader. "Introduction." In Chapman and Frader, eds., *Race in France: Interdisciplinary Perspectives on the Politics of Difference.* New York: Berghahn, 2004.

Chapman, Herrick, and Laura L. Frader, eds. *Race in France: Interdisciplinary Perspectives on the Politics of Difference.* New York: Berghahn, 2004.

Charlot, Bernard, and Madeleine Figeat. *Histoire de la formation des ouvriers 1789–1984.* Paris: Minerve, 1985.

Chauveau, Auguste. "Le travail professionnel: Recherches sur la physiologie du travail professionnel." *Bulletin mensuel de la statistique* 9 (1919): 333–50.

Chenelette, Mlle De. *La journée ménagère à l'école.* Lyon: Union du Sud-Est des syndicats agricoles, 1930.

Chenut, Helen Harden. *The Fabric of Gender: Working-Class Culture in Third Republic France.* University Park: Pennsylvania State University Press, 2005.

——. "The Gendering of Skill as Historical Process." In Laura L. Frader and Sonya O. Rose, eds., *Gender and Class in Modern Europe.* Ithaca, N.Y.: Cornell University Press, 1996. 77–107.

Childers, Kristen Stromberg. *Fathers, Families, and the French State, 1919–1945.* Ithaca, N.Y.: Cornell University Press, 2004.

——. "Paternity and the Politics of Citizenship in Interwar France." *Journal of Family History* 26 (January 2001): 90–111.

Christin, Olivier. "Les enjeux de la rationalisation industrielle (1901–1929)." Mémoire de Maîtrise. Université de Paris I. 1982.

Clancy-Smith, Julia. "Islam, Gender, and Identities in the Making of French Algeria, 1830–1962." In Julia Clancy-Smith and Frances Gouda, eds., *Domesticating the*

Empire: Race, Gender, and Family Life in French and Dutch Colonialism. Charlottesville: University Press of Virginia, 1998. 168–72.

Clapart (fils), Dr. *Maladies et accidents professionnels des téléphonistes à Paris.* Paris: Baillière et Fils, 1911.

Clark, Anna. "Manhood, Womanhood, and the Politics of Class in Britain, 1790–1845." In Laura L. Frader and Sonya O. Rose, eds., *Gender and Class in Modern Europe.* Ithaca, N.Y.: Cornell University Press, 1996, 263–79.

Clark, Linda, *The Rise of Professional Women in France: Gender and Public Administration since 1830.* Cambridge: Cambridge University Press, 2000.

———. *Schooling the Daughters of Marianne.* Albany: State University of New York Press, 1984.

Clément, Mlle J. *Le mouvement d'orientation professionnelle: Etude synthétique et critique.* Aix-en-Provence: Imprimerie d'éditions Paul Roubaud, 1924.

Cockburn, Cynthia. *Brothers: Male Dominance and Technological Change.* London: Pluto Press, 1983.

———. *Machinery of Dominance: Men, Women, and Technical Know-How.* London: Routledge, 1990.

Cohen, Miriam, and Michael Hanagan. "Politics, Industrialization and Citizenship: Unemployment Policy in England, France, and the United States, 1890–1950." *International Review of Social History* 40 (1995). Supplement 3, *Citizenship, Identity, and Social History,* edited by Charles Tilly.

Cohen, Yves. "Ernest Mattern chez Peugeot (1906–1918) ou comment peut-on être taylorien?" In Maurice de Montmollin and Olivier Pastré, eds., *Le taylorisme.* Paris: La Découverte, 1984. 115–26.

———. "Le travail social: Quand les techniciens sociaux parlent de leurs techniques." In Yves Cohen and Rémi Baudouï, eds., *Les chantiers de la paix sociale.* Fontenay aux Roses: ENS Editions, 1995. 105–26.

Colin, Madeleine. *Ce n'est pas d'aujourd'hui: Femmes, syndicats, luttes de classe.* Paris: Editions sociales, 1975.

Condorcet, Marie Jean Antoine Nicholas de Caritat, Marquis de. "On the Admission of Women to the Rights of Citizenship [July, 1790]." In Keith M. Baker, ed., *Condorcet: Selected Writings.* Indianapolis: Bobbs-Merrill, 1976. 97–104.

Conklin, Alice L. "Redefining 'Frenchness': Citizenship, Race Regeneration, and Imperial Motherhood in France and West Africa 1914–1940." In Julia Clancy-Smith and Frances Gouda, eds., *Domesticating the Empire: Race, Gender, and Family Life in French and Dutch Colonialism.* Charlottesville: University Press of Virginia, 1998. 65–83.

Cordelier, Suzanne F. *Femmes au travail: Etude pratique sur 17 carrières féminines.* Paris: Plon, 1935.

Cordier, Henri. "Le congrès de migrations." *Le Peuple,* July 12, 1926, 4.

Coron, Dr. "Pour une France libre, forte et heureuse." *Cahiers de Bolchévisme.* 13e année no. 12–13 (July 25, 1936): 807–22.

Cova, Anne. *Maternité et droits des femmes en France.* Paris: Anthropos, 1997.

Cronin, James E. *The Politics of State Expansion: War, State, and Society in Twentieth Century Britain*. London: Routledge, 1991.

Cross, Gary. *Immigrant Workers in Industrial France: The Making of a New Working Class*. Philadelphia: Temple University Press, 1983.

———.*The Quest for Time: The Reduction of Work in Britain and France, 1840–1914*. Berkeley: University of California Press, 1989.

———. "Redefining Workers' Control: Rationalization, Labor Time, and Union Politics in France, 1900–1928." In James E. Cronin and Carmen Sirianni, eds., *Work, Community, and Power: The Experience of Labor in Europe and America, 1900–1925*. Philadelphia: Temple University Press, 1983. 143–72.

Daniel, Christine, and Carole Tuchszirer. *L'état face au chômeurs*. Paris: Flammarion, 1999.

Darcy, Mlle. *Petit cours d'enseignement ménager*. Paris: Librairie Catholique, Emmanuel Vitte, 1924.

Daric, Jean. *L'activité professionnelle des femmes en France*. Institut national des études démographiques (INED). Travaux et Documents. Cahier no. 5. Paris: PUF, 1947.

Darrow, Margaret H. *French Women and the First World War: War Stories of the Home Front*. Oxford: Berg, 2000.

de Grazia, Victoria. *How Fascism Ruled Women*. Berkeley: University of California Press, 1992.

Del Re, Alisa. *Les femmes et l'état-providence: Les politiques sociales en France dans les années trentes*. Paris: L'Harmattan, 1994.

Delagrange, Mlle. "Le travail de la femme mariée." Asssociation des surintentantes d'usine. *Assemblée générale de 1934*. Paris: Association des surintendantes d'usine, 1934.

Delasalle, Eliane. *Le travail de la femme dans l'industrie textile et du vêtement dans l'arrondissement de Lille*. Loos: Imprimerie L. Davel, 1951.

Delatour, Yvonne. "Le travail de la femme pendant la première guerre mondiale et ses conséquences sur l'évolution de leur rôle dans la société." *Francia* 2 (1974): 482–501.

Deldyke, T., H. Gelders, and J.-M. Limbor. *La population active et sa structure*. Vol. 1. In *Les statistiques internationales rétrospectives* sous la direction de Paul Bairoch. Brussels: Institut de sociologie de l'Université libre de Bruxelles, 1968.

Depret, Paul. *Etude sur l'oeuvre sociale de la Compagnie des Chemins de Fer de l'Est*. Verdun: Imprimerie H. Frémont et Fils, 1936.

Depretto, Jean-Paul, and Sylvie V. Schweitzer. *Le Communisme à l'usine*. Roubaix: EDIRES, 1984.

Desanti, Dominique. *La femme au temps des années folles*. Paris: Stock/Laurence Pernoud, 1984.

Dogliani, Patrizia. "Une laboratoire de socialisme municipal: France, 1880–1920." Thèse de doctorat. Université de Paris VIII, 1992.

Downs, Laura Lee. *Manufacturing Inequality: Gender Division in the French and British Metalworking Industries, 1914–1939.* Ithaca, N.Y.: Cornell University Press, 1995.

———. "Women's Strikes and the Politics of Popular Egalitarianism in France, 1916–1918." In Leonard Berlanstein, ed., *Rethinking Labor History.* Urbana: University of Illinois Press, 1993. 114–48.

Doyen, F. "Pourquoi un programme de revendications pour les ouvrières." *L'Humanité,* February 18, 1925.

Droits de la femme. *Les femmes dans une société des inégalités.* Paris: La documentation française, 1982.

Dubesset, Mathilde, and Michelle Zancarini-Fournel. *Parcours des femmes: Réalités et représentations, Saint-Etienne 1880–1950.* Lyon: Presses universitaires de Lyon, 1993.

Dubesset, Mathilde, Françoise Thébaud, and Catherine Vincent. "Les munitionettes de la Seine." In Patrick Fridenson, ed., *L'autre front.* Paris: Les Editions ouvrières, 1977. 189–219.

———. "Quand les femmes entrent dans l'usine." Unpublished Mémoire de maîtrise. Université de Paris VII, 1973–74.

Dubief, Henri. *Le déclin de la IIIe république.* Paris: Seuil, 1976.

Dubois, Laurent. "Republican Anti-Racism and Racism: A Caribbean Genealogy." In Herrick Chapman and Laura L. Frader, eds., *Race in France: Interdisciplinary Perspectives on the Politics of Difference.* New York: Berghahn, 2004. 23–35.

Dubreuil, Hyacinthe. *Nouveaux standards.* Paris: B. Grasset, 1931.

———. *Standards.* Paris: B. Grasset, 1929.

Dugé de Bernonville, L. "Le travail professionnel: La selection des travailleurs." *Bulletin de la statistique de France* 9 (January 1920): 171–90.

———. "Travail professionnel: Recherches sur la physiologie du travail." *Bulletin de la statistique de France* 8 (July 1919): 333–79.

Dutton, Paul. *Origins of the French Welfare State: The Struggle for Social Reform in France, 1914–1947.* Cambridge: Cambridge University Press, 2002.

Duvergier, J. B. *Collection complète des lois, décrets, ordonnances, et règlements. Nouvelle série. Tome XVIII. 1918.* Paris: Sirey, 1918.

Ecole ménagère ambulant de la Sarthe. *Quelques recettes pratiques appliqués à l'école ménager.* Le Mans: Imprimerie Blanchet, 1926.

Ecole ménagère Les Fontenelles (Doubs). *Résumé des cours d'économie domestique.* Besançon: Imprimerie Catholique de l'Est, 1930.

Ehrenberg, Alain. *Le corps militaire: politique et pédagogie en démocratie.* Paris: Aubier Montaigne, 1983.

Eisenstein, Zillah. *Capitalist Patriarchy and the Case for Socialist Feminism.* New York: Monthly Review Press, 1979.

Elias, Norbert. *The Civilizing Process: Sociogenic and Psychogenic Investigations.*

Translated by Edmund Jephcott. Edited by Eric Danning, Johan Goudsblom, and Stephen Mennell. Oxford: Oxford University Press, 2000.

Enfière, André. *Le vote familial: La réforme electorale.* Paris: Marcel Giard, 1923.

Esping-Anderson, Gosta. *The Three Worlds of Welfare Capitalism.* Princeton, N.J.: Princeton University Press, 1990.

Evans, Peter, Dietrich Rueschemeyer, and Theda Skocpol, eds. *Bringing the State Back In.* London: Cambridge University Press, 1985.

Ewald, François. *Histoire de l'état-providence: Les origines de solidarité.* Paris: Librairie générale française, 1986.

Fabre, Clarisse. "Les députés débattent de l'égalité professionnelle hommes-femmes." *Le Monde,* March 8, 2000.

——. "La gauche vote sans enthusiasme le texte du PS sur l'égalité professionnelle hommes-femmes." *Le Monde,* March 9, 2000.

Fabre, Marie Antoinette. "Rapport de stage d'ouvrière du 10 au 22 janvier 1921 aux Ateliers de Construction Lavalette." In Archives de l'école des surintendantes d'Usine, Ecole supérieure du Travail social. Paris.

Fauchère, Germaine. *Le travail des femmes.* Paris: Libraririe populaire–Editions de la SFIO, 1934.

Faure, Alain. "Camille et Jeanne, ouvrières à la raffinerie Say." *Bulletin du Centre de l'Histoire de la France contemporaine* 11 (1990): 51–52.

Fields, Barbara J. "Ideology and Race in American History." In J. Morgan Kousser and James M. McPherson, eds., *Region, Race, and Reconstruction: Essays in Honor of C. Vann Woodward.* New York: Oxford University Press, 1982.

——. "Slavery, Race, and Ideology in the United States of America." *New Left Review* 181 (May–June, 1990): 95–118.

Fontaine, Arthur. "La journée de huit heures représent un progrès très important de la condition ouvrière." *Le Peuple* (October 1926).

Fontanon, Claudine, and André Grelon, eds. *Les professeurs du conservatoire national des arts et métiers: Dictionnaire biographique, 1794–1955.* 2 vols. Paris: INRP and CNAM, 1994.

Fontègne, Julien. *L'orientation professionnelle et la détermination des aptitudes.* Paris: Editions Delachaux and Niestlé, 1921.

Fontègne, Julien, and Emilio Solari. "Le travail de la téléphoniste: Essai de psychologie professonnelle." *Archives de Psychologie* 17, no. 66 (November 1918): 92.

Foucault, Michel. *The History of Sexuality.* Translated by Robert Hurley. Vol. 1. New York: Vintage, 1980.

Fourcaut, Annie. *Femmes à l'usine en France dans l'entre-deux guerres.* Paris: Maspéro, 1982.

Frader, Laura L. "La division sexuelle du travail à la lumière des recherches historiques." *Cahiers du MAGE* 3–4 (1995): 143–56.

——. "Engendering Work and Wages: The French Labor Movement and the Family Wage." In Frader and Sonya O. Rose, eds., *Gender and Class in Modern Europe.* Ithaca, N.Y.: Cornell University Press, 1996. 142–64.

——. "Social Citizens without Citizenship: Working-Class Women and Social Policy in Interwar France." *Social Politics* 3 (Summer–Fall, 1996): 111–35.

——. "Women, Work and Inequality in Contemporary France." In Peter Morris, ed., *Equalities and Inequalities in France*. London: Association for the Study of Modern and Contemporary France, 1984. 188–203.

Frader, Laura L., and Sonya O. Rose. "Introduction: Gender and the Reconstruction of European Working-Class History." In Frader and Rose, eds., *Gender and Class in Modern Europe*. Ithaca, N.Y.: Cornell University Press, 1996. 1–33.

Fraisse, Geneviève. *Muse de la raison: Démocratie et exclusion des femmes en France*. Paris: Gallimard, 1995.

Fraser, Nancy. *Justice Interruptus*. New York: Routledge, 1997.

——. "Struggle over Needs: Outline of a Socialist-Feminist Critical Theory of Late Capitalist Political Culture." In Linda Gordon, ed., *Women, the State, and Welfare*. Madison: University of Wisconsin Press, 1990. 199–225.

——. "What's Critical about Critical Theory." In Seyla Benhabib and Drucilla Cornell, eds., *Feminism as Critique: On the Politics of Gender*. Minneapolis: University of Minnesota Press, 1987. 31–56.

Fridenson, Patrick. *Histoire des usines Renault: Naissance d'une grande entreprise, 1898–1939*. Paris: Seuil, 1972.

——. "Un Tournant taylorien de la société, française (1904–1918)." *Annales ESC* 5 (September–October 1987): 1031–60.

Frischmann, Georges. *Histoire de la Fédération CGT des PTT*. Paris: Editions sociales, 1967.

Frois, Marcel. *La protection des ouvriers travaillant aux presses à métaux*. Geneva: Bureau international du Travail, 1930.

——. *La prévention des accidents au travail*. Vannes: Imprimerie La Foyle et J. de Lamarzelle, 1928.

——. *La santé et le travail des femmes pendant la guerre*. Paris: PUF and New Haven, Conn.: Yale University Press, 1926.

Funffrock, Gérard. "Les grèves ouvrières dans le département du Nord." Thèse du troisième cycle. Université de Paris I, 1988.

Fuss, Henri. "Chômage et placement des femmes." *Revue internationale du travail* 31 (April 1935): 493–530.

Ganay, Maurice de. "Pour la formation d'une élite rurale." *Dossiers de l'action populaire* 1 (1924): 6–20.

Gardey, Delphine, and Ilana Löwy, eds. *L'invention du naturel: Les sciences et la fabrication du féminine et du masculin*. Paris: Editions des archives contemporaines, 2000.

Gardey, Delphine. "Un monde en mutation: Les employées de bureau en France, 1890–1930: Féminisation, mécanisation, rationalisation." Thèse de Doctorat. Université de Paris VII, 1995.

Geoffroy, Mlle. "Rapport de Mademoiselle Geoffroy sur ce que font et peuvent faire les surintendantes pour 'l'éducation familiale,' et l'enseignement ménager." In

Association des surintendantes d'usine et des services sociaux. *Assemblée géné-*
rale, 21 février 1928. Paris: Moderne imprimerie, 1928. 29–34.

Gerrand, R-H, and M-A Rupp. *Brève histoire du service social en France.* Toulouse:
Privat, 1978.

Gilbert, Sandra M. "Soldier's Heart: Literary Men, Literary Women, and the Great
War." In Margaret Higonnet, Jane Jenson, Sonya Michel, and Margaret Collins
Weitz, eds., *Behind the Lines: Gender and the Two World Wars.* New Haven,
Conn.: Yale University Press, 1987. 197–226.

Gomar, Norbert. *L'émigration algérienne en France.* Paris: Les presses modernes,
1931.

Gordon, Bonnie. "Ouvrières et maladies professionnelles sous la troisième république: La victoire des allumettiers française sur la nécrose phosphorée de la
mâchoire." *Mouvement Social* 164 (July–September 1993): 77–93.

Goussault, Rémy. *Syndicats paysans.* Paris: Flammarion, 1937.

Gramsci, Antonio. *The Prison Notebooks of Antonio Gramsci.* Translated by Quentin
Hoare and Geoffrey Nowell Smith. New York: International Publishers, 1971.

Grayzel, Susan. *Women's Identities at War: Gender, Motherhood, and Politics in Britain and France during the First World War.* Chapel Hill: University of North
Carolina Press, 1999.

Green, Nancy L. *Ready-to-Wear and Ready-to-Work: A Century of Industry and
Immigrants in Paris and New York.* Durham, N.C.: Duke University Press, 1997.

Gucksmann, Miriam. *Women Assemble: Women Workers and the New Industries in
Interwar Britain.* London: Routledge, 1990.

Gueland-Léridon, Françoise. *Le travail des femmes en France.* INED. Travaux et Documents. Cahier no. 42. Paris: PUF, 1964.

Guelaud, Claire, "Les ressorts du non, 3: Promotion sociale–le modèle social français est à bout de souffle." *Le Monde,* June 3, 2005.

Guilbert, Madeleine. *Les femmes et le syndicalisme en France.* Paris: CNRS, 1968.

Hamp, Pierre. *Les métiers blessés.* Paris: Gallimard, 1919.

Hanagan, Michael. "Family, Work, and Wages: The Stéphanois Region of France,
1840–1914." *International Review of Social History* 42 (1997). Supplement: 129–51.

Harding, Sandra. *The "Racial" Economy of Science: Towards a Democratic Future.*
Bloomington: Indiana University Press, 1993.

Harris, Ruth. "The 'Child of the Barbarian': Rape, Race, and Nationalism in France
During the First World War." *Past and Present* no. 141 (November 1993): 170–
206.

Hartmann, Heidi. "Capitalism, Patriarchy and Job Segregation by Sex." *Signs: Journal of Women, Culture and Society* 1 (1976): 137–69.

Hause, Steven C. with Anne R. Kenney. *Women's Suffrage and Social Politics in the
French Third Republic.* Princeton, N.J.: Princeton University Press, 1984.

Hause, Steven. *Hubertine Auclert, the French Suffragette.* New Haven, Conn.: Yale
University Press, 1987.

Heinen, Jacqueline, and Heini Martiskainen de Koenigswater. "Framing Citizenship in France and Finland in the 1990s: Restructuring Motherhood, Work, and Care." *Social Politics* 8 (Summer 2001): 170–81.

Henri-Collet, Madame A. "Rapport de stage ouvrière fait à la manufacture de chaussures 'Incroyable' [Dressoir] du 6 au 21 janvier [1921]." In Archives de l'école des surintendantes d'usine. Ecole supérieure du travail social. Paris.

Hermann, Marie. "Rapport de stage à l'usine Jacob Delafond et Cie. Du 10 au 21 janvier 1921." In Archives de l'école des surintendantes d'Usine. Ecole supérieure du travail social. Paris.

Heyraud, Charles. *Vouloir vivre.* Paris: Perrin, 1925.

Higonnet, Margaret Randolph, and Patrice L-R.Higonnet. "The Double Helix." In Margaret Higonnet, Jane Jenson, Sonya Michel, and Margaret Collins Weitz, eds., *Behind the Lines: Gender and the Two World Wars.* New Haven, Conn.: Yale University Press, 1987. 31–47.

Hilden, Patricia. *Working Women and Socialist Politics in France, 1880–1914: A Regional Study.* Oxford: Oxford University Press, 1986.

Hobson, Barbara. "Feminist Strategies and Gendered Discourses in Welfare States: Married Women's Right to Work in the United States and Sweden." In Seth Koven and Sonya Michel, eds., *Mothers of a New World.* New York: Routledge, 1993. 396–429.

Hollis, Patricia. *Women in Public: The Women's Movement.* London: George Allen and Unwin, 1979.

Horne, Janet. "In Pursuit of Greater France: Visions of Empire among Musée Social Reformers, 1894–1931." In Julia Clancy-Smith and Frances Gouda, eds., *Domesticating the Empire: Race, Gender, and Family Life in French and Dutch Colonialism.* Charlottesville: University Press of Virginia, 1998. 37–41.

——. *A Social Laboratory for Modern France: The Musée Social and the Rise of the Welfare State.* Durham: Duke University Press, 2002.

Horne, John N., and Alan Kramer. *German Atrocities, 1914: A History of Denial.* New Haven, Conn.: Yale University Press, 2001.

Horne, John. "Immigrant Workers in France during World War I." *French Historical Studies* 24, no.1 (1985): 57–88.

——. *Labour at War: France and Britain, 1914–1918.* Oxford: Oxford University Press, 1991.

Hubert, Agnès, "The Rocky Road of Gender Equality." In Jytte Klausen and Charles Maier, eds., *Has Liberalism Failed Women?* New York: Westview Press, 2000.

Jack, Andrée. "Le chômage et le travail des femmes." *Revue politique et parlementaire* no. 501 (August 10, 1936): 272–88.

Janssens, Angélique. "The Rise and Decline of the Male Breadwinner Family? An Overview of the Debate." *International Review of Social History* 42 (1997) Supplement.

Jeannenay, Jean-Noël. *François de Wendel et la république: L'argent et le pouvoir, 1914–1940.* Paris: Seuil, 1976.

Jenson, Jane. "Friend or Foe? Women and State Welfare in Western Europe." In

Renate Bridenthal, Susan Stuard, and Merry Wiesner, eds., *Becoming Visible: Women in European History.* 3.† ed. Boston: Houghton Mifflin, 1998. 493–513.

——. "Gender and Reproduction or, Babies and the State." *Studies in Political Economy* 20 (Summer 1986): 9–46;

——. "Representations of Gender: Policies to 'Protect' Women Workers and Infants in France and the United States before 1914." In Linda Gordon, ed., *Women, the State, and Welfare.* Madison: University of Wisconsin Press, 1990.

Jenson, Jane, and Mariette Sineau. *Mitterrand et les françaises, un rendez-vous manqué.* Paris: Presses de la Fondation nationale des sciences politiques, 1995.

——. *Qui doit garder le jeune enfant? Modes d'acceuil et travail des mères dans l'Europe en crise.* Paris: Librairie générale de droit et de jurisprudence, 1998.

Jenson, Jane, Elizabeth Hagen, and Cellaigh Reddy, eds. *The Feminization of the Labor Force: Paradoxes and Promises.* New York: Oxford University Press, 1988.

Jouenne, Alice. "Migrations humaines." *Le Peuple,* July 9, 1926, 4.

Jouhaux, Germaine. "Le congrès de l'internationale des travailleuses." *La Voix du peuple* 53 (July–August, 1925): 332.

Juquelier, Pierre. "Le travail féminine dans l'industrie après la guerre." *Chimie et industrie* 2 (April 1, 1919): 485.

Kent, Susan Kingsley. *Gender and Power in Britain.* New York: Palgrave, 1999.

——. *Sex and Suffrage in Britain, 1860–1914.* Princeton, N.J.: Princeton, 1987.

Keranflech-Kernezne, Comtesse de. *La femme à la campagne: Ses épreuves et ses responsabilités.* Paris: Spès, 1933.

——. *Trois semaines rurales féminines: Causeries sur l'éducation.* St. Brieuc: Imprimerie-Librairies Prud'homme, 1925.

——. *La vie et les oeuvres à la campagne.* Autun: Perrot, 1920.

Kessler-Harris, Alice. "The Gendered Limits of Social Citizenship in the Depression Era." *Journal of American History* 86, no.3 (December 1999): 1251–79.

——. "In Pursuit of Economic Citizenship." *Social Politics: International Studies in the Gender, State, and Society* 10 (Summer 2003): 147–75.

——. *In Pursuit of Equity: Women, Men, and the Search for Economic Citizenship in Twentieth-Century America.* New York: Oxford University Press, 2001.

——. *Out to Work: A History of Wage-Earning Women in the United States.* New York: Oxford, 1982.

——. *A Woman's Wage.* Lexington: University Press of Kentucky, 1990.

Klaus, Alisa. *Every Child a Lion: The Origins of Maternal and Infant Health Policy in the United States and France, 1890–1920.* Ithaca, N.Y.: Cornell University Press, 1993.

Klejman, Laurence, and Florence Rochefort. *L'égalité en marche: Le féminisme sous la troisième république.* Paris: Des Femmes, 1989.

Knijn, Trudie, and Monique Kremer. "Gender and the Caring Dimension of Welfare States: Towards Inclusive Citizenship." *Social Politics* 4 (Fall 1997): 328–61.

Koonz, Claudia. *Mothers in the Fatherland: Women, the Family, and Nazi Politics.* New York: St. Martin's, 1987.

Koos, Cheryl, and Daniella Sarnoff. "France." In Kevin Passmore, ed., *Women, Gender and Fascism in Europe, 1919–1945*. Manchester: Manchester University Press, 2003. 168–88.

Korving, Robert, and Gerard Hogesteeger. "Psychotecnik bei der PTT Niederlands." In Helmut Gold and Annette Koch, eds., *Fraulein vom Amt*. München: Prestel, 1993.

Koven, Seth, and Sonya Michel, eds. *Mothers of a New World*. New York: Routledge, 1993.

Krémer, Pascale. "Les inégalités hommes-femmes persistent dans le monde du travail." *Le Monde,* September 3, 1999.

——. "Les inégalités professionelles hommes-femmes sont devenues plus injustes." *Le Monde,* March 28, 2000.

Kuisel, Richard. *Capitalism and the State in Modern France: Renovation and Economic Management in the Twentieth Century*. New York: Cambridge University Press, 1981.

Labat, Emmanuel. *L'âme paysan: La terre, la race, l'école*. Paris: Delagave, 1919.

Labriffe, Charles. *L'apprentissage dans l'industrie textile*. Paris: Editions de l'industrie textile, 1945.

Lahy, Jean Marie. "Les conflits du travail: Hommes et femmes typographes." *La Revue socialiste* 49 (1909): 289–308. Paris: Association des surintendantes d'usine et des services sociaux, 1930.

——. "Rapport de M. Lahy." *Xe Assemblée générale de l'association des surintendantes d'usine et des services sociaux 4 mars 1930.*

——. *La sélection psychophysiologique des travailleurs: Conducteurs de tramways et d'autobus*. Paris: Dunod, 1927.

——. *Le système taylor et la physiologie du travail professionnel*. Paris: Masson, 1916.

Lambérioux-Chapet, Marie-France. "Les ouvrières pendant l'entre-deux-guerres 1920–1936." Mémoire de Maîtrise. Université de Paris VII, 1980.

Lambert, Charles. *La France et les étrangers*. Paris: Delagrave, 1928.

Landes, Joan. *Women and the Public Sphere in the Age of the French Revolution*. Ithaca, N.Y.: Cornell University Press, 1988.

Lanri, Sophie. "Algériennes et mères françaises exemplaires, 1945–1962." *Mouvement social* (April–June 2002): 61–81.

La Voix du peuple. Special issue: "Assurances socials." September–October 1923.

Le Manifeste des Soixante Ouvriers de la Seine (1864). In Eric Cahm, ed., *Politics and Society in Contemporary France (1789–1971): A Documentary History*. London: George G. Harrap, 1972.

Le Blanc, René. *Enseignement ménager*. Paris: Larousse, 1918.

Le Guillou, Olivier. "L'émigration russe en France, Boulogne-Billancourt et les usines Renault: Lieux d'habitation et emplois des émigrés russes dans l'entre deux guerres." In Eric Guichard and Gérard Noiriel, eds., *Construction des nationalités et immigration dans la France contemporaine*. Paris: Presses de l'école normale supérieur, 1997.

Lebovics, Herman. *True France: The Wars over Cultural Identity, 1900–1945.* Ithaca, N.Y.: Cornell University Press, 1992.

Lefebvre, Madame. "Rapport de stage: Service psychotechnique de la Régie Renault. Stage effectuée par Madame Lefebvre du 22 mars au 31 mai 1955." In Archives de l'école des surintendantes d'usine. Paris.

Lefebvre-Dibon, P. "La crise économique et la femme au foyer." *La Revue de l'Alliance nationale pour l'accroissement de la population française* 233 (1931).

Legoux, Marie Louise. "La surintendante d'usine: Rôle social et situation juridique." Thèse pour le Doctorat. Université de Rennes. Faculté de Droit. Rennes: Imprimerie centrale de Rennes, 1942.

———. *La surintendante d'usine: rôle social et situation juridique.* Rennes: Imprimerie central, 1942.

Lequin, Yves, ed. *La mosaïque de la France: Histoire des étrangers et de l'immigration.* Paris: Larousse, 1988.

———. "La rationalisation du capitalisme française, a-t-elle eu lieu dans les années vingt?" *Cahiers d'histoire de l'Institut Maurice Thorez* no. 31 (1979): 115–36.

Letellier, Gabrielle, Jean Peret, H. E. Zuber, and A. Dauphin-Meunier. *Le chômage en France de 1930 à 1936.* 3 vols. Paris: Librairie de Recueil Sirey, 1938.

Lewis, Jane. "Economic Citizenship: A Comment." *Social Politics* 10 (Summer 2003): 176–85.

———. *Women and Social Policies in Europe: Work, Family, and the State.* Aldershot: Edward Elgar, 1993.

Lewis, Jane, and Ilona Ostner. "Gender and the Evolution of European Social Policy." In Stephan Liebfried and Paul Pierson, eds., *European Social Policy: Between Fragmentation and Integration.* Washington: Brookings Institution, 1995.

Lewis, Mary Dewhurst. *The Boundaries of the Republic: Migrant Rights and the Limits of Universalism in France 1918–1940.* Stanford, Calif.: Stanford University Press, 2007.

———. "Bring Us Your Labor, Your Children, Your Fecund Fathers: Naturalizing Immigrants in Interwar France." Unpublished paper cited by permission of the author.

———. "The Company of Strangers: Immigration and Citzenship in Interwar Lyon and Marseille. Ph.D. dissertation, New York University, 2000.

Lister, Ruth. "Citizenship: Towards a Feminist Synthesis." In Pnina Werbner and Nira Yuval-Davis, eds., *Citizenship: Pushing the Boundaries.* Special issue of *Feminist Review* 57 (1997): 29–33.

Lorcin, Patricia E. *Imperial Identities: Stereotyping Prejudice and Race in Colonial Algeria.* London: I. B. Tauris, 1999.

Lyons, Amelia. "Invisible Immigrants: Algerian Families and the French Welfare State in the Era of Decolonization, 1947–1974." Ph.D. dissertation, University of California, Irvine, 2004.

Macmillan, James. *Housewife or Harlot? The Place of Women in French Society.* New York: St. Martin's, 1981.

Magnier de Maisonneuve, Pierre. *Les institutions sociales en faveur des ouvrières d'usine.* Paris: Presses universitaires de la France, 1923.

Mahon, Rianne. "Child Care: Toward What Kind of Social Europe?" *Social Politics* 9 (Fall 2002): 343–79.

Maier, Charles. "Between Taylorism and Technocracy: European Ideologies and the Vision of Industrial Productivity in the 1920s." *Journal of Contemporary History* 5 (1970): 27–60.

Maitron, Jean, and Claude Pennetier. "Joseph Couergou." In Jean Maitron, ed., *Dictionnaire biographique du mouvement ouvrier français.* Part 4, volume 23. Paris: Editions ouvrières, 1984. 255–56.

Malik, Kenan. *The Meaning of Race: Race, History, and Culture in Western Society.* New York: New York University Press, 1996.

Maltrait, Henriette. "La Femme doit-elle travailler sans une nécessité absolue?" *La Française,* April 28, 1934, 1.

Marchand, Olivier, and Claude Thélot. *Le travail en France (1800–2000).* Paris: Nathan, 1997.

Marescal, Albert. *L'exode rural et l'école rurale.* Paris: Le Reveil économique, 1931.

Marpsat, Maryse. "Chômage et profession dans les années trente." *Economie et Statistique* 170 (October 1984).

——. "La statistique des chômeurs secourus en France de 1931 à 1939." *Actes de la journée d'étude "Sociologie et Statistique."* Vol. 2. Paris: Institut national de la statistique et des études économiques et de la société française de sociologie, 1982.

Marseille, Jacques. "Les origines 'inopportunes' de la crise de 1929 en France." *Revue économique* (July 1980): 648–84.

Marshall, T. H. *Citizenship and Social Class and Other Essays.* Cambridge: Cambridge University Press, 1950.

Martial, René. *Traité d'immigration et de la greffe interraciale.* Cuesmes-les-Mons: Imprimerie fédérale, Société coopérative, 1931.

Martin, Martine. "Femmes et société: Le travail ménager (1919–1939)." Thèse pour le doctorat du Troisième cycle. Université de Paris VII. 1984.

——. "Ménagère: Une profession? Les dilemmes de l'entre-deux-guerres." *Mouvement social* 140 (July–September 1987): 89–106.

Martin, Michèle. *"Hello Central": Gender, Technology, and Culture in the Formation of Telephone Systems.* Montréal: McGill-Queen's University Press, 1991.

Maruani, Margaret, ed. *Les nouvelles frontières de l'inégalité: Hommes et femmes sur le marché du travail.* Paris: La Découverte, 1998.

——. *Travail et emploi des femmes.* Paris: La Découverte, 2003.

Mauco, Georges. *Les étrangers en France: Leur rôle dans l'activité économique.* Paris: Armand Colin, 1932.

Mauzevin, Fernand. *Rose des métiers: Traité d'orientation professionnelle.* Paris: Editions littéraires et politiques, 1922.

McClelland, Keith. "Rational and Respectable Men: Gender, the Working Class, and Citizenship in Britain." In Laura L. Frader and Sonya O. Rose, eds., *Gender and Class in Modern Europe*. Ithaca, N.Y.: Cornell University Press, 1996. 280–93.

McClintock, Anne. "'No Longer in a Future Heaven': Nationalism, Gender, and Race." In Geoff Eley and Ronald Grigor Suny, eds., *Becoming National*. New York: Oxford, 1996. 260–84.

McLaren, Angus. *Sexuality and the Social Order: The Debate over the Fertility of Women and Workers in France, 1770–1920*. New York: Holmes and Meier, 1983.

Milkman, Ruth. "Women's Work and the Economic Crisis: Some Lessons from the Great Depresssion." In Nancy Cott and Elizabeth Pleck, eds., *A Heritage of Her Own: Towards a New Social History of American Women*. New York: Touchstone, 1979. 507–41.

Millerand, Alexandre. "Le Nouveau recrutement des téléphonistes." *L'Action*, February 23, 1910.

Milza, Pierre. *Les italiens en France de 1914 à 1940*. Paris: Bocard, 1987.

Misme, Jane. "Les françaises, doivent-elles épouser des étrangers?" *La Française*, November 19, 1921, 2.

Mitchell, Brian R. *European Historical Statistics, 1750–1970*. New York: 1978.

Moll-Weiss, Augusta. *Les écoles ménagères à l'étranger et en France*. Paris: Rousseau, 1908.

Morel, Edmond. "Action politique et social: le chômage à Paris." *La France libre*, January 19, 1919.

Morgan, Kimberly, and Kathrin Zippel. "The Origins and Effects of Care Leave Policies in Western Europe." *Social Politics* 10 (Spring 2003): 49–85.

Moses, Claire. "Debating the Present, Writing the Past: 'Feminism' in French History and Historiography." *Radical History Review* 52 (Winter 1992): 79–94.

——. *French Feminism in the Nineteenth Century*. Albany: State University of New York Press, 1984.

Mosse, George. *Fallen Soldiers: Reshaping the Memory of the World Wars*. New York: Oxford University Press, 1990.

——. *Nationalism and Sexuality: Respectability and Abnormal Sexuality in Modern Europe*. New York: Howard Fertig, 1985.

Moutet, Aimée. *Les logiques de l'entreprise: La rationalisation de l'industrie française de l'entre deux-guerres*. Paris: Editions de l'Ecole des hautes études en sciences sociales, 1997.

——. "Patrons du Progrès ou Patrons de Combat? La politique de rationalisation de l'industrie française au lendemain de la Première Guerre mondiale." In Lion Murard and Patrick Zylberman, eds., *Le soldat du travail: guerre, fascisme, et taylorisme*. Paris: Recherches, 1978.

Mouvet, E. *Orientation professionnelle des jeunes gens et enfants*. Brussels: Maison d'éditions A. De Boeck and Paris: Dunod, 1930.

Muret, Maurice. *La crépuscule des nations blanches*. Paris: Payot, 1925.

Nogaro, Bertrand, and Lucien Weil. *La main d'oeuvre étrangère et coloniale pendant*

la guerre. New Haven, Conn.: Yale University Press and Paris: Presses universitaires de France, 1926.

Noiriel, Gérard. *Le creuset français: Histoire de l'immigration XIX–XX siècles.* Paris:
Seuil, 1988.

——. *Les ouvriers dans la société française.* Paris: Seuil, 1986.

——. *Population, immigration, et identité nationale en France XIX–XX siècles.* Paris:
Hachette, 1992.

Nord, Philip. "The Welfare State in France: 1870–1914." *French Historical Studies* 18,
no.3 (Spring 1994): 821–38.

Nye, Robert A. *Crime, Madness, and Politics in Modern France: The Medical Concept
of National Decline.* Princeton, N.J.: Princeton University Press, 1984.

Offen, Karen. "Contextualizing the Theory and Practice of Feminism in Nineteenth Century Europe." In Renate Bridenthal, Susan Stuard, and Merry
Weisner-Hanks, eds., *Becoming Visible.* 3rd ed. Boston: Houghton Mifflin, 1998.
327–55.

——. "Defining Feminism: A Comparative Historical Approach." *Signs: Journal of
Women, Culture, and Society* 14 (Autumn 1988): 119–57.

——. "Depopulation, Nationalism and Feminism in Fin de Siècle France." *American
Historical Review* 89, no. 3 (June 1984): 648–76.

——. "The Theory and Practice of Feminism in Nineteenth Century Europe." In
Renate Bridenthal, Claudia Koonz, and Susan Stuard, eds., *Becoming Visible:
Women in European History.* Boston: Houghton Mifflin, 1987. 335–73.

——. "Women and the Politics of Motherhood in France, 1920–1940." European
University Institute Working Paper No.87/293.

——"Women, Work, and the Politics of Motherhood in France, 1920–1950." In
Gisela Bock and Pat Thane, eds., *Maternity and Gender Politics: Women and the
Rise of European Welfare States, 1880–1950.* London: Routledge, 1991.

Olson, Kevin. "Recognizing Gender, Redistributing Labor." *Social Politics* 9 (Fall
2002): 380–410.

Omnès, Catherine. *Ouvrières parisiennes: Marchés du travail et trajectoires professionelles au 20e siècle.* Paris: Editions de l'Ecole des Hautes études en sciences
sociales, 1997.

——. "La politique d'emploi de la Compagnie française des Téléphones Thomson-
Houston face à la crise des années 1930." *Mouvement social* no. 154 (January–
March 1991): 50.

Orloff, Ann. "Gender and the Social Rights of Citizenship." *American Sociological
Review* 58 (June 1993): 303–28.

——. "Gender and the Welfare State." Presented to the Workshop of the Research
Network on Gender, States, and Societies. Annual Meeting of the Social Science
History Assocation. Chicago, Ill. November 1995.

Ostner, Ilona. "From Equal Pay to Equal Employability: Four Decades of European
Gender Policies." In M. Rossilli, ed., *Gender Policies in the European Union.* New
York: Peter Lang, 2000.

Pairault, André. *L'immigration organisée et l'emploi de la main d'oeuvre en France.* Paris: Presses universitaires de France 1926.

Paraf, Pierre. "Budgets d'ouvriers, de fonctionnaires et de techniciens: Le budget minimum d'un travailleur parisien." *Information sociale* no. 361 (March 27, 1930): 8.

Parker, Andrew, Mary Russo, Doris Sommer, and Patricia Yaeger, eds. *Nationalisms and Sexualities.* London: Routledge, 1992.

Pasqualini-Bieganski, Esther. "La main d'oeuvre féminine textile dans l'arrondissement de Lille, 1919–1939." Mémoire de maîtrise d'histoire. Université de Lille III. 1973.

Pateman, Carole. *The Disorder of Women: Democracy, Feminism, and Political Theory.* Stanford, Calif.: Stanford University Press, 1989.

——. "Equality, Difference, Subordination: The Politics of Motherhood and Women's Citizenship." In Gisela Bock and Susan James, eds., *Beyond Equality and Difference: Citizenship, Feminist Politics, and Female Subjectivity.* London: Routledge, 1992. 17–31.

——. "Feminist Critiques of the Public/Private Dichotomy." In Anne Phillips, ed., *Feminism and Equality.* New York: NYU Press, 1987. 103–26.

——. *The Sexual Contract.* Stanford, Calif.: Stanford University Press, 1988.

Pedersen, Jeanne Elizabeth. " 'Special Customs,' Paternity Suits and Citizenship in France and the Colonies, 1870–1912." In Julia Clancy-Smith and Frances Gouda, eds., *Domesticating the Empire: Race, Gender, and Family Life in French and Dutch Colonialism.* Charlottesville: University Press of Virginia, 1998. 56–57.

Pedersen, Susan. "Catholicism, Feminism, and the Politics of the Family during the Late Third Republic." In Seth Koven and Sonya Michel, eds., *Mothers of a New World: Maternalist Politics and the Origins of Welfare States.* New York: Routledge, 1993. 246–76.

——. *Family, Dependence, and the Welfare State in France and Britain, 1914–1945.* Cambridge: Cambridge University Press, 1995.

Perochon, Ernest. *Les gardiennes.* Paris: Plon, 1924.

Perrot, Michelle. "L'éloge de la ménagère dans le discours des ouvriers français au XIXe siècle." *Romantisme: Mythes et Représentations de la Femme* 90 (1977): 105–23.

——. "The New Eve and the Old Adam: Changes in French Women's Condition at the Turn of the Century." In Margaret Randolph Higonnet, Jane Jenson, Sonya Michel, and Margaret Collins Weitz, eds., *Behind the Lines: Gender and the Two World Wars.* New Haven, Conn.: Yale University Press, 1987. 51–60.

——. "Préface." In Christine Bard, ed., *Un siècle d'antiféminisme en France.* Paris: Fayard, 1999.

Pezerat, Pierrette, and Danielle Poublan. "Femmes sans maris: Les employées des postes." In Arlette Farge and Christiane Klapisch-Zuber, eds., *Madame ou made-*

moiselle? Itinéraires de la solitude féminine, 18e–20e siècles. Paris: Editions Montalba, 1984.

Phan, Denis. "Productivité, emploi, et salaires ouvriers chez Renault des années 1930." *Mouvement social* no. 154 (January–March 1991).

Philips, Anne, and Barbara Taylor. "Sex and Skill: Notes Towards a Feminist Economics." *Feminist Review* 6 (October 1980): 79–88.

Pic, Paul. "Le mouvement législative ouvrier en France et à l'étranger et la crise mondiale: L'organisation de la lutte contre le chômage." *Revue politique et parlementaire* 448 (March 10 1932): 130–42.

Pieron, Henri, Henri Magne, and Marcel Frois. *Physiologie du travail: Contribution à l'étude du rendement de la main d'oeuvre et de la fatigue professionnelle.* Paris: Felix Alcan, 1922.

Pinot, Robert. *Les oeuvres sociales des industries métallurgiques.* Paris: Armand Colin, 1924.

Pluyette, Jean. *La doctrine des races et la sélection de l'immigration en France.* Paris: Editions et publications contemporaines, 1930.

Poovey, Mary. "The Abortion Question and the Death of Man." In Judith Butler and Joan W. Scott, eds., *Feminists Theorize the Political.* New York: Routledge, 1992.

Porter, Roy. "History of the Body." In Peter Burke, ed., *New Perspectives on Historical Writing.* University Park: Penn State University Press, 1992.

Première conférence internationale du service social, Paris 8–13 juillet 1928. Vol. 3. Paris: Imprimerie union, 1929.

Président du Conseil. Conseil national économique. *Le chômage dans les industries textiles.* Paris: Imprimerie des journaux officiels, 1936.

Prost, Antoine "L'évolution de la politique familiale en France de 1938 à 1981." *Mouvement social* 129 (1984): 7–28.

Quine, Maria. *Population Politics in Twentieth-Century Europe.* London: Routledge, 1996.

Rabinbach, Anson. "The European Science of Work: The Economy of the Body at the End of the Nineteenth Century." In Stephen Laurence Kaplan and Cynthia J. Koepp, eds., *Work in France: Representations, Meaning, Organization, and Practice.* Ithaca, N.Y.: Cornell University Press, 1986.

Rabinbach, Anson. *The Human Motor: Energy, Fatigue, and the Origins of Modernity.* New York: Basic Books, 1990.

Rageot, Gaston. *La natalité, ses lois économiques et psychologiques.* Paris, Flammarion, 1918.

Raymond, Dr. "La dépopulation et la misère d'enfance." *Cahiers de Bolchévisme.* 13e année no. 1–2 (January 15, 1936): 101–9.

Renard, Mlle. "Rapport de stage d'ouvrière à l'usine de Textilose du 12 au 15 octobre 1925." In Archives de l'école des surintendantes d'Usine, Ecole supérieure du travail social. Paris.

Rey, Eugénie. "Rapport de stage [de surintendante] fait aux usines de la Compagnie

Thomson Houston," du 17 au 30 juin 1921, 1, 3–4. In Archives de l'école des surintendants d'usine. Ecole supérieure du travail social. Paris.

Reynolds, Siân. *France between the Wars: Gender and Politics*. London: Routledge, 1996.

Rhein, Catherine. "Jeunes femmes au travail dans le Paris de l'entre-deux-guerres." Thèse de Doctorat de IIIe cycle. Université de Paris VII, 1977.

Ribeill, Georges. "Les débuts de l'ergonomie en France à la veille de la première guerre mondiale." *Mouvement social* 113 (October–December 1980): 3–36.

———. "Les organisations du mouvement ouvrier en France face à la rationalisation (1926–1932)." In Maurice de Montmollin and Olivier Pastré, eds., *Le Taylorism*. Paris: La Découverte, 1984.

Riot-Sarcey, Michèle. *La démocratie à l'épreuve des femmes*. Paris: Albin Michel, 1994.

Rioux, Jean-Pierre. *La France de la IVe république*. Vol. 1. *L'ardeur et la nécessité 1944–1952*. Paris: Seuil, 1980.

———. *La France de la IVe république*. Vol. 2. *L'expansion et l'impuissance*. Paris: Seuil, 1983.

Robert, Jean-Louis. "La CGT et la famille ouvrière, 1914–1918: Première approche." *Mouvement social* 116 (July–September 1981): 47–66.

———. "Ouvriers et mouvement ouvrier parisiens pendant la grande guerre et l'immédiat après guerre." Thèse de Doctorat d'Etat, Université de Paris I-Sorbonne, 1989.

———. "Women and Work in France during the First World War." In Richard Wall and Jay Winter, eds., *The Upheaval of War: Family, Work, and Welfare in Europe, 1914–1918*. Cambridge: Cambridge University Press, 1988.

Roberts, Mary Louise. *Civilization without Sexes: Reconstructing Gender in Postwar France, 1917–1927*. Chicago: University of Chicago Press, 1994.

Romier, Lucien. *L'explication de notre temps*. Paris: Grasset, 1925.

Ronsin, Françis. *La grève des ventres: Propagande néo-malthusienne et baisse de la natalité en France 19e–20e siècles*. Paris: Aubier Montaigne, 1980.

Rosanvallon, Pierre. *Le sacre du citoyen: Histoire du suffrage universel en France*. Paris: Gallimard, 1993.

Rose, Sonya O. "Gender Segregation in the Transition to the Factory: The English Hosiery Industry 1850–1910." *Feminist Studies* 13 (1987): 163–84.

———. *Limited Livelihoods: Gender and Class in Nineteenth Century England*. Berkeley: University of California Press, 1992.

Rosenberg, Clifford. "Albert Sarraut and Republican Racial Thought." In Herrick Chapman and Laura L. Frader, eds., *Race in France: Interdisciplinary Perspectives on the Politics of Difference*. New York: Berghahn, 2004. 36–53.

———. *Policing Paris: The Origins of Modern Immigration Control between the Wars*. Ithaca, N.Y.: Cornell University Press, 2006.

Ross, George W. "The EU Crisis in a Different Light: Social Model Anxieties and Hard Cases." Unpublished paper.

Rougé, Jeanne. "Le retour de la femme au foyer." *Cahiers du Bolchévisme* 10, no. 5 (March 1933).

Rougier, E. *Le vade-mecum de la téléphoniste.* Paris: Publications de l'indicateur universel des PTT, 1927.

Roulleaux-Dugage, Henri. "Le vote familial." *Familles de France* no. 11 (November 1933).

Salais, Robert, Nicolas Baverez, and Bénédicte Reynaud. *L'invention du chômage.* Paris: PUF, 1986.

Sauvy, Alfred. *Histoire économique de la France entre les deux guerres.* Volume 1. Paris: Fayard, 1967.

Sauvy, Alfred, and Pierre Depoid. *Salaires et pouvoir d'achat des ouvriers et des fonctionnaires entre les deux guerres.* Paris: Institut national d'étude du travail et d'orientation professionnelle, 1940.

Schneider, William H. *Quality and Quantity: The Quest for Biological Regeneration in Twentieth-Century France.* Cambridge: Cambridge University Press, 1990.

——. "The Scientific Study of Labor in Interwar France." *French Historical Studies* 17, no. 2 (Fall 1991): 410–46.

Schor, Ralph. *L'opinion française et les étrangers, 1919–1939.* Paris: Publications de la Sorbonne, 1985.

Schweitzer, Sylvie. *Des engrenages à la chaîne: Les usines Citroën, 1915–1935.* Lyon: Presses universitaires de Lyon, 1982.

——. *Les femmes ont toujours travaillé.* Paris: Odile Jacob, 2002.

Scott, Joan W. *Gender and the Politics of History.* New York: Columbia University Press, 1988.

——. *Only Paradoxes to Offer: French Feminists and the Rights of Man.* Cambridge, Mass.: Harvard University Press, 1996.

——. "L'ouvrière." In Geneviève Fraisse and Michelle Perrot, eds., *Le XIXe siècle.* Vol. 4 of *Histoire des femmes en occident,* edited by Georges Duby and Michelle Perrot. Paris: Plon, 1992. 399–426.

——. "Work Identities for Men and Women: The Politics of Work and Family in the Parisian Garment Trades in 1848." *Gender and the Politics of History.* New York: Columbia University Press, 1988. 93–112.

Sevegrand, Martine. *L'amour en toutes lettres: Questions à l'Abbé Viollet sur la sexualité 1924–1943.* Paris: Albin Michel, 1996.

——. *Les enfants du bon dieu: Les Catholiques français et la procréation au XXe siècle.* Paris: Albin Michel, 1995.

Sewell, William. *Work and Revolution in France: The Language of Labor from the Old Regime to 1848.* Cambridge: Cambridge University Press, 1980.

Sherman, Daniel J. *The Construction of Memory in Interwar France.* Chicago: University of Chicago Press, 1999.

——. "Monuments, Memory, and Masculinity in France after World War I." *Gender and History* 8 (1996): 82–107.

Showalter, Elaine. "Rivers and Sassoon: The Inscription of Male Gender Anxieties." In Margaret Higonnet, Jane Jenson, Sonya Michel, and Margaret Collins Weitz, eds., *Behind the Lines: Gender and the Two World Wars.* New Haven, Conn.: Yale University Press, 1987. 61–69.

Siau, René. *La fonction sociale d'une grande entreprise: L'oeuvre de la Compagnie parisienne de distribution d'électricité.* Paris: Les Presses modernes, 1932.

Siim, Birte. *Gender and Citizenship: Politics and Agency in France, Britain, and Denmark.* Cambridge: Cambridge University Press, 2000.

——. "Gender, Power, and Citizenship." Presented to the Groupe d'études sur la division sociale et sexuelle du travail (GEDISST). Paris, February 28, 1994.

——. "Welfare State, Gender Politics, and Equality Policies: Women's Citizenship in the Scandinavian Welfare States." In Elizabeth Meehan and Selma Sevenhuijsen, eds., *Equality Politics and Gender.* London: Sage, 1991.

Sirot, Stéphane. "Les conditions de travail et les grèves des ouvriers coloniaux à Paris des lendemains de la Première guerre mondiale à la veille du Front populaire." *Revue française d'histoire d'outre-mer* 83 (March 1996): 65–92.

Smith, Paul. *Feminism and the Third Republic: Women's Political and Civil Rights in France, 1918–1945.* Oxford: Oxford University Press, 1996.

Sohn, Anne-Marie. "Exemplarité et limites de la participation féminine à la vie syndicale: Les institutrices de la CGTU." *Revue d'Histoire moderne et contemporaine* (July–September 1977): 391–414.

——. "Féminisme et syndicalisme: Les institutrices de la Fédération unitaire de l'enseignement de 1919–1935." Thèse de doctorat en troisième cycle. Université de Paris X. 1976.

Sommestad, Lena. "Welfare State Attitudes to the Male Breadwinning System: The United States and Sweden in Comparative Perspective." *International Review of Social History* 42 (1997). Supplement: 153–74.

Sowerwine, Charles. *Sisters or Citizens? Women and Socialism in France since 1876.* Cambridge: Cambridge University Press, 1982.

Spengler, Joseph. *France Faces Depopulation.* Durham, N.C.: Duke University Press, 1979.

Stewart, Mary Lynn. *Women Workers and the French State: Labor Protection and Social Patriarchy, 1879–1919.* Montréal: McGill University Press, 1989.

Stoler, Ann Laura. "Carnal Knowledge and Imperial Power: Gender, Race, and Morality in Colonial Asia." In Michaela di Leonardo, ed., *Gender at the Crossroads of Knowledge: Feminist Anthropology in the Post Modern Era.* Berkeley: University of California Press, 1991.

——. "Racial Histories and their Regimes of Truth." *Political Power and Social Theory* 11 (1997): 183–206.

——. "Sexual Affronts and Racial Frontiers: National Identity, 'Mixed Bloods' and the Cultural Genealogies of Europeans in Colonial Southeast Asia." *Comparative Studies in Society and History* 34, no.3 (July 1992): 514–51.

Stoler, Ann Laura, and Frederick Cooper. "Between Metropole and Colony." In

Cooper and Stoler, eds., *Tensions of Empire: Colonial Cultures in a Bourgeois World.* Berkeley: University of California Press, 1997.

Stone, Judith. "The Republican Brotherhood: Gender and Ideology." In Eleanor A. Accampo, Rachel G. Fuchs, and Mary Lynn Stewart, eds., *Gender and the Politics of Social Reform in France.* Baltimore: Johns. Hopkins University Press, 1995. 28–58.

——. "Republican Ideology, Gender, and Class: France, 1860–1914." In Laura L. Frader and Sonya O. Rose, eds., *Gender and Class in Modern Europe.* Ithaca, N.Y.: Cornell University Press, 1996. 238–59.

——. *The Search for Social Peace: Reform Legislation in France, 1850–1914.* Albany: State University of New York Press, 1985.

Stoval, Tyler. "Color Blind France: Colonial Workers during the First World War." *Race and Class* 35, no. 2 (1993): 33–55.

——. "The Color Line behind the Lines: Racial Violence in France during the Great War." *American Historical Review* 103, no.3 (June 1998): 737–69.

——. *Paris Noir: African Americans in the City of Light.* Boston: Houghton Mifflin, 1996.

Tabili, Laura. "Women 'of a Very Low Type': Crossing Racial Boundaries in Imperial Britain." In Laura L. Frader and Sonya O. Rose, eds., *Gender and Class in Modern Europe.* Ithaca, N.Y.: Cornell University Press, 1996.

Talmy, Robert. *Histoire du mouvement familial, 1896–1939.* 2 vols. Aubenas: Union nationale des caisses d'allocations familiales, 1962.

Teyssot, Marthe. "Rapport fait sur mon stage d'ouvrière à l'usine Forman (July, 1920)." In Archives de l'école des surintendantes d'Usine. Ecole supérieure du travail social. Paris.

Thébaud, Françoise. *La femme au temps de la guerre de quatorze.* Paris: Stock, 1986.

——. "Le mouvement nataliste dans la France de l'entre-deux-guerres: L'Alliance nationale pour l'accroissement de la population française." *Revue d' histoire moderne et contemporaine* 32 (April–June 1985): 276–301.

——. *Quand nos grand-mères donnaient la vie: la maternité en France dans l'entre-deux-guerres.* Lyon: Presses universitaires de Lyon, 1986.

Thibault, Marie-Noëlle, and Michelle Riot-Sarcey. "La préhistoire de la protection: enquêtes et autres discours sur le travail des femmes." In Leora Auslander and Michelle Zancarini-Fournel, eds., *Différences des sexes et protection sociale.* St. Denis: Presses universitaires de Vincennes, 1995. 41–51.

Thibert, Marguerite. "Crise économique et le travail féminin, I." *Revue internationale du travail* 27 (April, 1933):465–93.

——. "Crise économique et le travail féminin, II." *Revue internationale du travail* 27 (May 1933): 647–57.

Thompson, Edward P. "Time, Work Discipline and Industrial Capitalism." *Past and Present* 38 (May 1969): 56–97.

Tilly, Charles. *Durable Inequality.* Berkeley: University of California Press, 1998.

Topalov, Christian. *La naissance du chômeur, 1880–1910.* Paris: Albin Michel, 1994.

Toulemon, André. *Le suffrage familial ou suffrage universel intégral: Le vote des femmes.* Préface par Georges Pernot. Paris: Librairie du Receuil Sirey, 1933.

Toulouse, Edouard. *La question sexuelle et la femme.* Paris: Bibliothèque Charpentier, 1918.

Toutain, J. C. *La population de la France de 1700 à 1959.* Cahiers de l' ISEA. Série AF No. 3. Supplément no. 3. Paris: I.S.E.A., 1963.

Turbin, Carole, Laura L. Frader, Sonya O. Rose, and Evelyn Nakano Glenn. "A Roundtable on Gender, Race, Class, Culture and Politics: Where Do We Go from Here?" *Social Science History* 22 (Spring 1998): 1–45.

Ungerson, Claire. "Social Politics and the Commodification of Care." *Social Politics* 4 (Fall 1977): 363–81.

Union patronale de la région d'Halluin. *Salaires et conditions du travail, 1929.* Halluin: Imprimerie spéciale de l'union patronale, 1929.

Valdour, Jacques. *Les parisiennes d'après guerre: Observations vécues.* Paris: Rousseau, 1921.

Verdès-Leroux, Janine. "Pouvoir et assistance: Cinquante ans de services sociales." *Actes de recherche en sciences sociales* no.6 (1976): 152–72.

Vidalenc, Jean. "La main-d'oeuvre étrangère en France et la première guerre mondiale (1901–1926)." *Francia* 2 (1974): 524–50.

Viêt, Vincent. *La France immigrée: Construction d'une politique, 1914–1997.* Paris: Fayard, 1998.

Vignes, Madeleine. *Les téléphonistes des PTT.* Préface de Madeleine Rebérioux. Paris: Vignes/RIV, 1984.

Villermé, Louis-René. *Tableau de l'état physique et moral des ouvriers employés dans les manufactures de coton, de laine, et de soie [1840].* Paris: Editions 10/18, 1971.

Vimont, Suzanne. *Un cours ménager volant.* Reims: Société des agriculteurs de France et l'Union centrale des syndicats, section des dames, 1914.

Viollet, Abbé Jean. *La bonne entente conjugale.* Paris: Bloud et Gay, 1927.

——. *Les devoirs du marriage.* Paris: Association du mariage chrétien [AMC], 1922.

——. *La loi chrétienne du mariage: Prescriptions et défenses.* Paris: Editions familiales de France, 1936.

——. *Le mariage.* Paris: Editions familiales de France, 1932.

von Oertzen, Christine, and Almut Rietzschel. "Comparing Post-War Germanies: Breadwinner Ideology and Women's Employment in the Divided Nation, 1948–1970." *International Review of Social History* 42 (1997). Supplement: 175–96.

Walby, Sylvia. *Patriarchy at Work.* Cambridge: Polity Press, 1989.

Weil, Patrick. *La France et ses étrangers.* Paris: Calman-Lévy, 1991.

Weil, Simone. *La condition ouvrière.* Paris: Gallimard, 1951.

Weindling, Paul. *Health, Race, and German Politics.* Cambridge: Cambridge University Press, 1989.

Werbner, Pnina, and Nira Yuval-Davis. *Citizenship: Pushing the Boundaries.* Special issue of *Feminist Review* 57 (1997).

Werner, Françoise. "Du ménage à l'art ménager: L'évolution du travail ménager et son echo dans la presse féminine française de 1919–1939." *Mouvement social* 129 (October–December 1984): 61–87.

Wiesner, Merry. "Guilds, Male Bonding, and Women's Work in Early Modern Germany." *Gender and History* 1 (Summer 1989): 125–37.

Winter, Jay. *The Great War and the Twentieth Century.* New Haven. Conn.: Yale University Press, 2000.

Wishnia, Judith. "Natalisme et nationalisme pendant la première guerre mondiale." *Vingtième Siècle* no.45 (January–March 1995): 30–39.

——. *The Proletarianizing of the Fonctionnaires: Civil Service Workers and the Labor Movement under the Third Republic.* Baton Rouge: Louisiana State University Press, 1991.

Yole, Jean. *La malaise paysanne.* Paris: Spès, 1929.

Young, Iris Marion. "Impartiality and the Civic Public: Some Implications of Feminist Critiques of Moral and Political Theory." In Seyla Benhabib and Drucilla Cornell, eds., *Feminism as Critique: On the Politics of Gender.* Minneapolis: University of Minnesota Press, 1987. 57–76.

Zancarini-Fournel, Michelle. "Archéologie de la loi de 1892 en France." In Leora Auslander and Michelle Zancarini-Fournel, eds., *Différences des sexes et protection sociale.* Saint-Denis: Presses universitaires de Vincennes, 1995. 75–92.

Zola, Emile. *La fécondité.* Paris: Charpentier, 1899.

Zylberberg-Hocquard, Marie-Héléne. *Féminisme et syndicalisme en France.* Paris: Anthropos, 1978.

women's bodies in, 284; wounded in, 41, 178

Weavers, 118

Weil, Lucien, 109

Weil, Simone, 72–73, 80, 103, 199, 200

Welfare, 1, 4, 6, 96, 168, 178, 231, 299; European, 4; fund for, 94, 96, 215; home visits and, 183; industrial, 5; reform of, 242; state, 3, 4, 6, 13, 20, 49, 245

Witte-Schlumberger, Marguerite, 22

Women: as breadwinners, 136–37; commissions for, 45, 162; dependence on men of, 222; "femme au foyer," 215; finances controlled by, 172; in labor force, 12, 28, 35, 39, 46, 47, 52, 55, 56, 87; moral superiority of, 231; nurturance and, 231; rights of, 13, 186; suffrage for, 33, 34

Wool industry, 199–200

Workers' compensation, 87

Worker-technicians, 68

Work permits, 87

Work stoppages, 157

World War I, 3, 4, 5, 7, 6, 8, 15, 16, 18, 46, 56, 74, 77, 78, 93, 100, 103, 107, 110, 124, 131, 186, 212

Xenophobia, 208, 210, 223, 227

Zola, Emile, 18

LAURA LEVINE FRADER is a professor of history at
Northeastern University.

Library of Congress Cataloging-in-Publication Data
Frader, Laura Levine, 1945–
Breadwinners and citizens : gender in the making of the
French social model / Laura Levine Frader.
p. cm.
Includes bibliographical references and index.
ISBN-13: 978-0-8223-4182-6 (cloth : alk. paper)
ISBN-13: 978-0-8223-4198-7 (pbk. : alk. paper)
1. Women—Employment—France—History—20th
century. 2. Sex discrimination in employment—
France—History—20th century. 3. Sex discrimination
against women—France—History—20th century. 4. Sex
role in the work environment—France—History—20th
century. I. Title.
HD6145.F66 2008
306.3'6150944—dc22   2007039434